MOODY

Hmm, What should I whip up today?

尾田栄一郎

It's always a gamble ordering the "Chef's Mood Pasta." What if his mood is "I'm not making any pasta today," or "I want to eat the pasta today"? You're out of a pasta. You'd really need to know the chef's latest state of mind. "The chef's daughter scored 100 on her test. Chef's Mood Pasta!!" Wow, that sounds yummy! "The chef's wife cheated on him... Chef's...Mood Pasta..." Umm... Anyway! Let's follow the adventures of our moody captain!! Volume 66 begins!!

–Eiichiro Oda, 2012

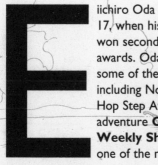

iichiro Oda began his manga career at the age of 17, when his one-shot cowboy manga **Wanted!** won second place in the coveted Tezuka manga awards. Oda went on to work as an assistant to some of the biggest manga artists in the industry, including Nobuhiro Watsuki, before winning the Hop Step Award for new artists. His pirate adventure **One Piece**, which debuted in **Weekly Shonen Jump** in 1997, quickly became one of the most popular manga in Japan.

ONE PIECE VOL. 66
NEW WORLD PART 6

SHONEN JUMP Manga Edition

STORY AND ART BY EIICHIRO ODA

Translation/Stephen Paul
Touch-up Art & Lettering/Vanessa Satone
Design/Fawn Lau
Editor/Alexis Kirsch

Printed in the U.S.A.

Published by VIZ Media, LLC
P.O. Box 77010
San Francisco, CA 94107

10 9 8 7 6 5 4 3 2 1
First printing, March 2013

www.viz.com

PARENTAL ADVISORY
ONE PIECE is rated T for Teen and is recommended
for ages 13 and up. This volume contains fantasy
violence and tobacco usage.
ratings.viz.com

THE WORLD'S
MOST POPULAR MANGA
www.shonenjump.com

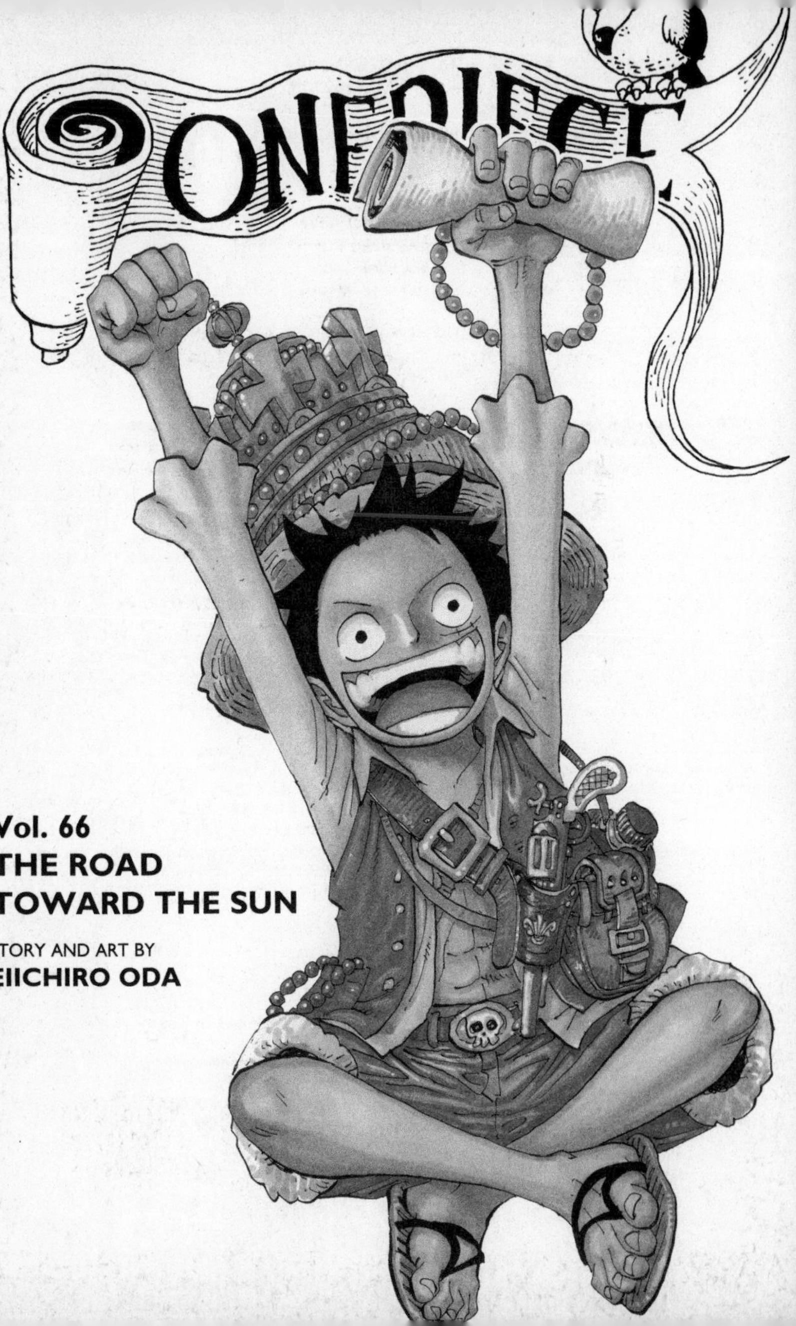
ONE PIECE

Vol. 66

THE ROAD TOWARD THE SUN

STORY AND ART BY

EIICHIRO ODA

The Straw Hat Crew

Monkey D. Luffy

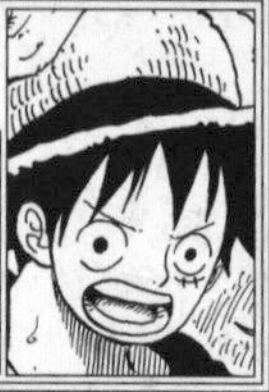

A young man who dreams of becoming the Pirate King. After training with Rayleigh, he and his crew head for the New World!

Captain, Bounty: 400 million berries

Roronoa Zolo

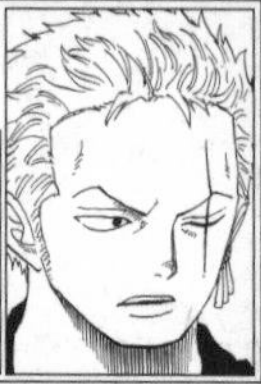

He swallowed his pride and asked to be trained by Mihawk on Gloom Island before reuniting with the rest of the crew.

Fighter, Bounty: 120 million berries

Tony Tony Chopper

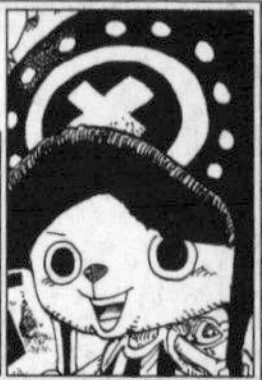

After researching powerful medicine in Birdie Kingdom, he reunites with the rest of the crew.

Ship's Doctor, Bounty: 50 berries

Nami

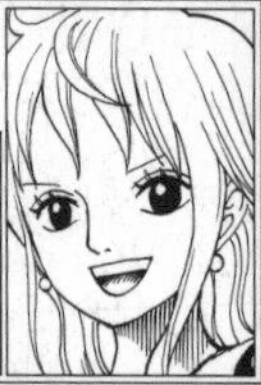

She studied the weather of the New World on the small Sky Island Weatheria, a place where weather is studied as a science.

Navigator, Bounty: 16 million berries

Nico Robin

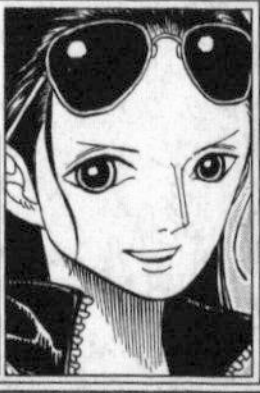

She spent her time in Baltigo with the leader of the Revolutionary Army: Luffy's father, Dragon.

Archeologist, Bounty: 80 million berries

Usopp

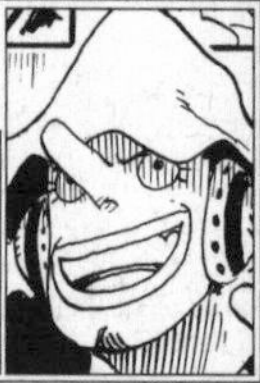

He trained under Heracles at the Bowin Islands to become the King of Snipers.

Sniper, Bounty: 30 million berries

Franky

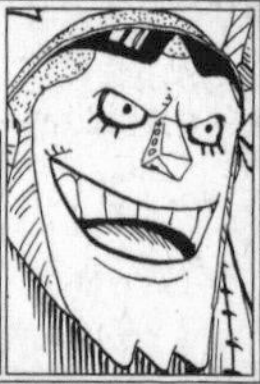

He modified himself in Future Land Baldimore and turned himself into Armored Franky before reuniting with the rest of the crew.

Shipwright, Bounty: 44 million berries

Sanji

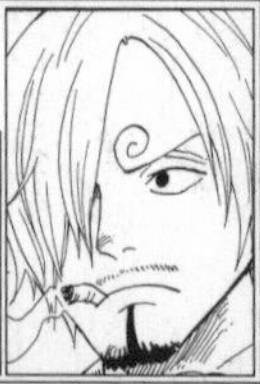

After fighting the New Kama Karate masters in the Kamabakka Kingdom, he returned to the crew.

Cook, Bounty: 77 million berries

Brook

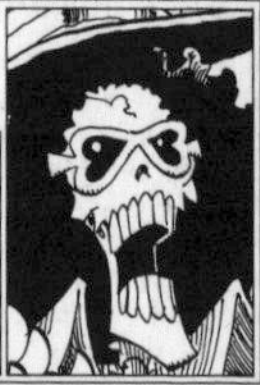

After being captured and used as a freak show by the Longarm Tribe, he became a famous rock star called "Soul King" Brook.

Musician, Bounty: 33 million berries

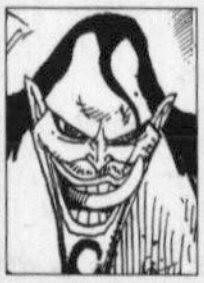

Wet-Haired Caribou

Captain of the Caribou Pirates

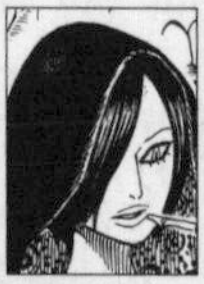

Madam Sharley

Owner of the Mermaid Café

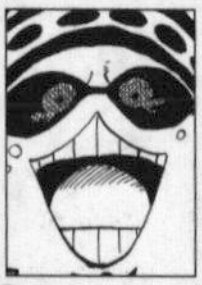

Pappagu

The Designer/President of the Criminal brand

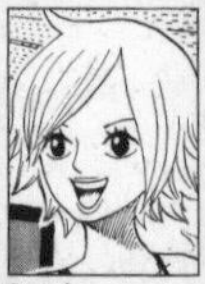

Camie

Works at the Mermaid Café

The story of ONE PIECE 1»66

Shanks

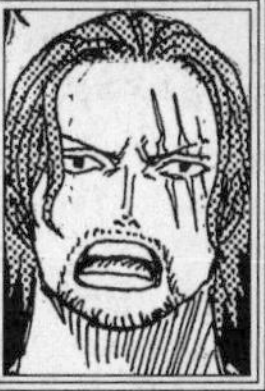

One of the Four Emperors. He continues to wait for Luffy in the second half of the Grand Line, called the New World.

Captain of the Red-Haired Pirates

Jimbei

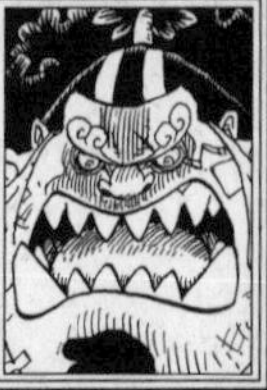

Reunited with Luffy at Fish-Man Island, where he tries to stop Hody's plot.

Former Warlord of the Sea

The Ryugu Kingdom

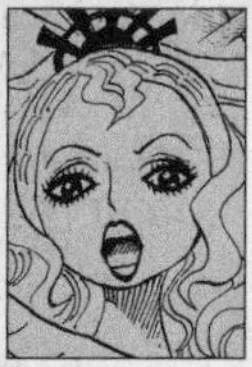

Queen Otohime

Neptune's Wife

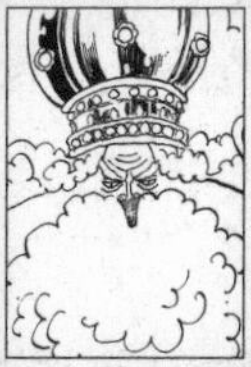

Neptune the Sea God

King of the Ryugu Kingdom

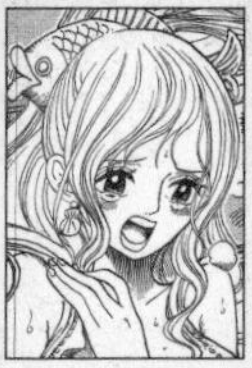

Princess Shirahoshi

Princess of the Ryugu Kingdom

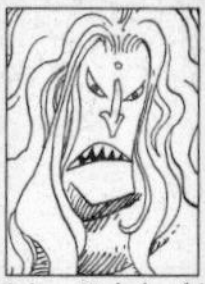

Prince Fukaboshi

Eldest of Neptune's Three Sons

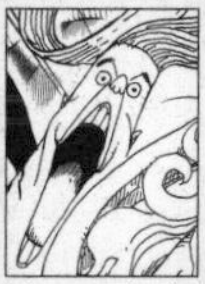

Prince Ryuboshi

Second of Neptune's Three Sons

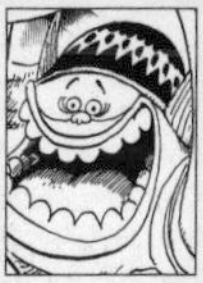

Prince Mamboshi

Youngest of Neptune's Three Sons

Proposed to

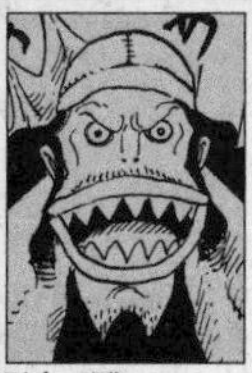

Fisher Tiger

Sun Pirates Captain

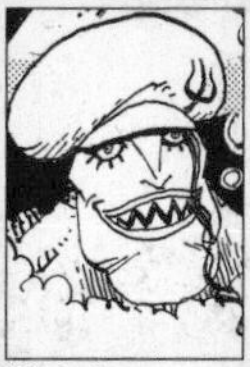

Hody Jones

Captain of the New Fish-Man Pirates

Alliance Broken

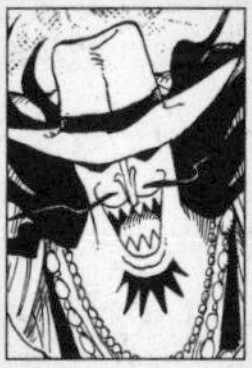

Vander Decken IX

Captain of the Flying Pirates

Flying Pirates

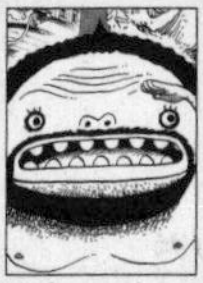

Wadatsumi

Member of the Flying Pirates

The New Fish-Man Pirates

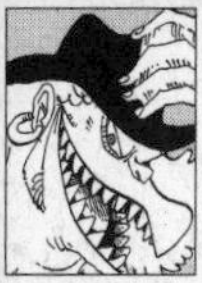

Hammond

New Fish-Man Pirate

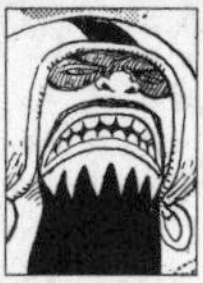

Ikaros Much

New Fish-Man Pirate

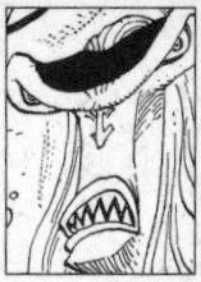

Dosun

New Fish-Man Pirate

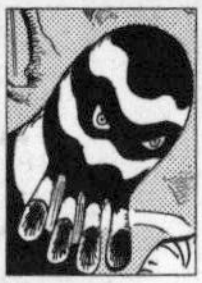

Zeo

New Fish-Man Pirate

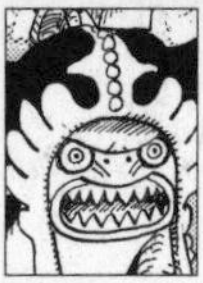

Daruma

New Fish-Man Pirate

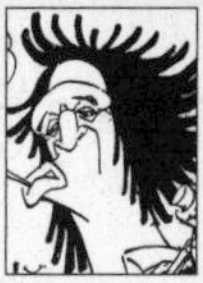

Hyouzou

New Fish-Man Pirate

Story

Having finished their two years of training, the Straw Hat crew reunites on the Sabaody Archipelago. They set sail more determined than ever to reach The New World!

The Straw Hats finally reach Fish-Man Island but are quickly ambushed by the New Fish-Man Pirates. Their hatred of humans was caused by a long and terrible history of oppression. Now Hody Jones has sworn to destroy the Ryugu Kingdom, become the *new* king of Fish-Man Island and eliminate anyone who hopes for peace with humankind!! Princess Shirahoshi and her brothers want peace, and they stand up to Hody with Luffy's help!! But now the giant ark *Noah* is bearing down on Fish-Man Island! Luffy's crew defeats the Fish-Man officers, but *Noah*'s downward plunge continues. The island is in great danger!!

Vol. 66
The Road Toward the Sun

CONTENTS

Chapter 647:
STOP, NOAH

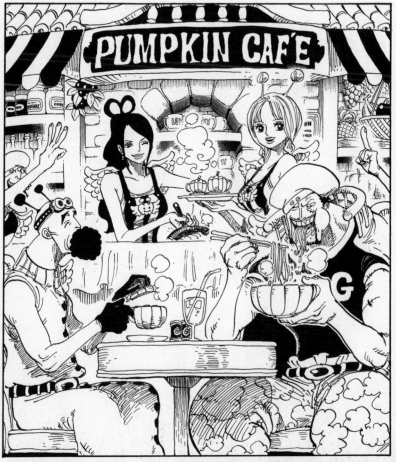

DECKS OF THE WORLD, VOL. 30: "SKYPIEA—RAKI AND
CONIS' PUMPKIN CAFÉ SPECIALTY: PUMPKIN NOODLES"

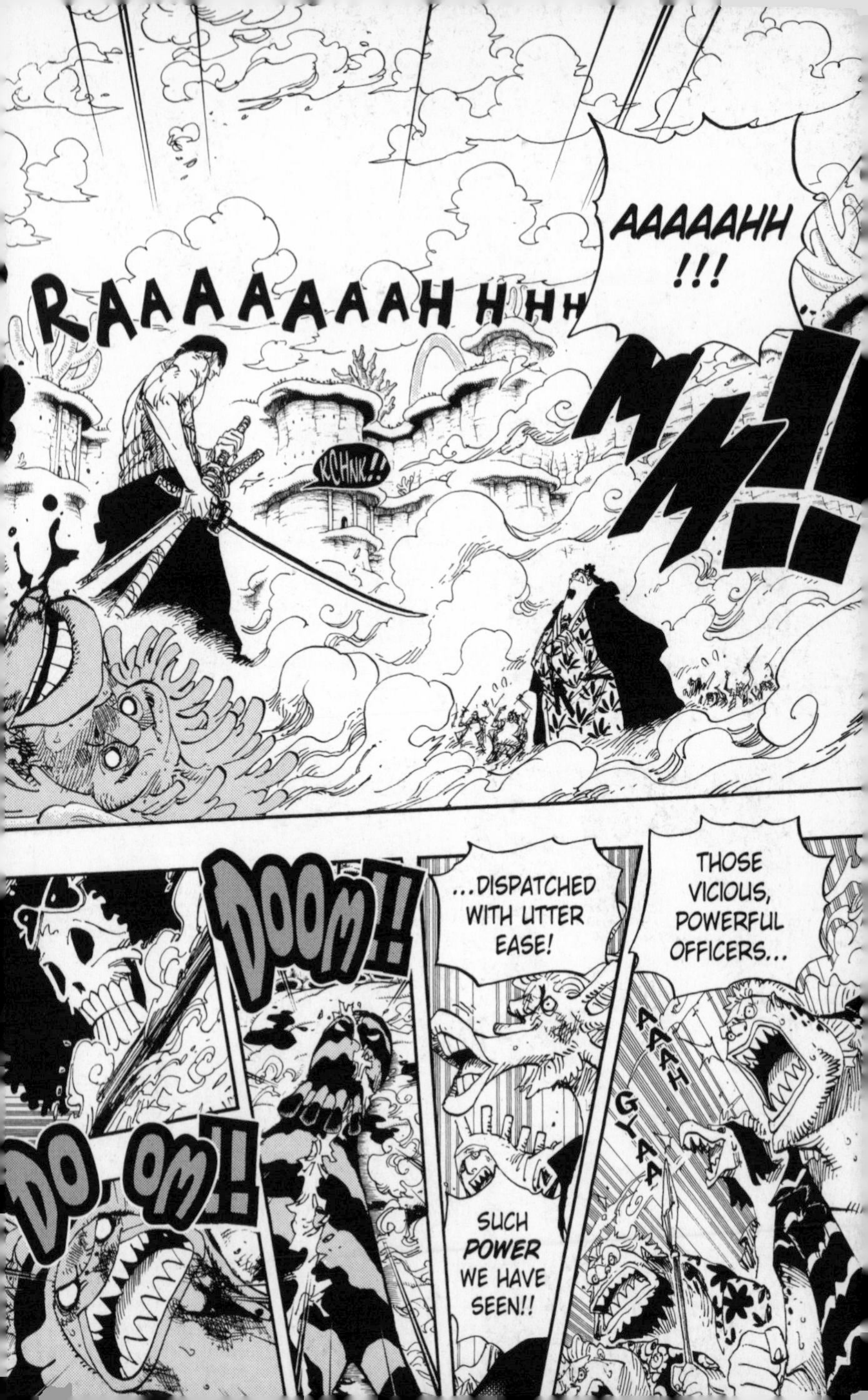
AAAAAHH!!!
RAAAAAAAHHHH
KCHNK!!
THOSE VICIOUS, POWERFUL OFFICERS...
AAAH
GYAA
...DISPATCHED WITH UTTER EASE!
SUCH POWER WE HAVE SEEN!!
DOOM!!
DO..OM!!

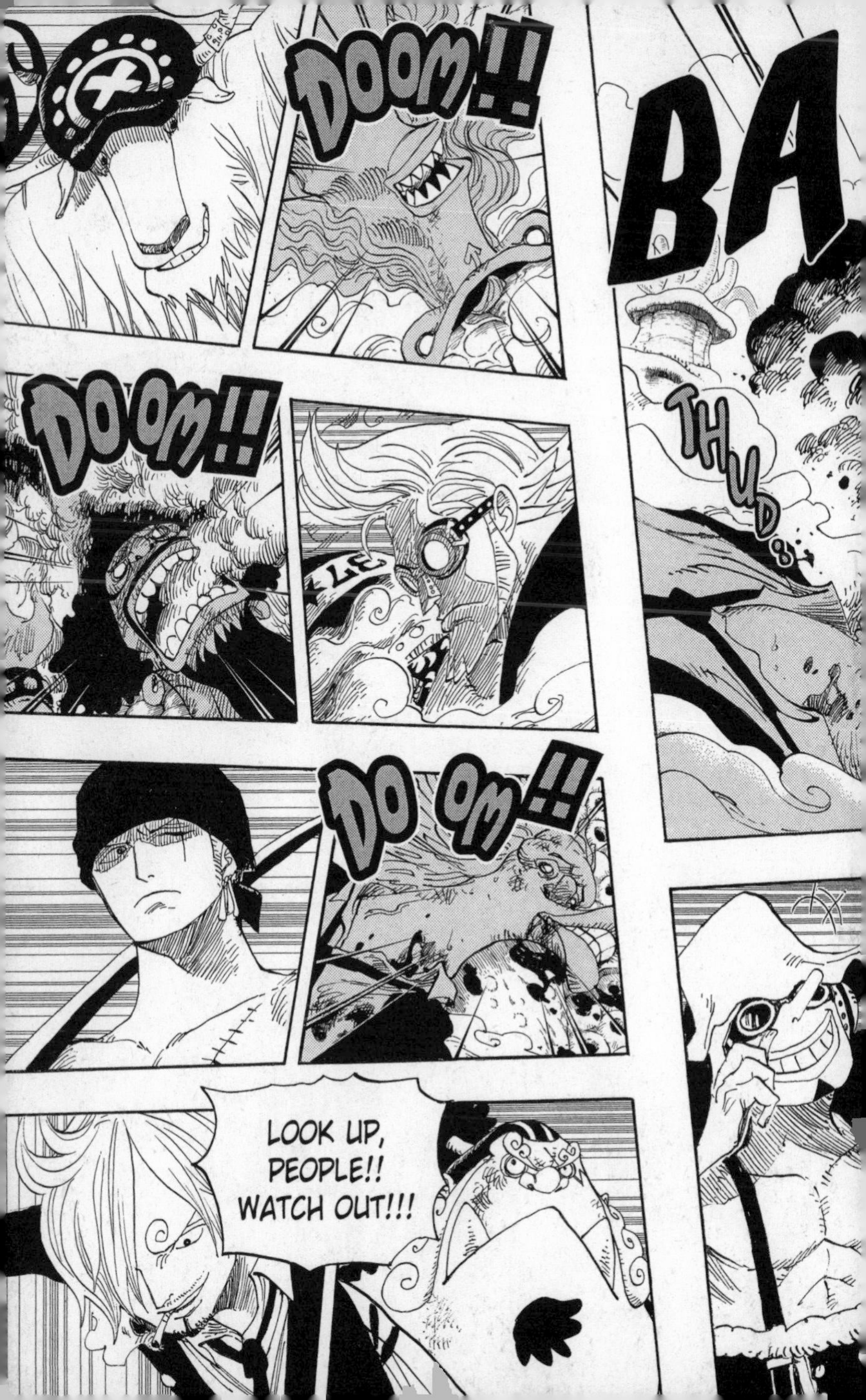
BA
THUD
DOOM!!
DOOM!!
DO OM!!
LOOK UP, PEOPLE!! WATCH OUT!!!

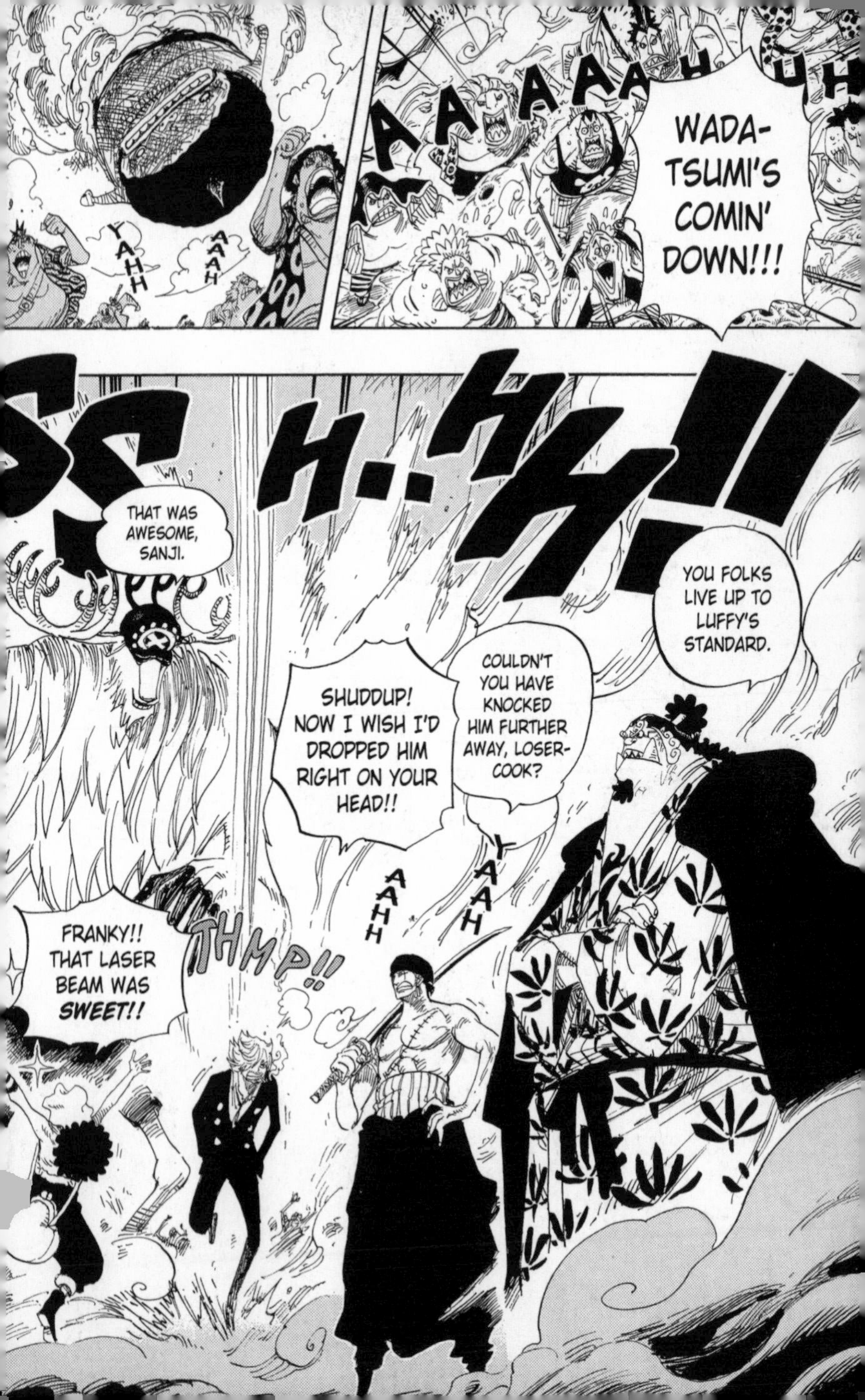
UH
AAAAAH
WADA-TSUMI'S COMIN' DOWN!!!
YAHH
AAAH
YOU FOLKS LIVE UP TO LUFFY'S STANDARD.
COULDN'T YOU HAVE KNOCKED HIM FURTHER AWAY, LOSER-COOK?
SHUDDUP! NOW I WISH I'D DROPPED HIM RIGHT ON YOUR HEAD!!
THAT WAS AWESOME, SANJI.
YAAAH
AAHH
THMP!!
FRANKY!! THAT LASER BEAM WAS SWEET!!

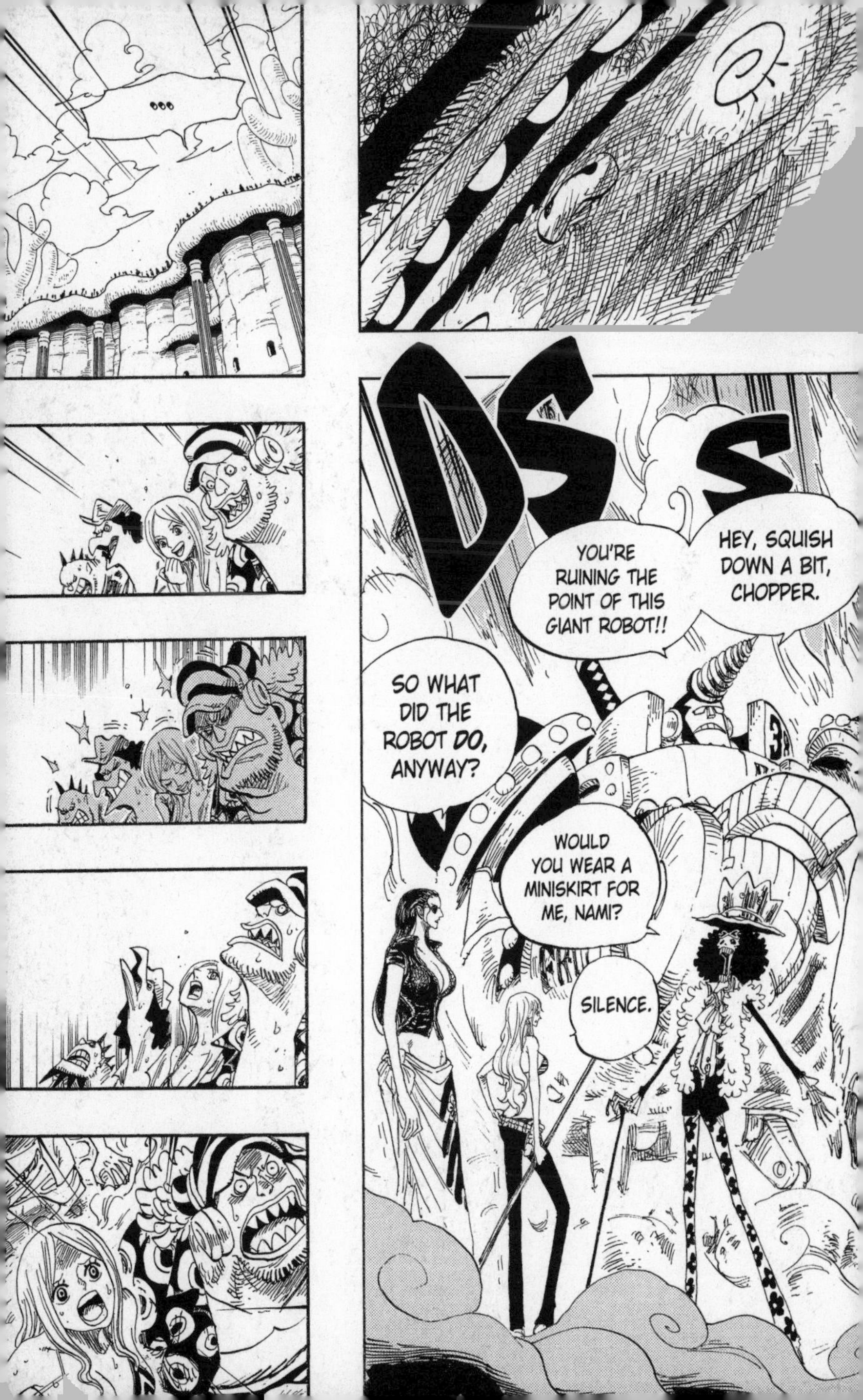
•••
DSS
HEY, SQUISH DOWN A BIT, CHOPPER.
YOU'RE RUINING THE POINT OF THIS GIANT ROBOT!!
SO WHAT DID THE ROBOT *DO*, ANYWAY?
WOULD YOU WEAR A MINISKIRT FOR ME, NAMI?
SILENCE.

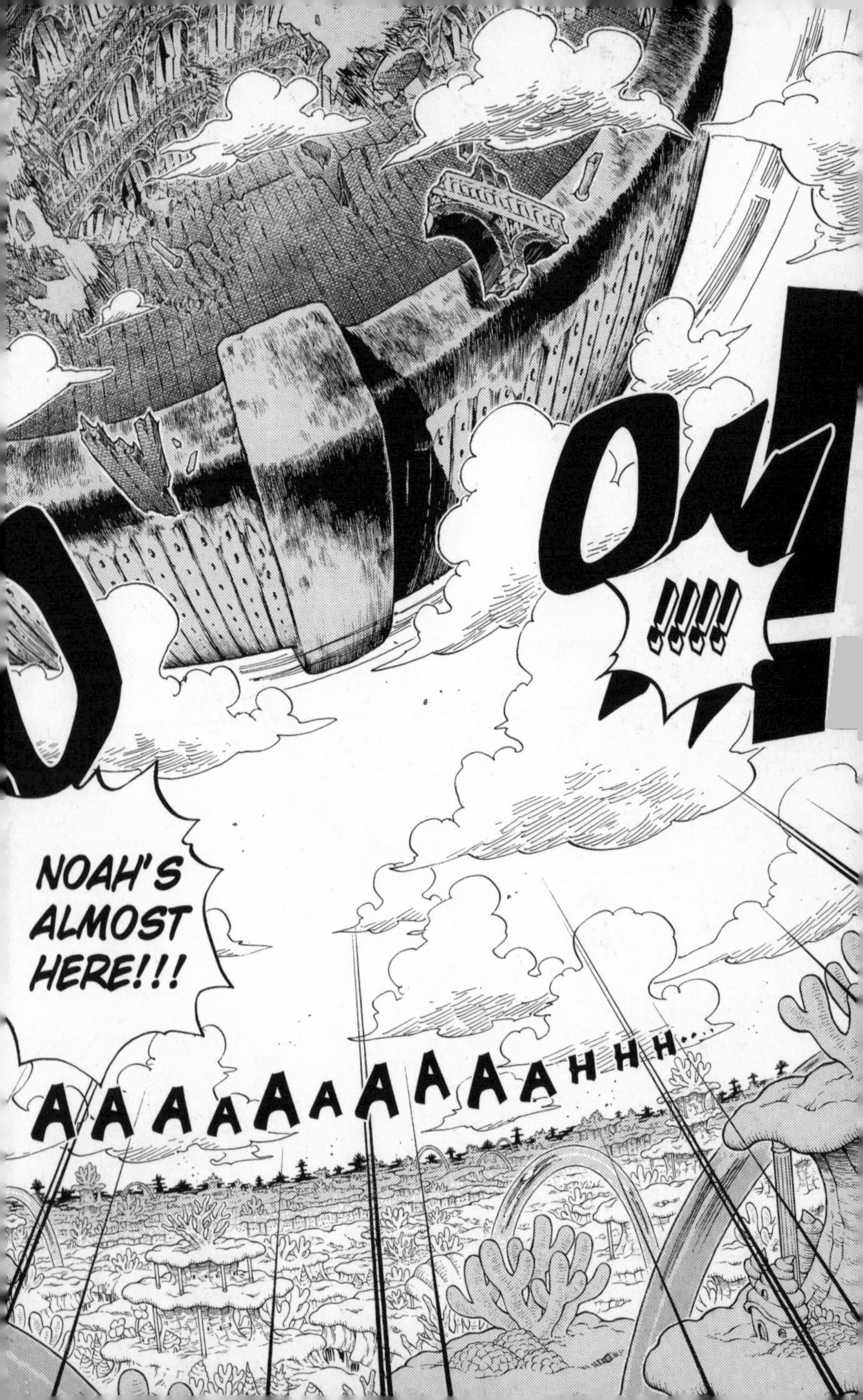
NOAH'S ALMOST HERE!!!
AAAAAAAAAAHHH...

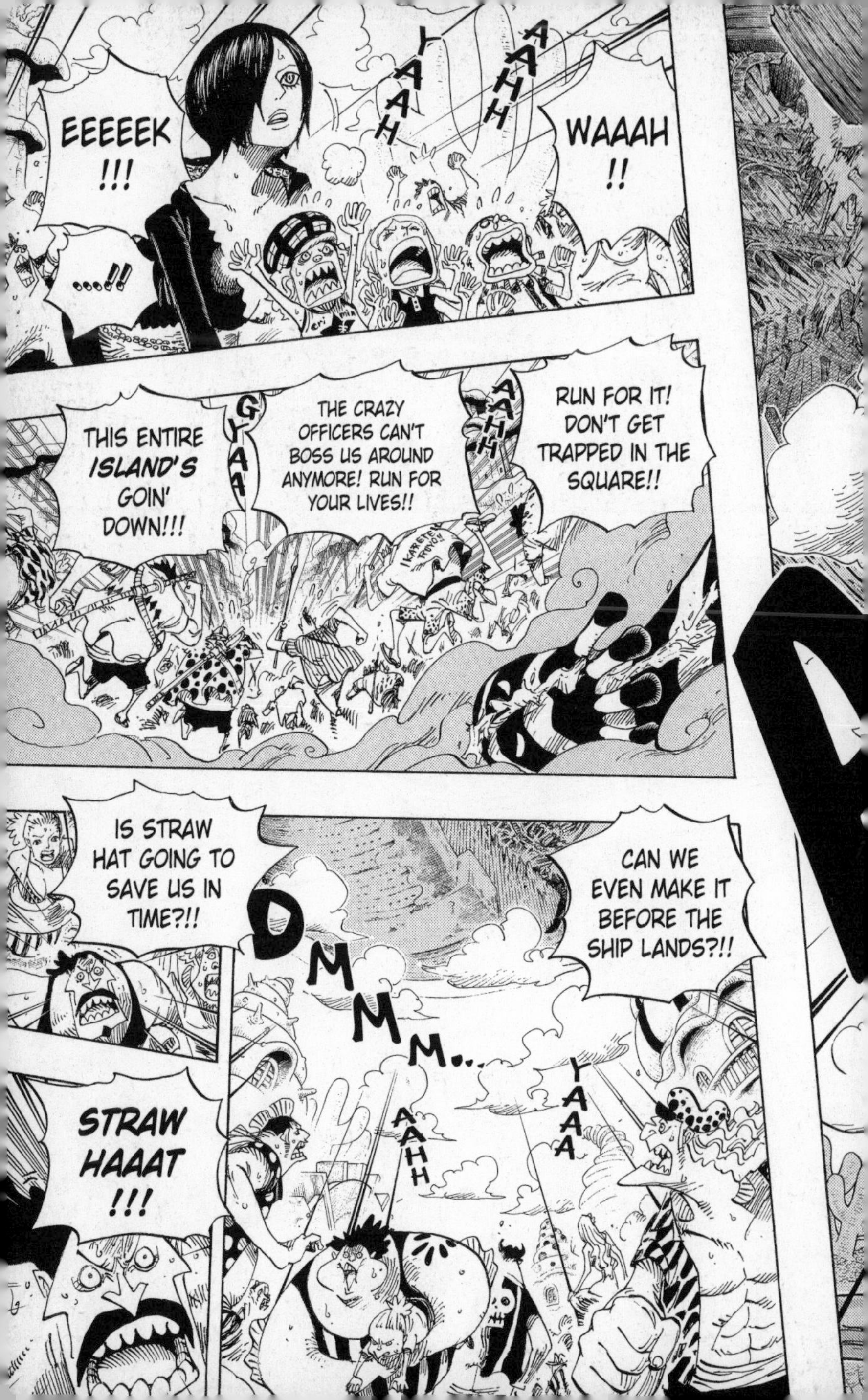
WAAAH !!
AAHH
YAAAH
EEEEEK !!!
...!!
RUN FOR IT! DON'T GET TRAPPED IN THE SQUARE!!
AAHH
THE CRAZY OFFICERS CAN'T BOSS US AROUND ANYMORE! RUN FOR YOUR LIVES!!
GYAA
THIS ENTIRE ISLAND'S GOIN' DOWN!!!
CAN WE EVEN MAKE IT BEFORE THE SHIP LANDS?!!
DMMM...
IS STRAW HAT GOING TO SAVE US IN TIME?!!
YAAA
AAHH
STRAW HAAAT !!!

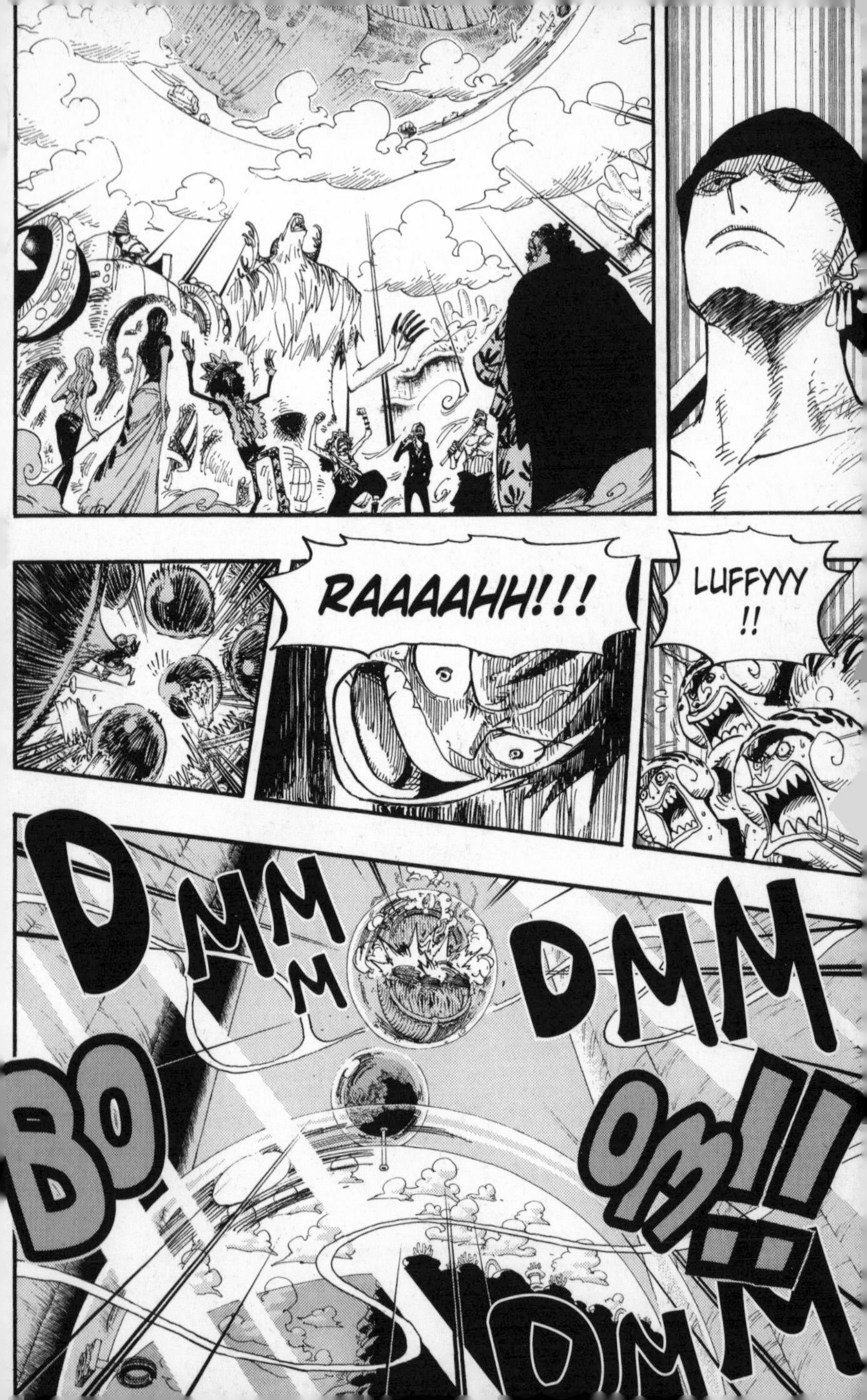
LUFFYYY !!
RAAAAHH!!!
DMM
DMMM
BOOM!!

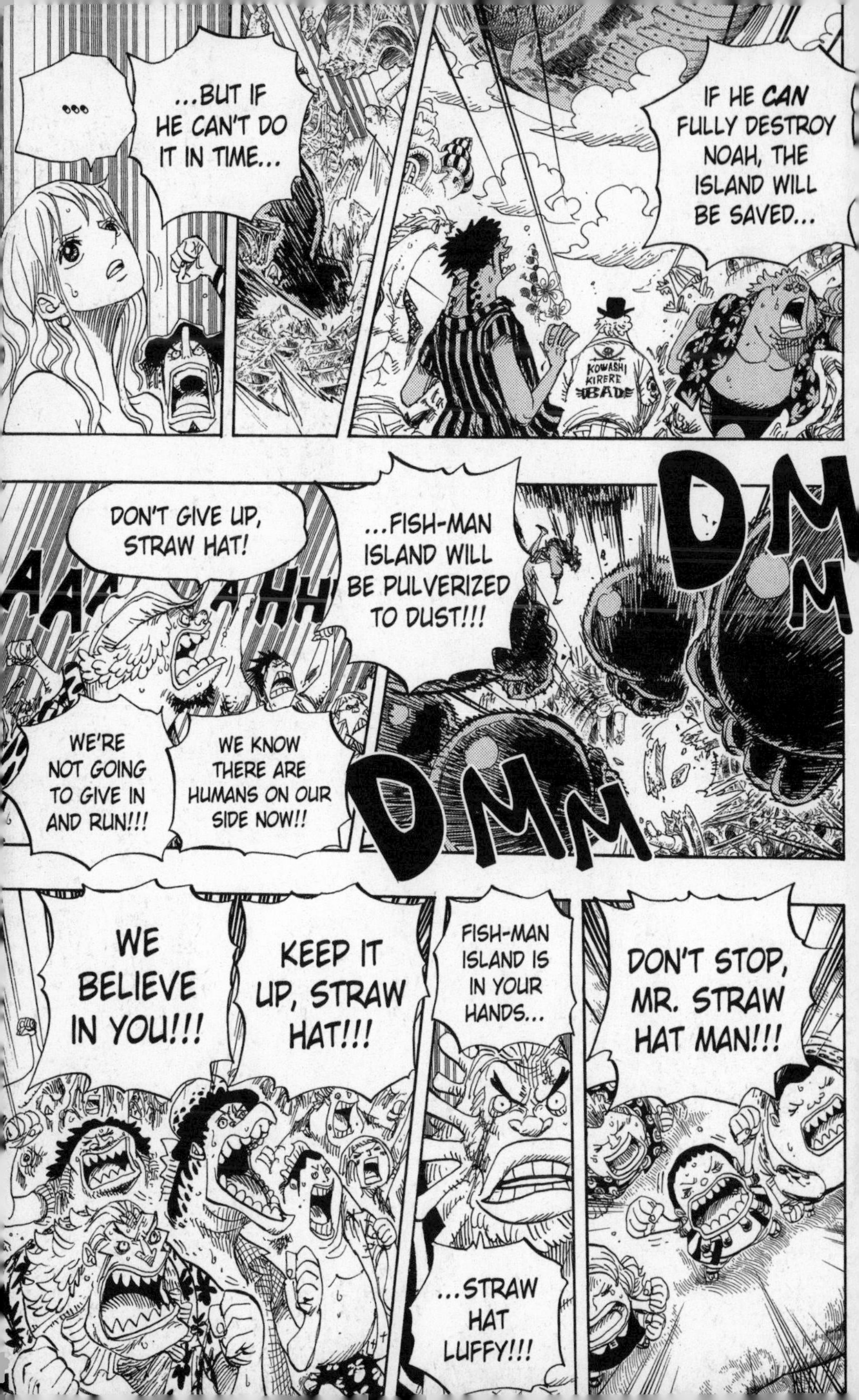
IF HE CAN FULLY DESTROY NOAH, THE ISLAND WILL BE SAVED...
...BUT IF HE CAN'T DO IT IN TIME...
...
KOWASHI KIRERE BAD
DMM
...FISH-MAN ISLAND WILL BE PULVERIZED TO DUST!!!
DMM
DON'T GIVE UP, STRAW HAT!
WE KNOW THERE ARE HUMANS ON OUR SIDE NOW!!
WE'RE NOT GOING TO GIVE IN AND RUN!!!
DON'T STOP, MR. STRAW HAT MAN!!!
FISH-MAN ISLAND IS IN YOUR HANDS...
...STRAW HAT LUFFY!!!
KEEP IT UP, STRAW HAT!!!
WE BELIEVE IN YOU!!!

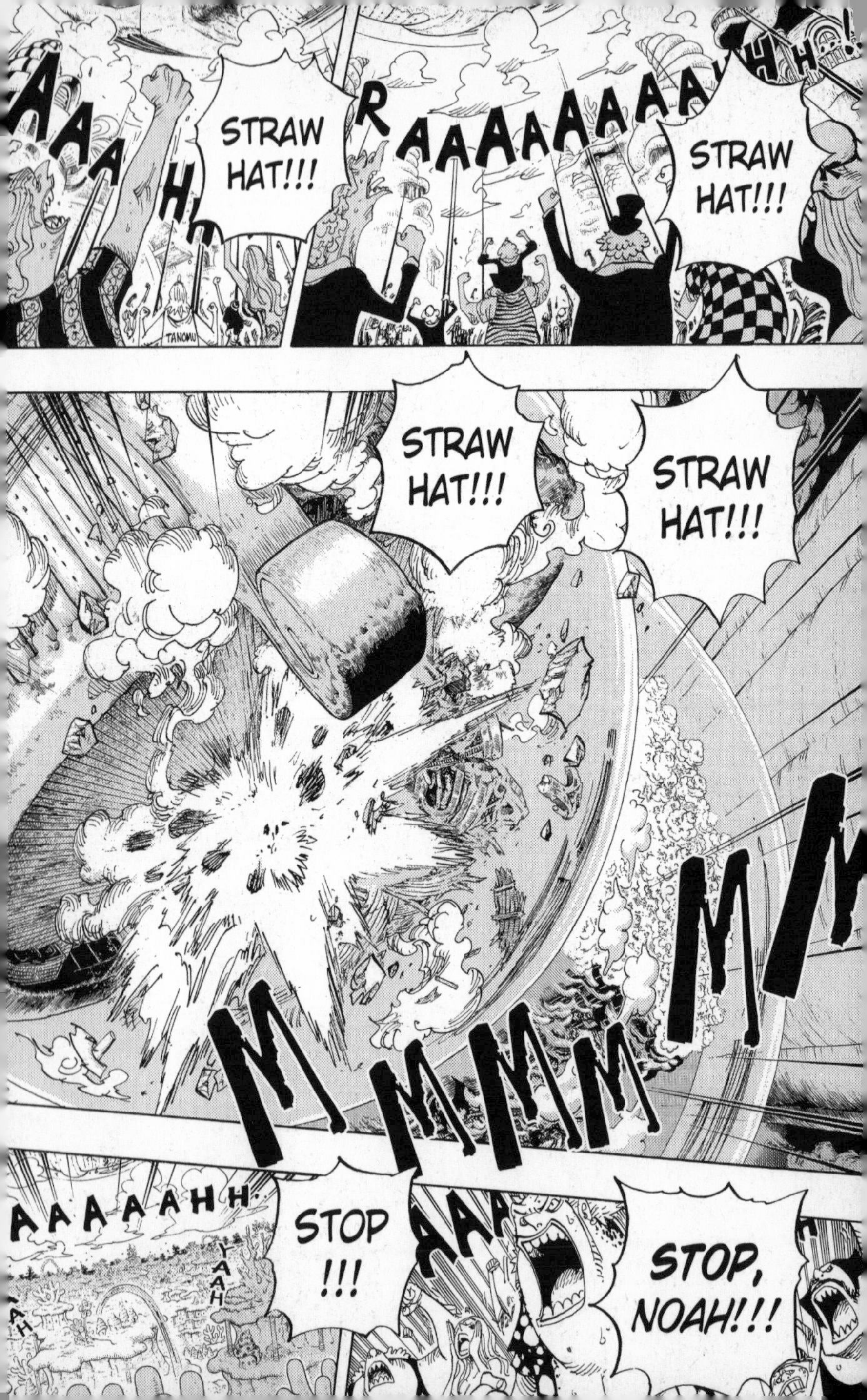
STRAW HAT!!!
RAAAAAAAAHH!
STRAW HAT!!!
AAAAH
TANOMU
STRAW HAT!!!
STRAW HAT!!!
MMMMMM
STOP, NOAH!!!
AAA
STOP !!!
AAAAAAHH
YAAH

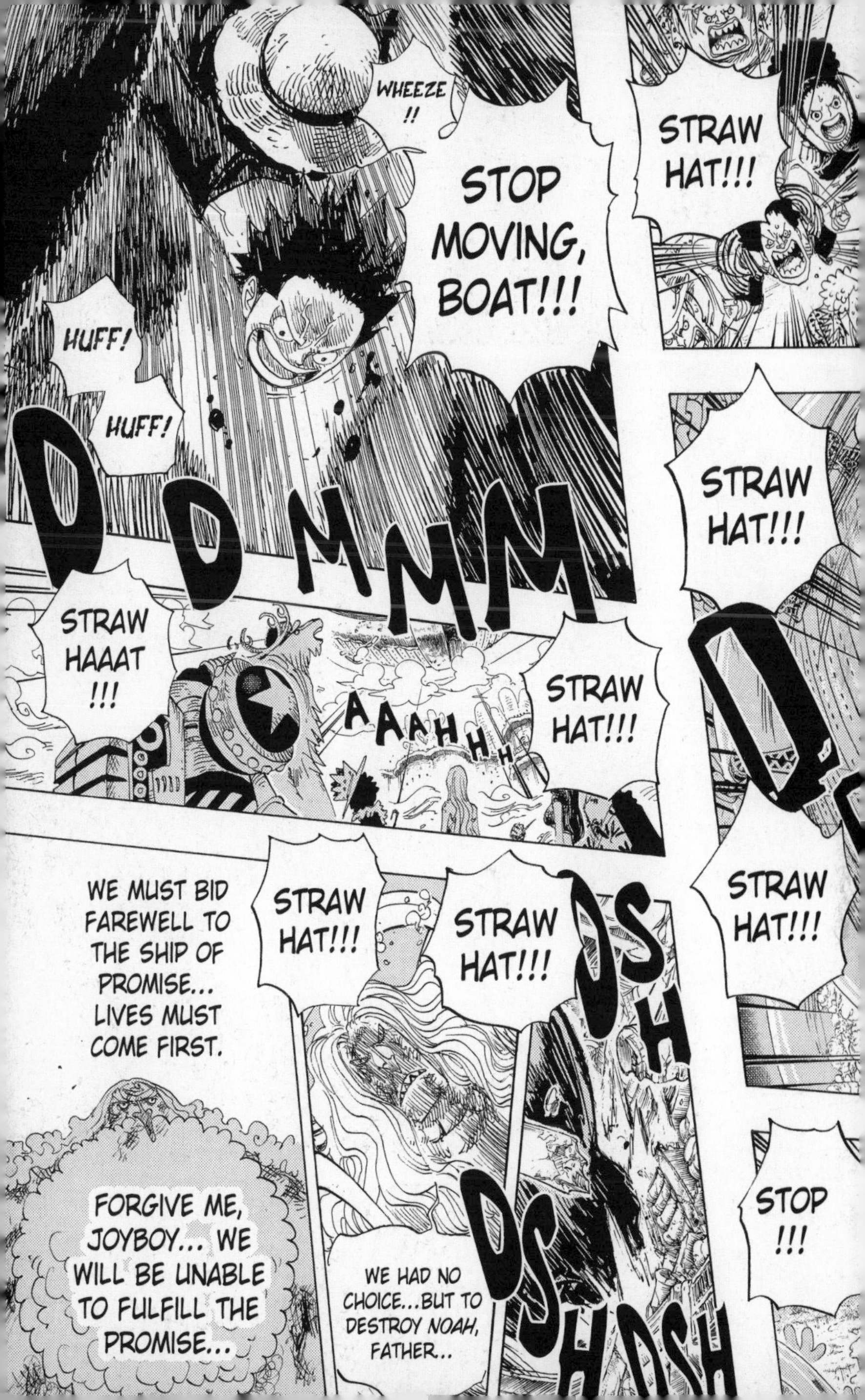
STRAW HAT!!!
WHEEZE !!
STOP MOVING, BOAT!!!
HUFF!
HUFF!
DDMMM
STRAW HAT!!!
STRAW HAT!!!
AAAHHH
STRAW HAAAT !!!
STRAW HAT!!!
STOP !!!
STRAW HAT!!!
STRAW HAT!!!
WE HAD NO CHOICE...BUT TO DESTROY NOAH, FATHER...
WE MUST BID FAREWELL TO THE SHIP OF PROMISE... LIVES MUST COME FIRST.
FORGIVE ME, JOYBOY... WE WILL BE UNABLE TO FULFILL THE PROMISE...

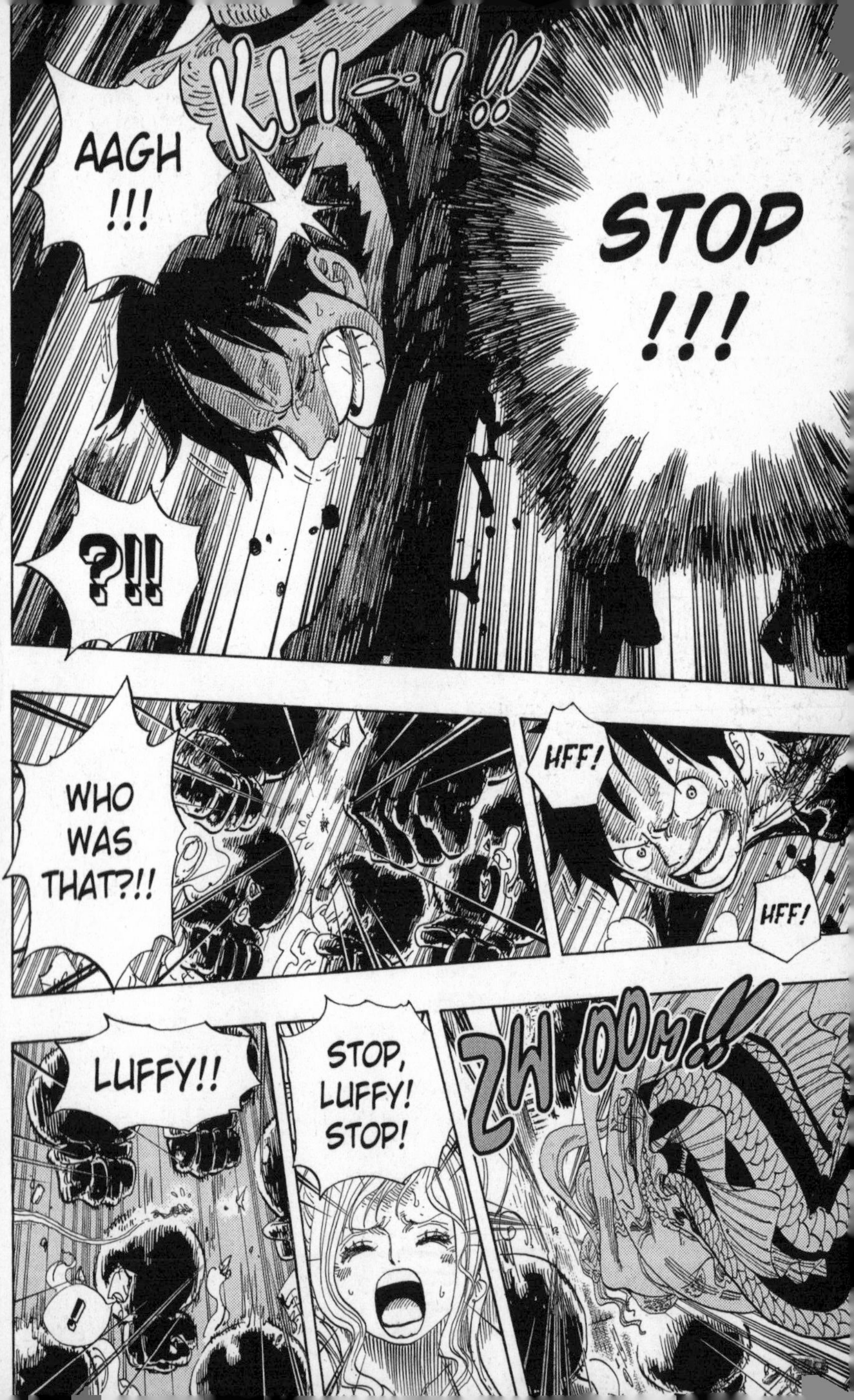
KI--!!
STOP!!!
AAGH!!!
?!!
HFF!
HFF!
WHO WAS THAT?!!
ZWOOM!!
STOP, LUFFY! STOP!
LUFFY!!
!

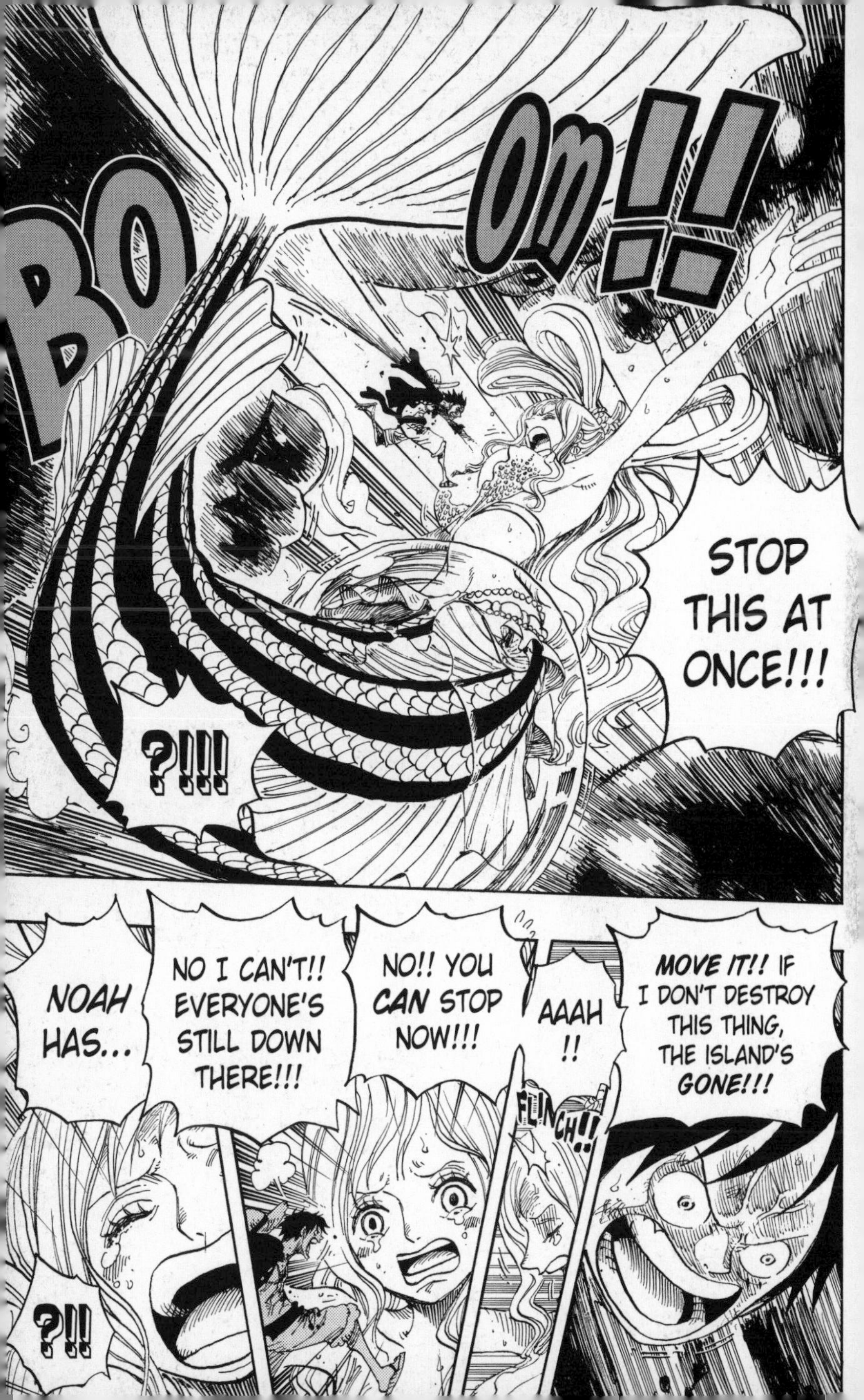
STOP THIS AT ONCE!!!
BOOM!!
?!!!
MOVE IT!! IF I DON'T DESTROY THIS THING, THE ISLAND'S GONE!!!
FLINCH!!
AAAH !!
NO!! YOU CAN STOP NOW!!!
NO I CAN'T!! EVERYONE'S STILL DOWN THERE!!!
NOAH HAS...
?!!

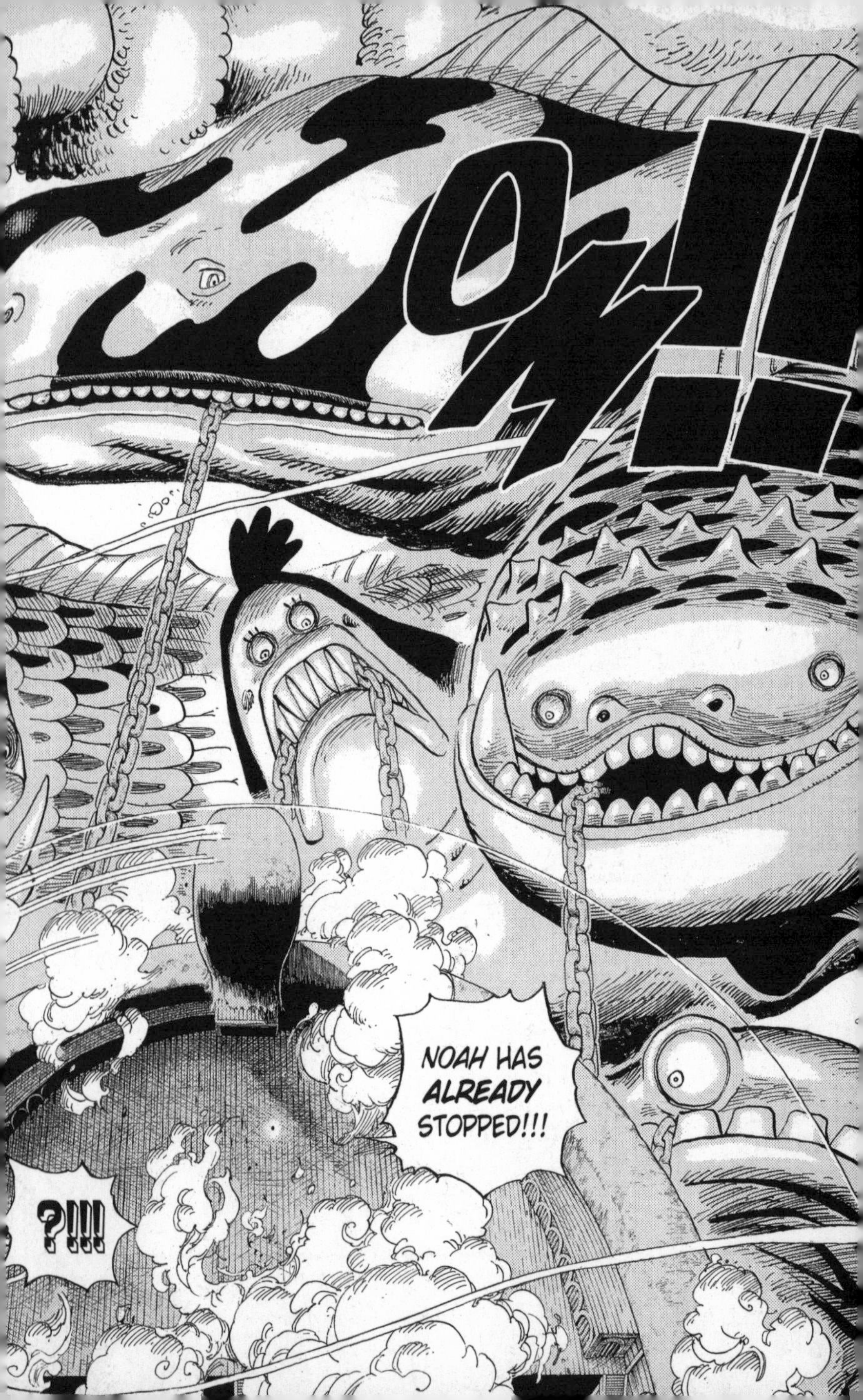
NOAH HAS ALREADY STOPPED!!!
?!!!

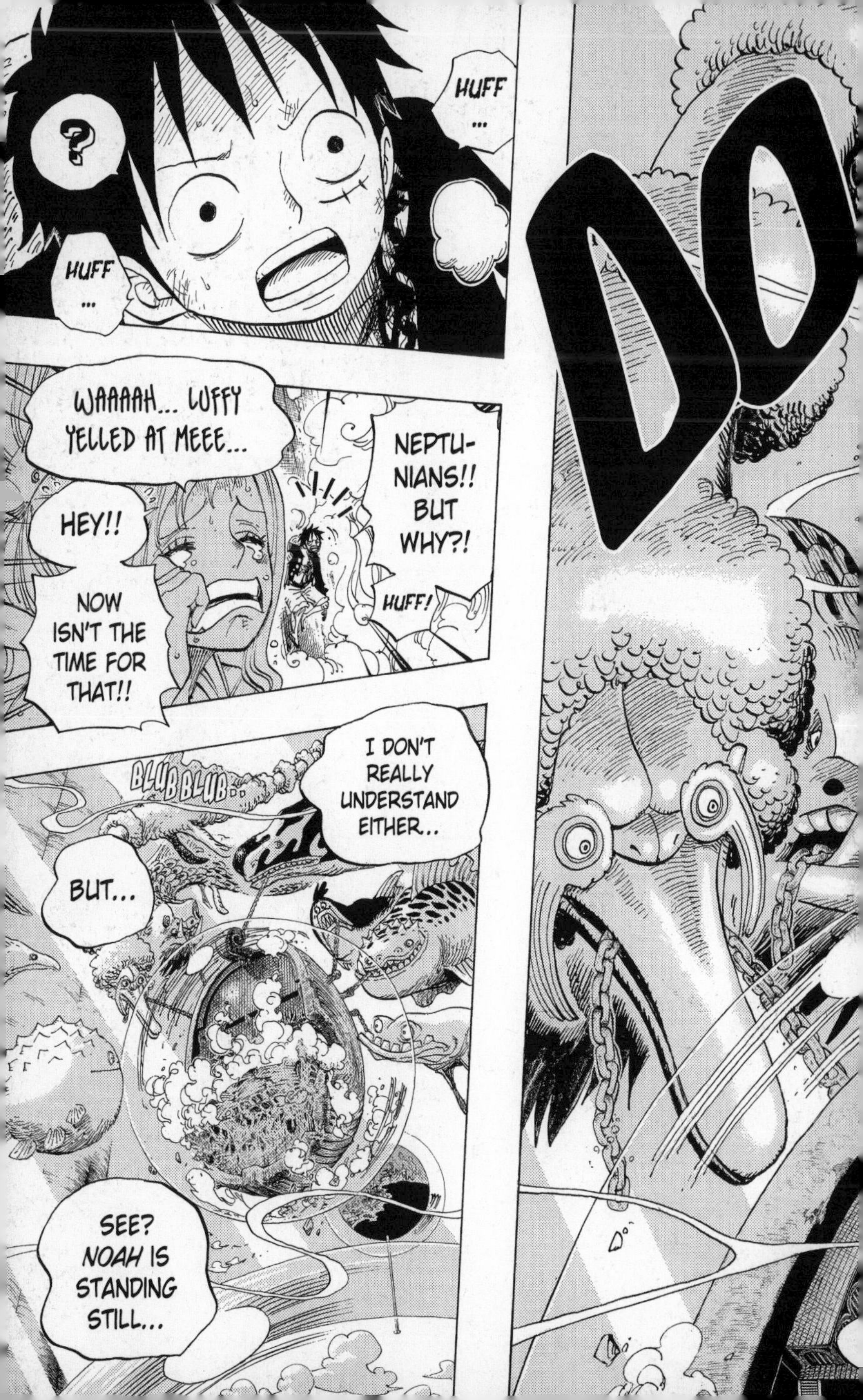
DO
?
HUFF ...
HUFF ...
NEPTUNIANS!! BUT WHY?!
HUFF!
WAAAAH... LUFFY YELLED AT MEEE...
HEY!!
NOW ISN'T THE TIME FOR THAT!!
I DON'T REALLY UNDERSTAND EITHER...
BLUB BLUB
BUT...
SEE? *NOAH* IS STANDING STILL...
DO

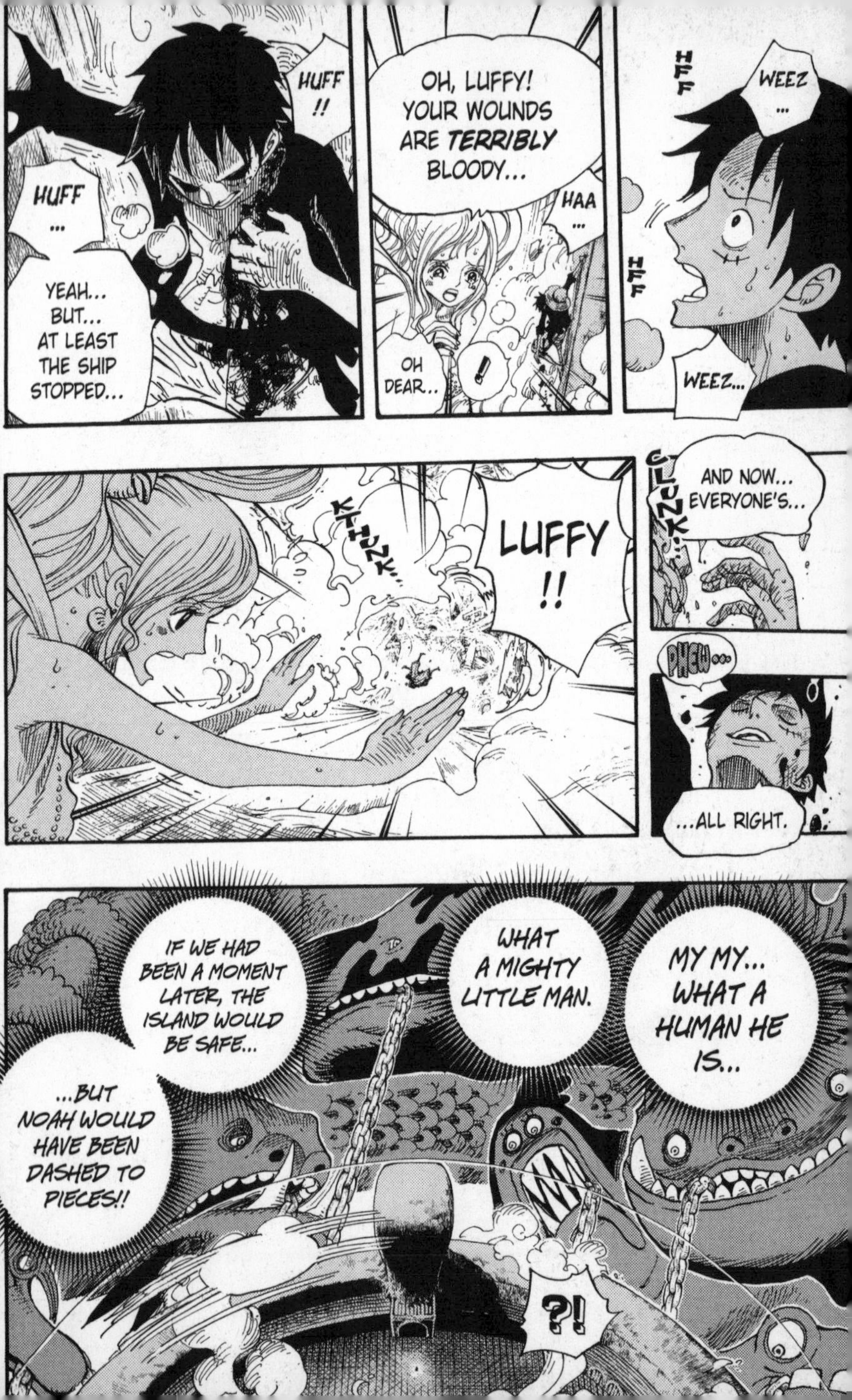
WEEZ ...
HFF
HFF
WEEZ...
OH, LUFFY! YOUR WOUNDS ARE TERRIBLY BLOODY...
HAA ...
!
OH DEAR..
HUFF !!
HUFF ...
YEAH... BUT... AT LEAST THE SHIP STOPPED...
CLUNK...
AND NOW... EVERYONE'S...
PHEW...
...ALL RIGHT.
LUFFY !!
KTHUNK...
MY MY... WHAT A HUMAN HE IS...
WHAT A MIGHTY LITTLE MAN.
IF WE HAD BEEN A MOMENT LATER, THE ISLAND WOULD BE SAFE...
...BUT NOAH WOULD HAVE BEEN DASHED TO PIECES!!
?!

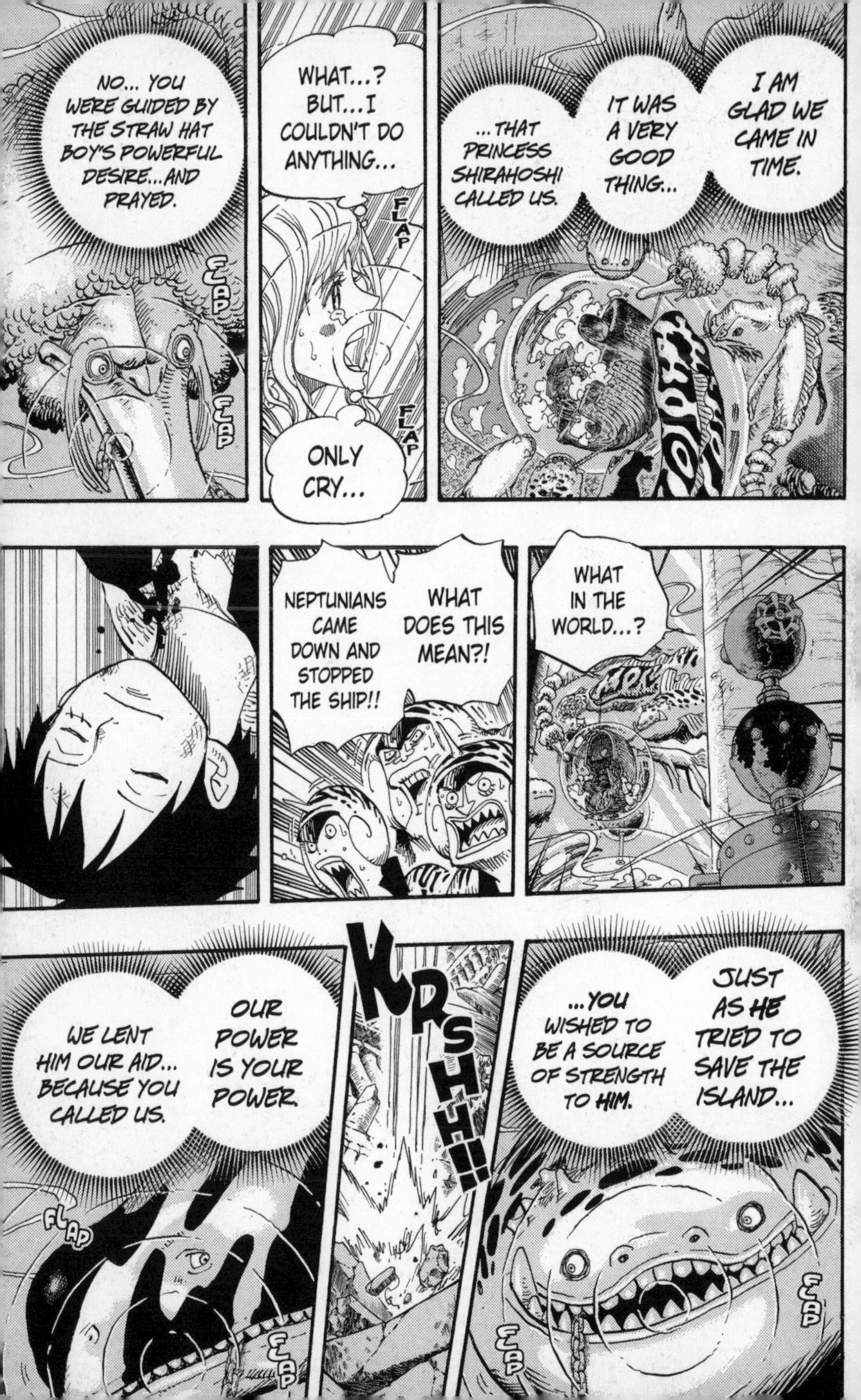
I AM GLAD WE CAME IN TIME.
IT WAS A VERY GOOD THING...
...THAT PRINCESS SHIRAHOSHI CALLED US.
WHAT...? BUT...I COULDN'T DO ANYTHING...
FLAP
FLAP
ONLY CRY...
NO... YOU WERE GUIDED BY THE STRAW HAT BOY'S POWERFUL DESIRE...AND PRAYED.
FLAP
FLAP
WHAT IN THE WORLD...?
WHAT DOES THIS MEAN?!
NEPTUNIANS CAME DOWN AND STOPPED THE SHIP!!
JUST AS HE TRIED TO SAVE THE ISLAND...
...YOU WISHED TO BE A SOURCE OF STRENGTH TO HIM.
FLAP
FLAP
KRSHH!!
OUR POWER IS YOUR POWER.
WE LENT HIM OUR AID... BECAUSE YOU CALLED US.
FLAP
FLAP

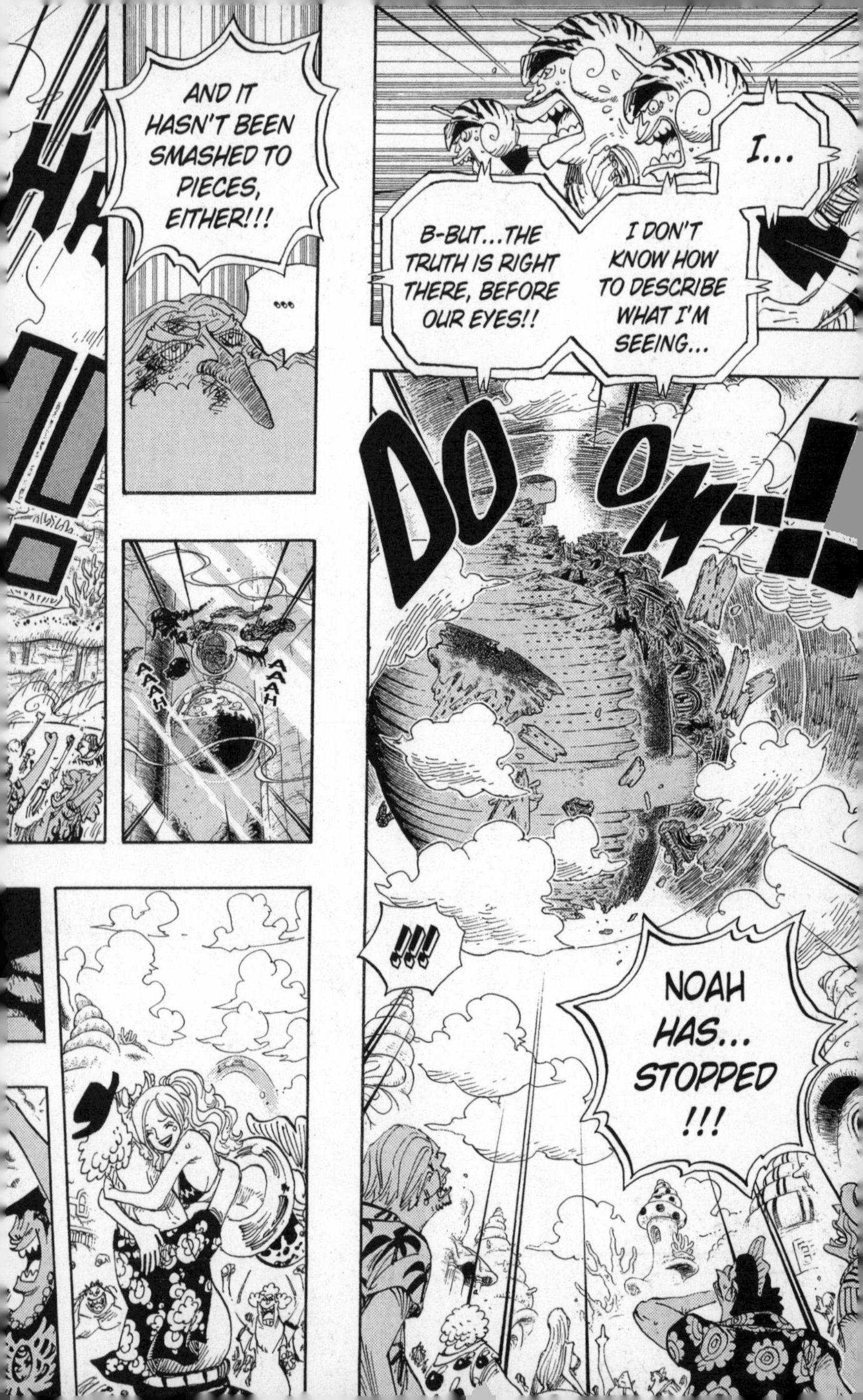
I...
I DON'T KNOW HOW TO DESCRIBE WHAT I'M SEEING...
B-BUT...THE TRUTH IS RIGHT THERE, BEFORE OUR EYES!!
AND IT HASN'T BEEN SMASHED TO PIECES, EITHER!!!
...
AAAH
AAAH
DOOM!!
!!!
NOAH HAS... STOPPED!!!

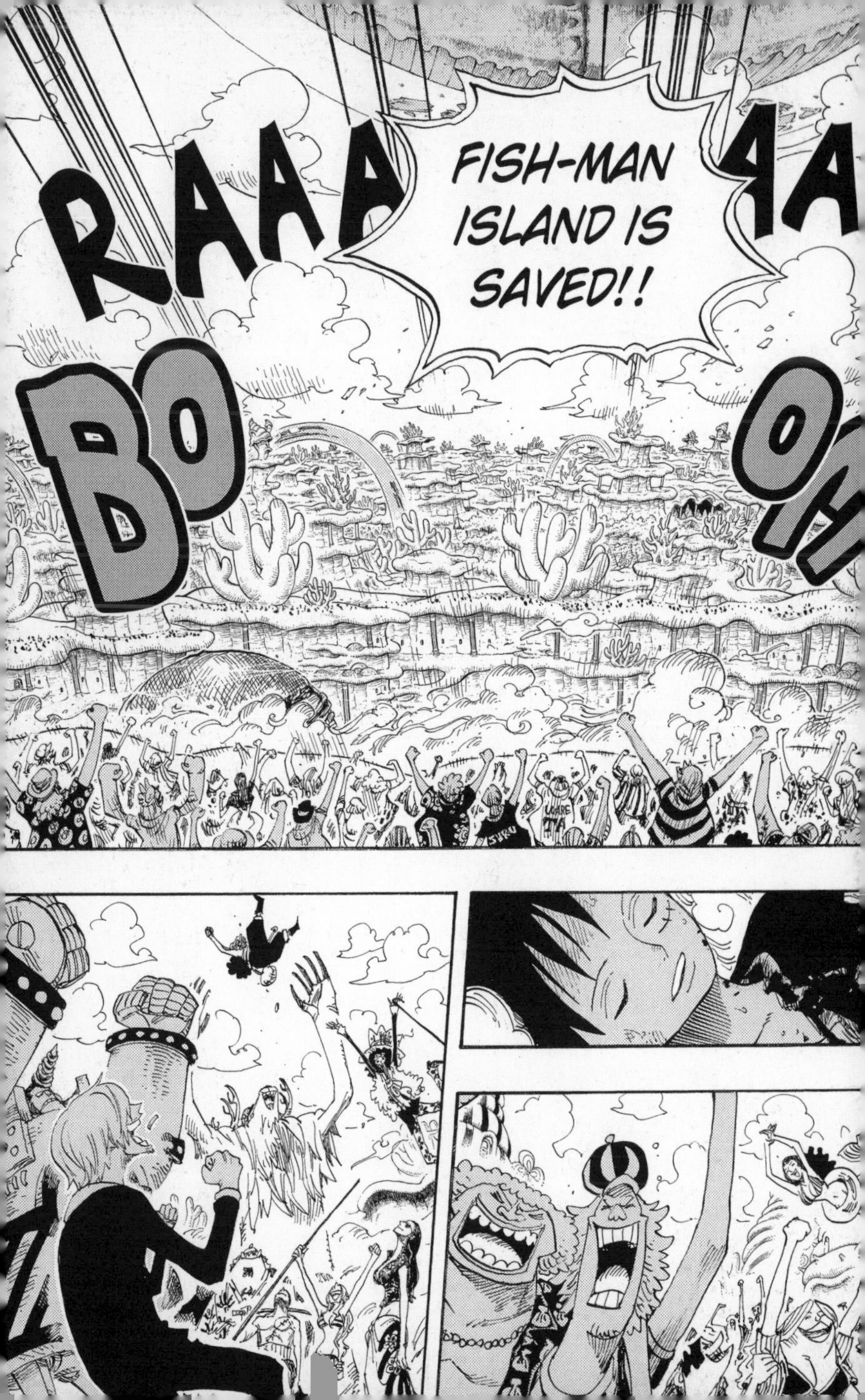
FISH-MAN ISLAND IS SAVED!!
RAAA AA
BO OH

SBS Question Corner

(Ponio, Aichi)

Q: Greetings, Mr. Oda and readers of *One Piece*. I am a bonafide **psychic,** and I am going to correctly predict what Mr. Oda wants to say right now.

"Start the SBS." Well? Impressive, isn't it?

--M. Mimori

A: You're right!!! Huh?! How did you know?! Geez, that was freaky!!

Q: Is Akainu's wiener magma-y? --Wi

A: Hey!

Q: Is Aokiji's wiener chilly? -en

A: Stop that!

Q: Is Kizaru's wiener flashy? -Er

A: Knock it off!! Are these questions really appropriate for the start of the book? Yes to all three!!!

Q: Odacchi, Odacchi, when does the New World Nami full-body pillow come out?

--Captain Nobuo

A: I don't know!! Look, I'm not involved with merchandising, nor do I know everything about every product! Although, if I could design one, I'd love to have Franky's arms. You could put them on over your arms and grab people's heads with them. And they'd make cool sounds and everything. Bandai, can you start working on that?

Q: Why do you draw yourself as a fish? Knowing you, I'm sure there's a very deep and thoughtful meaning behind it!

--Emi@3!04

A: There's no meaning behind it at all!

Q: If you cooked the giant kraken, how many octopus fritters could you make?

--Hunting Pirates

A: Good question. Even if you were on the generous side in terms of doling out the portions...you could probably make ten million fritters. So, at eight per pack....that's one and a quarter million servings! Food for one and a quarter million people! Wait, don't eat your friends!!

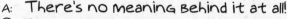

26

Chaper 648:
THE ROAD TOWARD THE SUN

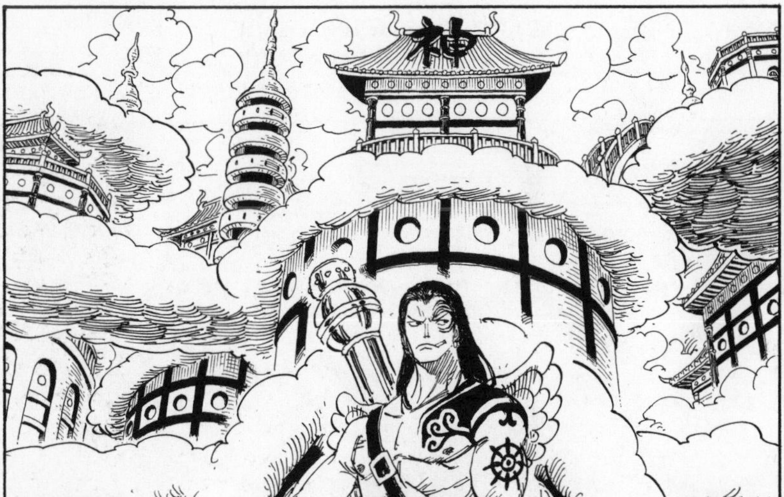
神

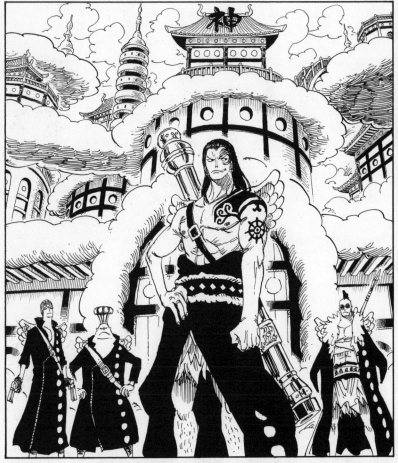

DECKS OF THE WORLD, VOL. 31:
"SKYPIEA—KAMI'S GUARDIANS"

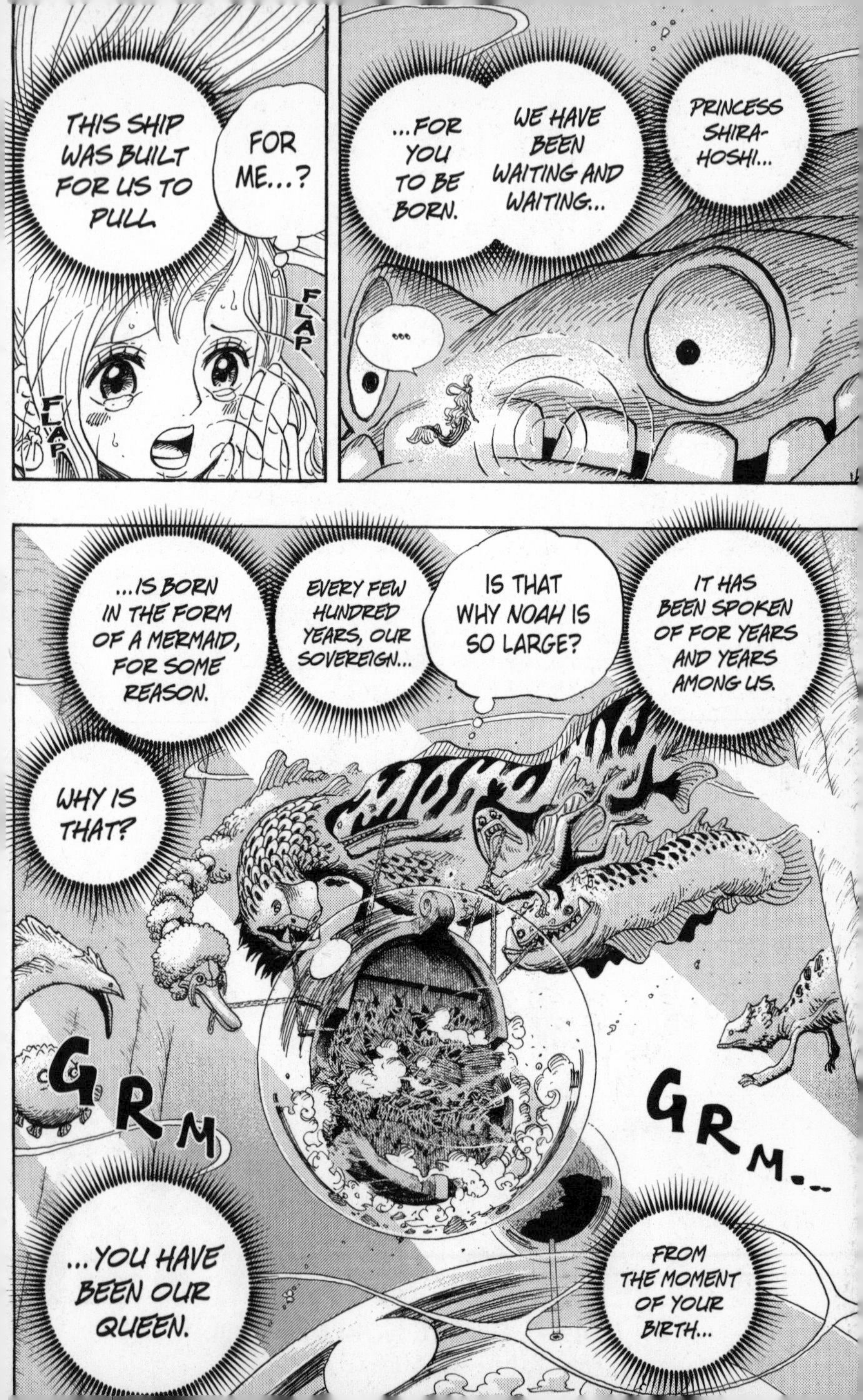
PRINCESS SHIRAHOSHI...
WE HAVE BEEN WAITING AND WAITING...
...FOR YOU TO BE BORN.
...
FOR ME...?
THIS SHIP WAS BUILT FOR US TO PULL
FLAP
FLAP
IT HAS BEEN SPOKEN OF FOR YEARS AND YEARS AMONG US.
IS THAT WHY NOAH IS SO LARGE?
EVERY FEW HUNDRED YEARS, OUR SOVEREIGN...
...IS BORN IN THE FORM OF A MERMAID, FOR SOME REASON.
WHY IS THAT?
GRM...
GRM
FROM THE MOMENT OF YOUR BIRTH...
...YOU HAVE BEEN OUR QUEEN.

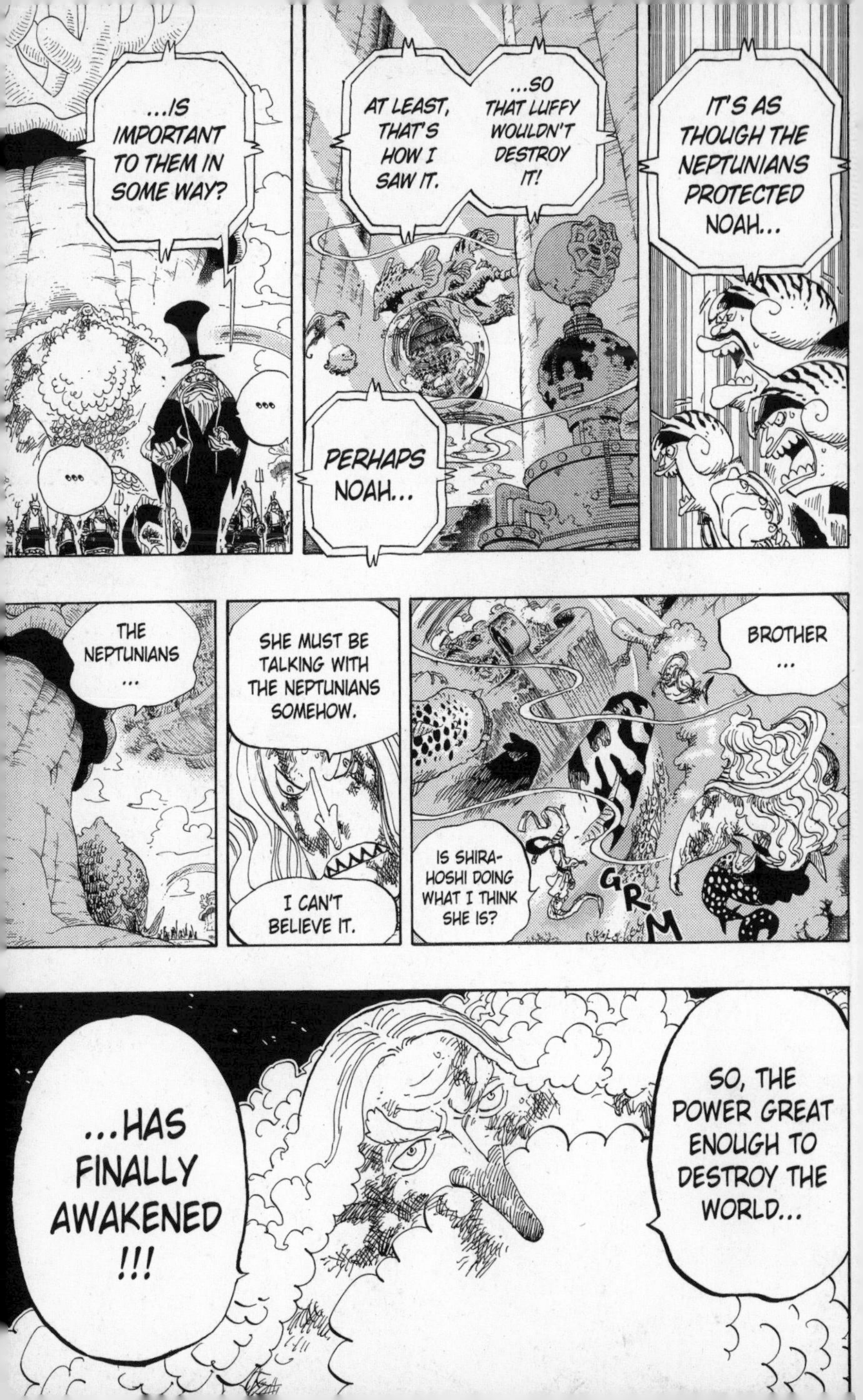
IT'S AS THOUGH THE NEPTUNIANS PROTECTED NOAH...
...SO THAT LUFFY WOULDN'T DESTROY IT!
AT LEAST, THAT'S HOW I SAW IT.
PERHAPS NOAH...
...IS IMPORTANT TO THEM IN SOME WAY?
...
...
BROTHER ...
IS SHIRA-HOSHI DOING WHAT I THINK SHE IS?
GRM
SHE MUST BE TALKING WITH THE NEPTUNIANS SOMEHOW.
I CAN'T BELIEVE IT.
THE NEPTUNIANS ...
SO, THE POWER GREAT ENOUGH TO DESTROY THE WORLD...
...HAS FINALLY AWAKENED !!!

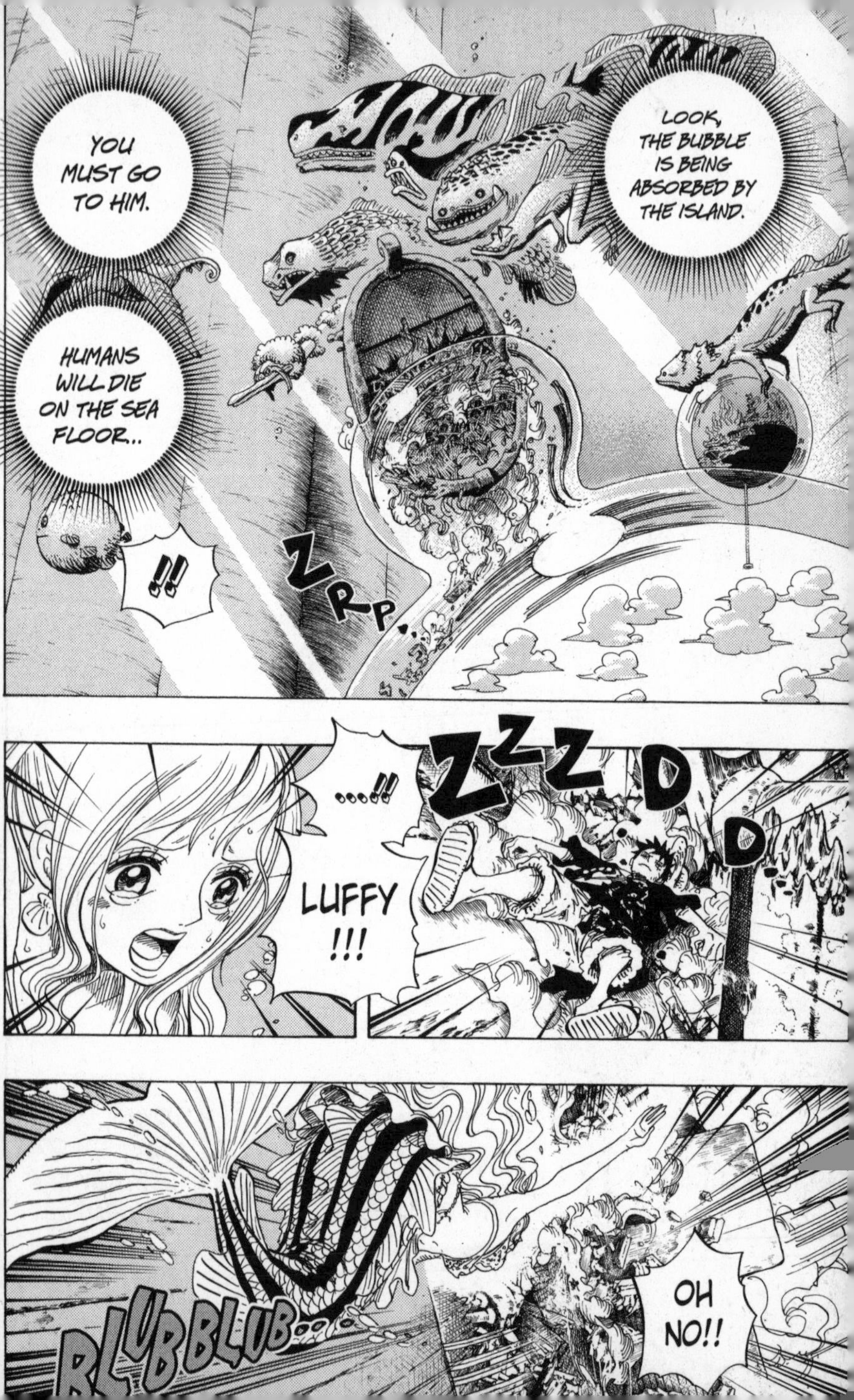
LOOK, THE BUBBLE IS BEING ABSORBED BY THE ISLAND.
YOU MUST GO TO HIM.
HUMANS WILL DIE ON THE SEA FLOOR...
ZRP..
!!
ZZZD D..
...!!
LUFFY !!!
OH NO!!
BLUBBLUB..

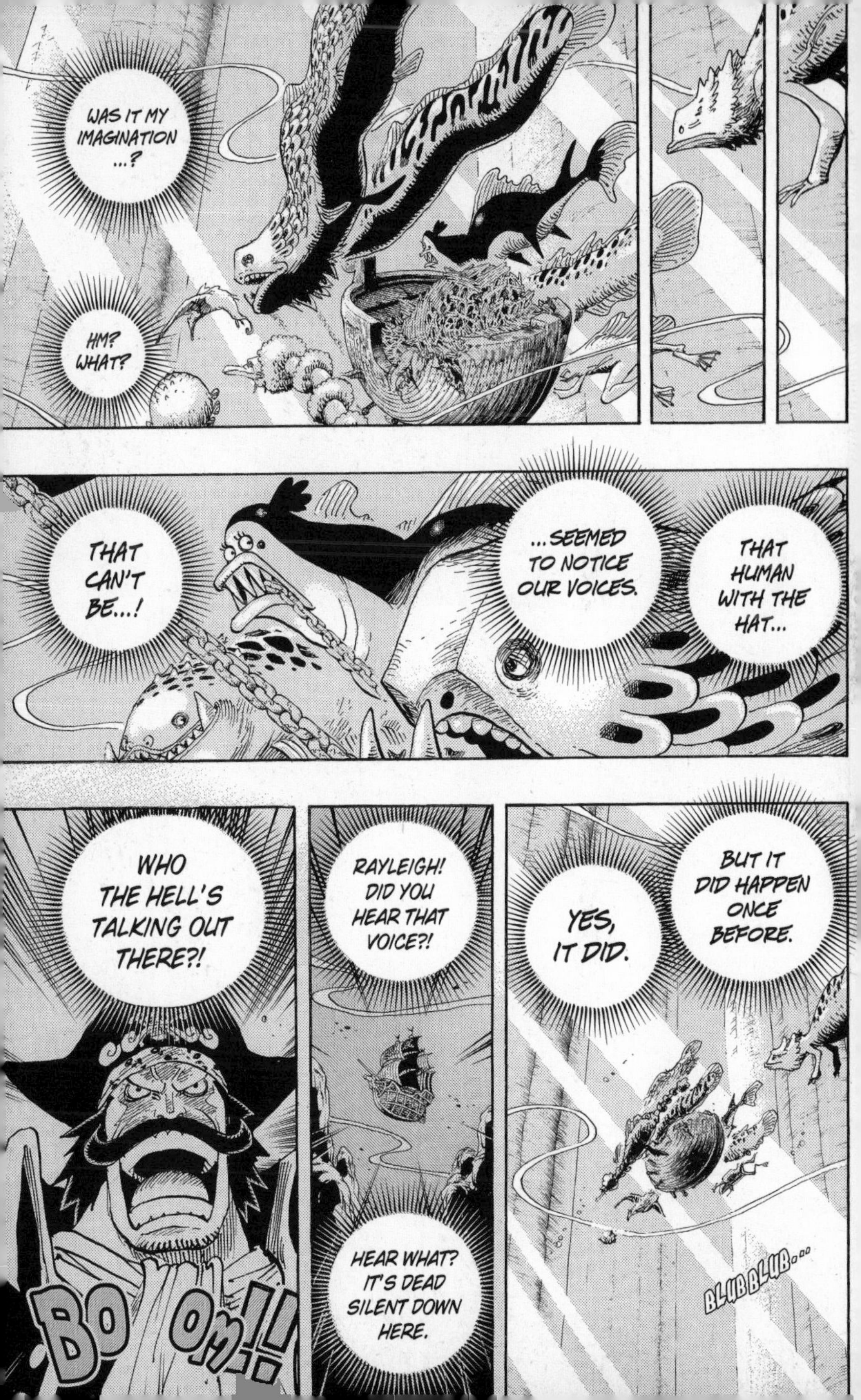
WAS IT MY IMAGINATION ...?
HM? WHAT?
THAT HUMAN WITH THE HAT...
...SEEMED TO NOTICE OUR VOICES.
THAT CAN'T BE...!
BUT IT DID HAPPEN ONCE BEFORE.
YES, IT DID.
BLUB BLUB...
RAYLEIGH! DID YOU HEAR THAT VOICE?!
HEAR WHAT? IT'S DEAD SILENT DOWN HERE.
WHO THE HELL'S TALKING OUT THERE?!
BOOM!!

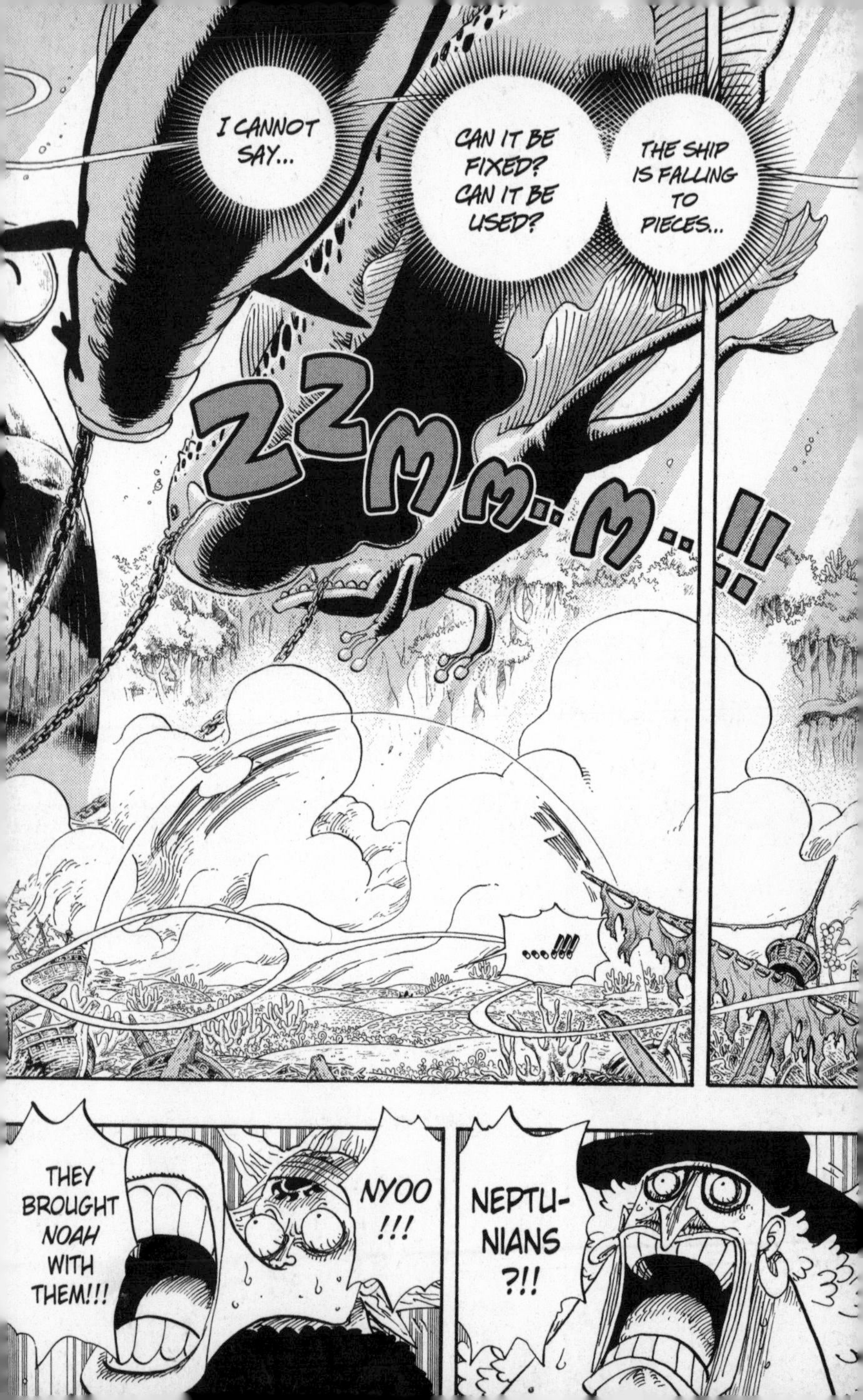
THE SHIP IS FALLING TO PIECES...
CAN IT BE FIXED? CAN IT BE USED?
I CANNOT SAY...
ZZMM..M..!!
...!!!
NEPTUNIANS?!!
NYOO!!!
THEY BROUGHT NOAH WITH THEM!!!

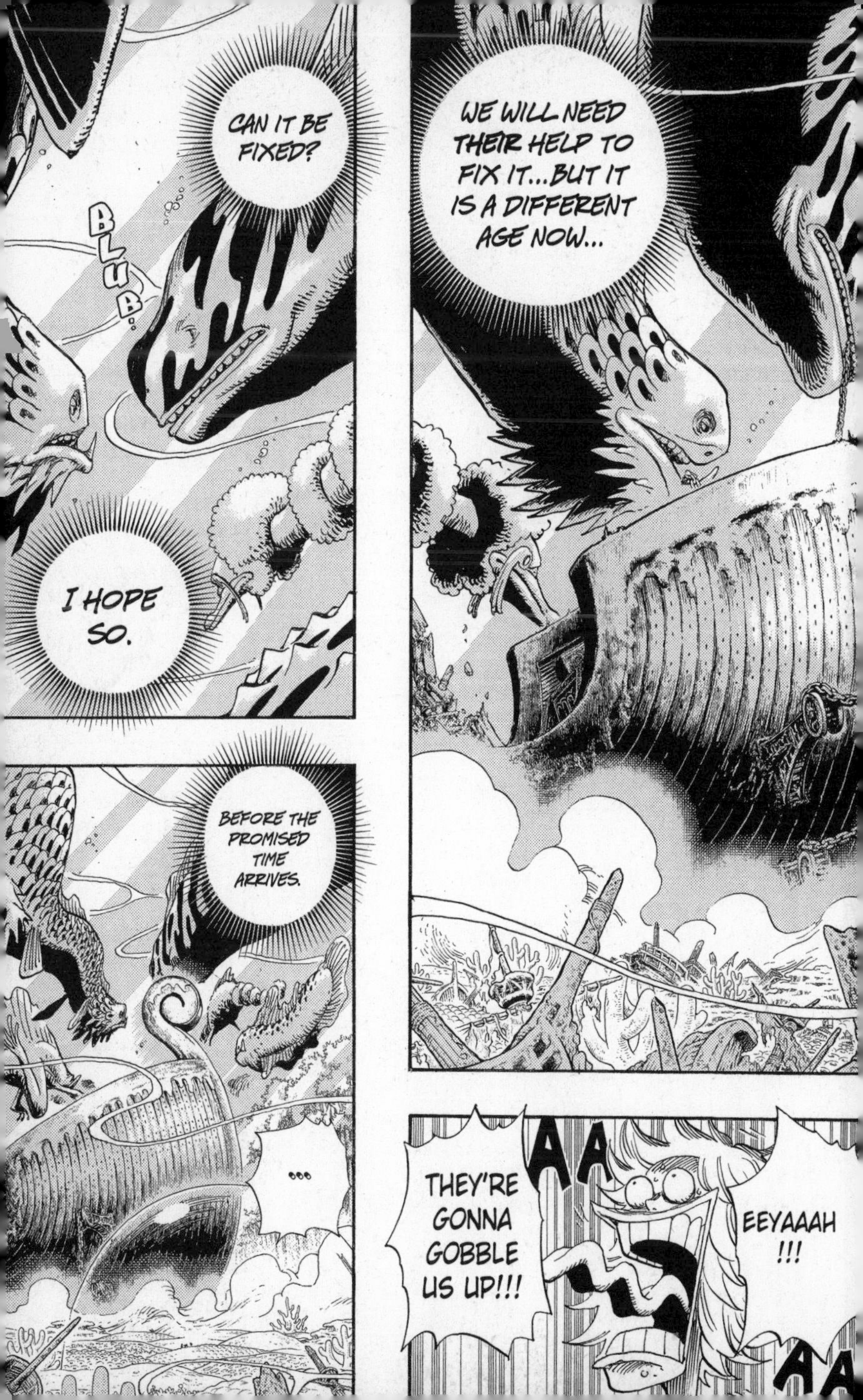

WE WILL NEED THEIR HELP TO FIX IT...BUT IT IS A DIFFERENT AGE NOW...
CAN IT BE FIXED?
BLUB..
I HOPE SO.
BEFORE THE PROMISED TIME ARRIVES.
...
AA
THEY'RE GONNA GOBBLE US UP!!!
EEYAAAH !!!
AA

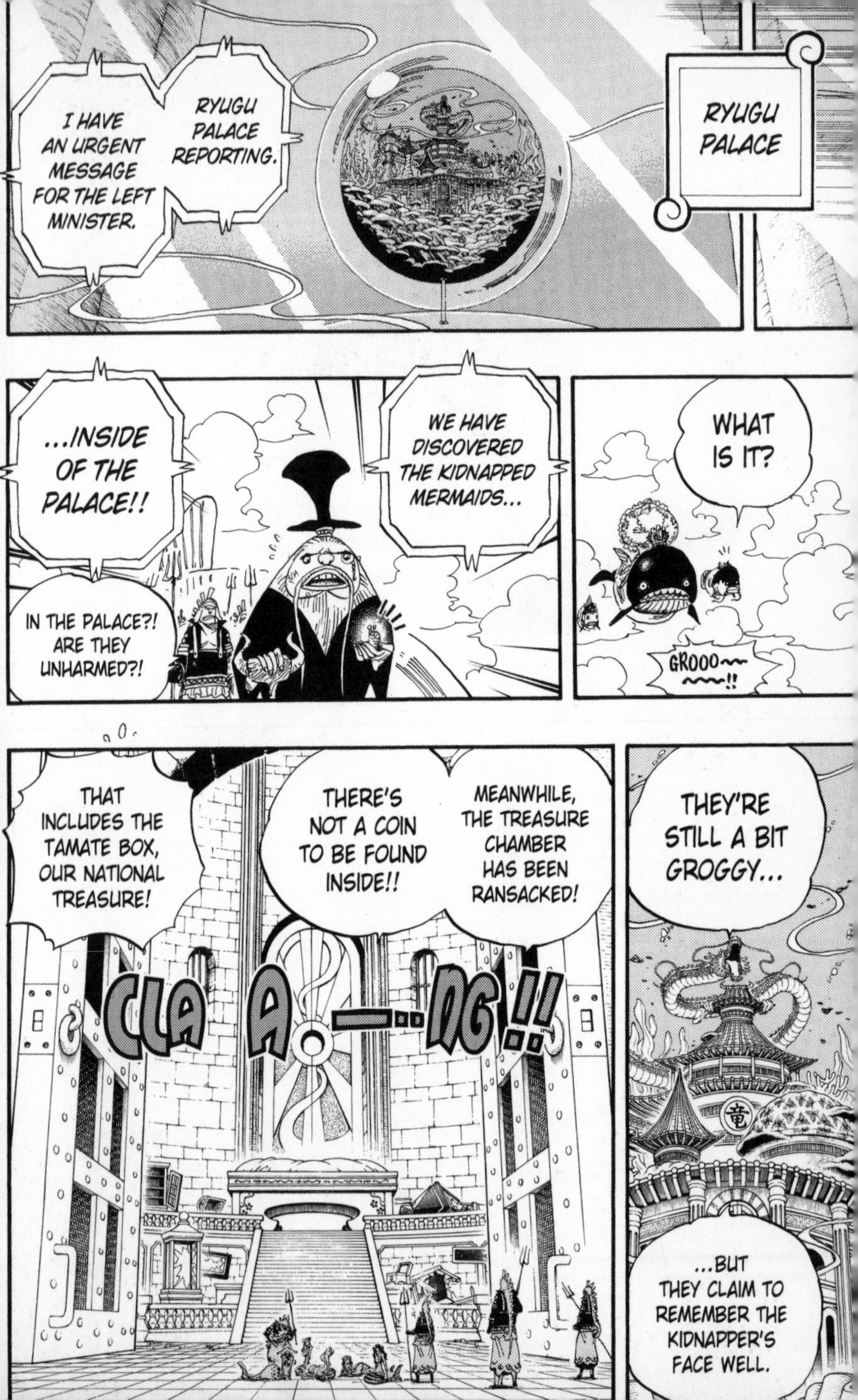
RYUGU PALACE
RYUGU PALACE REPORTING.
I HAVE AN URGENT MESSAGE FOR THE LEFT MINISTER.
WHAT IS IT?
GROOO~~ ~~~!!
WE HAVE DISCOVERED THE KIDNAPPED MERMAIDS...
...INSIDE OF THE PALACE!!
IN THE PALACE?! ARE THEY UNHARMED?!
THEY'RE STILL A BIT GROGGY...
...BUT THEY CLAIM TO REMEMBER THE KIDNAPPER'S FACE WELL.
MEANWHILE, THE TREASURE CHAMBER HAS BEEN RANSACKED!
THERE'S NOT A COIN TO BE FOUND INSIDE!!
THAT INCLUDES THE TAMATE BOX, OUR NATIONAL TREASURE!
CLA A—..NG!!

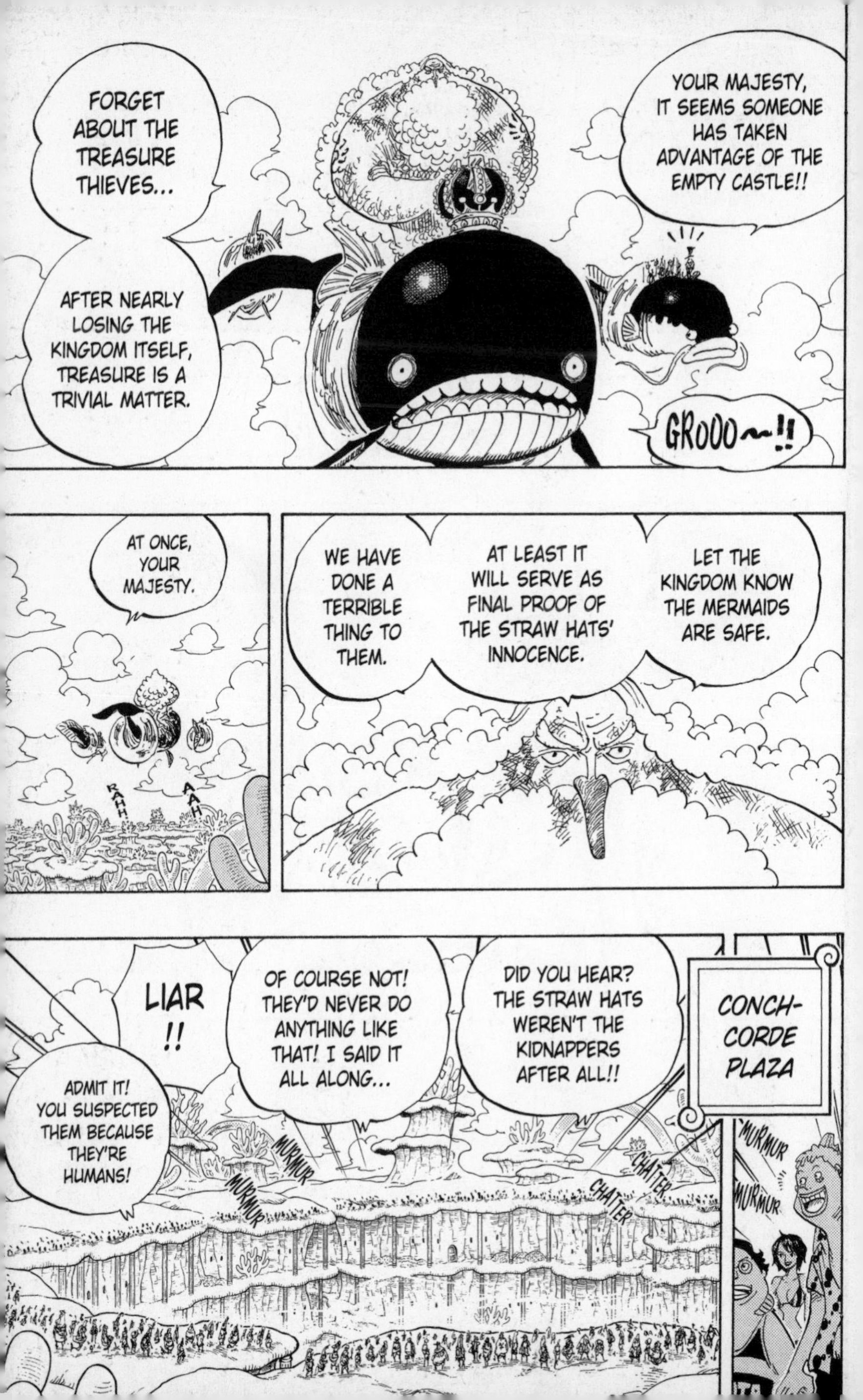
YOUR MAJESTY, IT SEEMS SOMEONE HAS TAKEN ADVANTAGE OF THE EMPTY CASTLE!!
GROOO~!!
FORGET ABOUT THE TREASURE THIEVES...
AFTER NEARLY LOSING THE KINGDOM ITSELF, TREASURE IS A TRIVIAL MATTER.
LET THE KINGDOM KNOW THE MERMAIDS ARE SAFE.
AT LEAST IT WILL SERVE AS FINAL PROOF OF THE STRAW HATS' INNOCENCE.
WE HAVE DONE A TERRIBLE THING TO THEM.
AT ONCE, YOUR MAJESTY.
AAH
RAHH!
CONCH-CORDE PLAZA
MURMUR
MURMUR
DID YOU HEAR? THE STRAW HATS WEREN'T THE KIDNAPPERS AFTER ALL!!
CHATTER
CHATTER
OF COURSE NOT! THEY'D NEVER DO ANYTHING LIKE THAT! I SAID IT ALL ALONG...
MURMUR
MURMUR
LIAR!!
ADMIT IT! YOU SUSPECTED THEM BECAUSE THEY'RE HUMANS!

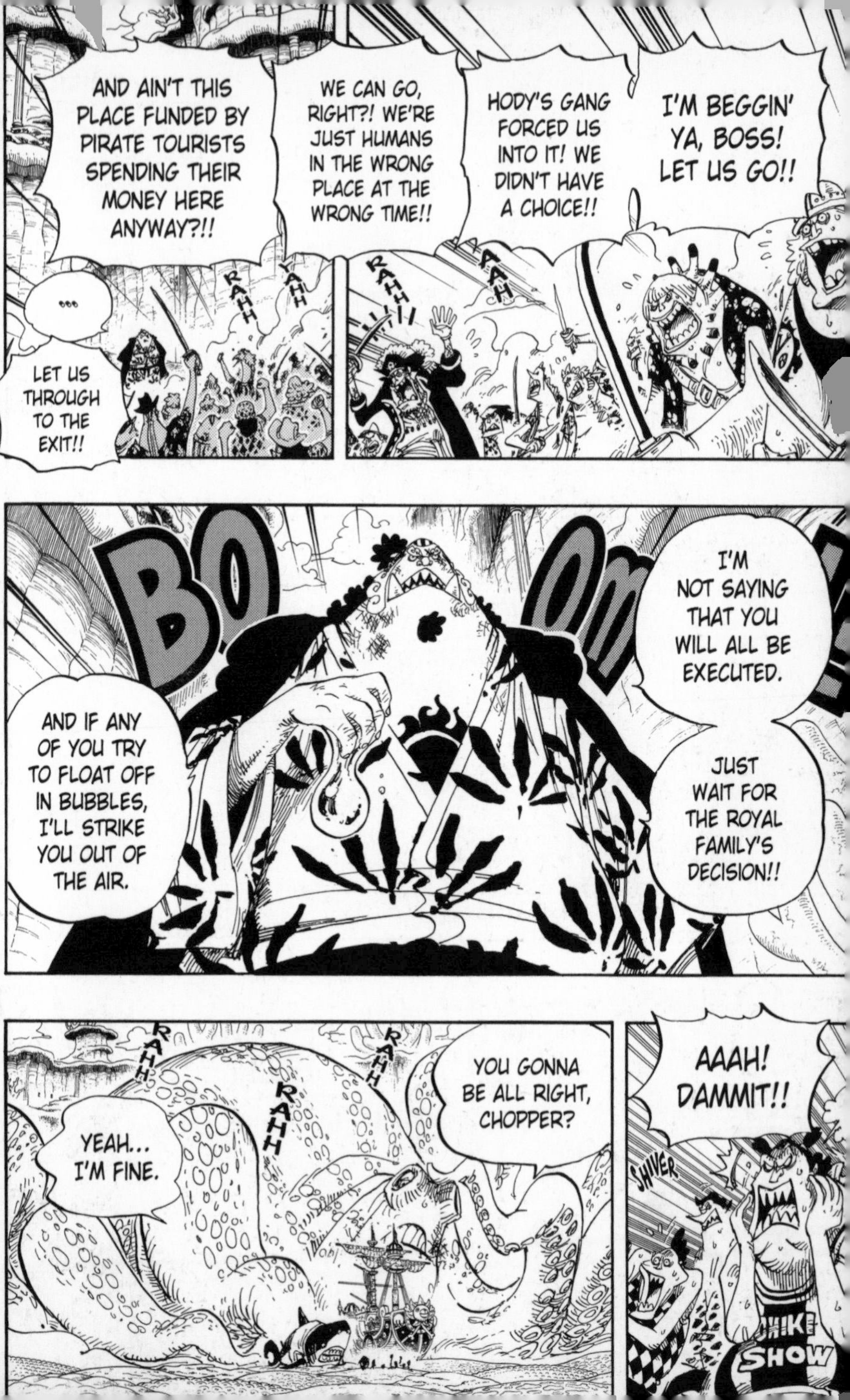
I'M BEGGIN' YA, BOSS! LET US GO!!
HODY'S GANG FORCED US INTO IT! WE DIDN'T HAVE A CHOICE!!
AAAH
RAHH
WE CAN GO, RIGHT?! WE'RE JUST HUMANS IN THE WRONG PLACE AT THE WRONG TIME!!
AND AIN'T THIS PLACE FUNDED BY PIRATE TOURISTS SPENDING THEIR MONEY HERE ANYWAY?!!
YAHH
RAHH
...
LET US THROUGH TO THE EXIT!!
BOOM
I'M NOT SAYING THAT YOU WILL ALL BE EXECUTED.
JUST WAIT FOR THE ROYAL FAMILY'S DECISION!!
AND IF ANY OF YOU TRY TO FLOAT OFF IN BUBBLES, I'LL STRIKE YOU OUT OF THE AIR.
AAAH! DAMMIT!!
SHIVER
SHOW
YOU GONNA BE ALL RIGHT, CHOPPER?
RAHH
RAHH
RAHH
YEAH... I'M FINE.

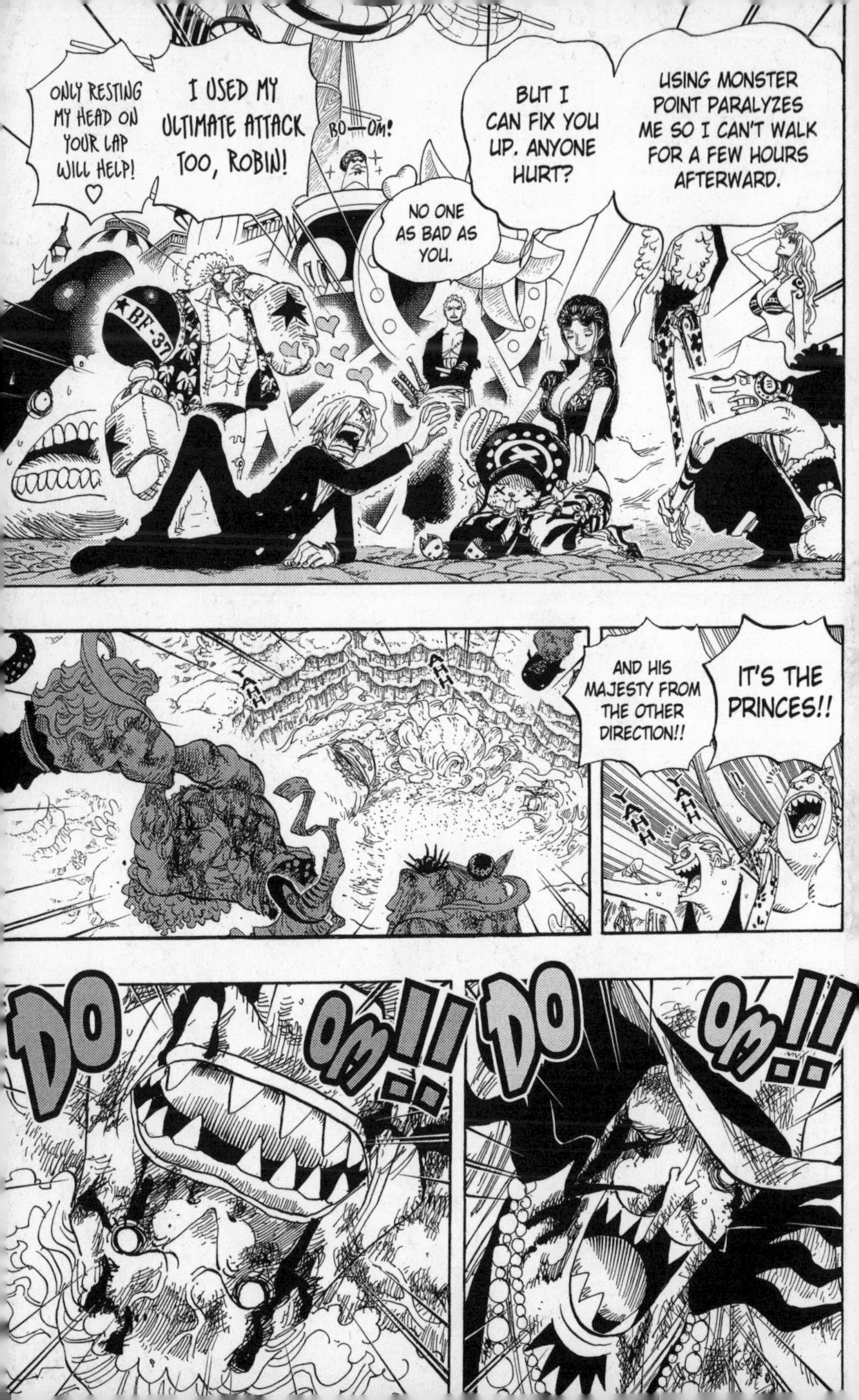
USING MONSTER POINT PARALYZES ME SO I CAN'T WALK FOR A FEW HOURS AFTERWARD.
BUT I CAN FIX YOU UP. ANYONE HURT?
NO ONE AS BAD AS YOU.
BO—OM!
I USED MY ULTIMATE ATTACK TOO, ROBIN!
ONLY RESTING MY HEAD ON YOUR LAP WILL HELP! ♡
IT'S THE PRINCES!!
AND HIS MAJESTY FROM THE OTHER DIRECTION!!
YAHH
YAHH
AHH
YAHH
DO OM!!
DO OM!!

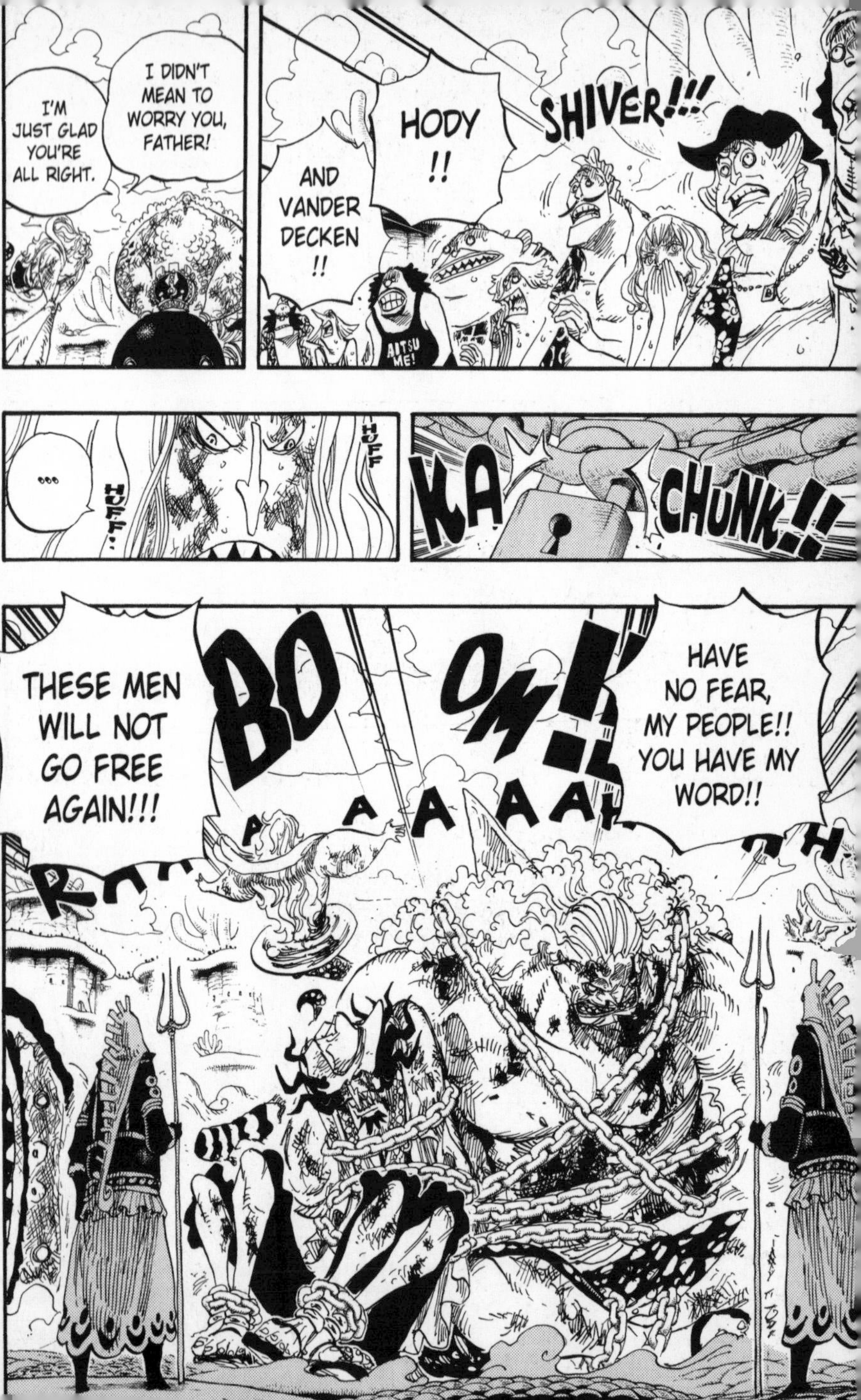
SHIVER!!!
HODY !!
AND VANDER DECKEN !!
I DIDN'T MEAN TO WORRY YOU, FATHER!
I'M JUST GLAD YOU'RE ALL RIGHT.
KA CHUNK!!
HUFF HUFF
...
HAVE NO FEAR, MY PEOPLE!! YOU HAVE MY WORD!!
BOOM!!
THESE MEN WILL NOT GO FREE AGAIN!!!

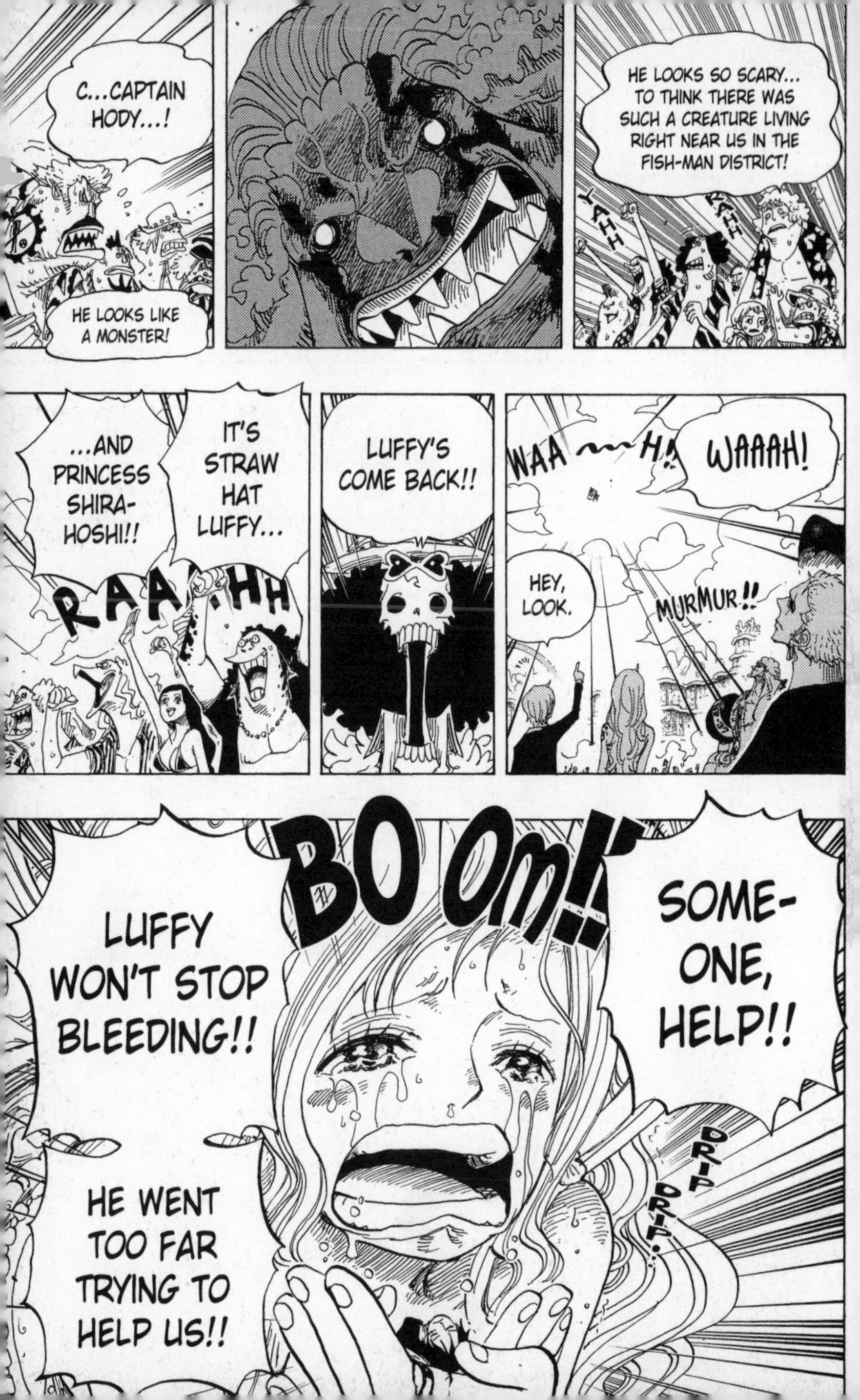
HE LOOKS SO SCARY... TO THINK THERE WAS SUCH A CREATURE LIVING RIGHT NEAR US IN THE FISH-MAN DISTRICT!
RAHH
YAHH
C...CAPTAIN HODY...!
HE LOOKS LIKE A MONSTER!
WAAAH!
WAA~~H!
HEY, LOOK.
MURMUR!!
LUFFY'S COME BACK!!
IT'S STRAW HAT LUFFY...
...AND PRINCESS SHIRA-HOSHI!!
RAAAHH
BOOM!!
SOME-ONE, HELP!!
LUFFY WON'T STOP BLEEDING!!
DRIP
DRIP
HE WENT TOO FAR TRYING TO HELP US!!

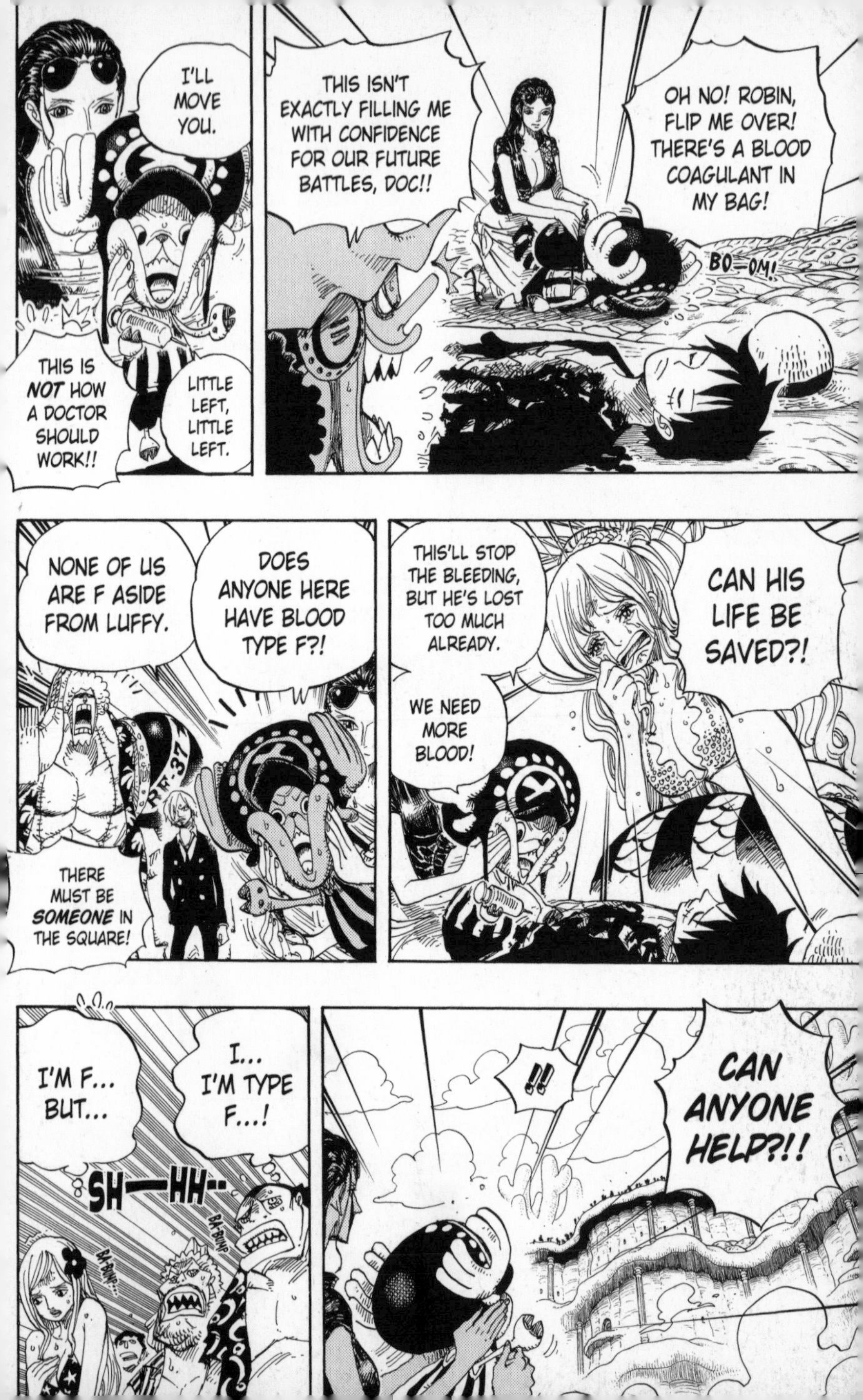
OH NO! ROBIN, FLIP ME OVER! THERE'S A BLOOD COAGULANT IN MY BAG!
BO-OM!
THIS ISN'T EXACTLY FILLING ME WITH CONFIDENCE FOR OUR FUTURE BATTLES, DOC!!
I'LL MOVE YOU.
LITTLE LEFT, LITTLE LEFT.
THIS IS **NOT** HOW A DOCTOR SHOULD WORK!!
CAN HIS LIFE BE SAVED?!
THIS'LL STOP THE BLEEDING, BUT HE'S LOST TOO MUCH ALREADY.
WE NEED MORE BLOOD!
DOES ANYONE HERE HAVE BLOOD TYPE F?!
NONE OF US ARE F ASIDE FROM LUFFY.
RF-37
THERE MUST BE **SOMEONE** IN THE SQUARE!
CAN ANYONE HELP?!!
!!
I... I'M TYPE F...!
I'M F... BUT...
SH—HH--
BA-BUMP
BA-BUMP

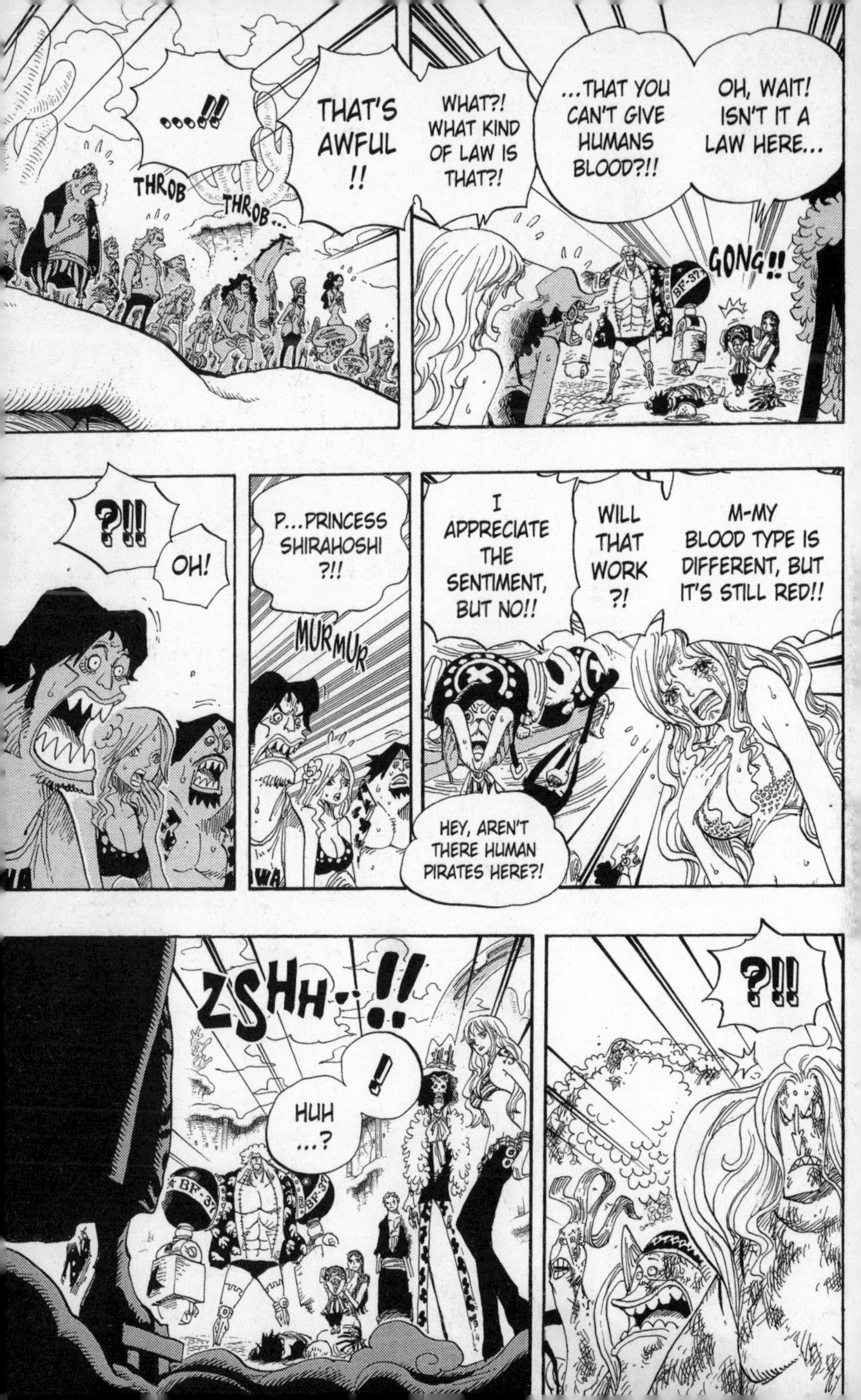
OH, WAIT! ISN'T IT A LAW HERE...
...THAT YOU CAN'T GIVE HUMANS BLOOD?!!
GONG!!
WHAT?! WHAT KIND OF LAW IS THAT?!
THAT'S AWFUL !!
....!!
THROB
THROB...
M-MY BLOOD TYPE IS DIFFERENT, BUT IT'S STILL RED!!
WILL THAT WORK ?!
I APPRECIATE THE SENTIMENT, BUT NO!!
HEY, AREN'T THERE HUMAN PIRATES HERE?!
P...PRINCESS SHIRAHOSHI ?!!
MURMUR
?!!
OH!
?!!
ZSHH-..!!
!
HUH ...?

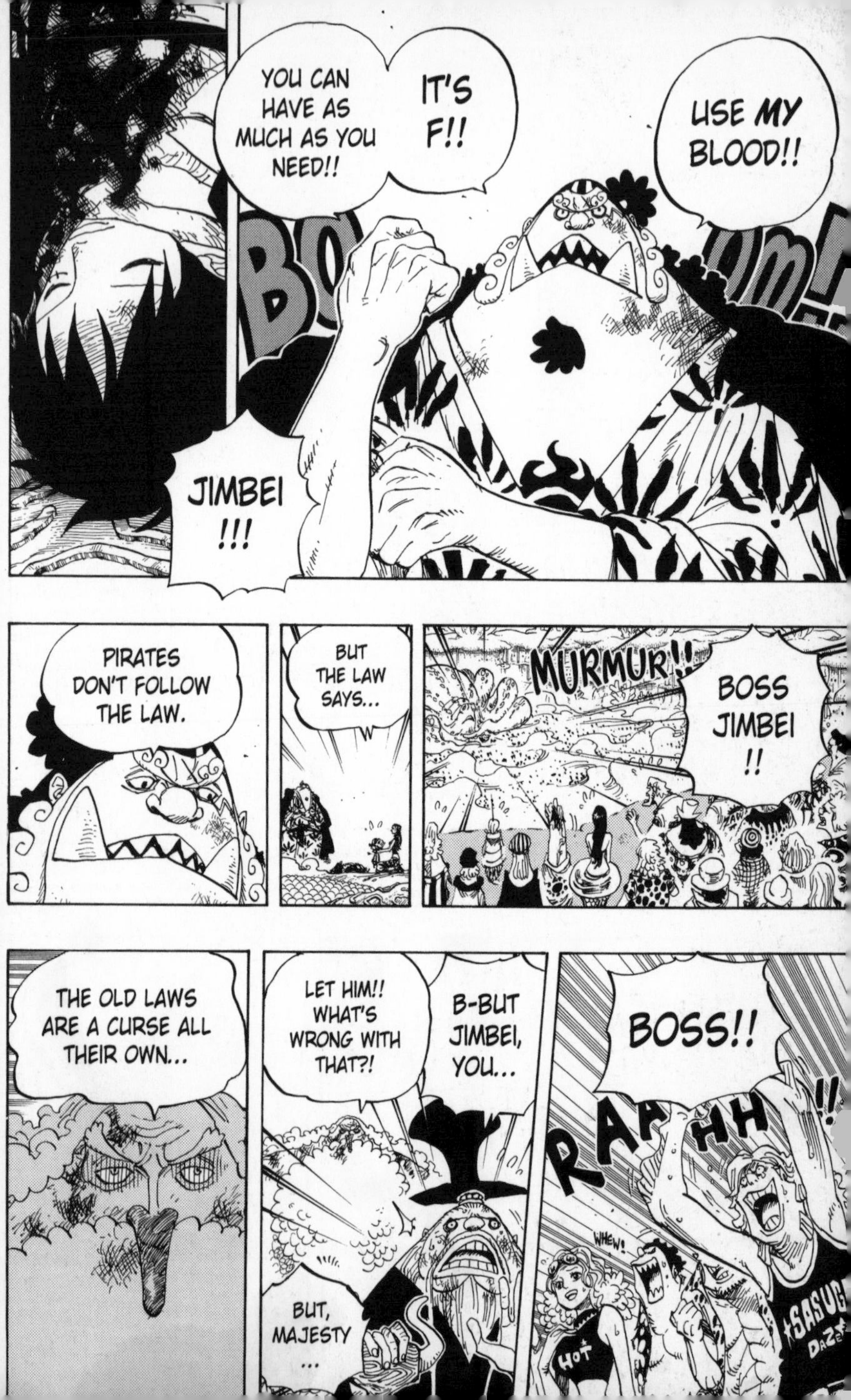
USE MY BLOOD!!
IT'S F!!
YOU CAN HAVE AS MUCH AS YOU NEED!!
BO
OM!!
JIMBEI!!!
MURMUR!!
BOSS JIMBEI!!
BUT THE LAW SAYS...
PIRATES DON'T FOLLOW THE LAW.
BOSS!!
RAAHH!!
WHEW!
HOT
B-BUT JIMBEI, YOU...
LET HIM!! WHAT'S WRONG WITH THAT?!
BUT, MAJESTY ...
THE OLD LAWS ARE A CURSE ALL THEIR OWN...

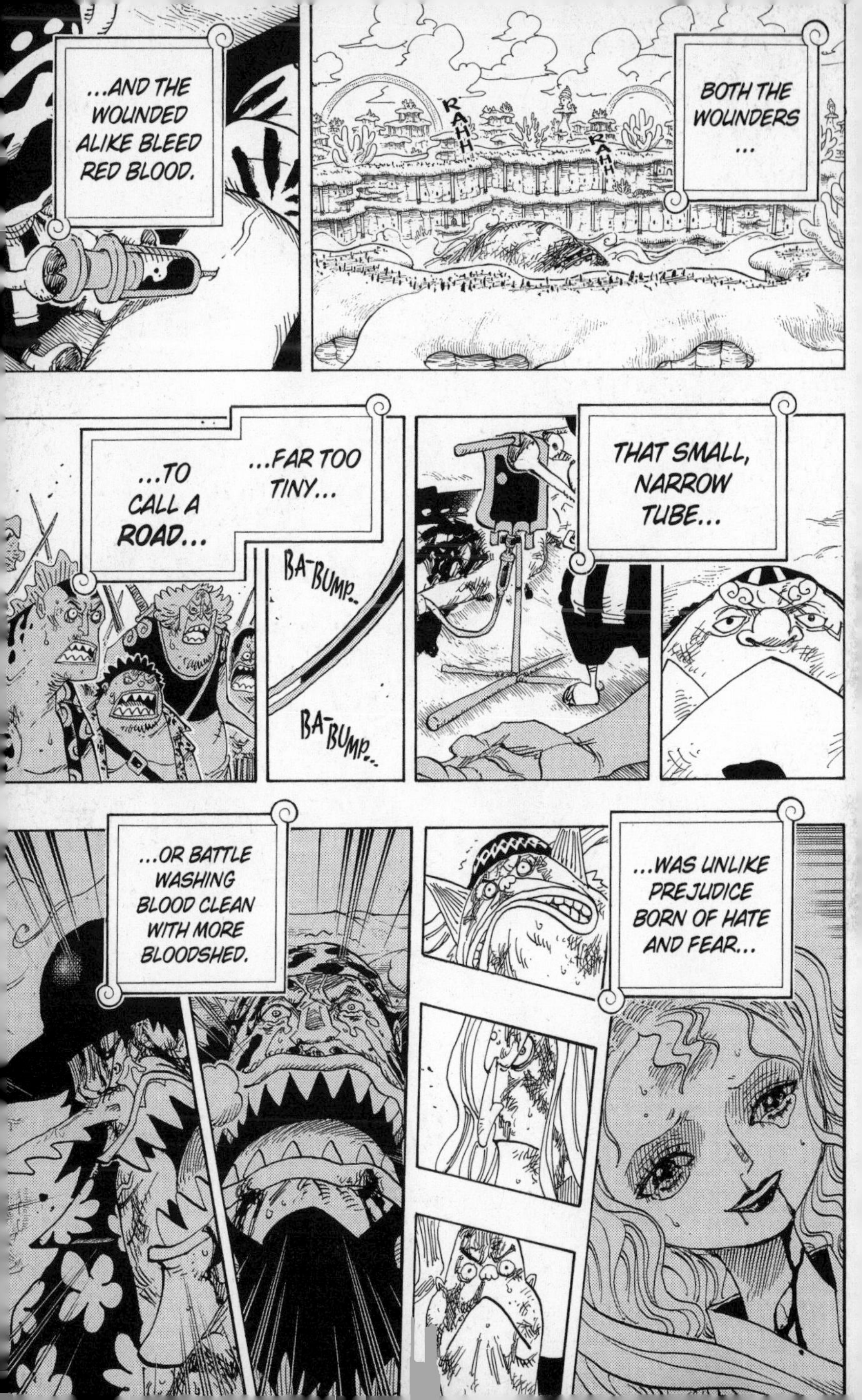
BOTH THE WOUNDERS ...
RAHH
RAHH
...AND THE WOUNDED ALIKE BLEED RED BLOOD.
THAT SMALL, NARROW TUBE...
...FAR TOO TINY...
...TO CALL A ROAD...
BA-BUMP..
BA-BUMP...
...WAS UNLIKE PREJUDICE BORN OF HATE AND FEAR...
...OR BATTLE WASHING BLOOD CLEAN WITH MORE BLOODSHED.

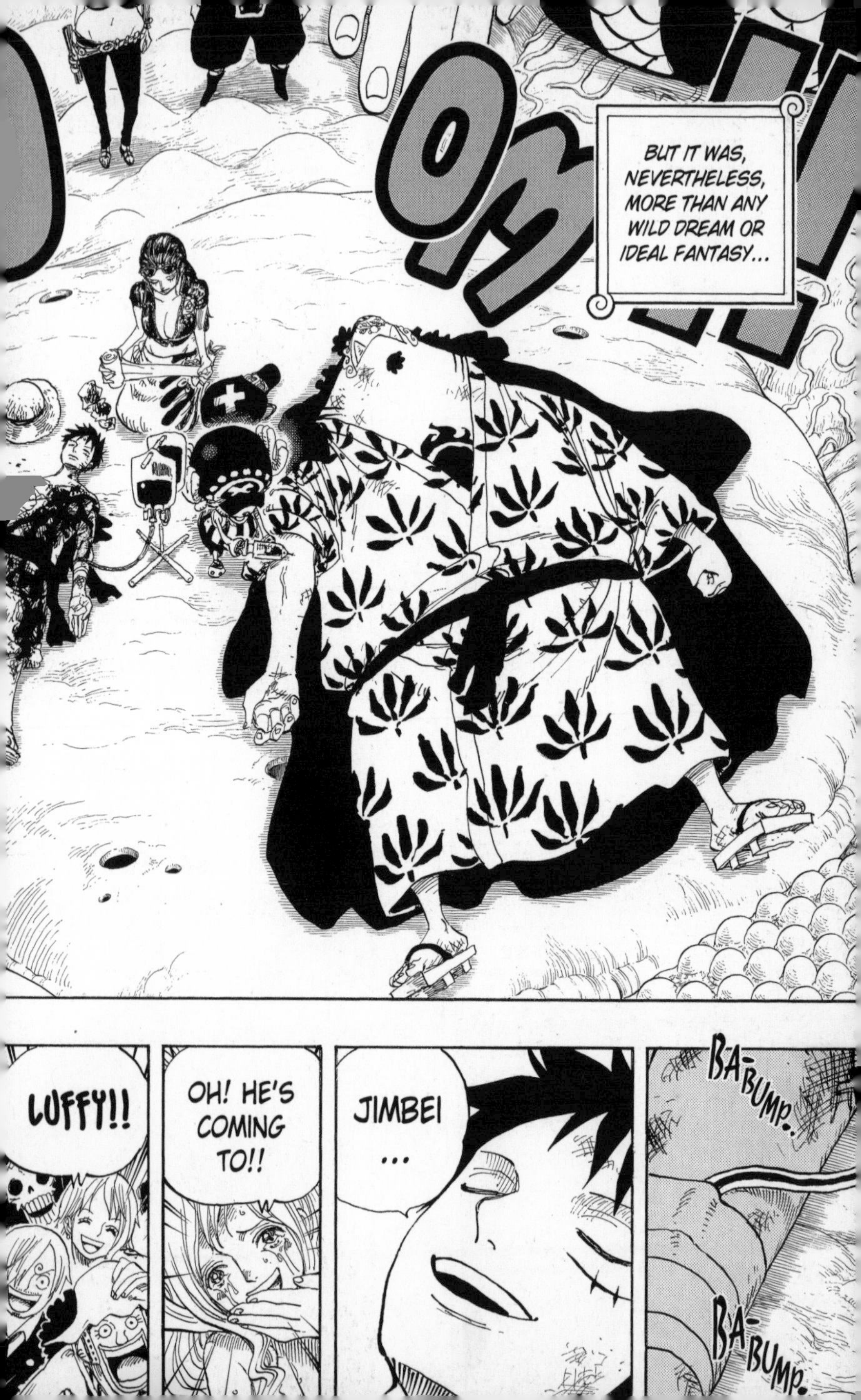
BUT IT WAS, NEVERTHELESS, MORE THAN ANY WILD DREAM OR IDEAL FANTASY...
BA-BUMP..
BA-BUMP.
JIMBEI ...
OH! HE'S COMING TO!!
LUFFY!!

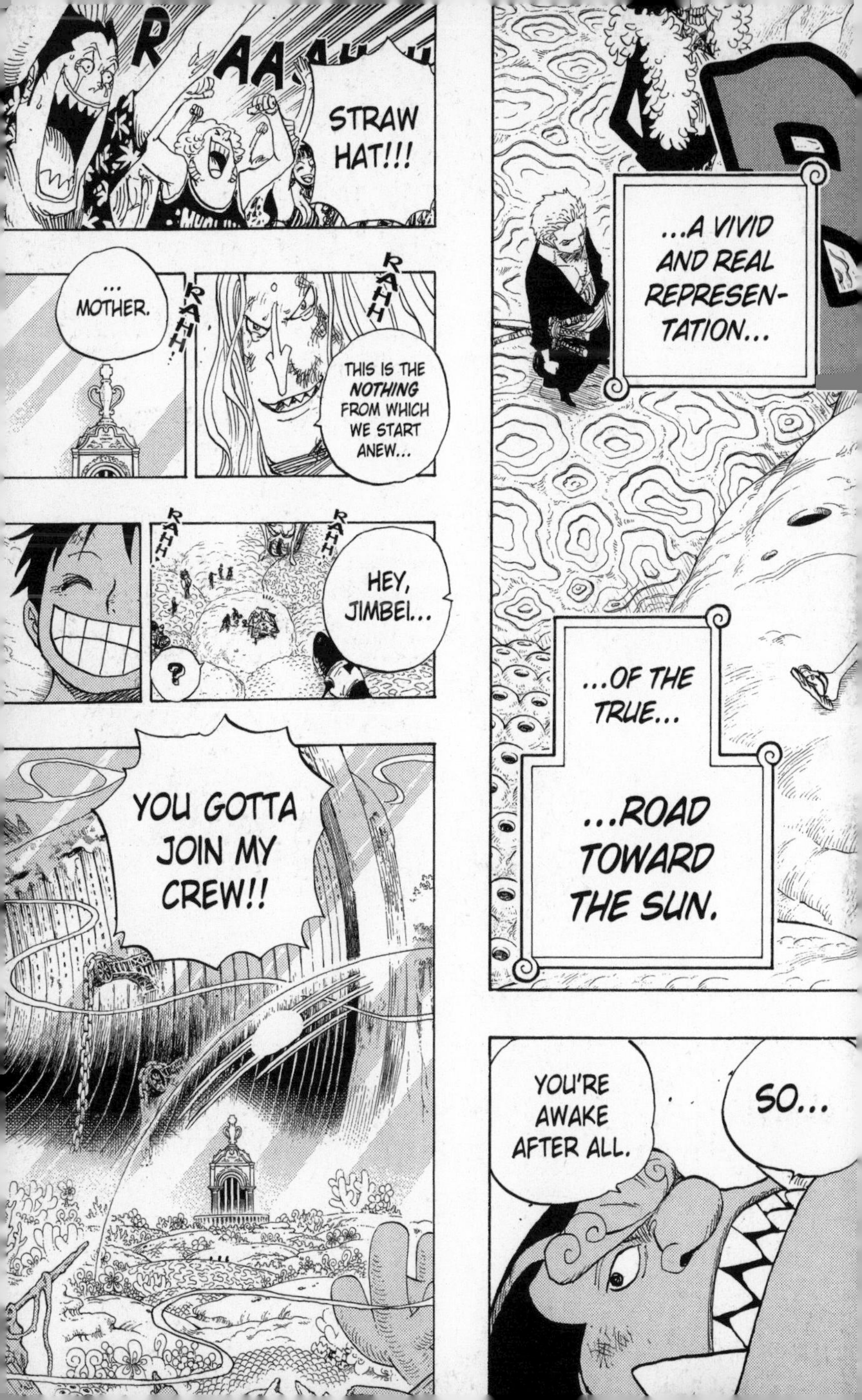
...A VIVID AND REAL REPRESEN-TATION...
...OF THE TRUE...
...ROAD TOWARD THE SUN.
SO...
YOU'RE AWAKE AFTER ALL.
RAA
STRAW HAT!!!
RAHH
THIS IS THE *NOTHING* FROM WHICH WE START ANEW...
RAHH!
... MOTHER.
RAHH
HEY, JIMBEI...
RAHH!
?
YOU GOTTA JOIN MY CREW!!

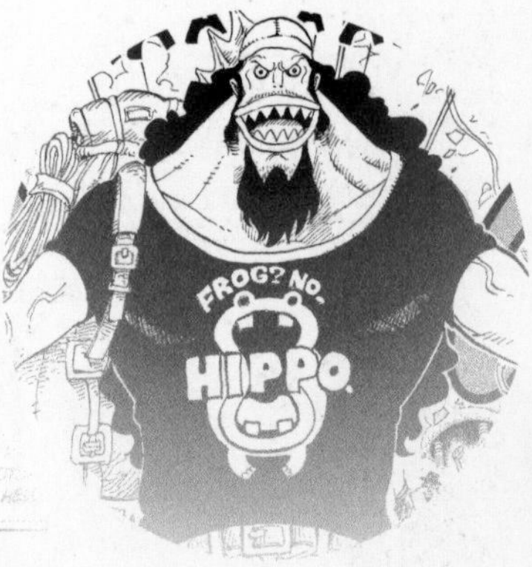
FROG? NO.
HIPPO.

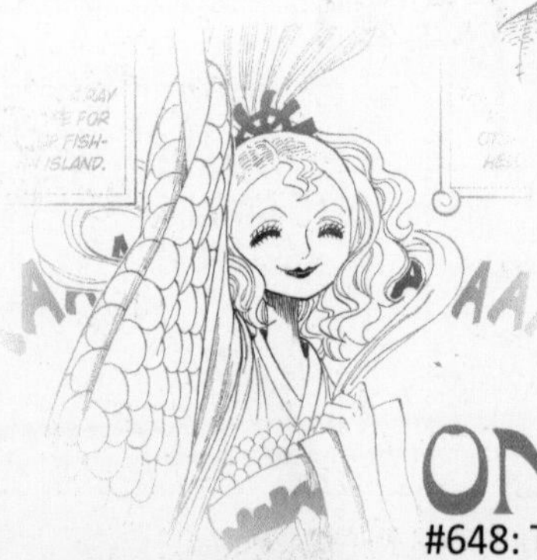

vol.66

ONE PIECE

#648: The Road Toward the Sun

Chaper 649:
THE DANCE OF BREAMS AND PLAICES

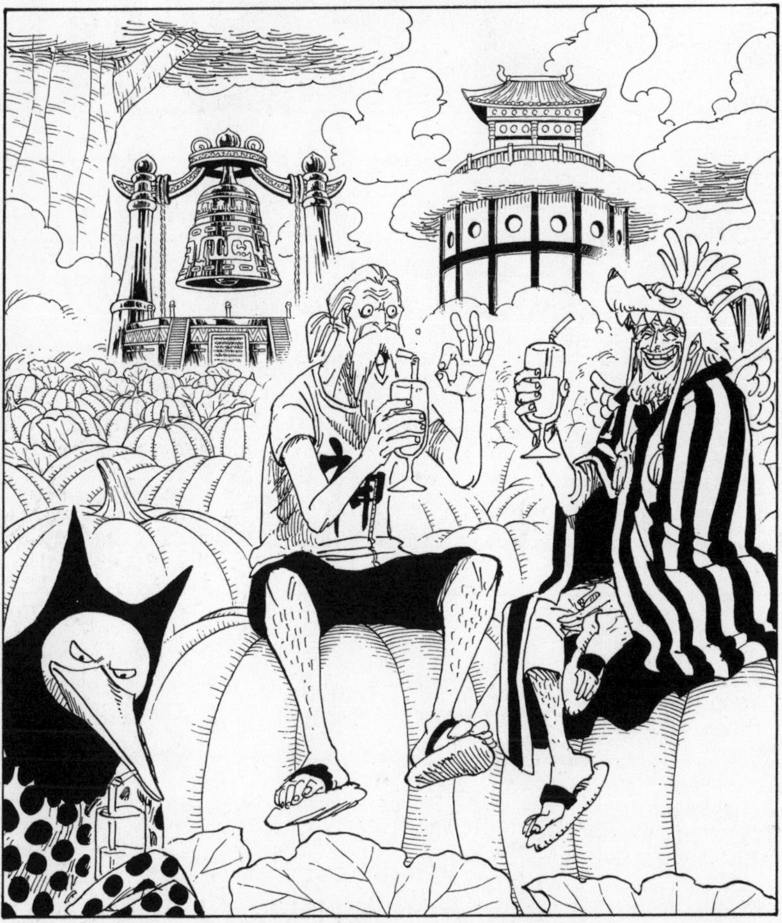

DECKS OF THE WORLD, VOL. 32:
"SKYPIEA—GOD IS PLEASED WITH THIS YEAR'S CROP"

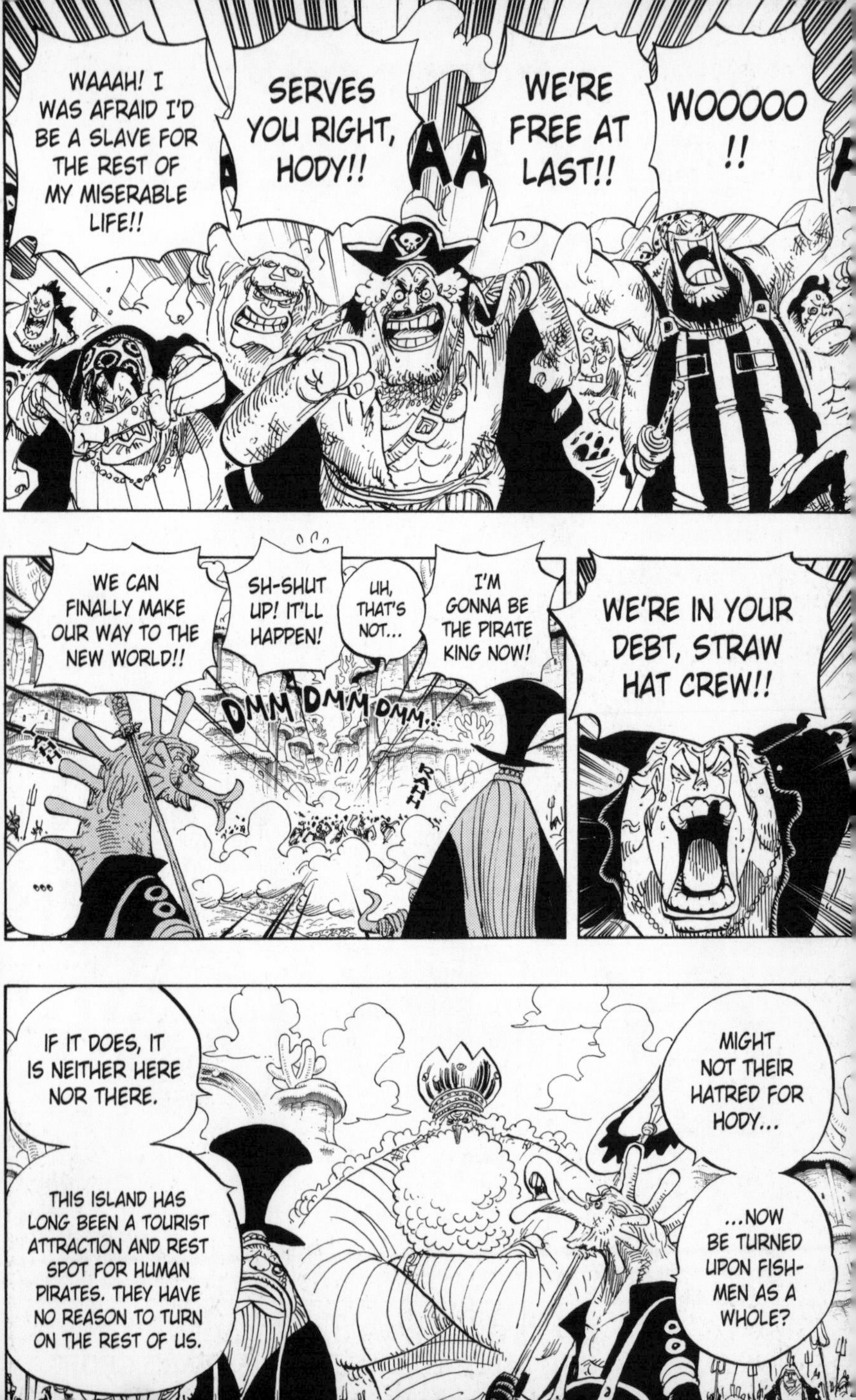
WOOOOO!!
WE'RE FREE AT LAST!!
AA
SERVES YOU RIGHT, HODY!!
WAAAH! I WAS AFRAID I'D BE A SLAVE FOR THE REST OF MY MISERABLE LIFE!!
WE'RE IN YOUR DEBT, STRAW HAT CREW!!
I'M GONNA BE THE PIRATE KING NOW!
UH, THAT'S NOT...
SH-SHUT UP! IT'LL HAPPEN!
WE CAN FINALLY MAKE OUR WAY TO THE NEW WORLD!!
DMM DMM DMM..
RAHH
...
MIGHT NOT THEIR HATRED FOR HODY...
...NOW BE TURNED UPON FISH-MEN AS A WHOLE?
IF IT DOES, IT IS NEITHER HERE NOR THERE.
THIS ISLAND HAS LONG BEEN A TOURIST ATTRACTION AND REST SPOT FOR HUMAN PIRATES. THEY HAVE NO REASON TO TURN ON THE REST OF US.

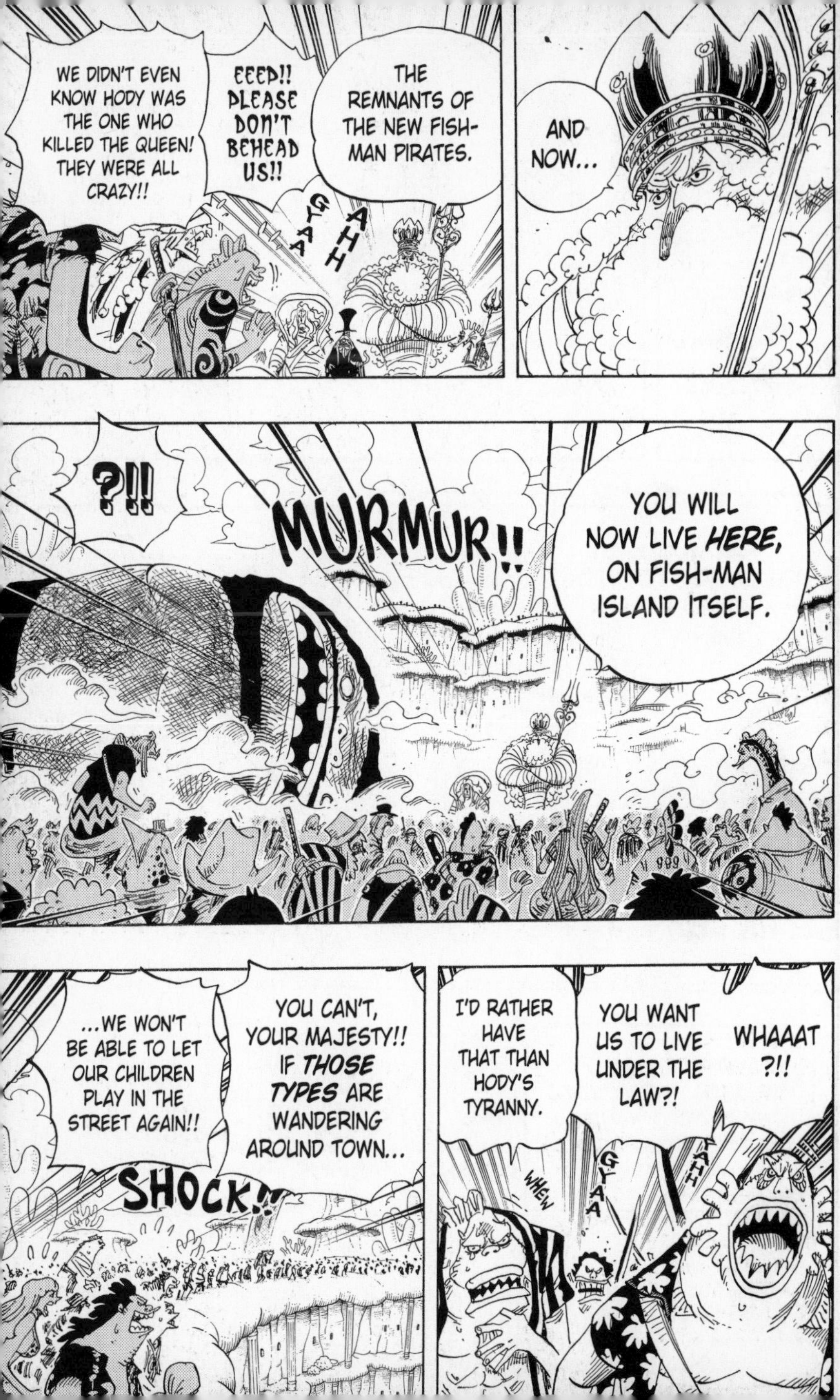
AND NOW...
THE REMNANTS OF THE NEW FISH-MAN PIRATES.
EEEP!! PLEASE DON'T BEHEAD US!!
GYAA
AHH
WE DIDN'T EVEN KNOW HODY WAS THE ONE WHO KILLED THE QUEEN! THEY WERE ALL CRAZY!!
YOU WILL NOW LIVE *HERE*, ON FISH-MAN ISLAND ITSELF.
MURMUR!!
?!!
WHAAAT?!!
YOU WANT US TO LIVE UNDER THE LAW?!
I'D RATHER HAVE THAT THAN HODY'S TYRANNY.
GYAA
AHH
WHEW
YOU CAN'T, YOUR MAJESTY!! IF *THOSE TYPES* ARE WANDERING AROUND TOWN...
...WE WON'T BE ABLE TO LET OUR CHILDREN PLAY IN THE STREET AGAIN!!
SHOCK!!

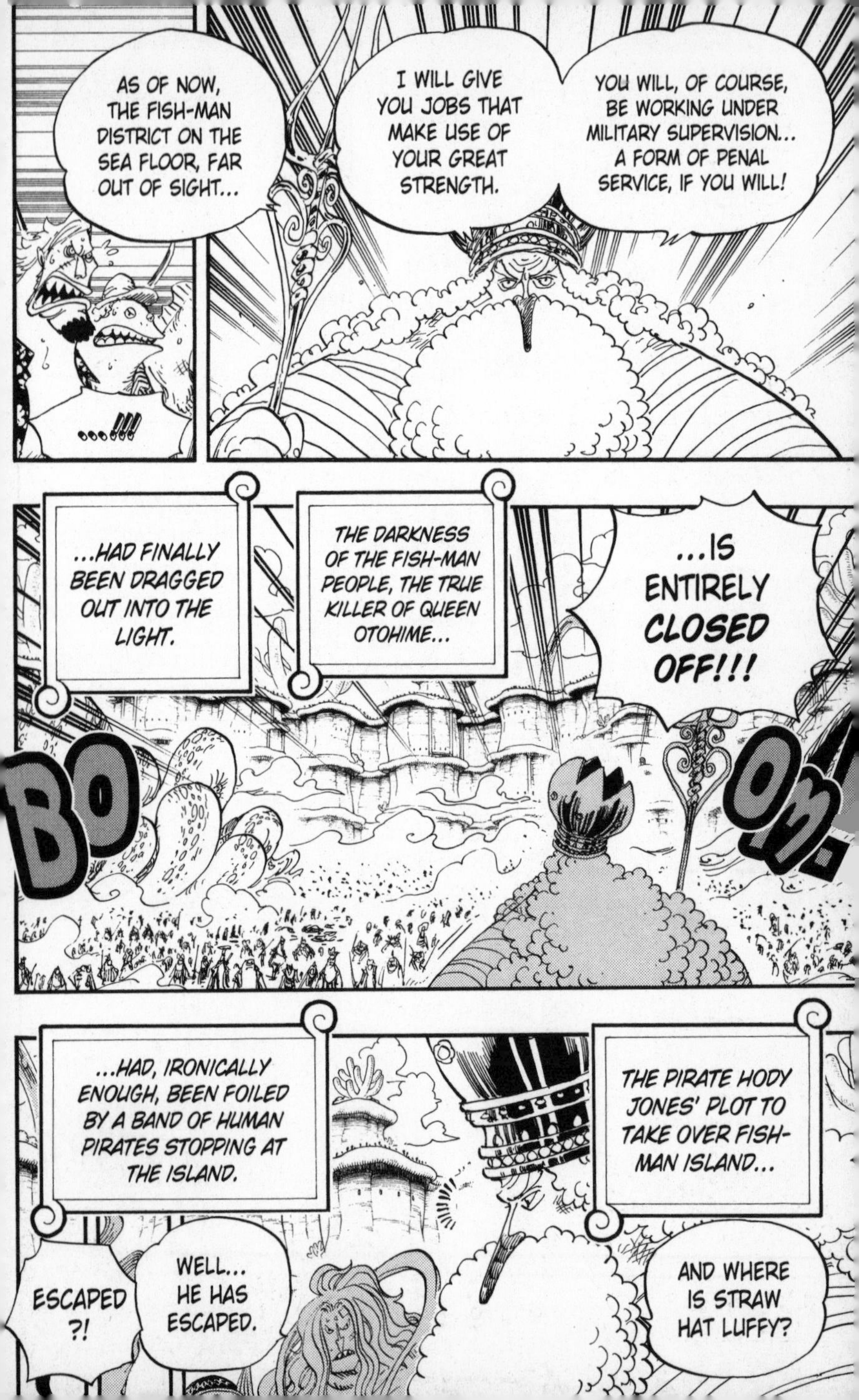
YOU WILL, OF COURSE, BE WORKING UNDER MILITARY SUPERVISION... A FORM OF PENAL SERVICE, IF YOU WILL!
I WILL GIVE YOU JOBS THAT MAKE USE OF YOUR GREAT STRENGTH.
AS OF NOW, THE FISH-MAN DISTRICT ON THE SEA FLOOR, FAR OUT OF SIGHT...
...!!!
...IS ENTIRELY CLOSED OFF!!!
THE DARKNESS OF THE FISH-MAN PEOPLE, THE TRUE KILLER OF QUEEN OTOHIME...
...HAD FINALLY BEEN DRAGGED OUT INTO THE LIGHT.
BOOM!
THE PIRATE HODY JONES' PLOT TO TAKE OVER FISH-MAN ISLAND...
AND WHERE IS STRAW HAT LUFFY?
...HAD, IRONICALLY ENOUGH, BEEN FOILED BY A BAND OF HUMAN PIRATES STOPPING AT THE ISLAND.
WELL... HE HAS ESCAPED.
ESCAPED ?!

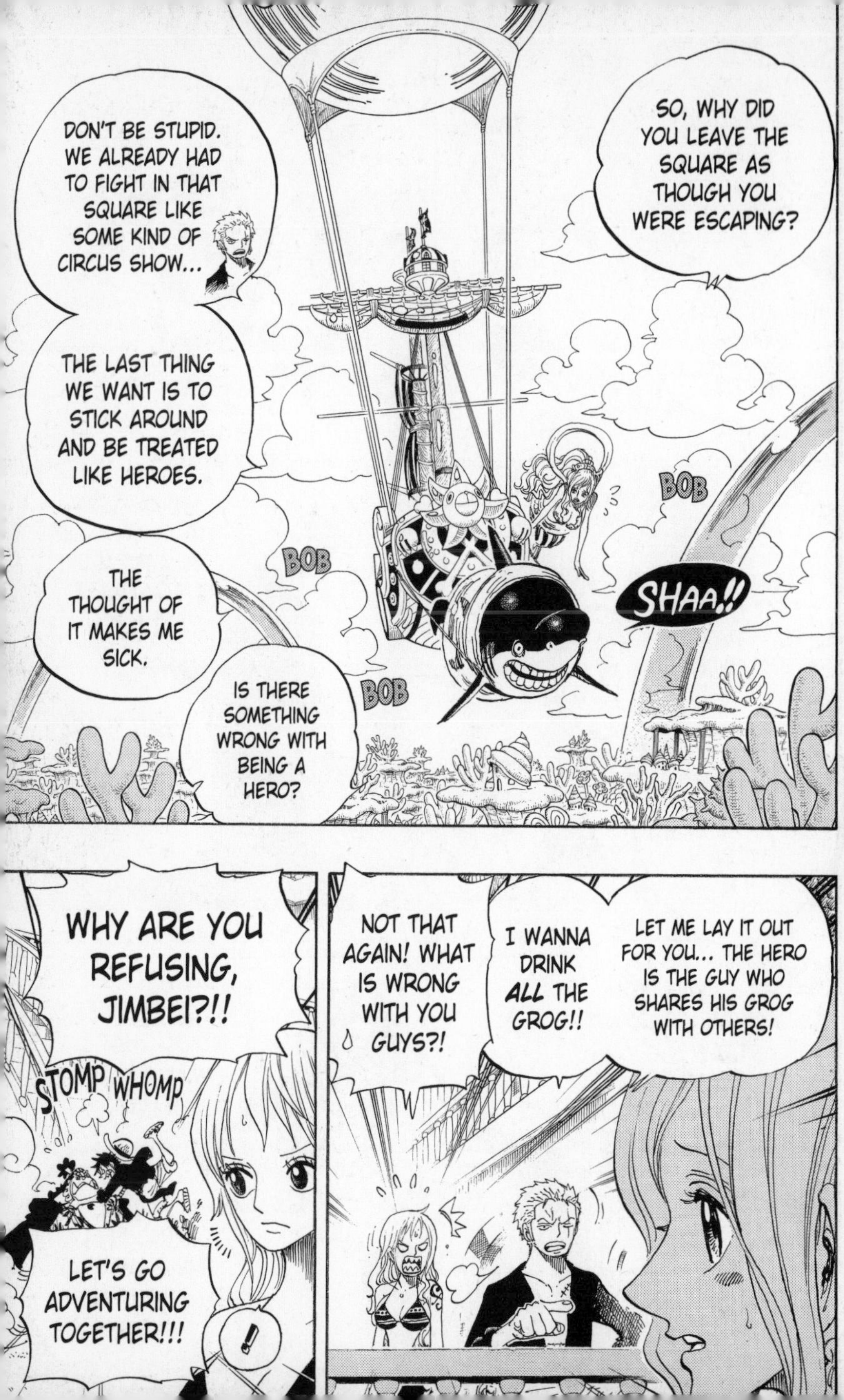
SO, WHY DID YOU LEAVE THE SQUARE AS THOUGH YOU WERE ESCAPING?
DON'T BE STUPID. WE ALREADY HAD TO FIGHT IN THAT SQUARE LIKE SOME KIND OF CIRCUS SHOW...
THE LAST THING WE WANT IS TO STICK AROUND AND BE TREATED LIKE HEROES.
BOB
SHAA!!
THE THOUGHT OF IT MAKES ME SICK.
BOB
IS THERE SOMETHING WRONG WITH BEING A HERO?
BOB
LET ME LAY IT OUT FOR YOU... THE HERO IS THE GUY WHO SHARES HIS GROG WITH OTHERS!
I WANNA DRINK ALL THE GROG!!
NOT THAT AGAIN! WHAT IS WRONG WITH YOU GUYS?!
WHY ARE YOU REFUSING, JIMBEI?!!
STOMP WHOMP
LET'S GO ADVENTURING TOGETHER!!!

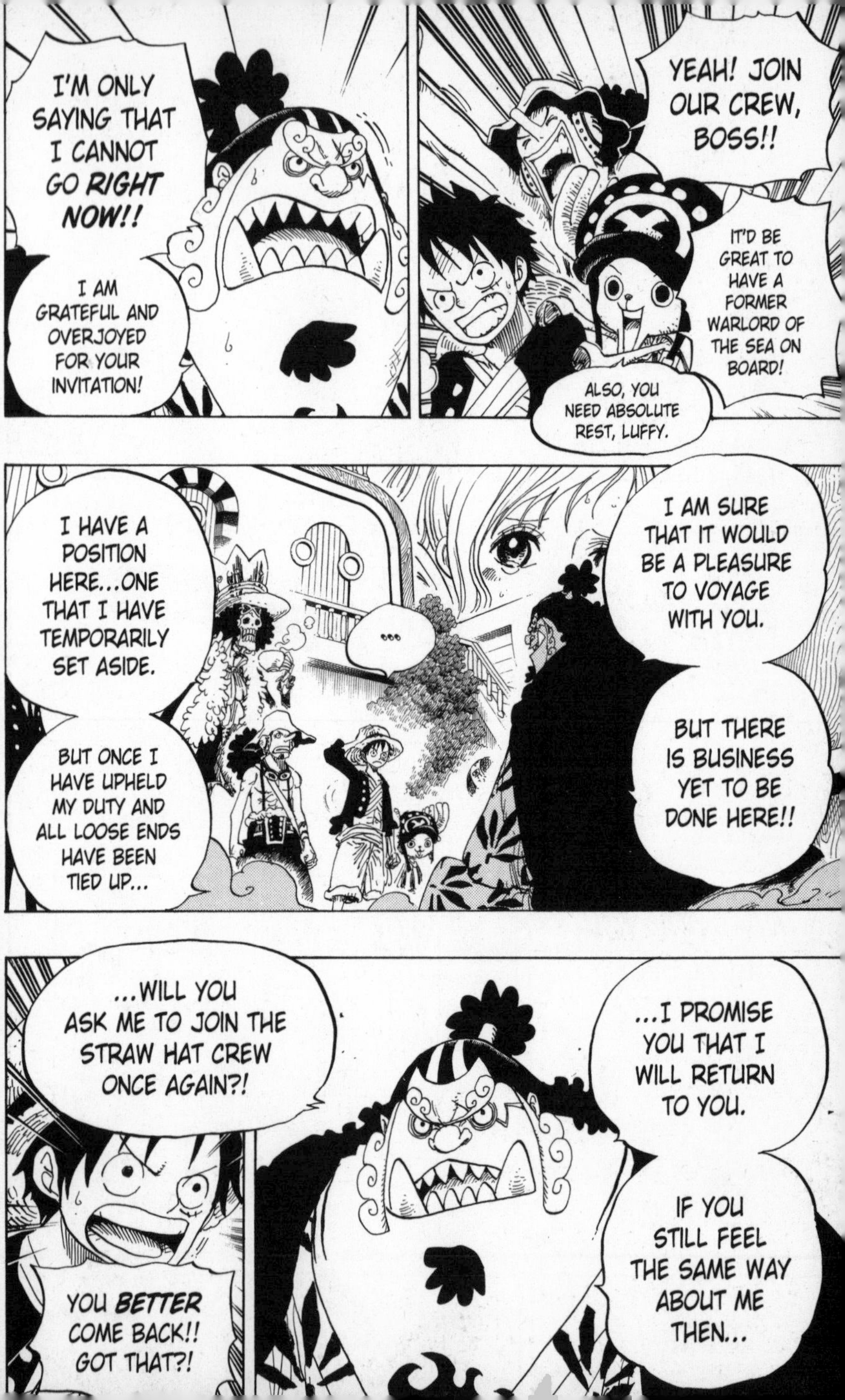
YEAH! JOIN OUR CREW, BOSS!!
IT'D BE GREAT TO HAVE A FORMER WARLORD OF THE SEA ON BOARD!
ALSO, YOU NEED ABSOLUTE REST, LUFFY.
I'M ONLY SAYING THAT I CANNOT GO *RIGHT NOW!!*
I AM GRATEFUL AND OVERJOYED FOR YOUR INVITATION!
I AM SURE THAT IT WOULD BE A PLEASURE TO VOYAGE WITH YOU.
BUT THERE IS BUSINESS YET TO BE DONE HERE!!
...
I HAVE A POSITION HERE...ONE THAT I HAVE TEMPORARILY SET ASIDE.
BUT ONCE I HAVE UPHELD MY DUTY AND ALL LOOSE ENDS HAVE BEEN TIED UP...
...I PROMISE YOU THAT I WILL RETURN TO YOU.
IF YOU STILL FEEL THE SAME WAY ABOUT ME THEN...
...WILL YOU ASK ME TO JOIN THE STRAW HAT CREW ONCE AGAIN?!
YOU *BETTER* COME BACK!! GOT THAT?!

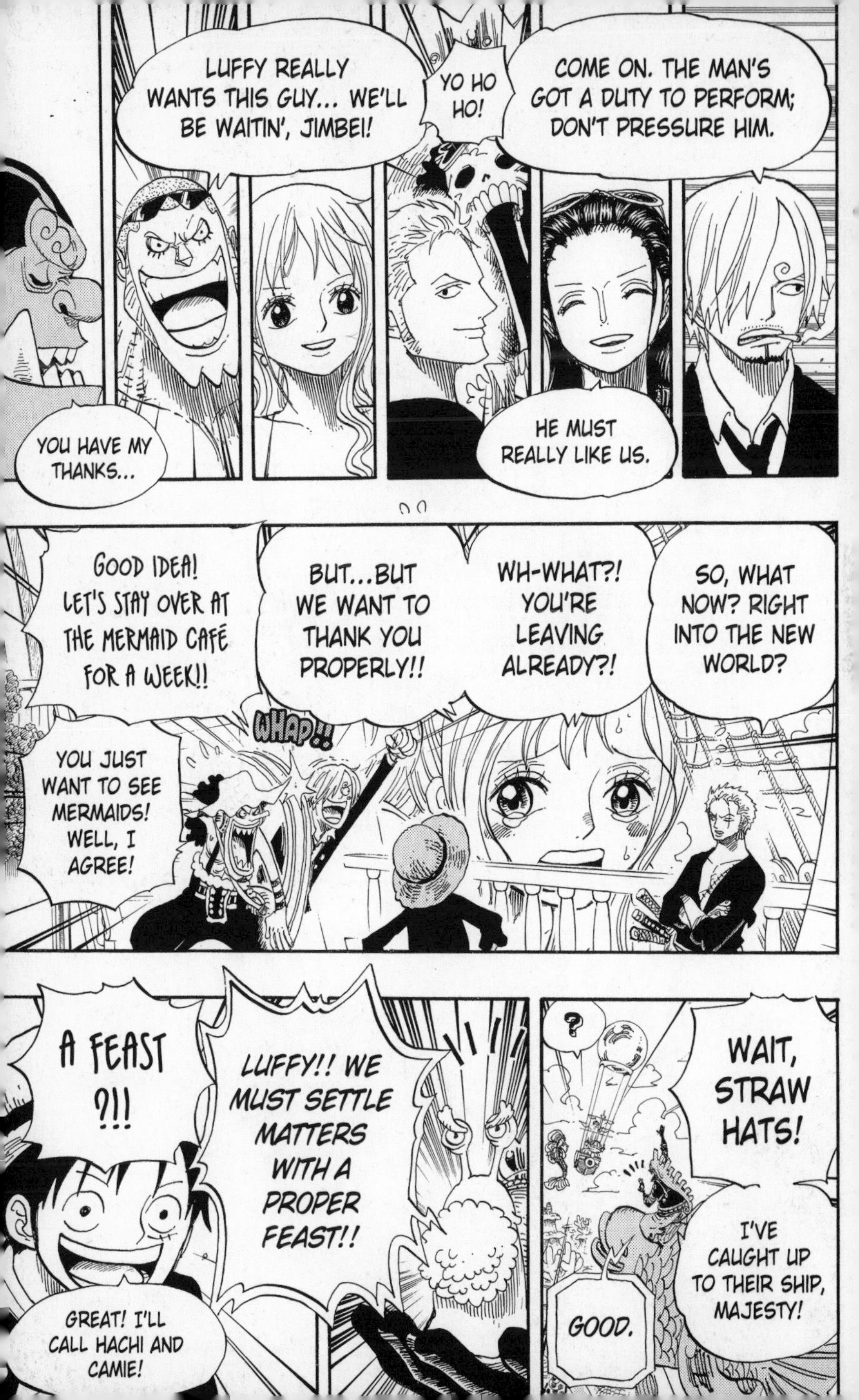
COME ON. THE MAN'S GOT A DUTY TO PERFORM; DON'T PRESSURE HIM.
HE MUST REALLY LIKE US.
YO HO HO!
LUFFY REALLY WANTS THIS GUY... WE'LL BE WAITIN', JIMBEI!
YOU HAVE MY THANKS...
SO, WHAT NOW? RIGHT INTO THE NEW WORLD?
WH-WHAT?! YOU'RE LEAVING ALREADY?!
BUT...BUT WE WANT TO THANK YOU PROPERLY!!
GOOD IDEA! LET'S STAY OVER AT THE MERMAID CAFÉ FOR A WEEK!!
WHAP!!
YOU JUST WANT TO SEE MERMAIDS! WELL, I AGREE!
?
WAIT, STRAW HATS!
I'VE CAUGHT UP TO THEIR SHIP, MAJESTY!
GOOD.
LUFFY!! WE MUST SETTLE MATTERS WITH A PROPER FEAST!!
A FEAST ?!!
GREAT! I'LL CALL HACHI AND CAMIE!

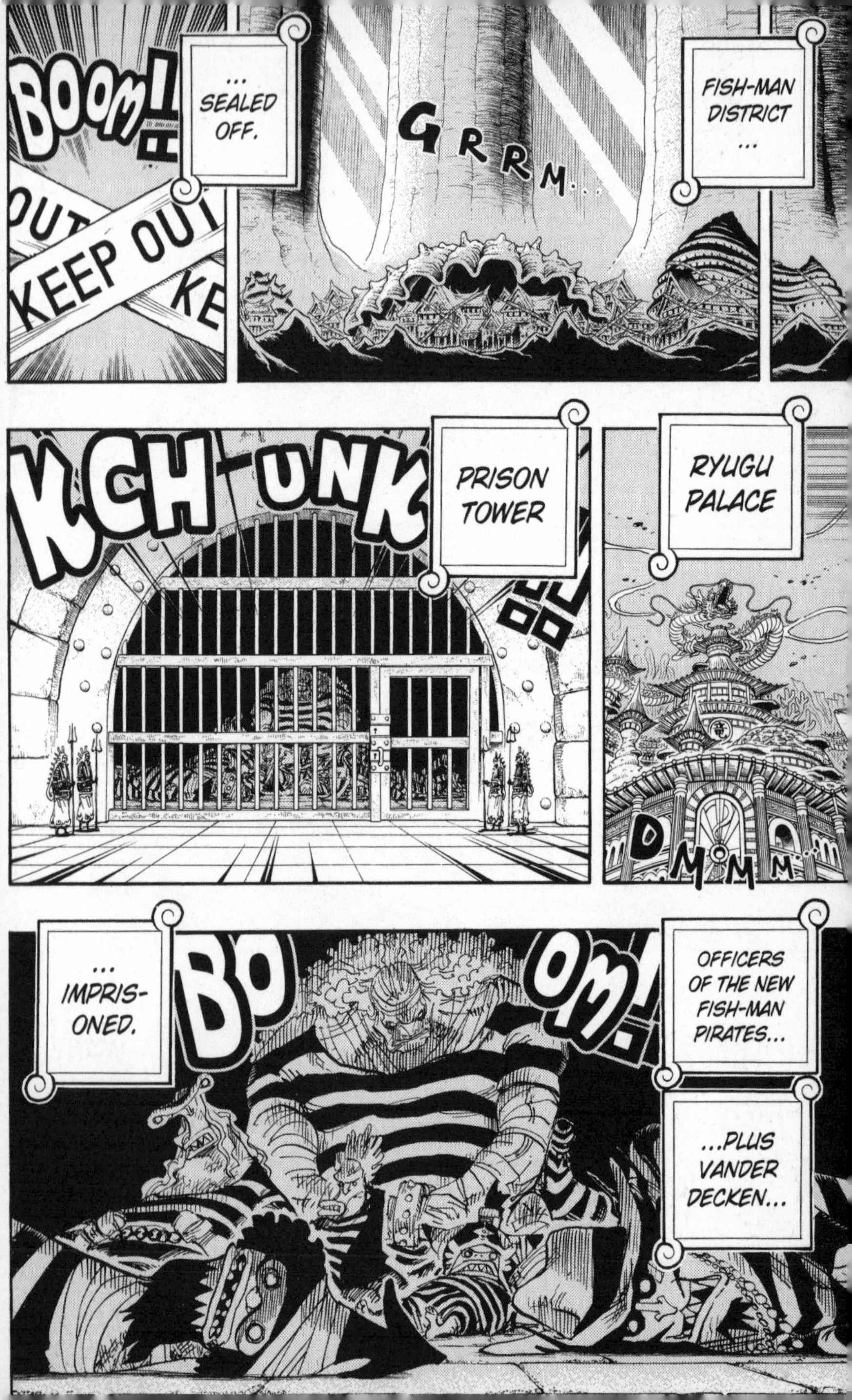
FISH-MAN DISTRICT...
GRRRM...
...SEALED OFF.
BOOM!!
KEEP OUT
RYUGU PALACE
DMMM...
PRISON TOWER
KCH-UNK
OFFICERS OF THE NEW FISH-MAN PIRATES...
...PLUS VANDER DECKEN...
BOOM!!
...IMPRIS-ONED.

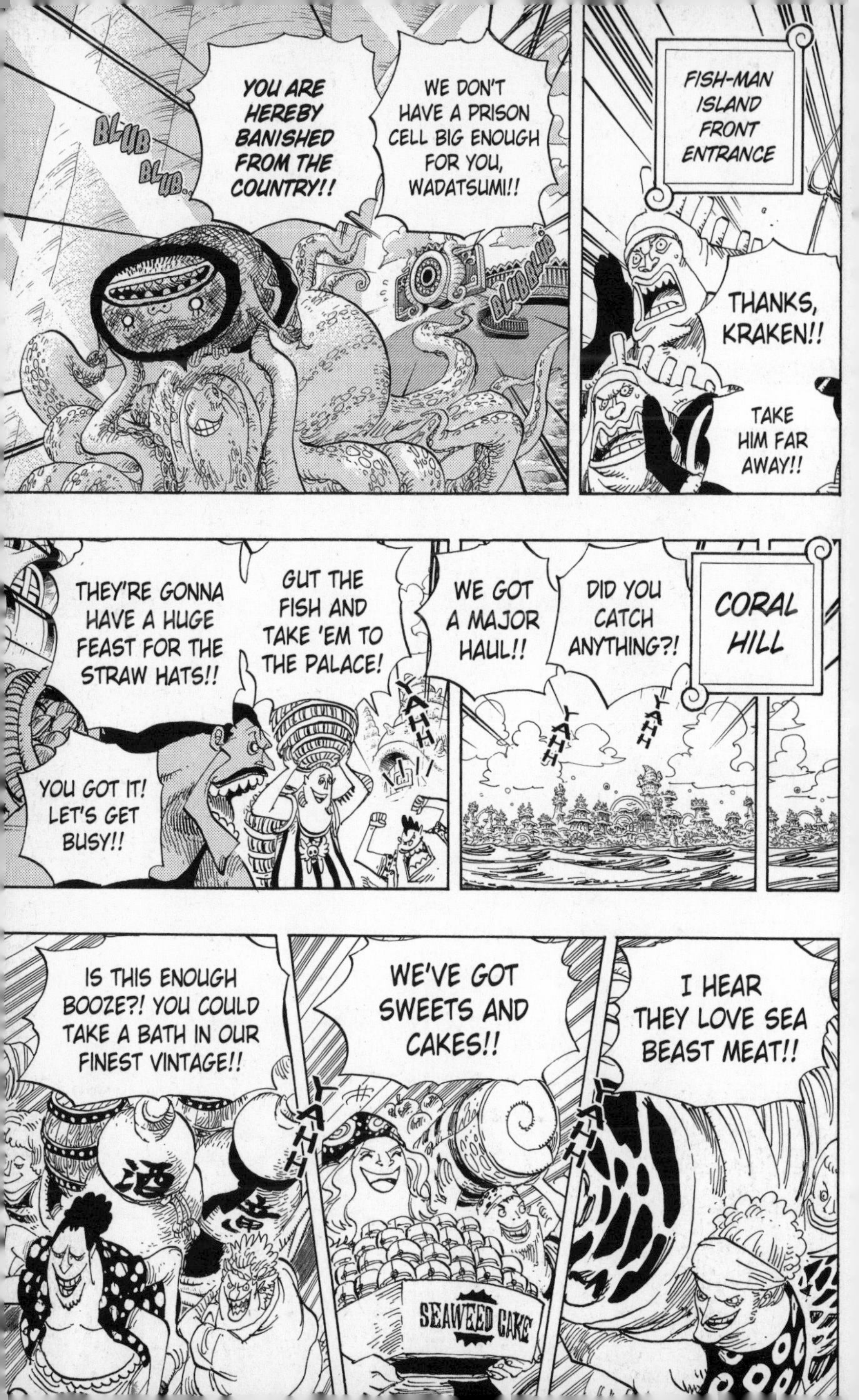
FISH-MAN ISLAND FRONT ENTRANCE
THANKS, KRAKEN!!
TAKE HIM FAR AWAY!!
WE DON'T HAVE A PRISON CELL BIG ENOUGH FOR YOU, WADATSUMI!!
YOU ARE HEREBY BANISHED FROM THE COUNTRY!!
BLUB
BLUB..
CORAL HILL
DID YOU CATCH ANYTHING?!
WE GOT A MAJOR HAUL!!
YAHH
YAHH
GUT THE FISH AND TAKE 'EM TO THE PALACE!
THEY'RE GONNA HAVE A HUGE FEAST FOR THE STRAW HATS!!
YAHH
YOU GOT IT! LET'S GET BUSY!!
I HEAR THEY LOVE SEA BEAST MEAT!!
YAHH
WE'VE GOT SWEETS AND CAKES!!
SEAWEED CAKE
YAHH
IS THIS ENOUGH BOOZE?! YOU COULD TAKE A BATH IN OUR FINEST VINTAGE!!

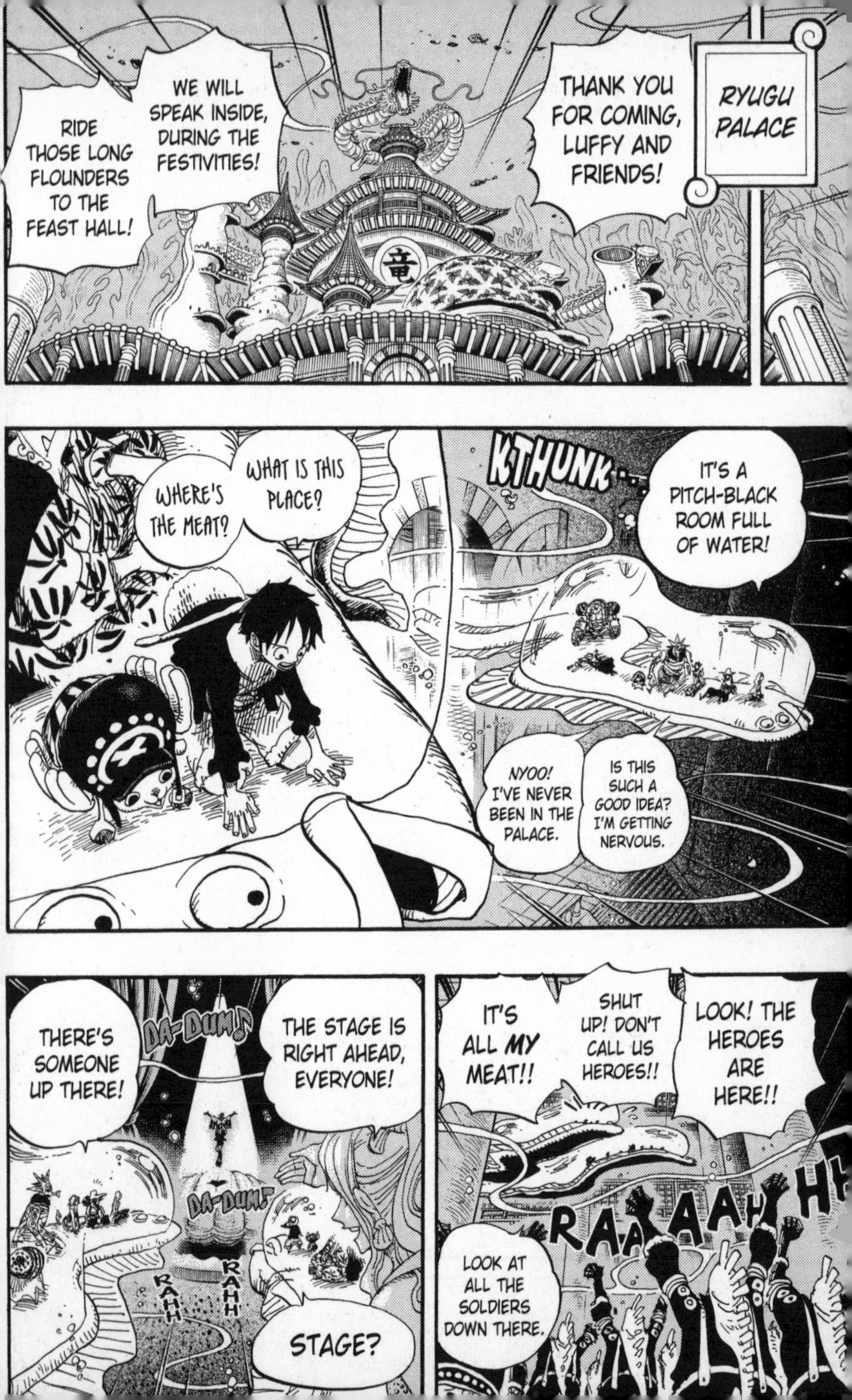
RYUGU PALACE
THANK YOU FOR COMING, LUFFY AND FRIENDS!
WE WILL SPEAK INSIDE, DURING THE FESTIVITIES!
RIDE THOSE LONG FLOUNDERS TO THE FEAST HALL!
KTHUNK
IT'S A PITCH-BLACK ROOM FULL OF WATER!
IS THIS SUCH A GOOD IDEA? I'M GETTING NERVOUS.
NYOO! I'VE NEVER BEEN IN THE PALACE.
WHAT IS THIS PLACE?
WHERE'S THE MEAT?
LOOK! THE HEROES ARE HERE!!
SHUT UP! DON'T CALL US HEROES!!
IT'S ALL MY MEAT!!
RAAAAHH
LOOK AT ALL THE SOLDIERS DOWN THERE.
THE STAGE IS RIGHT AHEAD, EVERYONE!
DA-DUM
THERE'S SOMEONE UP THERE!
DA-DUM
RAHH
RAHH
STAGE?

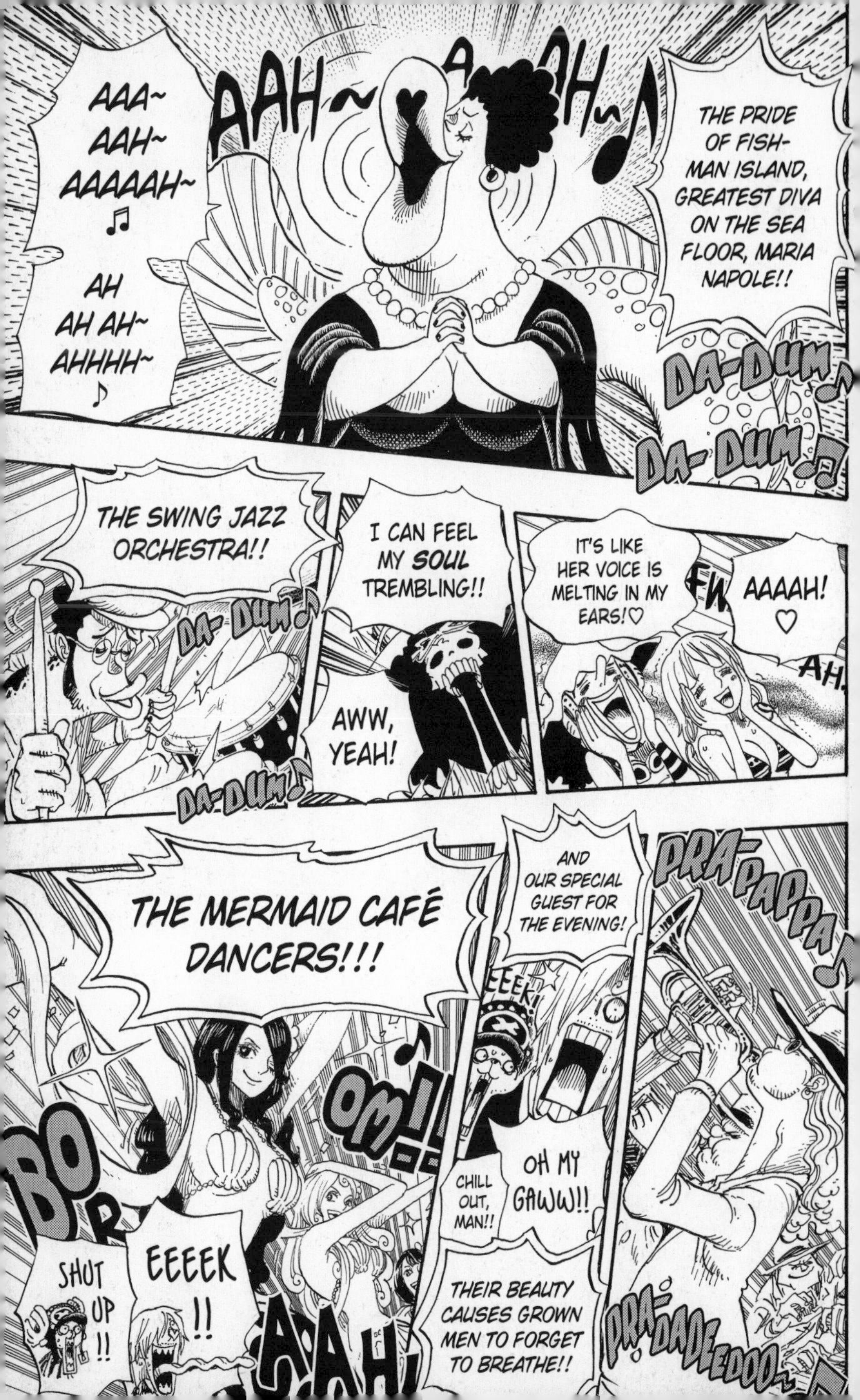
THE PRIDE OF FISH-MAN ISLAND, GREATEST DIVA ON THE SEA FLOOR, MARIA NAPOLE!!
AAH~ A AH~♪
AAA~ AAH~ AAAAAH~ ♫
AH AH AH~ AHHHH~ ♪
DA-DUM♪
DA-DUM♫
AAAAH! ♡
IT'S LIKE HER VOICE IS MELTING IN MY EARS!♡
I CAN FEEL MY **SOUL** TREMBLING!!
AWW, YEAH!
THE SWING JAZZ ORCHESTRA!!
DA-DUM♪
DA-DUM♪
PRA-PAPPA♪
AND OUR SPECIAL GUEST FOR THE EVENING!
OH MY GAWW!!
CHILL OUT, MAN!!
THEIR BEAUTY CAUSES GROWN MEN TO FORGET TO BREATHE!!
PRA-DADEEDOO
THE MERMAID CAFÉ DANCERS!!!
EEEEK !!
SHUT UP !!

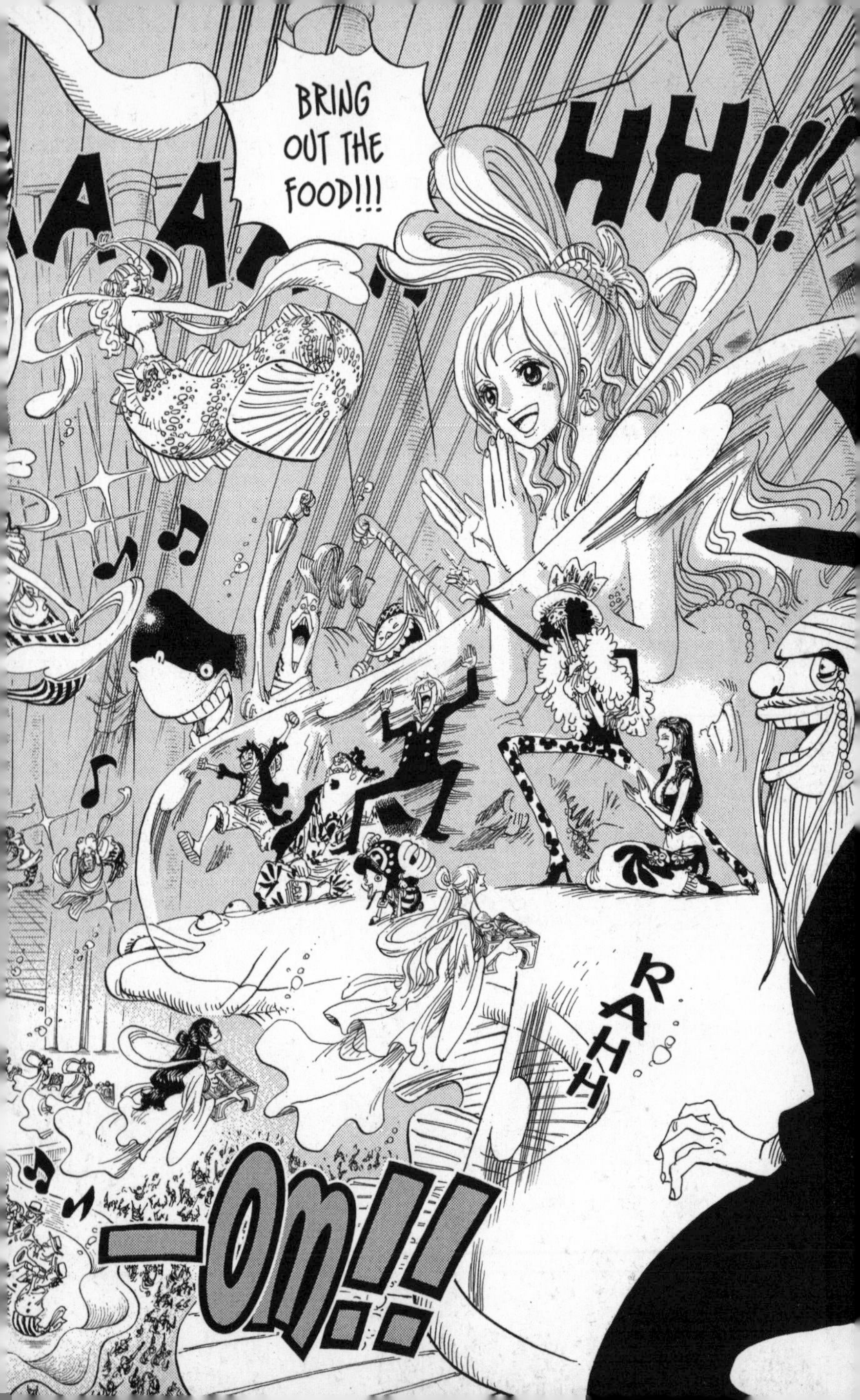

HH!!
BRING OUT THE FOOD!!!
A..A..!!
RAHHH
-OM!!

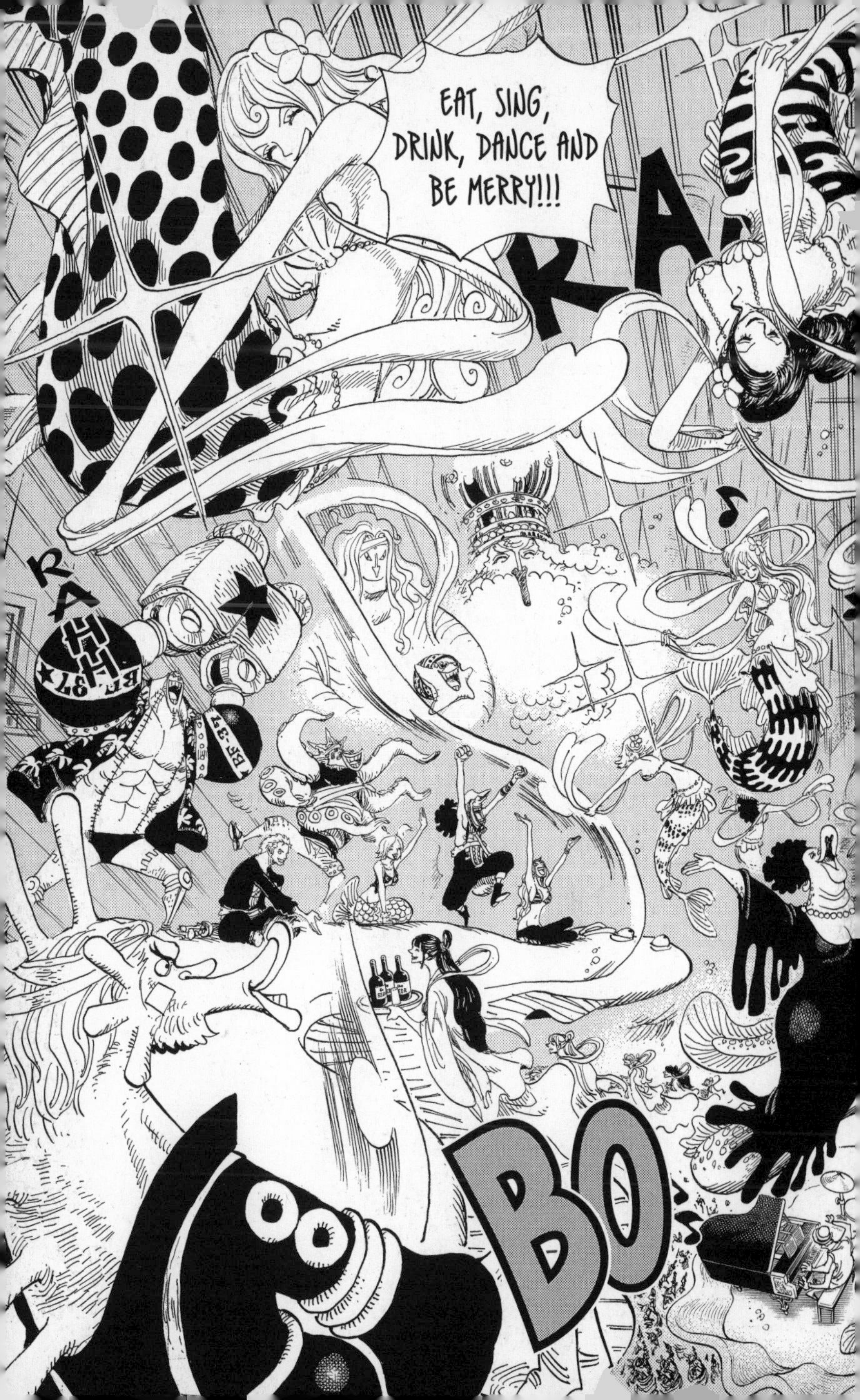
EAT, SING, DRINK, DANCE AND BE MERRY!!!
KA
RA
BF-37
BO

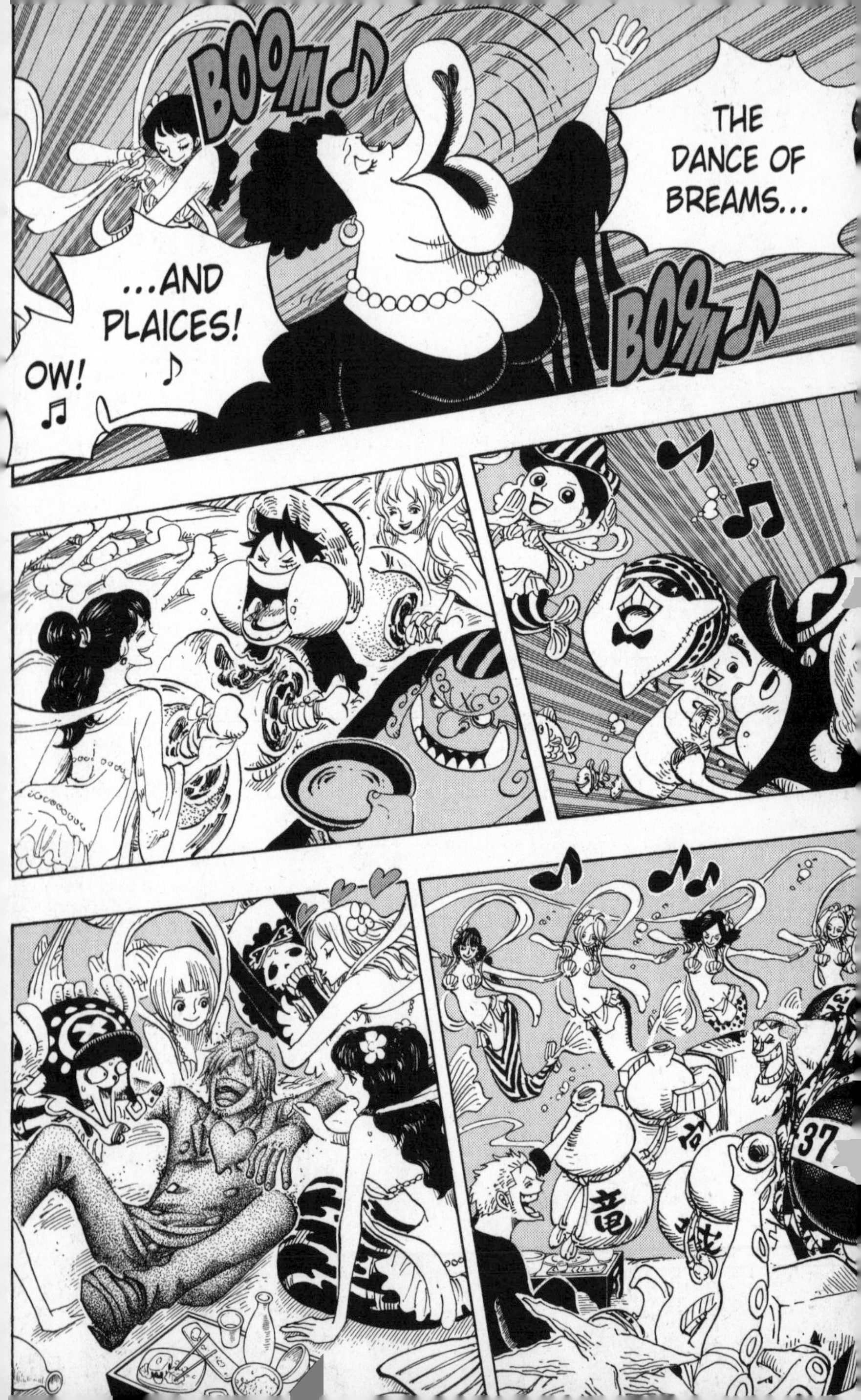
THE DANCE OF BREAMS...
BOOM ♪
BOOM ♪
...AND PLAICES! ♪
OW! ♫
37
竜

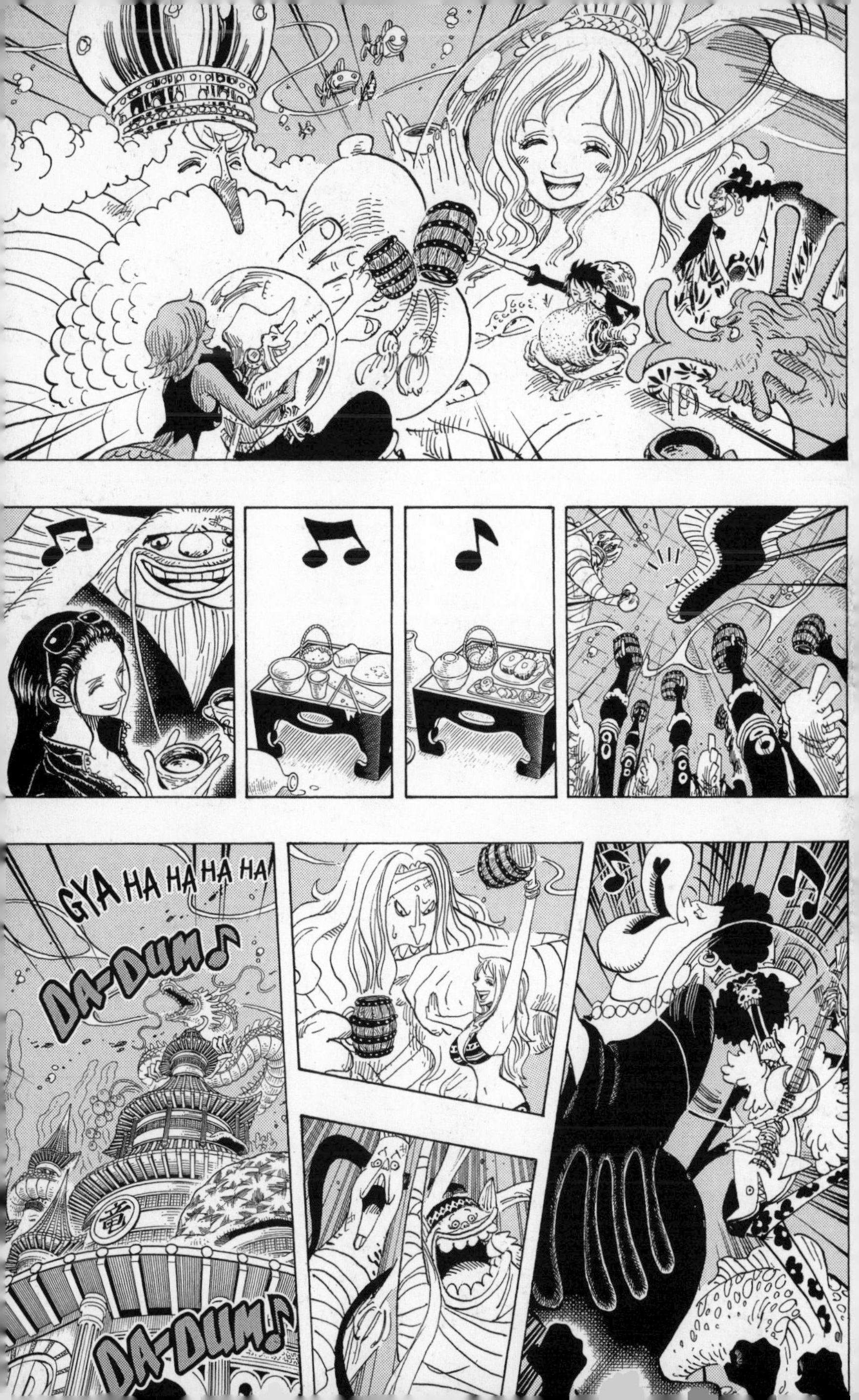

GYA HA HA HA HA
DA-DUM♪
DA-DUM♪

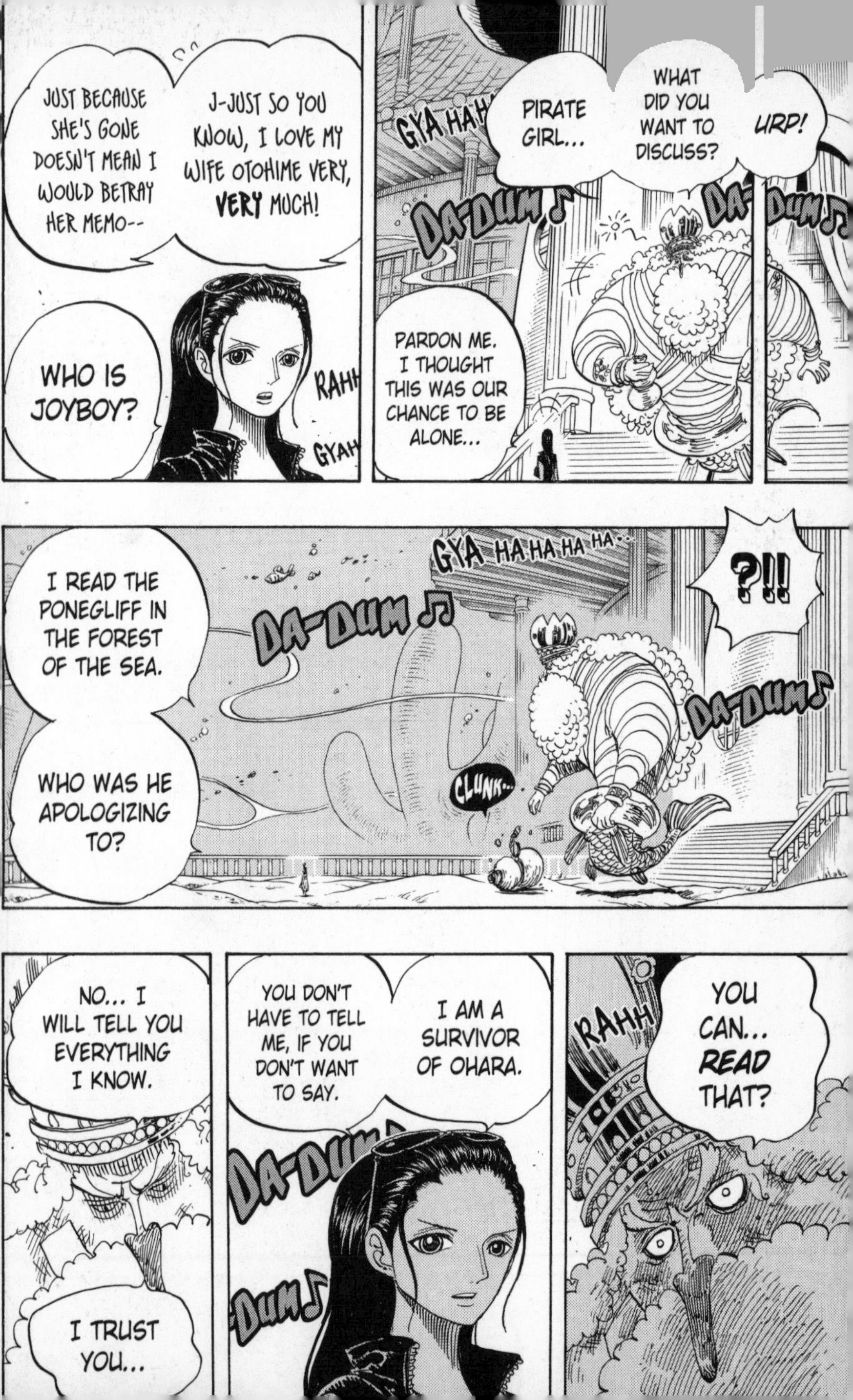
URP!
DA-DUM♪
GYA HAH
PIRATE GIRL...
WHAT DID YOU WANT TO DISCUSS?
DA-DUM♪
PARDON ME. I THOUGHT THIS WAS OUR CHANCE TO BE ALONE...
J-JUST SO YOU KNOW, I LOVE MY WIFE OTOHIME VERY, VERY MUCH!
JUST BECAUSE SHE'S GONE DOESN'T MEAN I WOULD BETRAY HER MEMO--
RAHH
GYAH
WHO IS JOYBOY?
?!!
GYA HA HA HA HA..
DA-DUM♪
DA-DUM♪
I READ THE PONEGLIFF IN THE FOREST OF THE SEA.
WHO WAS HE APOLOGIZING TO?
CLUNK..
YOU CAN... READ THAT?
RAHH
I AM A SURVIVOR OF OHARA.
YOU DON'T HAVE TO TELL ME, IF YOU DON'T WANT TO SAY.
DA-DU
-DUM♪
NO... I WILL TELL YOU EVERYTHING I KNOW.
I TRUST YOU...

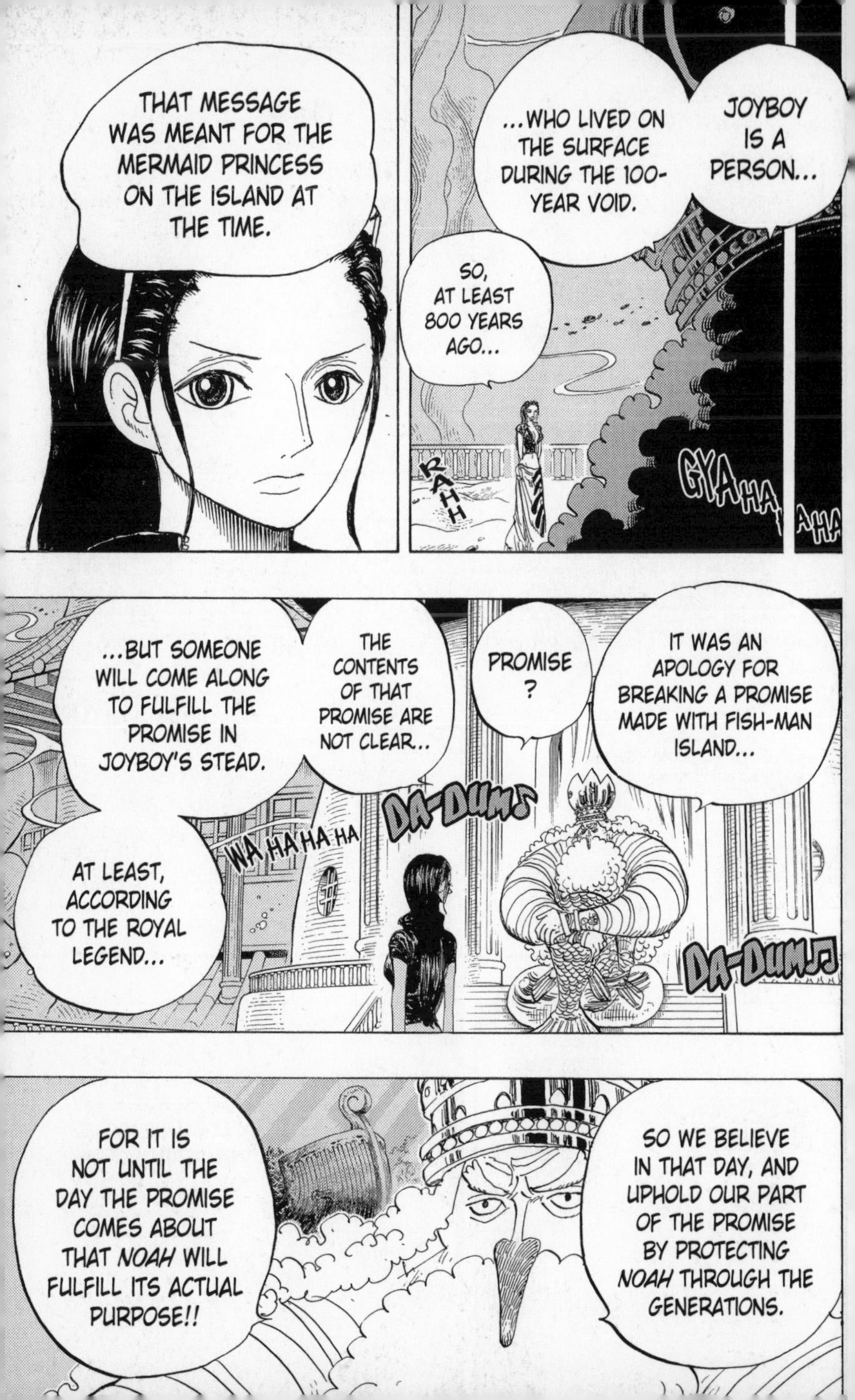
JOYBOY IS A PERSON...
...WHO LIVED ON THE SURFACE DURING THE 100-YEAR VOID.
SO, AT LEAST 800 YEARS AGO...
GYAHAHAHA
RAHH
THAT MESSAGE WAS MEANT FOR THE MERMAID PRINCESS ON THE ISLAND AT THE TIME.
IT WAS AN APOLOGY FOR BREAKING A PROMISE MADE WITH FISH-MAN ISLAND...
PROMISE?
THE CONTENTS OF THAT PROMISE ARE NOT CLEAR...
...BUT SOMEONE WILL COME ALONG TO FULFILL THE PROMISE IN JOYBOY'S STEAD.
DA-DUM
DA-DUM
WAHAHAHA
AT LEAST, ACCORDING TO THE ROYAL LEGEND...
SO WE BELIEVE IN THAT DAY, AND UPHOLD OUR PART OF THE PROMISE BY PROTECTING *NOAH* THROUGH THE GENERATIONS.
FOR IT IS NOT UNTIL THE DAY THE PROMISE COMES ABOUT THAT *NOAH* WILL FULFILL ITS ACTUAL PURPOSE!!

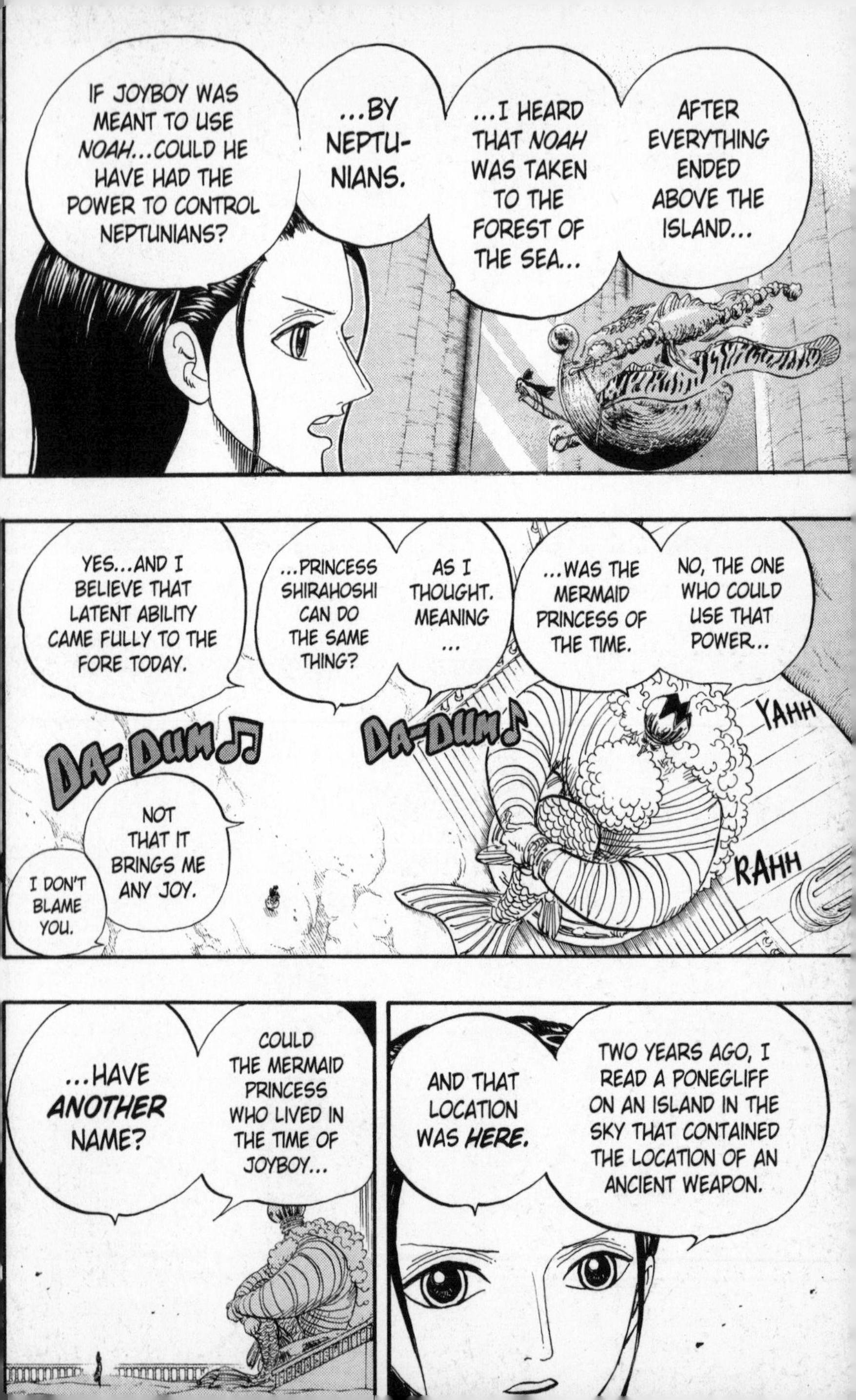
AFTER EVERYTHING ENDED ABOVE THE ISLAND...
...I HEARD THAT NOAH WAS TAKEN TO THE FOREST OF THE SEA...
...BY NEPTUNIANS.
IF JOYBOY WAS MEANT TO USE NOAH...COULD HE HAVE HAD THE POWER TO CONTROL NEPTUNIANS?
NO, THE ONE WHO COULD USE THAT POWER...
...WAS THE MERMAID PRINCESS OF THE TIME.
YAHH
RAHH
AS I THOUGHT. MEANING ...
...PRINCESS SHIRAHOSHI CAN DO THE SAME THING?
DA-DUM♪
YES...AND I BELIEVE THAT LATENT ABILITY CAME FULLY TO THE FORE TODAY.
DA-DUM♫
NOT THAT IT BRINGS ME ANY JOY.
I DON'T BLAME YOU.
TWO YEARS AGO, I READ A PONEGLIFF ON AN ISLAND IN THE SKY THAT CONTAINED THE LOCATION OF AN ANCIENT WEAPON.
AND THAT LOCATION WAS HERE.
COULD THE MERMAID PRINCESS WHO LIVED IN THE TIME OF JOYBOY...
...HAVE ANOTHER NAME?

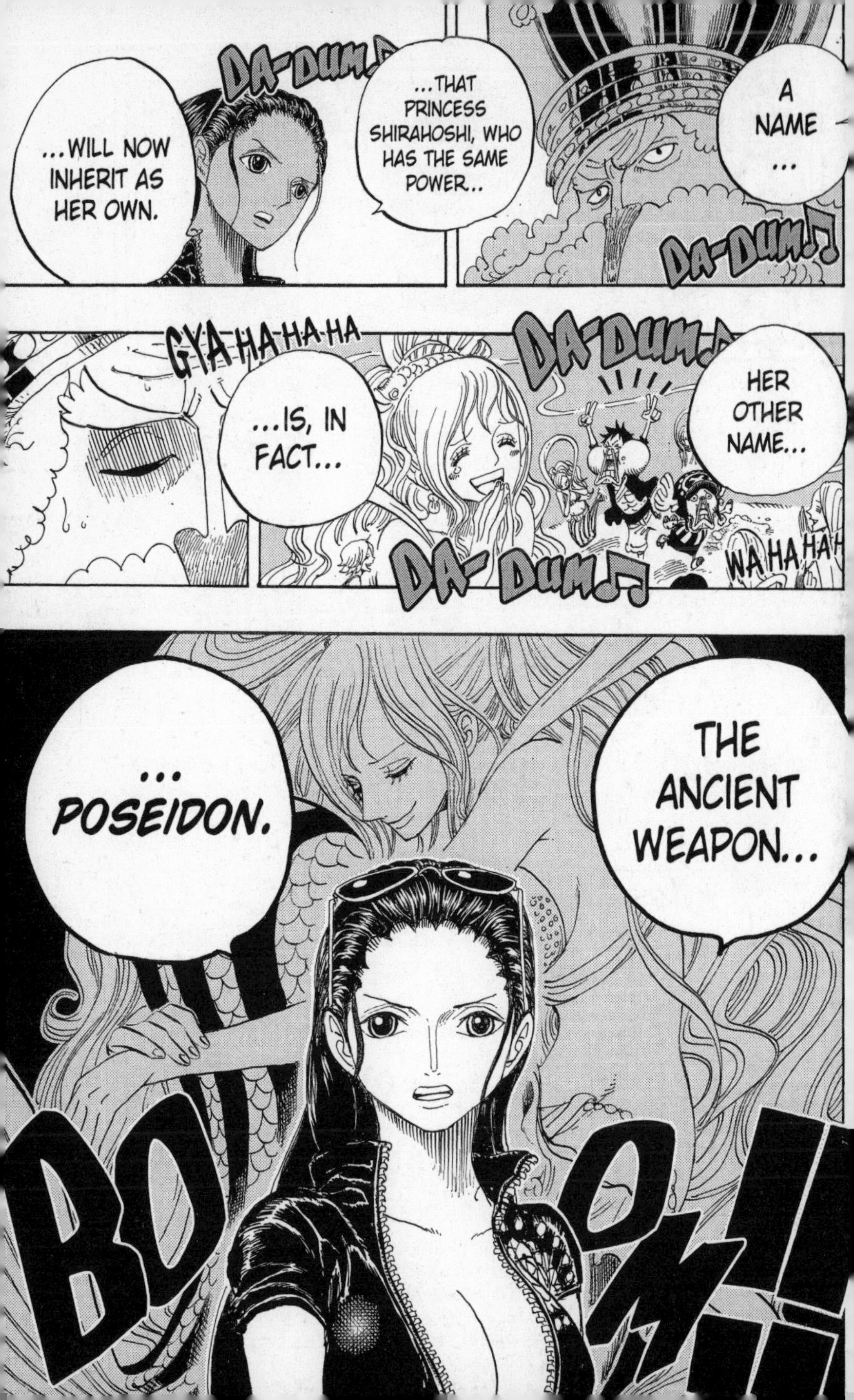
A NAME...
DA-DUM♫
...THAT PRINCESS SHIRAHOSHI, WHO HAS THE SAME POWER...
...WILL NOW INHERIT AS HER OWN.
DA-DUM♫
DA-DUM♫
HER OTHER NAME...
WA HA HAH
...IS, IN FACT...
DA-DUM♫
GYA HA HA HA
THE ANCIENT WEAPON...
...POSEIDON.
BOOM!!

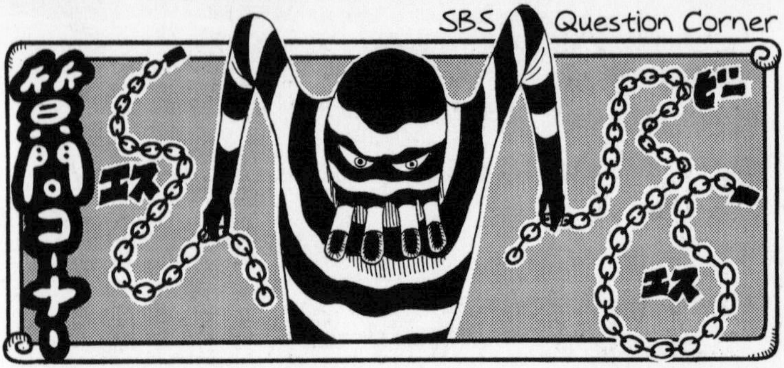
質問コーナー
エス
ビー
エス

(Yutaka Harada, Hokkaido)

Q: Hello, Mr. Oda! Hody turned his dorsal fin into a blade using Shark Slicer. Can Fish-Men remove their dorsal fins? Are they reversible or something? Or is it sticking out of the side? Please explain!!

--Nyaa

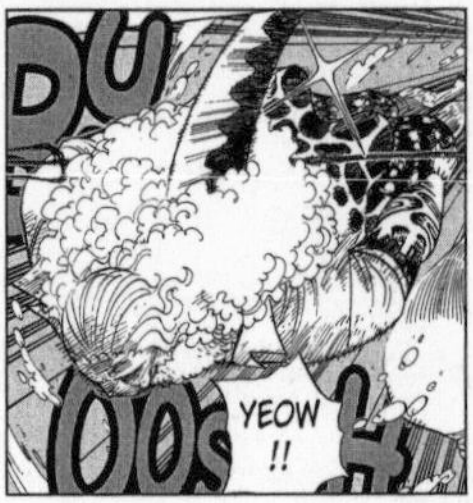
YEOW !!

A: Oh, that's a weapon that fits over the top.

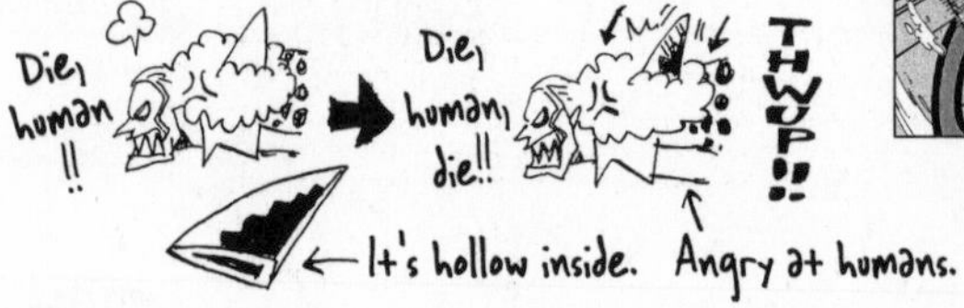
Die, human!!
Die, human, die!!
THWUP!!
It's hollow inside.
Angry at humans.

Q: Howdy, Odacchi! I love One Piece so much, I'll make time for it no matter how busy I am! So I put together a list of Fish-Man emotion T-shirts found in the manga. (it might not be all of them, though) What do you think?! ☆

--Horo Horo Butterfly

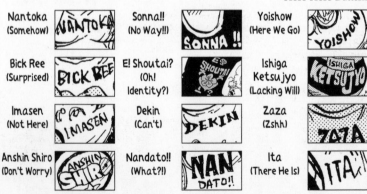

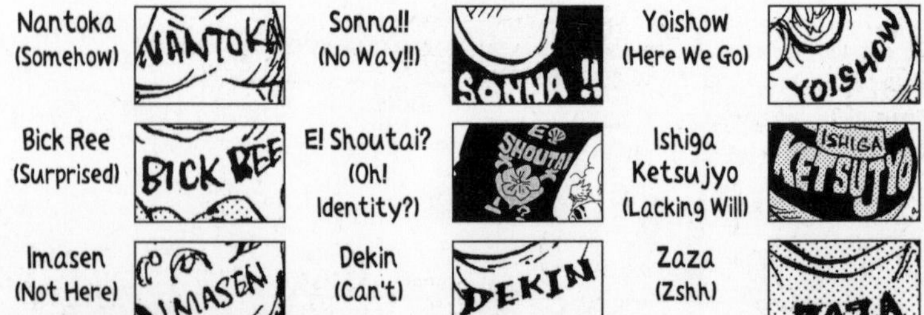
Nantoka (Somehow)
NANTOKA
Sonna!! (No Way!!)
SONNA !!
Yoishow (Here We Go)
YOISHOW
Bick Ree (Surprised)
BICK REE
E! Shoutai? (Oh! Identity?)
E SHOUTAI
Ishiga Ketsujyo (Lacking Will)
ISHIGA KETSUJYO
Imasen (Not Here)
IMASEN
Dekin (Can't)
DEKIN
Zaza (Zshh)
ZAZA
Anshin Shiro (Don't Worry)
ANSHIN SHIRO
Nandato!! (What?!)
NAN DATO!!
Ita (There He Is)
ITA

A: Ooh! There were a bunch. Thanks for finding them! They sure don't make much sense when you remove the context, do they? Not very useful. Aloha shirt style is the traditional style on Fish-Man Island, and the Criminal brand and explanation shirts seem to be the latest trend.

Chaper 650:

TWO CHANGES TO BE AWARE OF

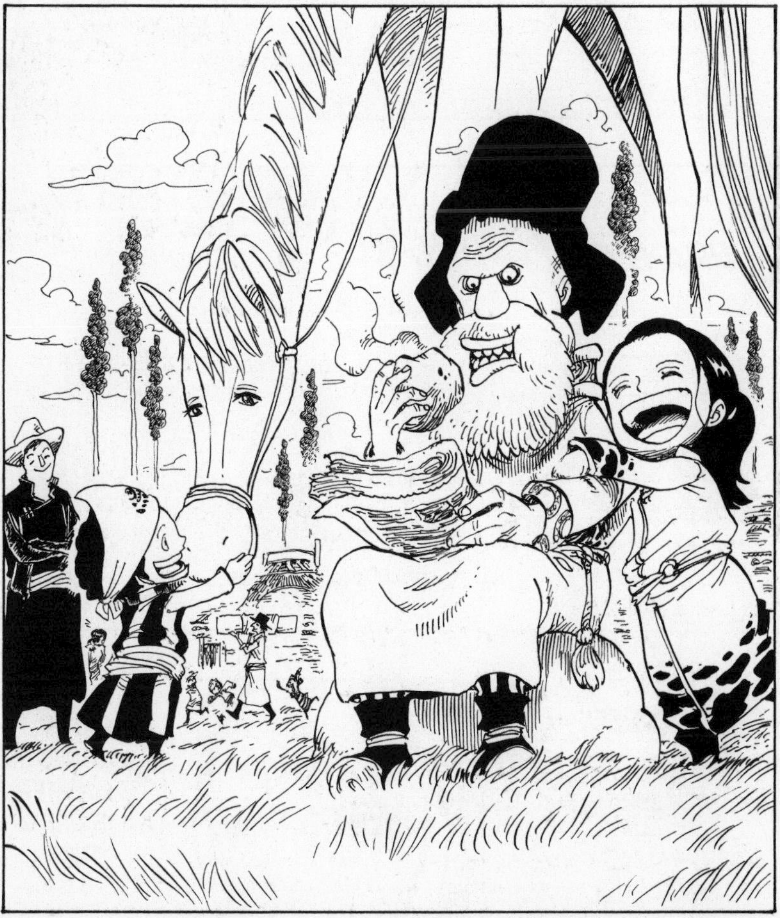

DECKS OF THE WORLD, VOL. 33 "LONG RING LONG LAND—TONJIT MEETS HIS GRANDCHILDREN"

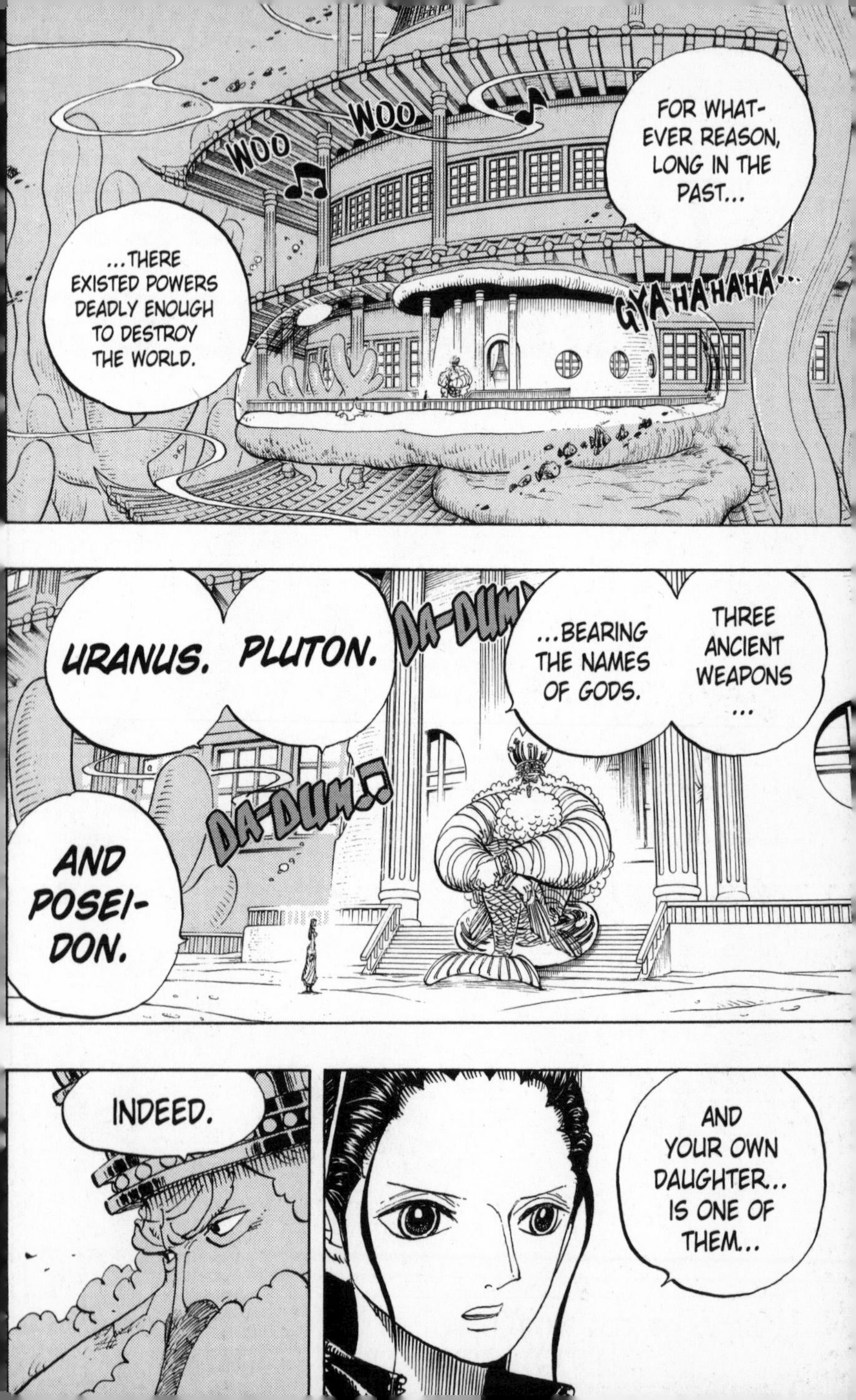
FOR WHAT-EVER REASON, LONG IN THE PAST...
WOO WOO
GYA HA HA HA...
...THERE EXISTED POWERS DEADLY ENOUGH TO DESTROY THE WORLD.
THREE ANCIENT WEAPONS ...
...BEARING THE NAMES OF GODS.
DA-DUM
PLUTON.
URANUS.
DA-DUM
AND POSEI-DON.
AND YOUR OWN DAUGHTER.. IS ONE OF THEM...
INDEED.

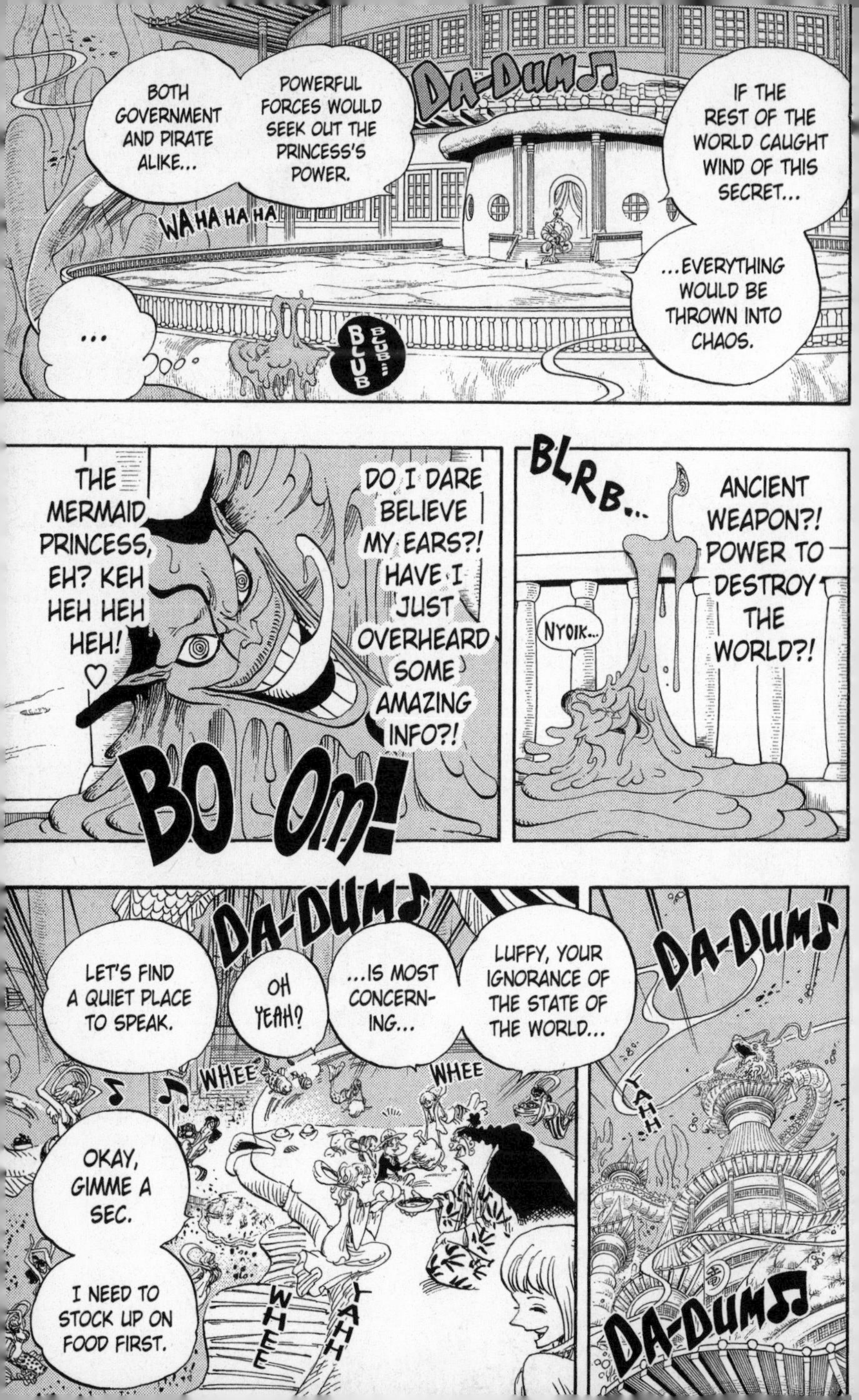
IF THE REST OF THE WORLD CAUGHT WIND OF THIS SECRET...
...EVERYTHING WOULD BE THROWN INTO CHAOS.
DA-DUM♫
POWERFUL FORCES WOULD SEEK OUT THE PRINCESS'S POWER.
BOTH GOVERNMENT AND PIRATE ALIKE...
WA HA HA HA
BLUB BLUB!!
...
BLRB...
ANCIENT WEAPON?! POWER TO DESTROY THE WORLD?!
NYOIK...
DO I DARE BELIEVE MY EARS?! HAVE I JUST OVERHEARD SOME AMAZING INFO?!
THE MERMAID PRINCESS, EH? KEH HEH HEH HEH! ♡
BOOM!
DA-DUM♪
YAHH
DA-DUM♫
DA-DUM♪
LUFFY, YOUR IGNORANCE OF THE STATE OF THE WORLD...
...IS MOST CONCERN-ING...
OH YEAH?
LET'S FIND A QUIET PLACE TO SPEAK.
WHEE
WHEE
OKAY, GIMME A SEC.
I NEED TO STOCK UP ON FOOD FIRST.
YAHH
WHEE

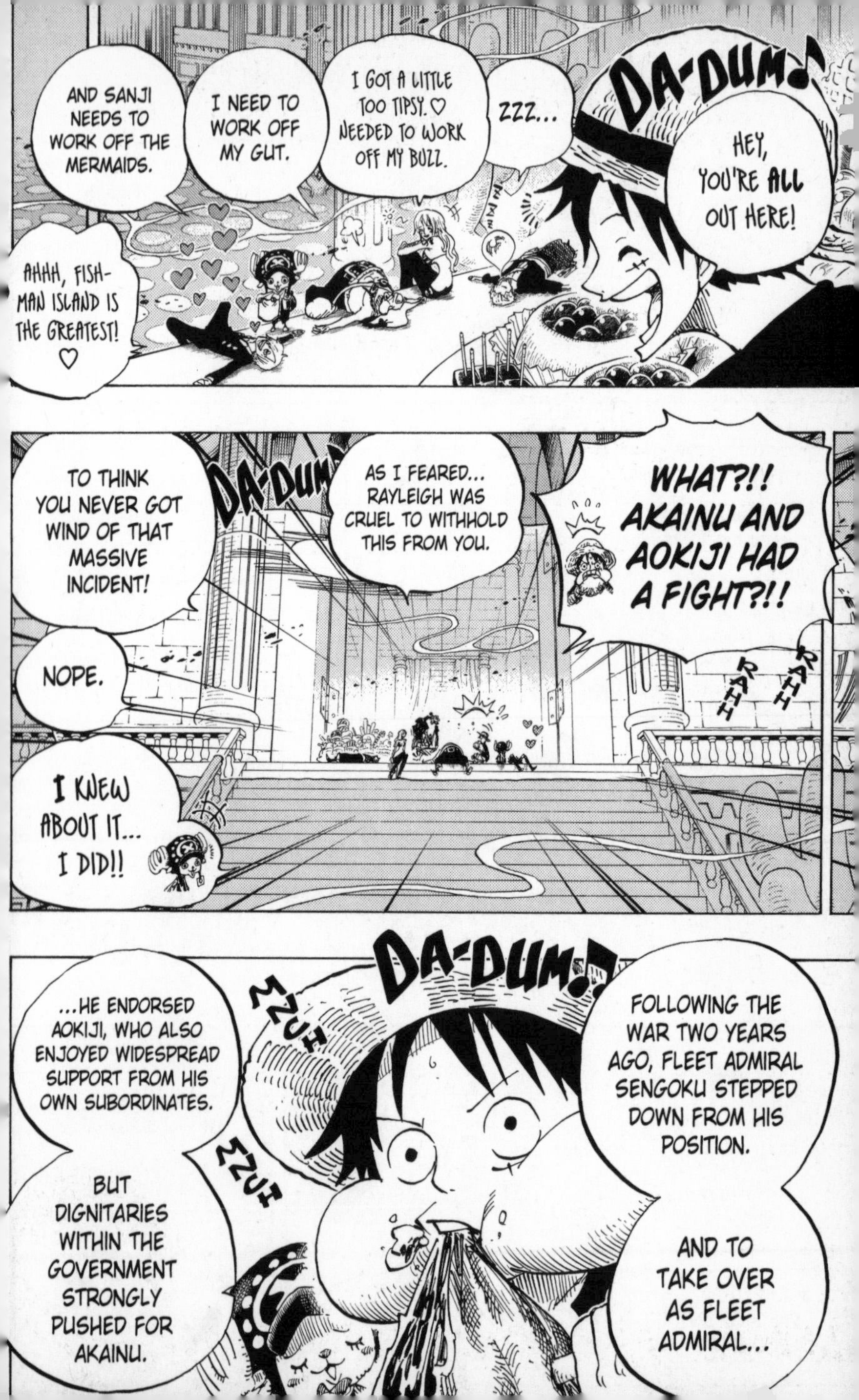
DA-DUM♪
HEY, YOU'RE ALL OUT HERE!
ZZZ...
I GOT A LITTLE TOO TIPSY. ♡ NEEDED TO WORK OFF MY BUZZ.
I NEED TO WORK OFF MY GUT.
AND SANJI NEEDS TO WORK OFF THE MERMAIDS.
AHHH, FISH-MAN ISLAND IS THE GREATEST! ♡
WHAT?!! AKAINU AND AOKIJI HAD A FIGHT?!!
RAHH
RAHH
AS I FEARED... RAYLEIGH WAS CRUEL TO WITHHOLD THIS FROM YOU.
DA-DUM
TO THINK YOU NEVER GOT WIND OF THAT MASSIVE INCIDENT!
NOPE.
I KNEW ABOUT IT... I DID!!
DA-DUM♪
FOLLOWING THE WAR TWO YEARS AGO, FLEET ADMIRAL SENGOKU STEPPED DOWN FROM HIS POSITION.
AND TO TAKE OVER AS FLEET ADMIRAL...
...HE ENDORSED AOKIJI, WHO ALSO ENJOYED WIDESPREAD SUPPORT FROM HIS OWN SUBORDINATES.
BUT DIGNITARIES WITHIN THE GOVERNMENT STRONGLY PUSHED FOR AKAINU.

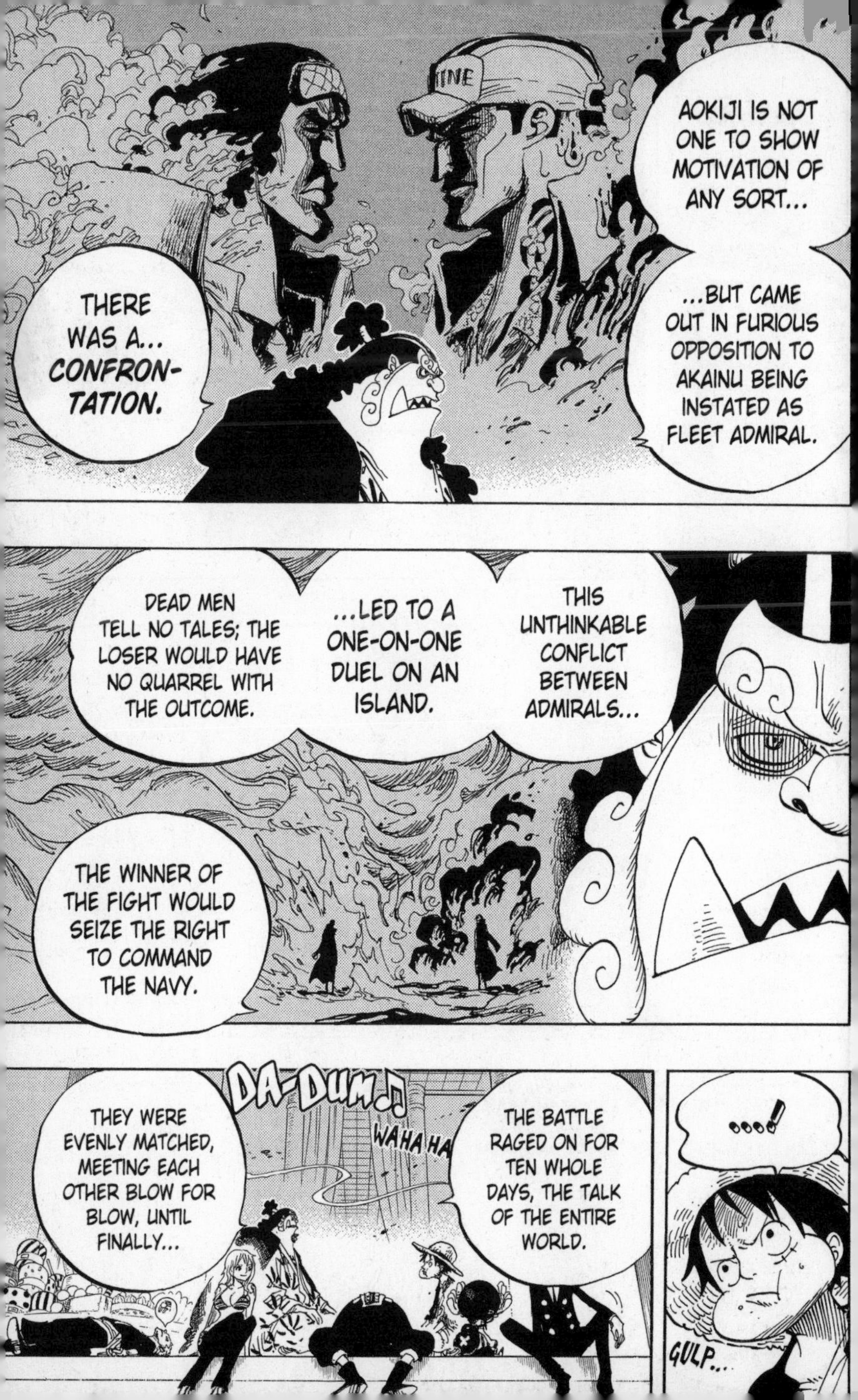
AOKIJI IS NOT ONE TO SHOW MOTIVATION OF ANY SORT...
...BUT CAME OUT IN FURIOUS OPPOSITION TO AKAINU BEING INSTATED AS FLEET ADMIRAL.
THERE WAS A... CONFRONTATION.
THIS UNTHINKABLE CONFLICT BETWEEN ADMIRALS...
...LED TO A ONE-ON-ONE DUEL ON AN ISLAND.
DEAD MEN TELL NO TALES; THE LOSER WOULD HAVE NO QUARREL WITH THE OUTCOME.
THE WINNER OF THE FIGHT WOULD SEIZE THE RIGHT TO COMMAND THE NAVY.
...!
GULP...
THE BATTLE RAGED ON FOR TEN WHOLE DAYS, THE TALK OF THE ENTIRE WORLD.
DA-DUM♫
WAHAHA
THEY WERE EVENLY MATCHED, MEETING EACH OTHER BLOW FOR BLOW, UNTIL FINALLY...

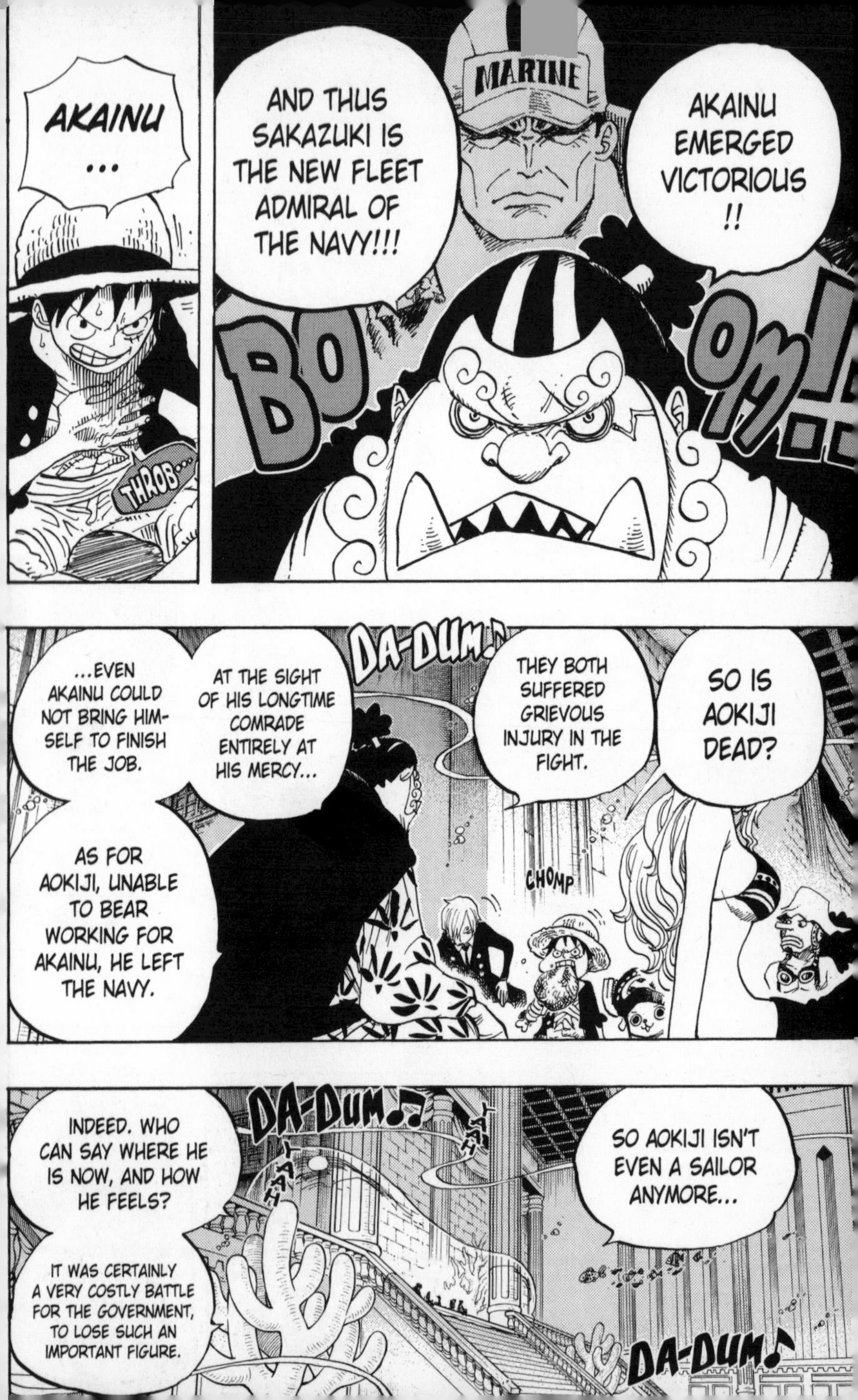
AKAINU EMERGED VICTORIOUS !!
AND THUS SAKAZUKI IS THE NEW FLEET ADMIRAL OF THE NAVY!!!
MARINE
BOOM!!
AKAINU ...
THROB...
SO IS AOKIJI DEAD?
DA-DUM
THEY BOTH SUFFERED GRIEVOUS INJURY IN THE FIGHT.
AT THE SIGHT OF HIS LONGTIME COMRADE ENTIRELY AT HIS MERCY...
...EVEN AKAINU COULD NOT BRING HIMSELF TO FINISH THE JOB.
AS FOR AOKIJI, UNABLE TO BEAR WORKING FOR AKAINU, HE LEFT THE NAVY.
CHOMP
SO AOKIJI ISN'T EVEN A SAILOR ANYMORE...
DA-DUM♫
YAAH
YAAH
INDEED. WHO CAN SAY WHERE HE IS NOW, AND HOW HE FEELS?
IT WAS CERTAINLY A VERY COSTLY BATTLE FOR THE GOVERNMENT, TO LOSE SUCH AN IMPORTANT FIGURE.
DA-DUM♪

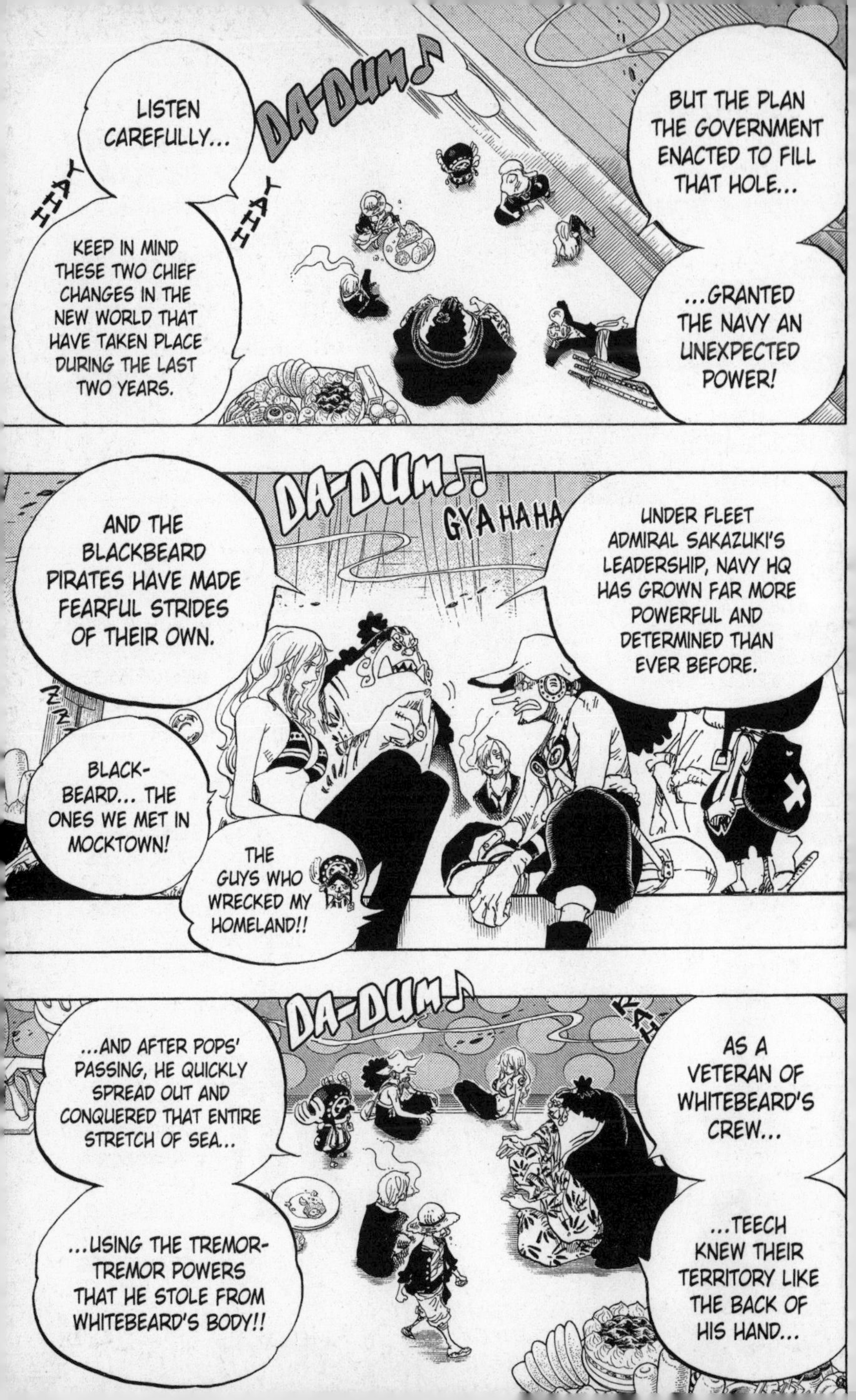
BUT THE PLAN THE GOVERNMENT ENACTED TO FILL THAT HOLE...
...GRANTED THE NAVY AN UNEXPECTED POWER!
DA-DUM♪
YAHH
YAHH
LISTEN CAREFULLY...
KEEP IN MIND THESE TWO CHIEF CHANGES IN THE NEW WORLD THAT HAVE TAKEN PLACE DURING THE LAST TWO YEARS.
UNDER FLEET ADMIRAL SAKAZUKI'S LEADERSHIP, NAVY HQ HAS GROWN FAR MORE POWERFUL AND DETERMINED THAN EVER BEFORE.
GYA HA HA
DA-DUM♫
AND THE BLACKBEARD PIRATES HAVE MADE FEARFUL STRIDES OF THEIR OWN.
BLACK-BEARD... THE ONES WE MET IN MOCKTOWN!
THE GUYS WHO WRECKED MY HOMELAND!!
AS A VETERAN OF WHITEBEARD'S CREW...
...TEECH KNEW THEIR TERRITORY LIKE THE BACK OF HIS HAND...
DA-DUM♪
...AND AFTER POPS' PASSING, HE QUICKLY SPREAD OUT AND CONQUERED THAT ENTIRE STRETCH OF SEA...
...USING THE TREMOR-TREMOR POWERS THAT HE STOLE FROM WHITEBEARD'S BODY!!

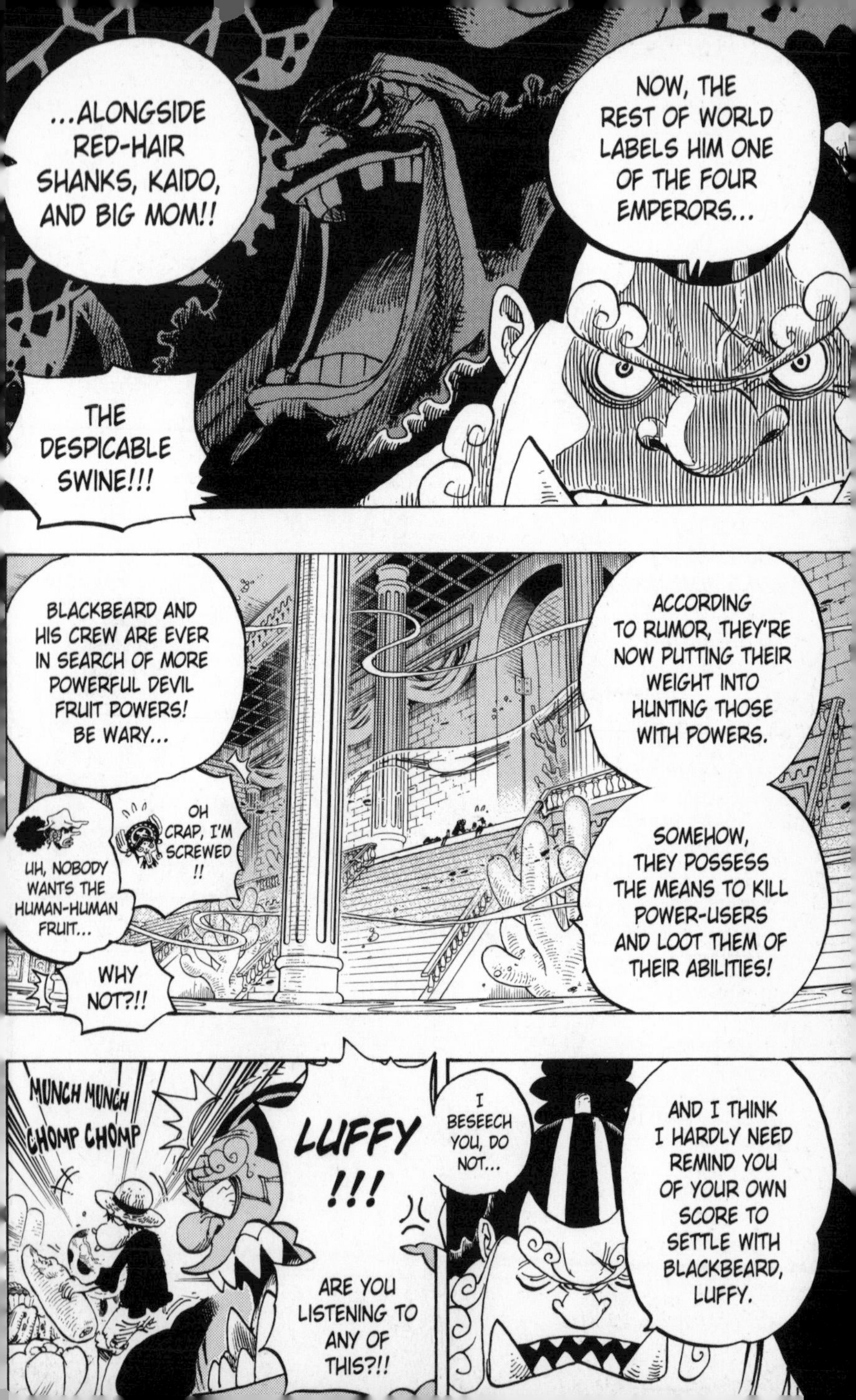
NOW, THE REST OF WORLD LABELS HIM ONE OF THE FOUR EMPERORS...
...ALONGSIDE RED-HAIR SHANKS, KAIDO, AND BIG MOM!!
THE DESPICABLE SWINE!!!
ACCORDING TO RUMOR, THEY'RE NOW PUTTING THEIR WEIGHT INTO HUNTING THOSE WITH POWERS.
SOMEHOW, THEY POSSESS THE MEANS TO KILL POWER-USERS AND LOOT THEM OF THEIR ABILITIES!
BLACKBEARD AND HIS CREW ARE EVER IN SEARCH OF MORE POWERFUL DEVIL FRUIT POWERS! BE WARY...
OH CRAP, I'M SCREWED!!
UH, NOBODY WANTS THE HUMAN-HUMAN FRUIT...
WHY NOT?!!
AND I THINK I HARDLY NEED REMIND YOU OF YOUR OWN SCORE TO SETTLE WITH BLACKBEARD, LUFFY.
I BESEECH YOU, DO NOT...
LUFFY!!!
ARE YOU LISTENING TO ANY OF THIS?!!
MUNCH MUNCH CHOMP CHOMP

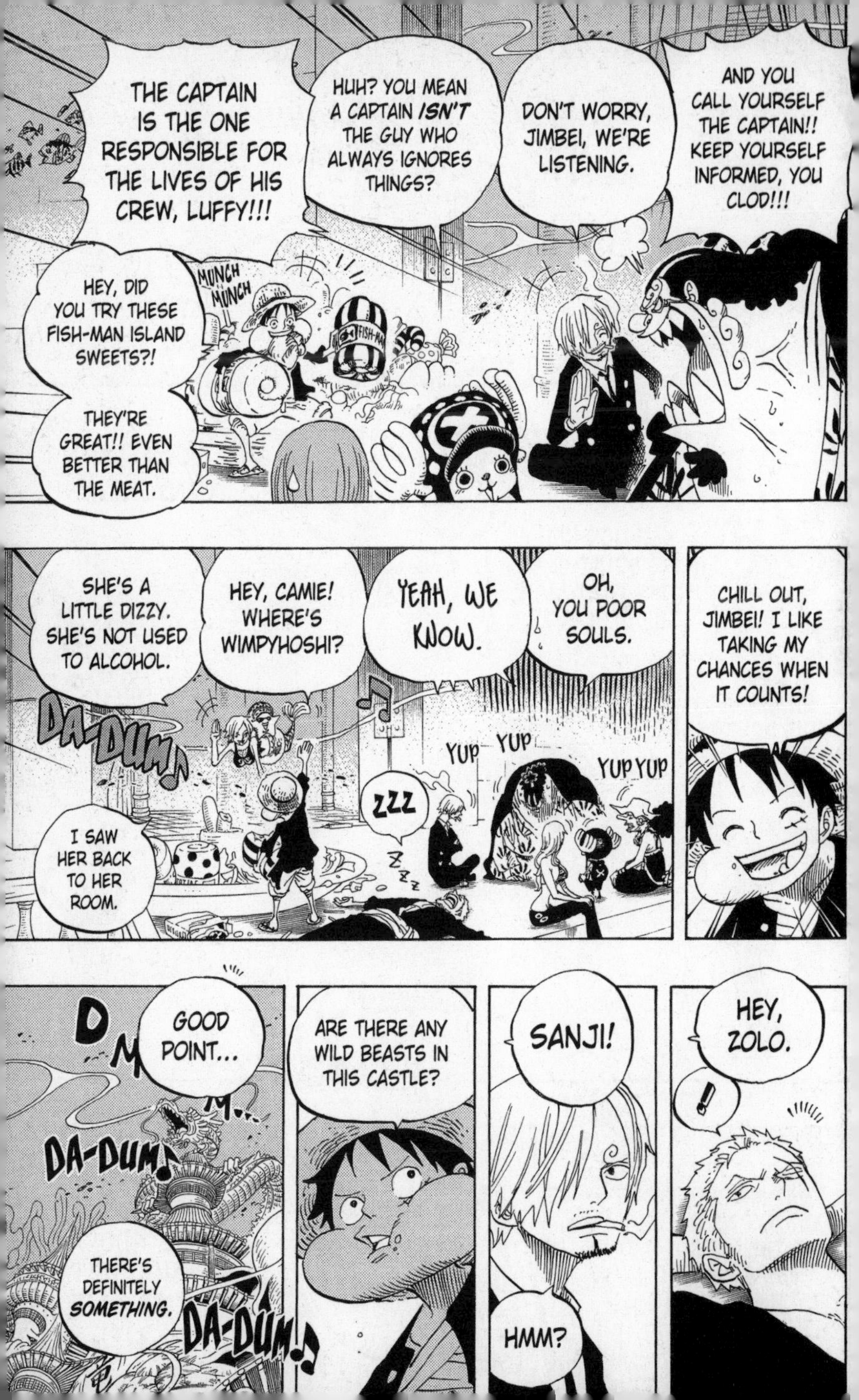
AND YOU CALL YOURSELF THE CAPTAIN!! KEEP YOURSELF INFORMED, YOU CLOD!!!
DON'T WORRY, JIMBEI, WE'RE LISTENING.
HUH? YOU MEAN A CAPTAIN *ISN'T* THE GUY WHO ALWAYS IGNORES THINGS?
THE CAPTAIN IS THE ONE RESPONSIBLE FOR THE LIVES OF HIS CREW, LUFFY!!!
MUNCH MUNCH
HEY, DID YOU TRY THESE FISH-MAN ISLAND SWEETS?!
THEY'RE GREAT!! EVEN BETTER THAN THE MEAT.
CHILL OUT, JIMBEI! I LIKE TAKING MY CHANCES WHEN IT COUNTS!
OH, YOU POOR SOULS.
YEAH, WE KNOW.
YUP YUP
YUPYUP
HEY, CAMIE! WHERE'S WIMPYHOSHI?
SHE'S A LITTLE DIZZY. SHE'S NOT USED TO ALCOHOL.
ZZZ
DA-DUM
I SAW HER BACK TO HER ROOM.
HEY, ZOLO.
!
SANJI!
HMM?
ARE THERE ANY WILD BEASTS IN THIS CASTLE?
GOOD POINT...
DA-DUM
THERE'S DEFINITELY *SOMETHING.*
DA-DUM

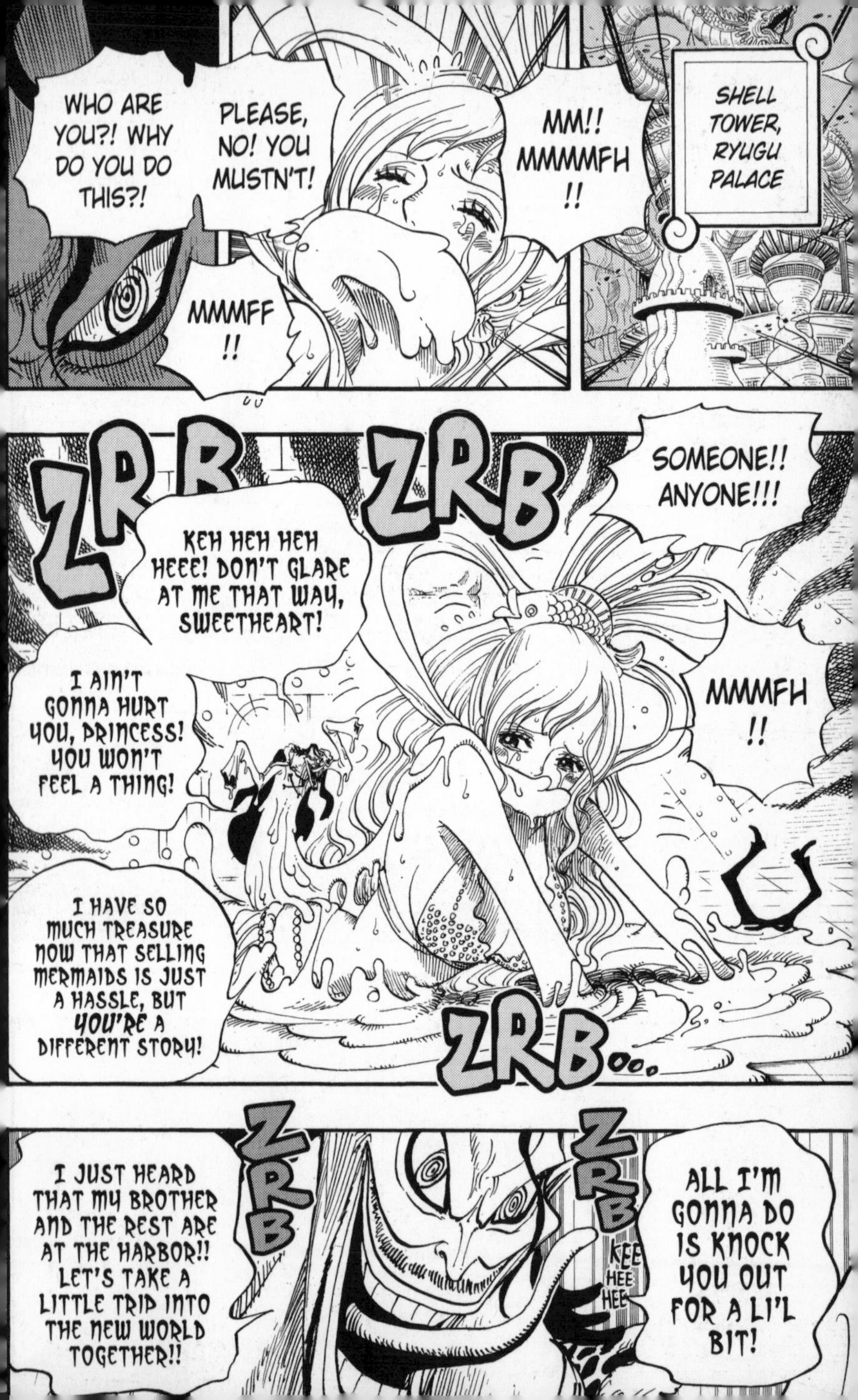
SHELL TOWER, RYUGU PALACE
MM!! MMMMFH !!
PLEASE, NO! YOU MUSTN'T!
WHO ARE YOU?! WHY DO YOU DO THIS?!
MMMFF !!
ZRB
SOMEONE!! ANYONE!!!
ZRB
KEH HEH HEH HEEE! DON'T GLARE AT ME THAT WAY, SWEETHEART!
MMMFH !!
I AIN'T GONNA HURT YOU, PRINCESS! YOU WON'T FEEL A THING!
I HAVE SO MUCH TREASURE NOW THAT SELLING MERMAIDS IS JUST A HASSLE, BUT *YOU'RE* A DIFFERENT STORY!
ZRB...
ALL I'M GONNA DO IS KNOCK YOU OUT FOR A LI'L BIT!
ZRB
KEE HEE HEE
ZRB
I JUST HEARD THAT MY BROTHER AND THE REST ARE AT THE HARBOR!! LET'S TAKE A LITTLE TRIP INTO THE NEW WORLD TOGETHER!!

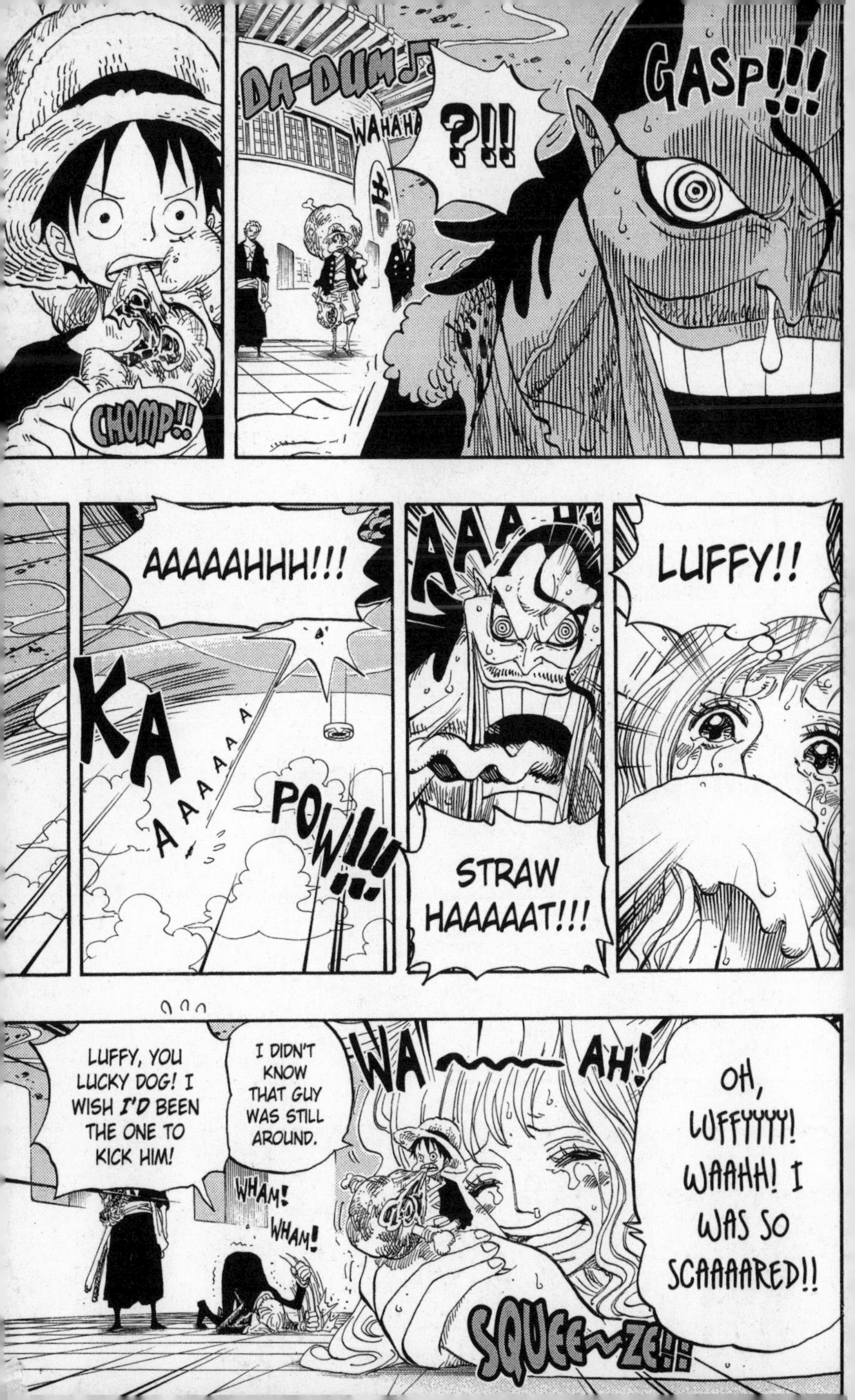
GASP!!!
?!!
DA-DUM♫
WAHAH
CHOMP!!
LUFFY!!
STRAW HAAAAAT!!!
AAAAAHHH!!!
KA
AAAAAA
POW!!!
OH, LUFFYYYY! WAAHH! I WAS SO SCAAAARED!!
WA~~AH!
SQUEE~ZE!!
I DIDN'T KNOW THAT GUY WAS STILL AROUND.
WHAM!
WHAM!
LUFFY, YOU LUCKY DOG! I WISH *I'D* BEEN THE ONE TO KICK HIM!

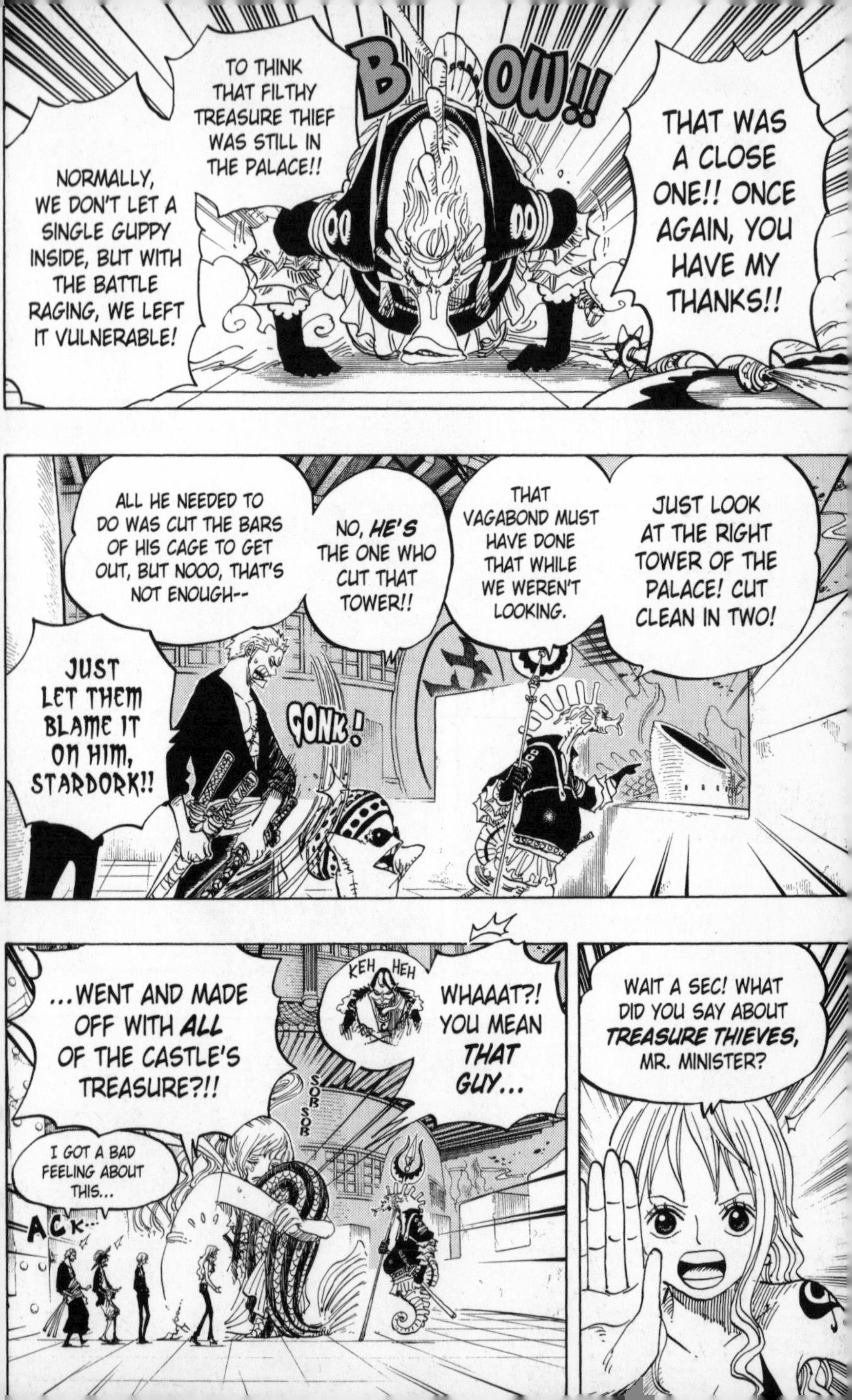
THAT WAS A CLOSE ONE!! ONCE AGAIN, YOU HAVE MY THANKS!!
BOW!!
TO THINK THAT FILTHY TREASURE THIEF WAS STILL IN THE PALACE!!
NORMALLY, WE DON'T LET A SINGLE GUPPY INSIDE, BUT WITH THE BATTLE RAGING, WE LEFT IT VULNERABLE!
JUST LOOK AT THE RIGHT TOWER OF THE PALACE! CUT CLEAN IN TWO!
THAT VAGABOND MUST HAVE DONE THAT WHILE WE WEREN'T LOOKING.
NO, *HE'S* THE ONE WHO CUT THAT TOWER!!
ALL HE NEEDED TO DO WAS CUT THE BARS OF HIS CAGE TO GET OUT, BUT NOOO, THAT'S NOT ENOUGH--
JUST LET THEM BLAME IT ON HIM, STARDORK!!
GONK!
WAIT A SEC! WHAT DID YOU SAY ABOUT *TREASURE THIEVES,* MR. MINISTER?
WHAAAT?! YOU MEAN *THAT GUY...*
KEH HEH
...WENT AND MADE OFF WITH *ALL* OF THE CASTLE'S TREASURE?!!
SOB SOB
I GOT A BAD FEELING ABOUT THIS...
ACK...

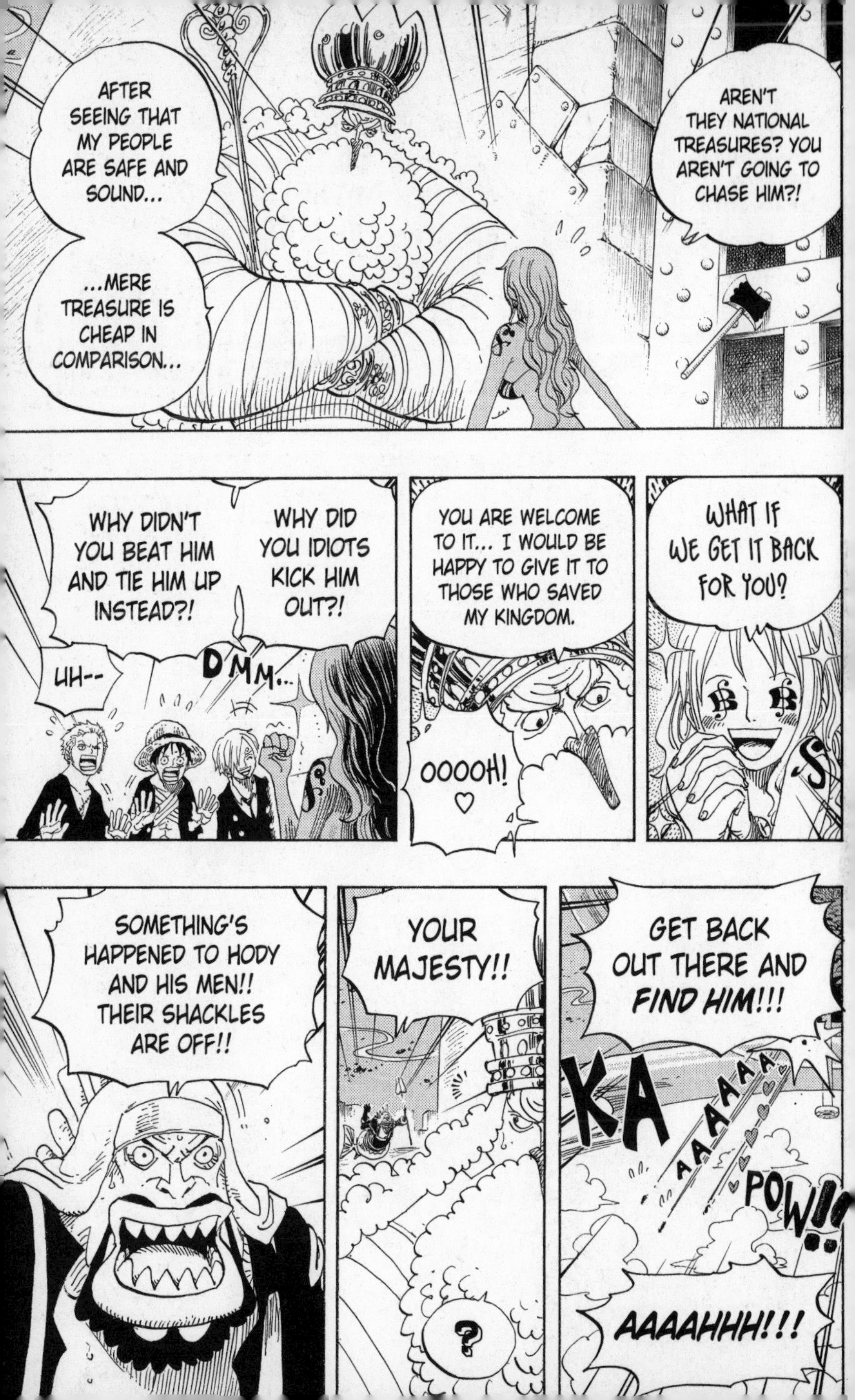
AREN'T THEY NATIONAL TREASURES? YOU AREN'T GOING TO CHASE HIM?!
AFTER SEEING THAT MY PEOPLE ARE SAFE AND SOUND...
...MERE TREASURE IS CHEAP IN COMPARISON...
WHAT IF WE GET IT BACK FOR YOU?
YOU ARE WELCOME TO IT... I WOULD BE HAPPY TO GIVE IT TO THOSE WHO SAVED MY KINGDOM.
OOOOH! ♡
WHY DID YOU IDIOTS KICK HIM OUT?!
WHY DIDN'T YOU BEAT HIM AND TIE HIM UP INSTEAD?!
DMM...
UH--
GET BACK OUT THERE AND *FIND HIM!!!*
KAAAAAAA
POW!!
AAAAHHH!!!
YOUR MAJESTY!!
?
SOMETHING'S HAPPENED TO HODY AND HIS MEN!! THEIR SHACKLES ARE OFF!!

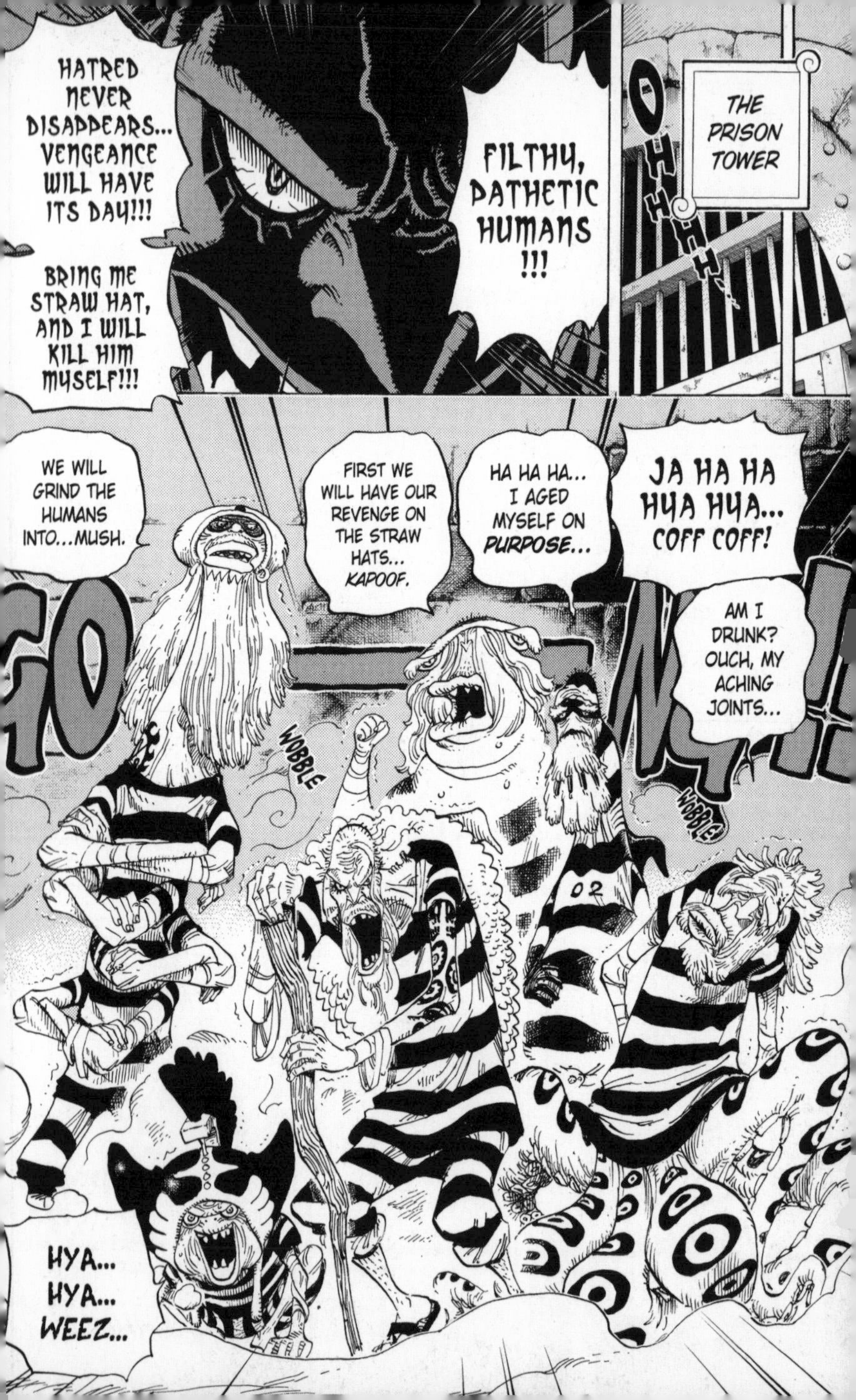
THE PRISON TOWER
OHHHHH
FILTHY, PATHETIC HUMANS!!!
HATRED NEVER DISAPPEARS... VENGEANCE WILL HAVE ITS DAY!!!
BRING ME STRAW HAT, AND I WILL KILL HIM MYSELF!!!
JA HA HA HYA HYA... COFF COFF!
AM I DRUNK? OUCH, MY ACHING JOINTS...
WOBBLE
HA HA HA... I AGED MYSELF ON *PURPOSE*...
FIRST WE WILL HAVE OUR REVENGE ON THE STRAW HATS... *KAPOOF.*
WE WILL GRIND THE HUMANS INTO...MUSH.
WOBBLE
HYA... HYA... WEEZ...

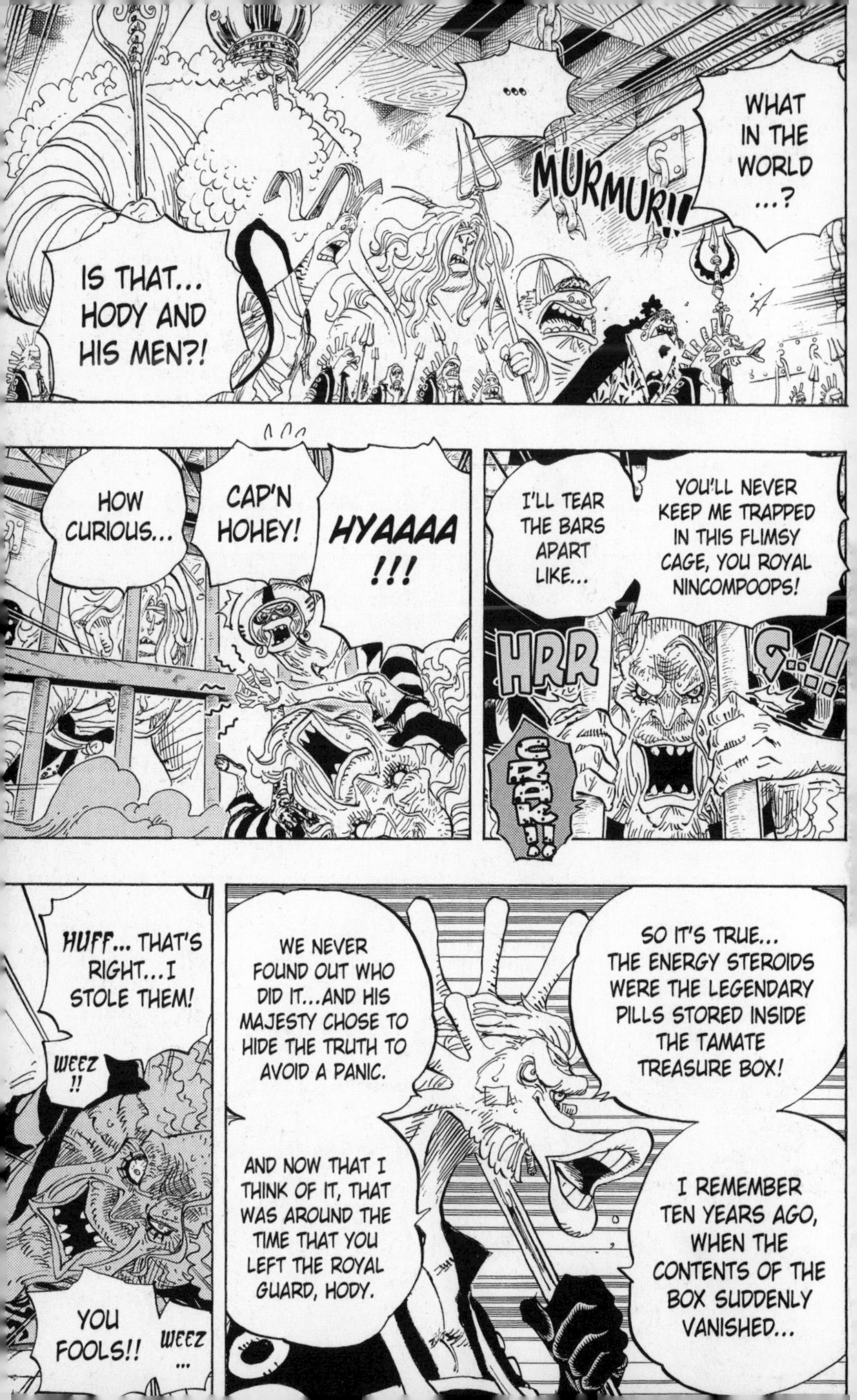
WHAT IN THE WORLD ...?
MURMUR!!
...
IS THAT... HODY AND HIS MEN?!
YOU'LL NEVER KEEP ME TRAPPED IN THIS FLIMSY CAGE, YOU ROYAL NINCOMPOOPS!
I'LL TEAR THE BARS APART LIKE...
HRRG..!!
GRRK!!
HYAAAA!!!
CAP'N HOHEY!
HOW CURIOUS...
SO IT'S TRUE... THE ENERGY STEROIDS WERE THE LEGENDARY PILLS STORED INSIDE THE TAMATE TREASURE BOX!
WE NEVER FOUND OUT WHO DID IT...AND HIS MAJESTY CHOSE TO HIDE THE TRUTH TO AVOID A PANIC.
I REMEMBER TEN YEARS AGO, WHEN THE CONTENTS OF THE BOX SUDDENLY VANISHED...
AND NOW THAT I THINK OF IT, THAT WAS AROUND THE TIME THAT YOU LEFT THE ROYAL GUARD, HODY.
HUFF... THAT'S RIGHT...I STOLE THEM!
WEEZ!!
YOU FOOLS!!
WEEZ...

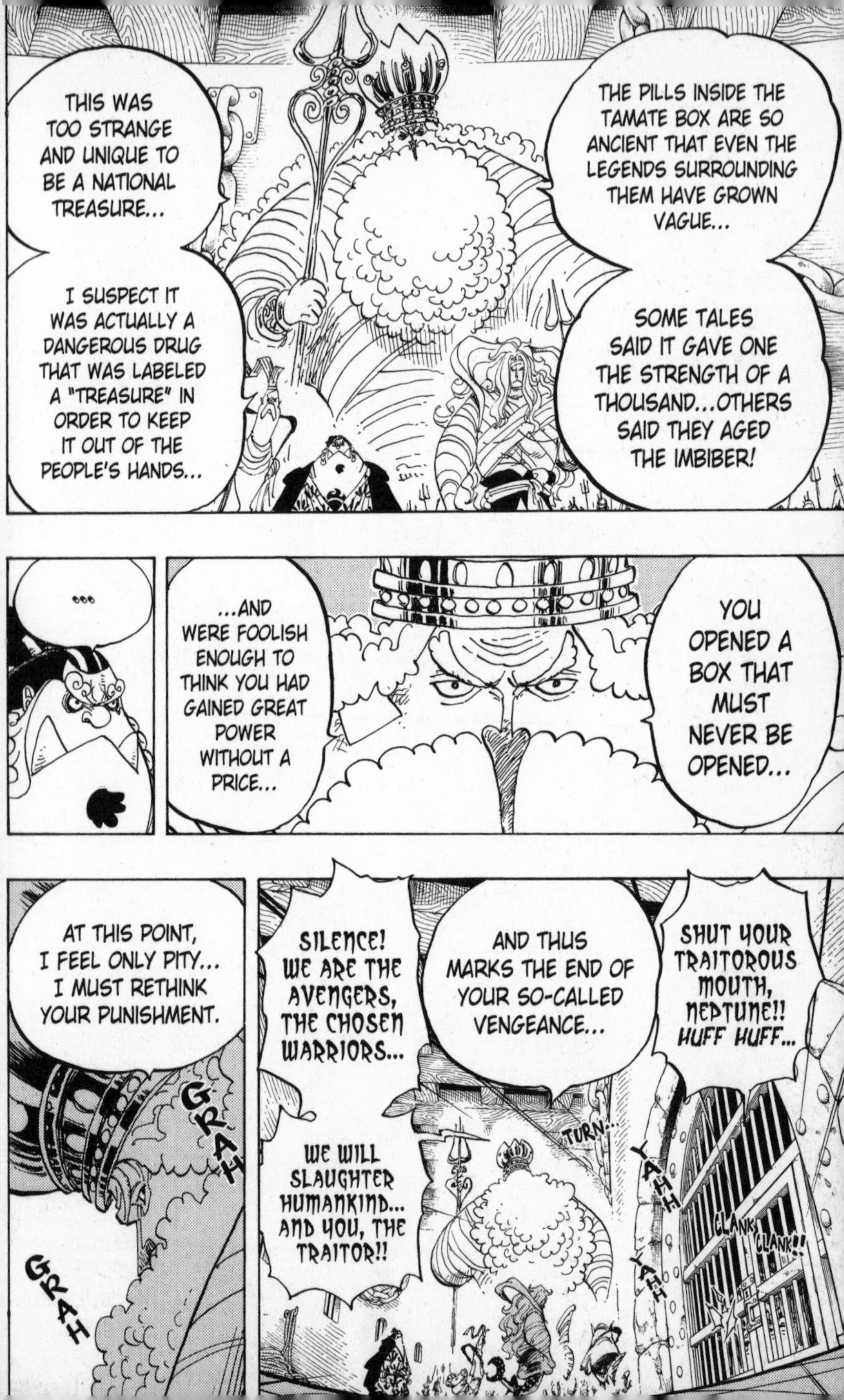
THE PILLS INSIDE THE TAMATE BOX ARE SO ANCIENT THAT EVEN THE LEGENDS SURROUNDING THEM HAVE GROWN VAGUE...
SOME TALES SAID IT GAVE ONE THE STRENGTH OF A THOUSAND...OTHERS SAID THEY AGED THE IMBIBER!
THIS WAS TOO STRANGE AND UNIQUE TO BE A NATIONAL TREASURE...
I SUSPECT IT WAS ACTUALLY A DANGEROUS DRUG THAT WAS LABELED A "TREASURE" IN ORDER TO KEEP IT OUT OF THE PEOPLE'S HANDS...
YOU OPENED A BOX THAT MUST NEVER BE OPENED...
...AND WERE FOOLISH ENOUGH TO THINK YOU HAD GAINED GREAT POWER WITHOUT A PRICE...
...
SHUT YOUR TRAITOROUS MOUTH, NEPTUNE!! HUFF HUFF...
AND THUS MARKS THE END OF YOUR SO-CALLED VENGEANCE...
SILENCE! WE ARE THE AVENGERS, THE CHOSEN WARRIORS...
TURN...
YAHH
YAHH
CLANK
CLANK!!
WE WILL SLAUGHTER HUMANKIND... AND YOU, THE TRAITOR!!
AT THIS POINT, I FEEL ONLY PITY... I MUST RETHINK YOUR PUNISHMENT.
GRAH
GRAH

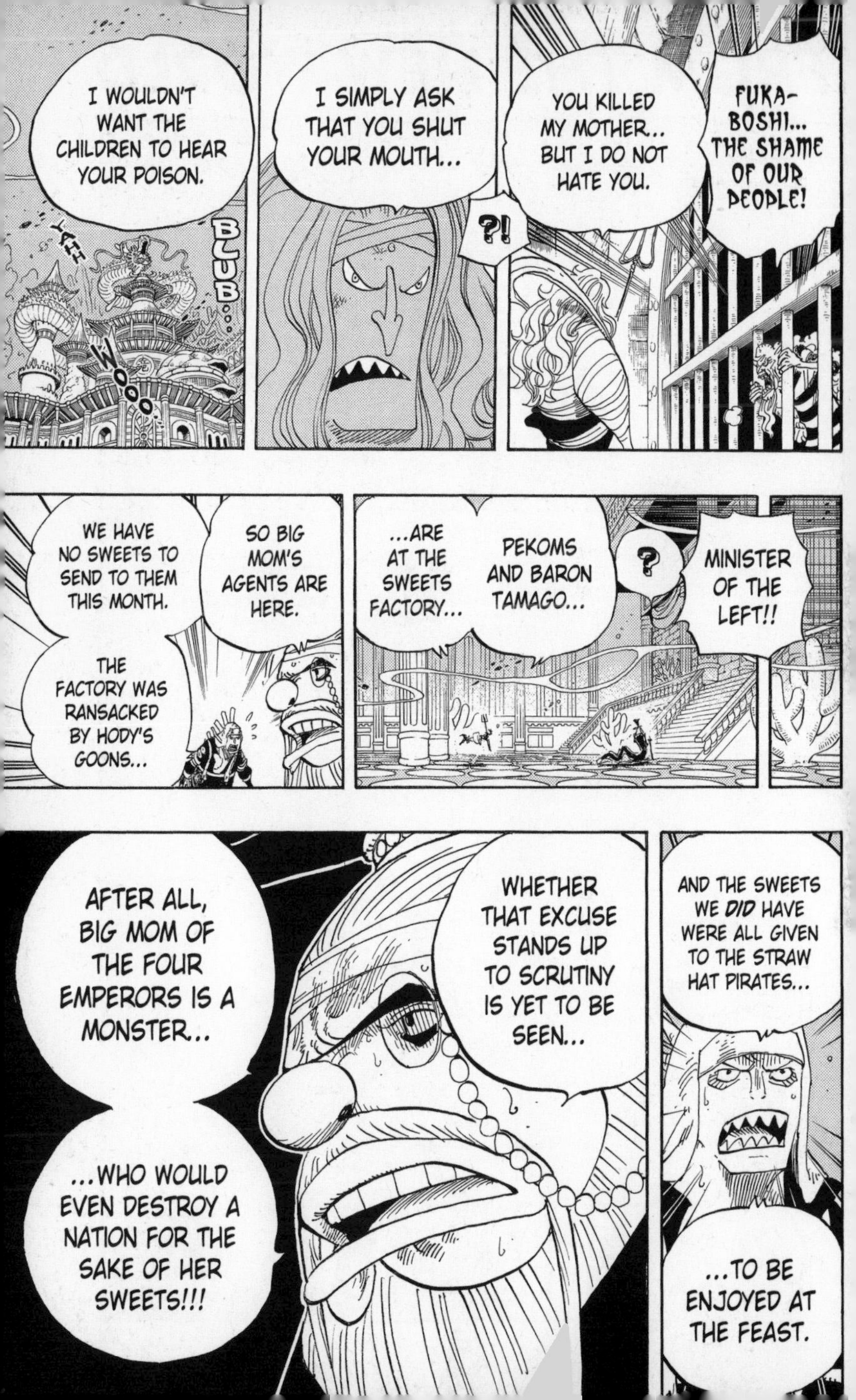
FUKA-BOSHI... THE SHAME OF OUR PEOPLE!
YOU KILLED MY MOTHER... BUT I DO NOT HATE YOU.
?!
I SIMPLY ASK THAT YOU SHUT YOUR MOUTH...
I WOULDN'T WANT THE CHILDREN TO HEAR YOUR POISON.
BLUB...
YAHH
WOOO...
?
MINISTER OF THE LEFT!!
PEKOMS AND BARON TAMAGO...
...ARE AT THE SWEETS FACTORY...
SO BIG MOM'S AGENTS ARE HERE.
WE HAVE NO SWEETS TO SEND TO THEM THIS MONTH.
THE FACTORY WAS RANSACKED BY HODY'S GOONS...
AND THE SWEETS WE *DID* HAVE WERE ALL GIVEN TO THE STRAW HAT PIRATES...
...TO BE ENJOYED AT THE FEAST.
WHETHER THAT EXCUSE STANDS UP TO SCRUTINY IS YET TO BE SEEN...
AFTER ALL, BIG MOM OF THE FOUR EMPERORS IS A MONSTER...
...WHO WOULD EVEN DESTROY A NATION FOR THE SAKE OF HER SWEETS!!!

FROM THE NEW WORLD

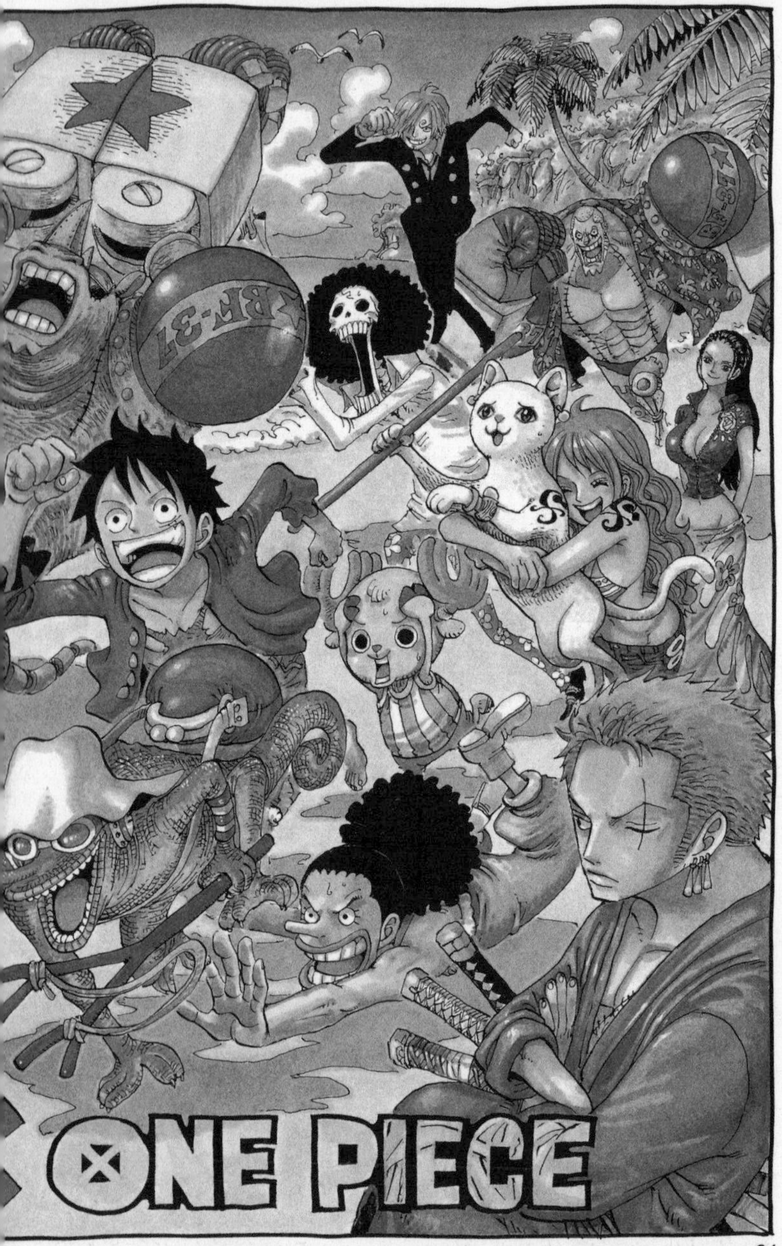
ONE PIECE

Chapter 651: A VOICE

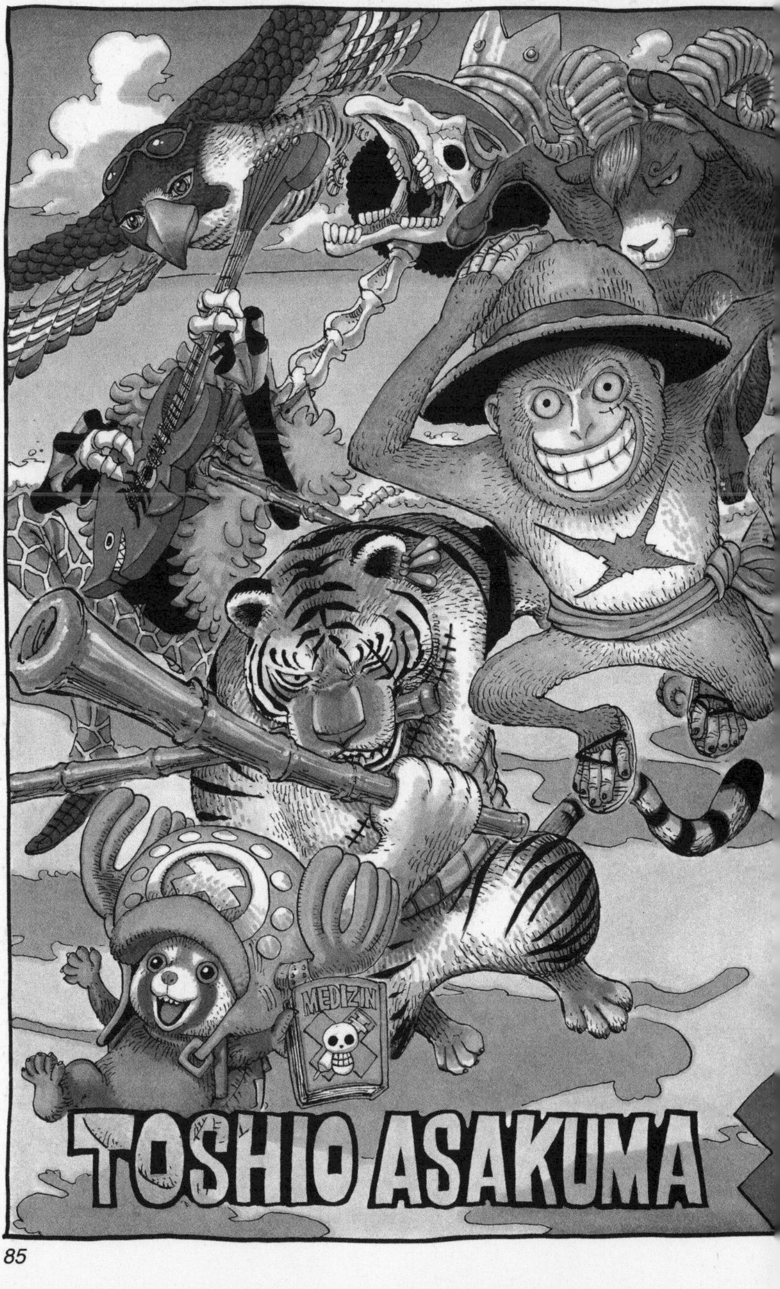
MEDIZIN
TOSHIO ASAKUMA

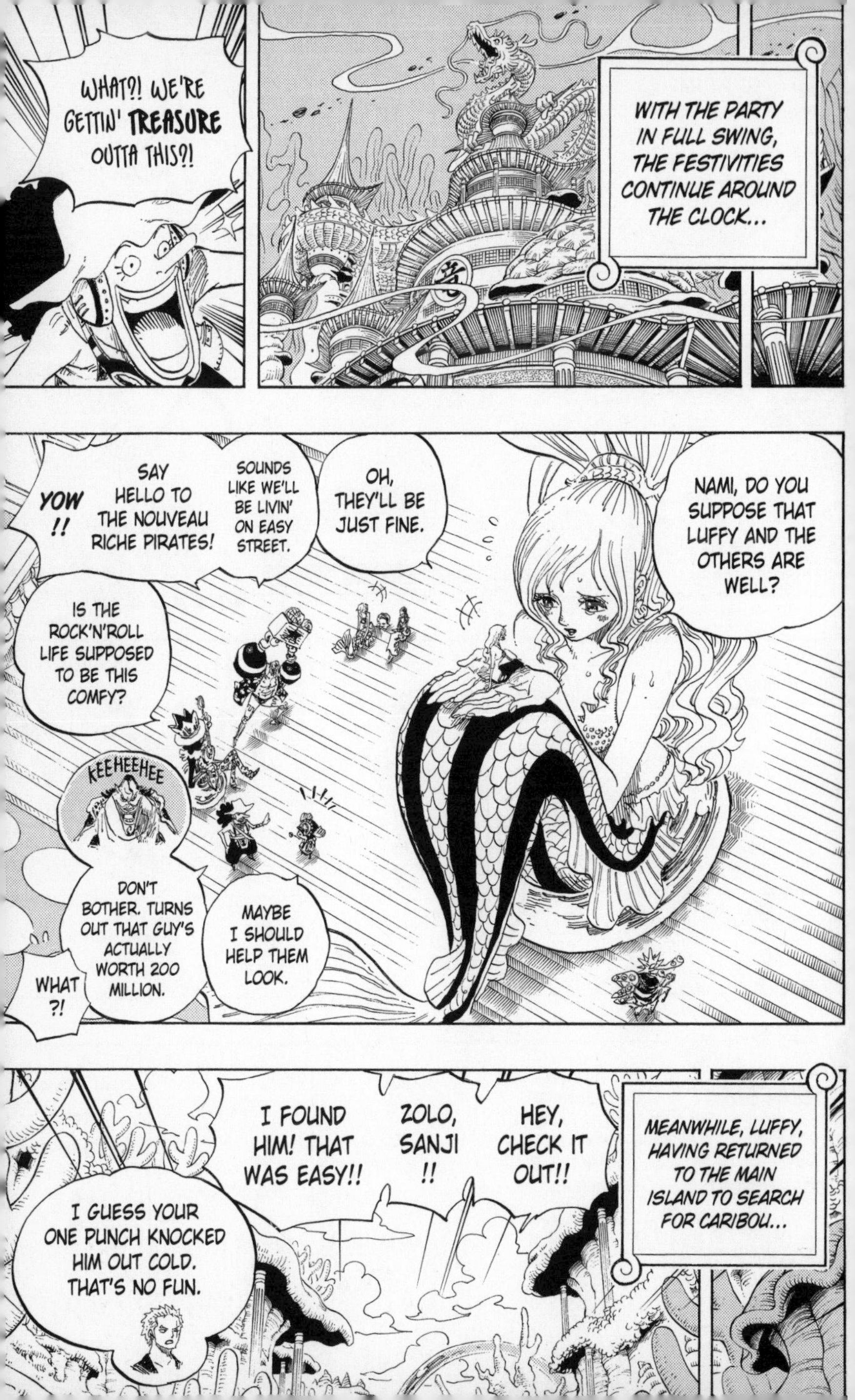
WITH THE PARTY IN FULL SWING, THE FESTIVITIES CONTINUE AROUND THE CLOCK...
WHAT?! WE'RE GETTIN' TREASURE OUTTA THIS?!
NAMI, DO YOU SUPPOSE THAT LUFFY AND THE OTHERS ARE WELL?
OH, THEY'LL BE JUST FINE.
SOUNDS LIKE WE'LL BE LIVIN' ON EASY STREET.
SAY HELLO TO THE NOUVEAU RICHE PIRATES!
YOW!!
IS THE ROCK'N'ROLL LIFE SUPPOSED TO BE THIS COMFY?
KEEHEEHEE
MAYBE I SHOULD HELP THEM LOOK.
DON'T BOTHER. TURNS OUT THAT GUY'S ACTUALLY WORTH 200 MILLION.
WHAT?!
MEANWHILE, LUFFY, HAVING RETURNED TO THE MAIN ISLAND TO SEARCH FOR CARIBOU...
HEY, CHECK IT OUT!!
ZOLO, SANJI!!
I FOUND HIM! THAT WAS EASY!!
I GUESS YOUR ONE PUNCH KNOCKED HIM OUT COLD. THAT'S NO FUN.

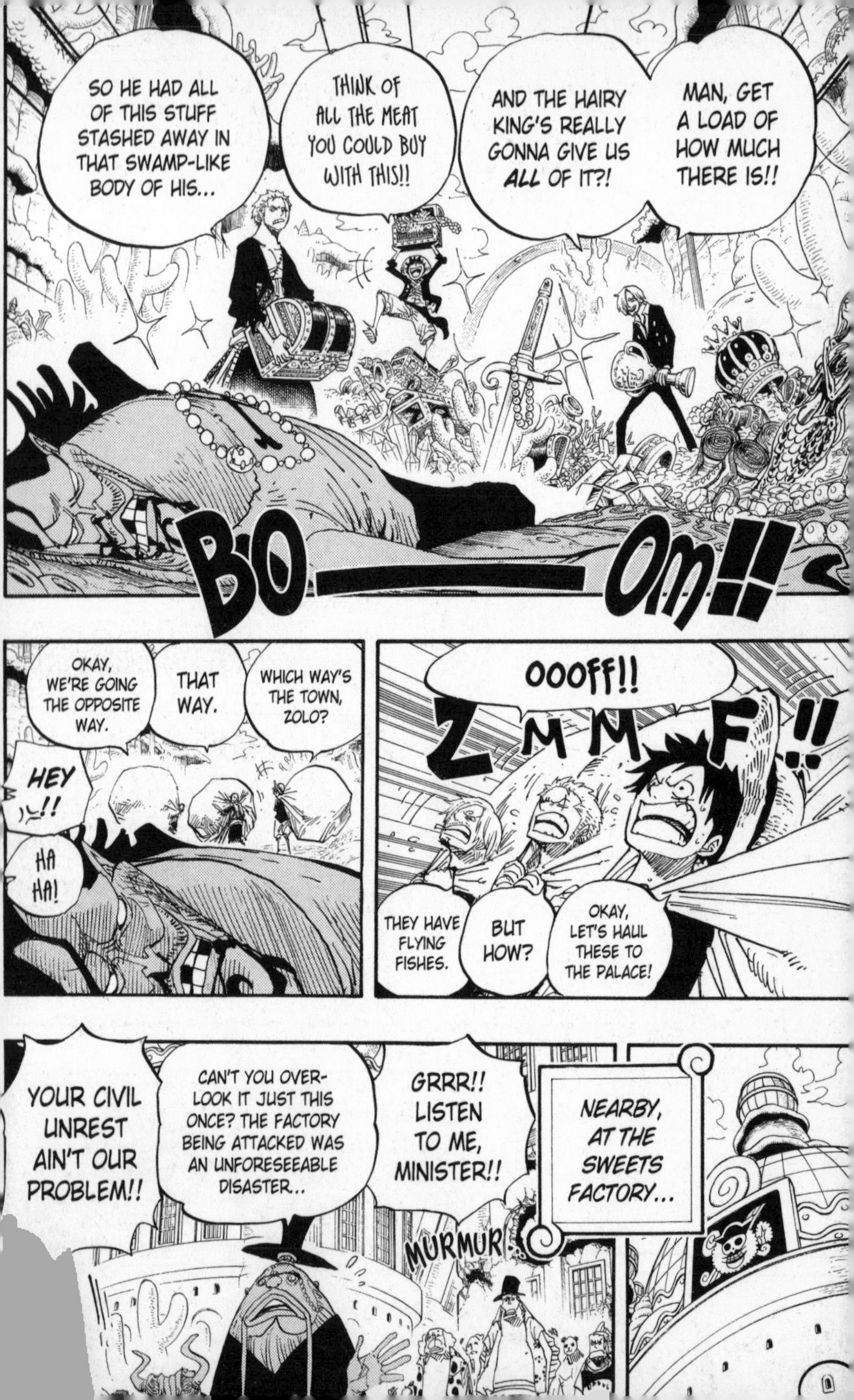
MAN, GET A LOAD OF HOW MUCH THERE IS!!
AND THE HAIRY KING'S REALLY GONNA GIVE US ALL OF IT?!
THINK OF ALL THE MEAT YOU COULD BUY WITH THIS!!
SO HE HAD ALL OF THIS STUFF STASHED AWAY IN THAT SWAMP-LIKE BODY OF HIS...
BO—OM!!
OOOFF!!
ZMMF!!
OKAY, LET'S HAUL THESE TO THE PALACE!
BUT HOW?
THEY HAVE FLYING FISHES.
WHICH WAY'S THE TOWN, ZOLO?
THAT WAY.
OKAY, WE'RE GOING THE OPPOSITE WAY.
HEY!!
HA HA!
NEARBY, AT THE SWEETS FACTORY...
GRRR!! LISTEN TO ME, MINISTER!!
CAN'T YOU OVER-LOOK IT JUST THIS ONCE? THE FACTORY BEING ATTACKED WAS AN UNFORESEEABLE DISASTER...
YOUR CIVIL UNREST AIN'T OUR PROBLEM!!
MURMUR

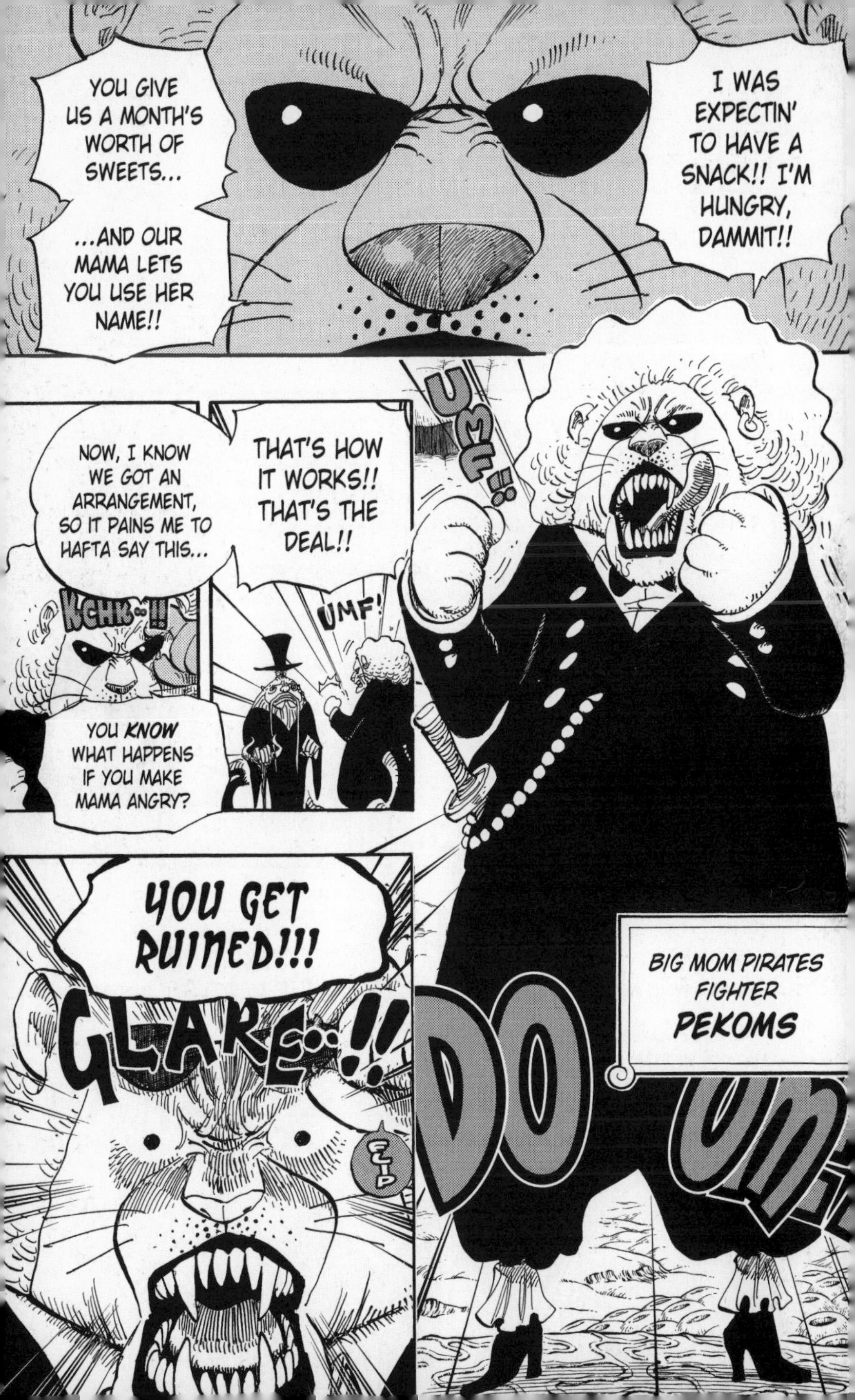
I WAS EXPECTIN' TO HAVE A SNACK!! I'M HUNGRY, DAMMIT!!
YOU GIVE US A MONTH'S WORTH OF SWEETS...
...AND OUR MAMA LETS YOU USE HER NAME!!
UMF!!
BIG MOM PIRATES FIGHTER PEKOMS
DOOM
THAT'S HOW IT WORKS!! THAT'S THE DEAL!!
UMF!
NOW, I KNOW WE GOT AN ARRANGEMENT, SO IT PAINS ME TO HAFTA SAY THIS...
KCHK!!
YOU KNOW WHAT HAPPENS IF YOU MAKE MAMA ANGRY?
YOU GET RUINED!!!
GLARE!!
FLIP

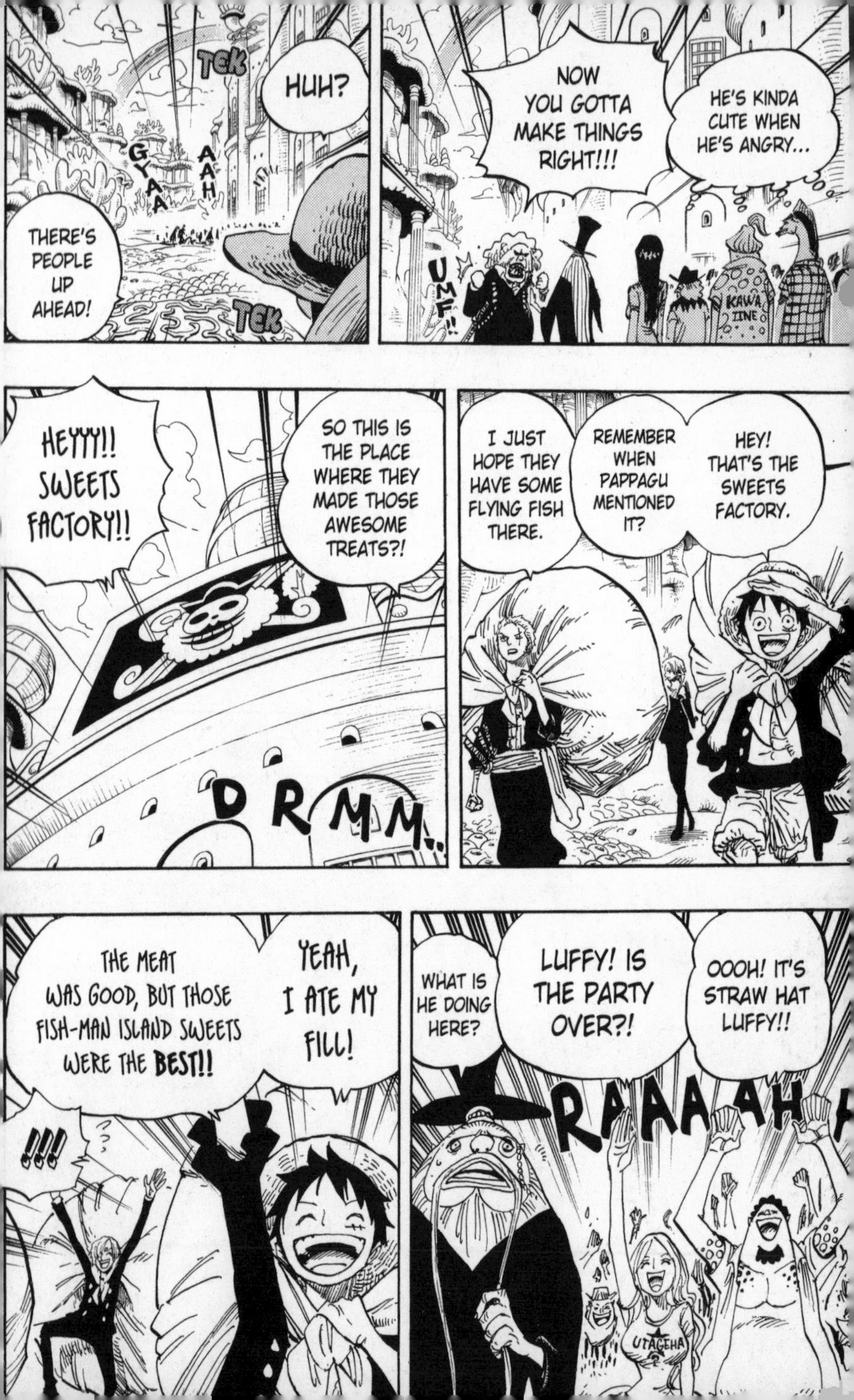
HE'S KINDA CUTE WHEN HE'S ANGRY...
NOW YOU GOTTA MAKE THINGS RIGHT!!!
UMF!!
HUH?
TEK
GYAA
AAH
THERE'S PEOPLE UP AHEAD!
TEK
HEY! THAT'S THE SWEETS FACTORY.
REMEMBER WHEN PAPPAGU MENTIONED IT?
I JUST HOPE THEY HAVE SOME FLYING FISH THERE.
SO THIS IS THE PLACE WHERE THEY MADE THOSE AWESOME TREATS?!
HEYYY!! SWEETS FACTORY!!
DRMM..
OOOH! IT'S STRAW HAT LUFFY!!
LUFFY! IS THE PARTY OVER?!
WHAT IS HE DOING HERE?
RAAAAH
UTAGEHA
YEAH, I ATE MY FILL!
THE MEAT WAS GOOD, BUT THOSE FISH-MAN ISLAND SWEETS WERE THE **BEST**!!
!!!

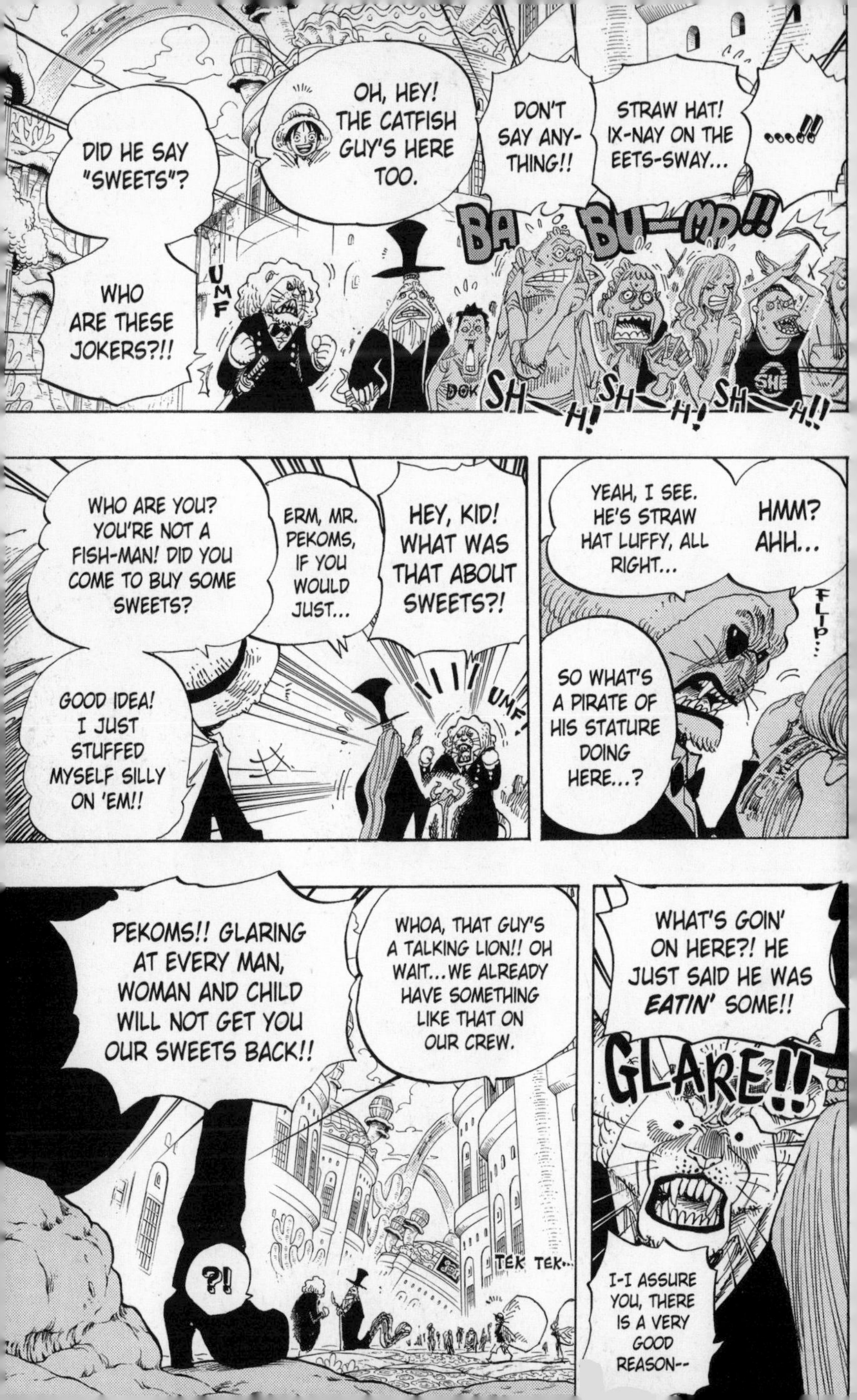

....!!
STRAW HAT! IX-NAY ON THE EETS-SWAY...
DON'T SAY ANY-THING!!
OH, HEY! THE CATFISH GUY'S HERE TOO.
DID HE SAY "SWEETS"?
BA-BU-MP!!
WHO ARE THESE JOKERS?!!
UMF
DOK
SH-H! SH-H! SH-H!!
HMM? AHH...
YEAH, I SEE. HE'S STRAW HAT LUFFY, ALL RIGHT...
FLIP..
SO WHAT'S A PIRATE OF HIS STATURE DOING HERE...?
HEY, KID! WHAT WAS THAT ABOUT SWEETS?!
ERM, MR. PEKOMS, IF YOU WOULD JUST...
WHO ARE YOU? YOU'RE NOT A FISH-MAN! DID YOU COME TO BUY SOME SWEETS?
UMF..
GOOD IDEA! I JUST STUFFED MYSELF SILLY ON 'EM!!
WHAT'S GOIN' ON HERE?! HE JUST SAID HE WAS *EATIN'* SOME!!
GLARE!!
I-I ASSURE YOU, THERE IS A VERY GOOD REASON--
WHOA, THAT GUY'S A TALKING LION!! OH WAIT...WE ALREADY HAVE SOMETHING LIKE THAT ON OUR CREW.
PEKOMS!! GLARING AT EVERY MAN, WOMAN AND CHILD WILL NOT GET YOU OUR SWEETS BACK!!
TEK TEK...
?!

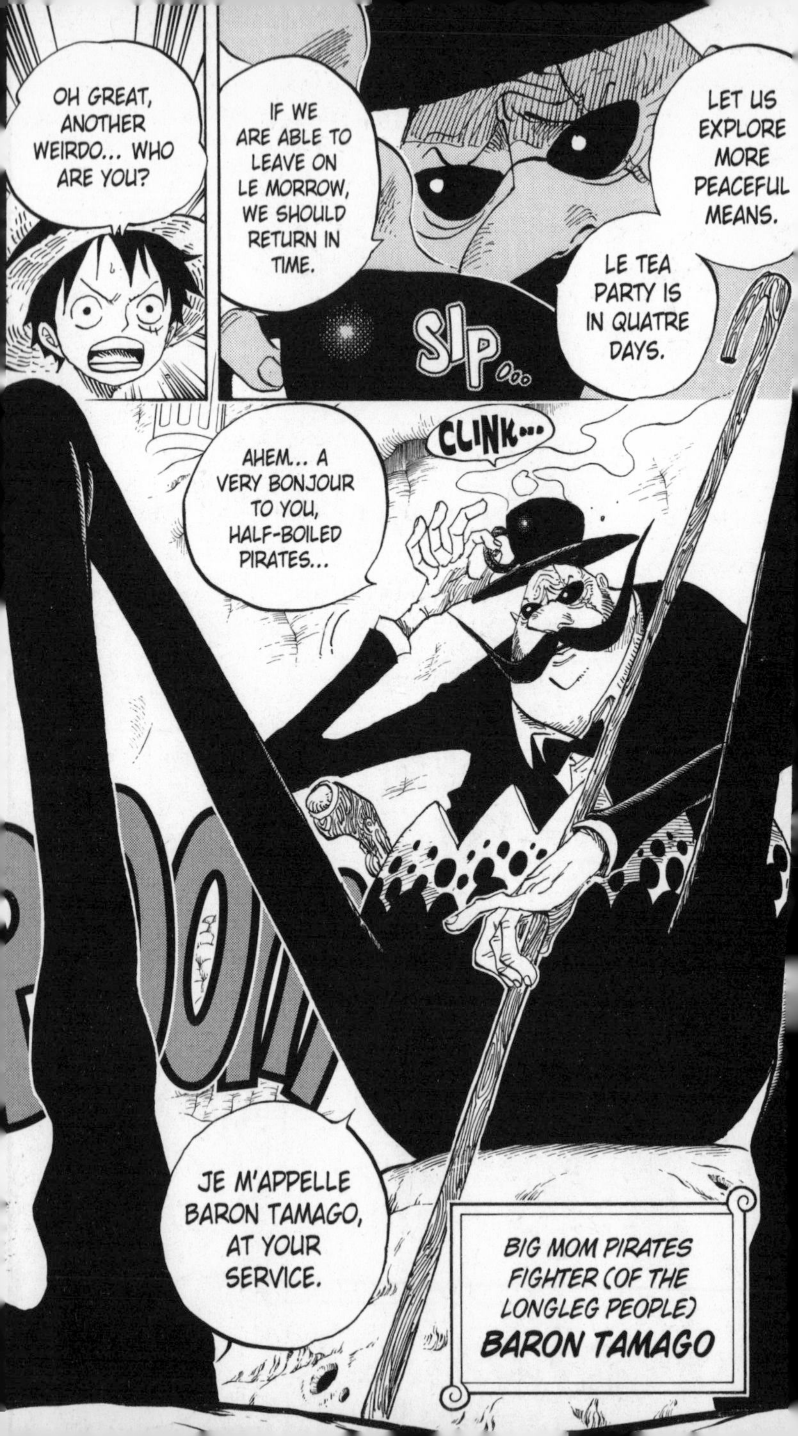
LET US EXPLORE MORE PEACEFUL MEANS.
LE TEA PARTY IS IN QUATRE DAYS.
IF WE ARE ABLE TO LEAVE ON LE MORROW, WE SHOULD RETURN IN TIME.
SIP...
OH GREAT, ANOTHER WEIRDO... WHO ARE YOU?
CLINK...
AHEM... A VERY BONJOUR TO YOU, HALF-BOILED PIRATES...
JE M'APPELLE BARON TAMAGO, AT YOUR SERVICE.
BIG MOM PIRATES FIGHTER (OF THE LONGLEG PEOPLE)
BARON TAMAGO

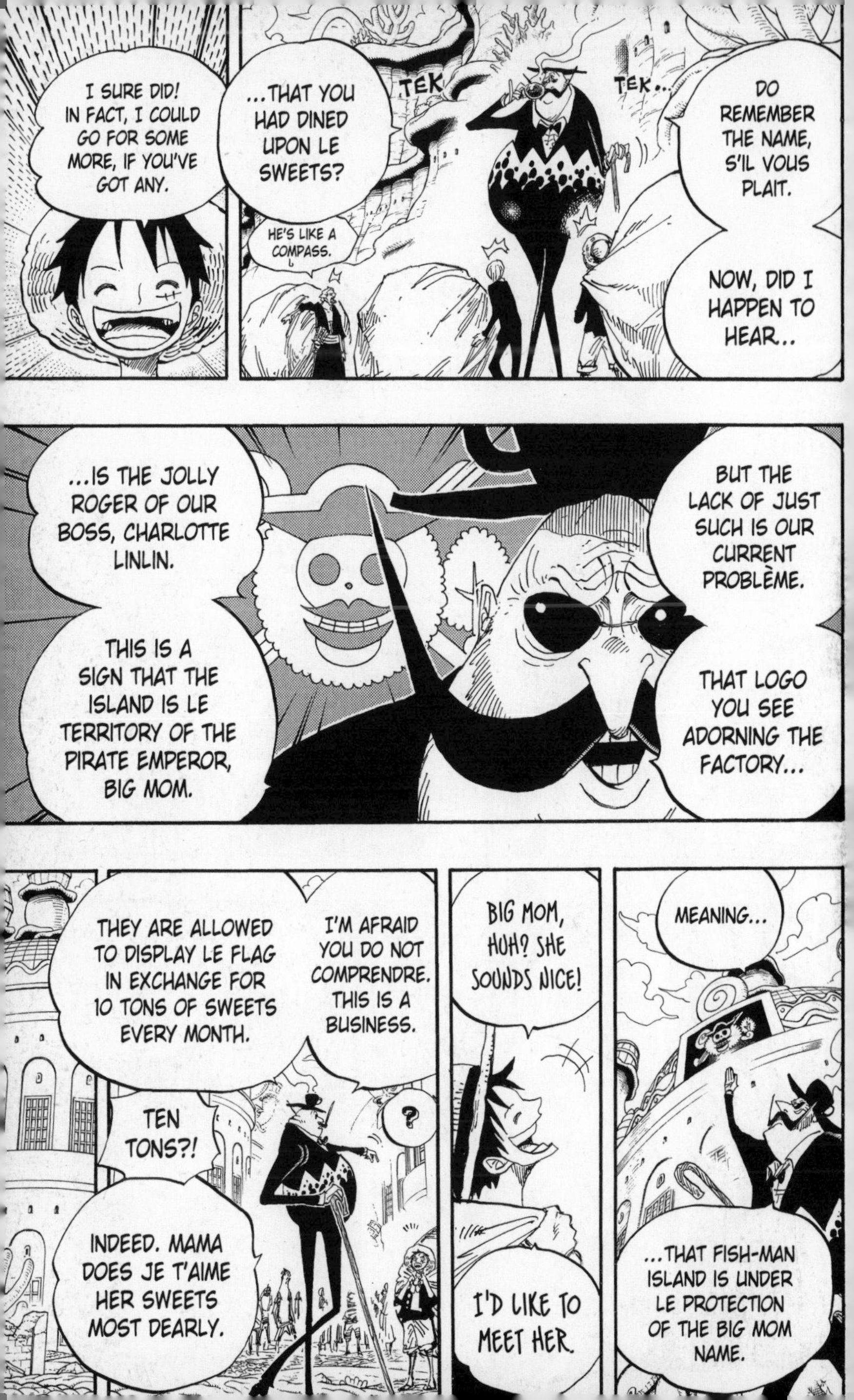
DO REMEMBER THE NAME, S'IL VOUS PLAIT.
NOW, DID I HAPPEN TO HEAR...
TEK...
TEK
...THAT YOU HAD DINED UPON LE SWEETS?
HE'S LIKE A COMPASS.
I SURE DID! IN FACT, I COULD GO FOR SOME MORE, IF YOU'VE GOT ANY.
BUT THE LACK OF JUST SUCH IS OUR CURRENT PROBLÈME.
THAT LOGO YOU SEE ADORNING THE FACTORY...
...IS THE JOLLY ROGER OF OUR BOSS, CHARLOTTE LINLIN.
THIS IS A SIGN THAT THE ISLAND IS LE TERRITORY OF THE PIRATE EMPEROR, BIG MOM.
MEANING...
...THAT FISH-MAN ISLAND IS UNDER LE PROTECTION OF THE BIG MOM NAME.
BIG MOM, HUH? SHE SOUNDS NICE!
I'D LIKE TO MEET HER.
I'M AFRAID YOU DO NOT COMPRENDRE. THIS IS A BUSINESS.
THEY ARE ALLOWED TO DISPLAY LE FLAG IN EXCHANGE FOR 10 TONS OF SWEETS EVERY MONTH.
?
TEN TONS?!
INDEED. MAMA DOES JE T'AIME HER SWEETS MOST DEARLY.

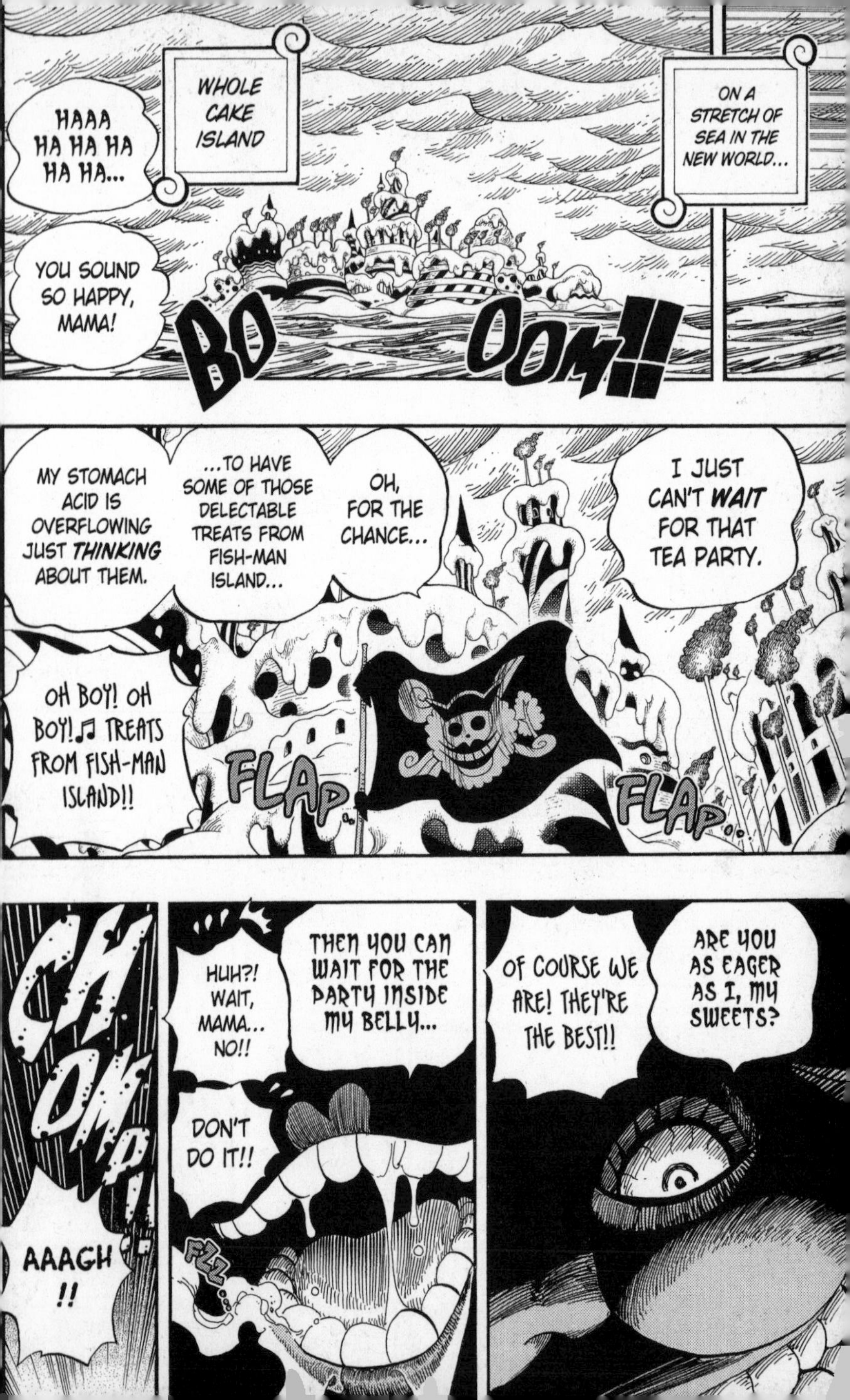
ON A STRETCH OF SEA IN THE NEW WORLD...
WHOLE CAKE ISLAND
HAAAA HA HA HA HA HA...
YOU SOUND SO HAPPY, MAMA!
BOOOM!!
I JUST CAN'T WAIT FOR THAT TEA PARTY.
OH, FOR THE CHANCE...
...TO HAVE SOME OF THOSE DELECTABLE TREATS FROM FISH-MAN ISLAND...
MY STOMACH ACID IS OVERFLOWING JUST THINKING ABOUT THEM.
FLAP
FLAP
OH BOY! OH BOY!♫ TREATS FROM FISH-MAN ISLAND!!
ARE YOU AS EAGER AS I, MY SWEETS?
OF COURSE WE ARE! THEY'RE THE BEST!!
THEN YOU CAN WAIT FOR THE PARTY INSIDE MY BELLY...
HUH?! WAIT, MAMA... NO!!
DON'T DO IT!!
FZZ
CHOMP!
AAAGH!!

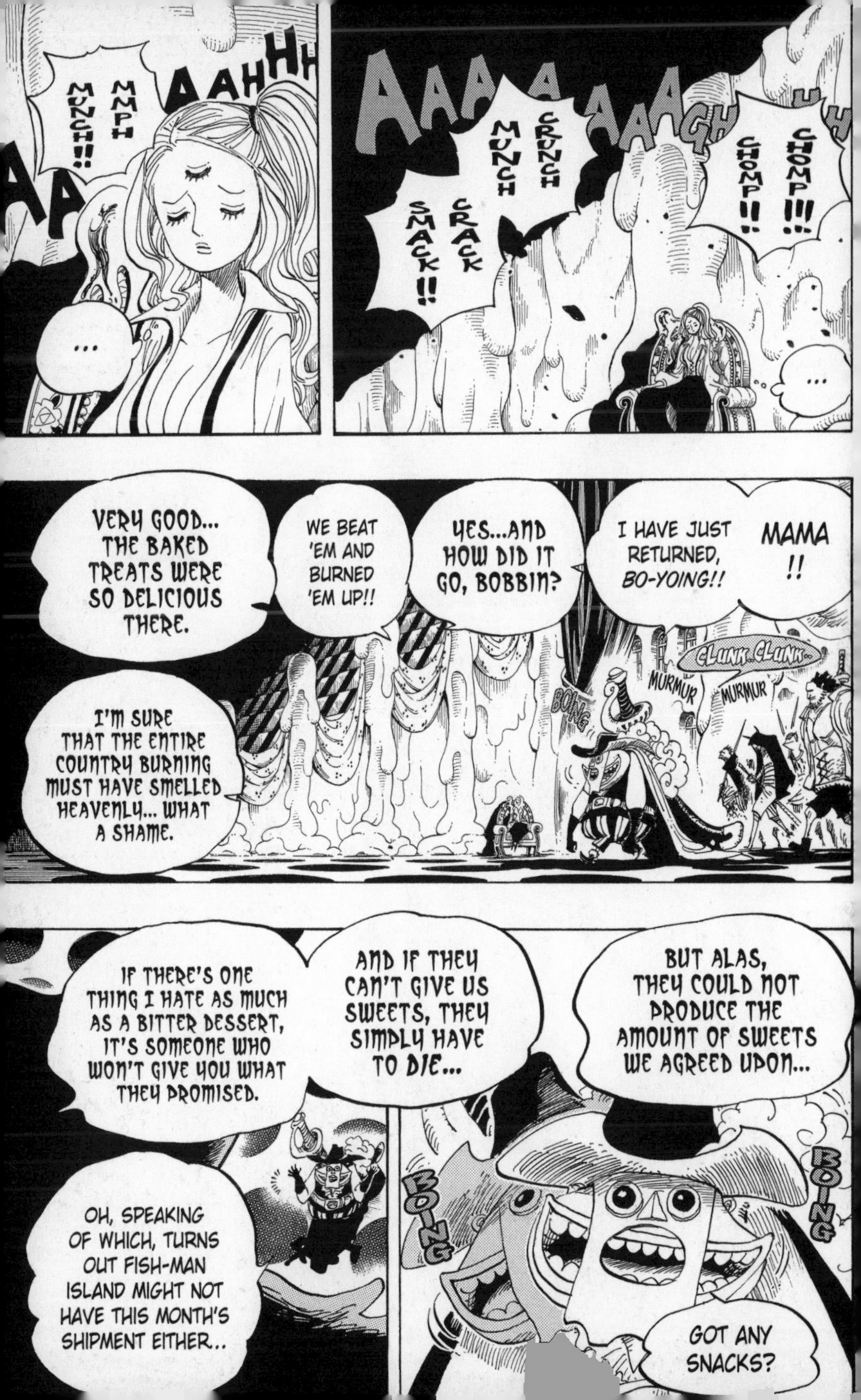
AAAA AAAGH
CHOMP!!!
CHOMP!!
CRUNCH
MUNCH
CRACK
SMACK!!
...
...
AAHHH
MMPH
MUNCH!!
AA
...
MAMA!!
I HAVE JUST RETURNED, BO-YOING!!
YES...AND HOW DID IT GO, BOBBIN?
WE BEAT 'EM AND BURNED 'EM UP!!
VERY GOOD... THE BAKED TREATS WERE SO DELICIOUS THERE.
I'M SURE THAT THE ENTIRE COUNTRY BURNING MUST HAVE SMELLED HEAVENLY... WHAT A SHAME.
CLUNK CLUNK
MURMUR
MURMUR
BOING
BUT ALAS, THEY COULD NOT PRODUCE THE AMOUNT OF SWEETS WE AGREED UPON...
AND IF THEY CAN'T GIVE US SWEETS, THEY SIMPLY HAVE TO DIE...
BOING
BOING
GOT ANY SNACKS?
IF THERE'S ONE THING I HATE AS MUCH AS A BITTER DESSERT, IT'S SOMEONE WHO WON'T GIVE YOU WHAT THEY PROMISED.
OH, SPEAKING OF WHICH, TURNS OUT FISH-MAN ISLAND MIGHT NOT HAVE THIS MONTH'S SHIPMENT EITHER...

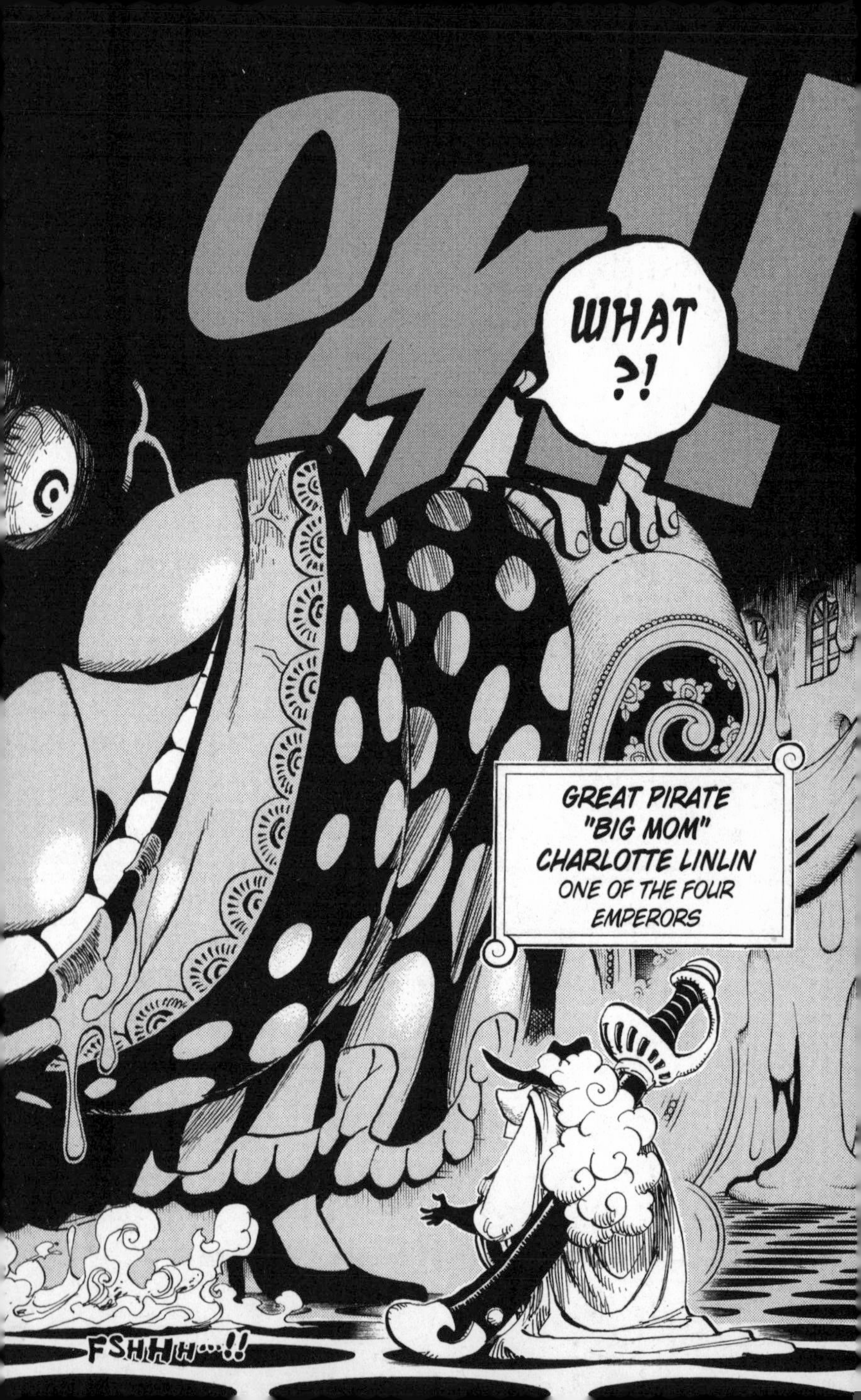
OH!!
WHAT ?!
GREAT PIRATE "BIG MOM" CHARLOTTE LINLIN ONE OF THE FOUR EMPERORS
FSHHHH...!!

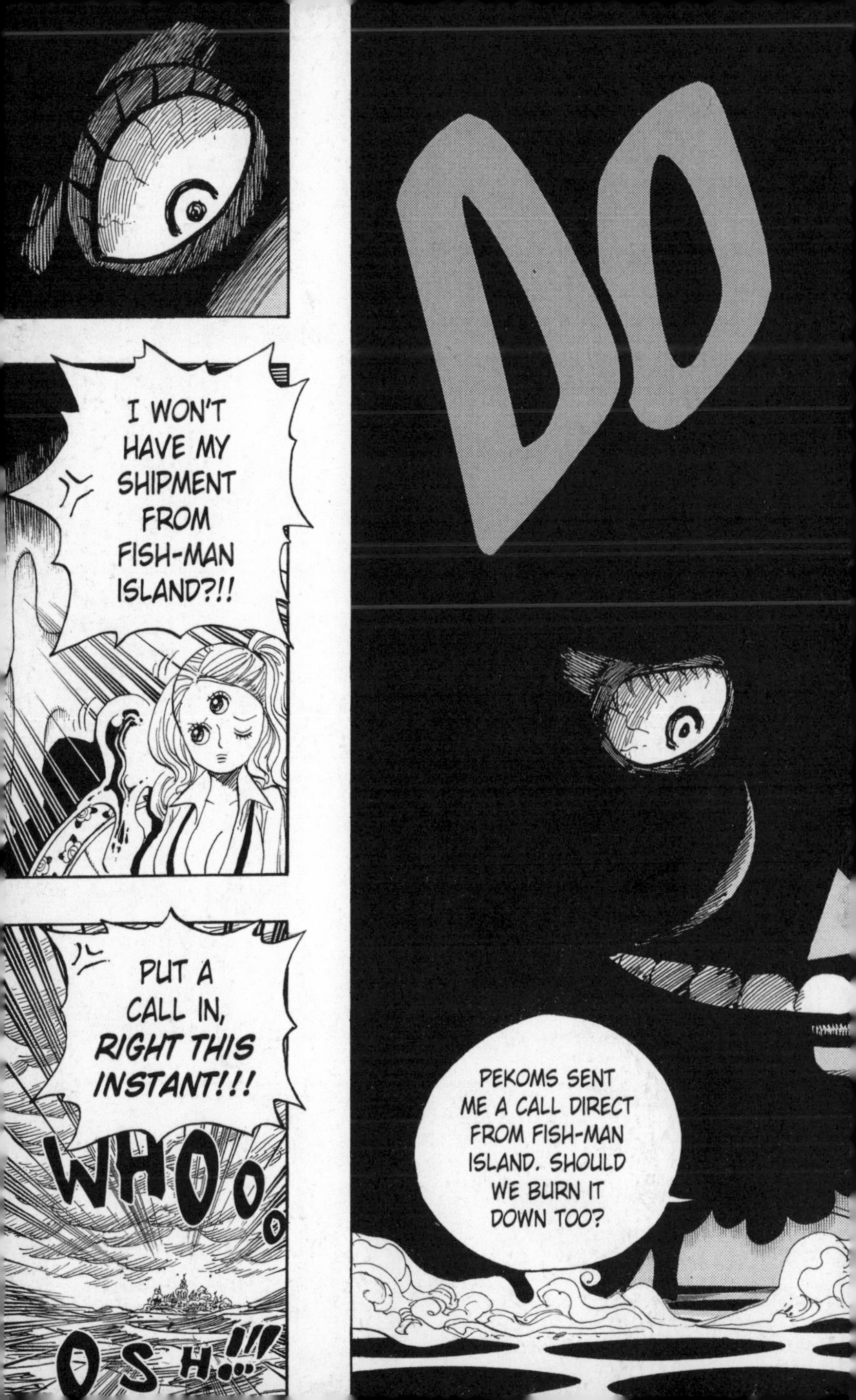
DO
PEKOMS SENT ME A CALL DIRECT FROM FISH-MAN ISLAND. SHOULD WE BURN IT DOWN TOO?
I WON'T HAVE MY SHIPMENT FROM FISH-MAN ISLAND?!!
PUT A CALL IN, *RIGHT THIS INSTANT!!!*
WHOOOOSH!!!

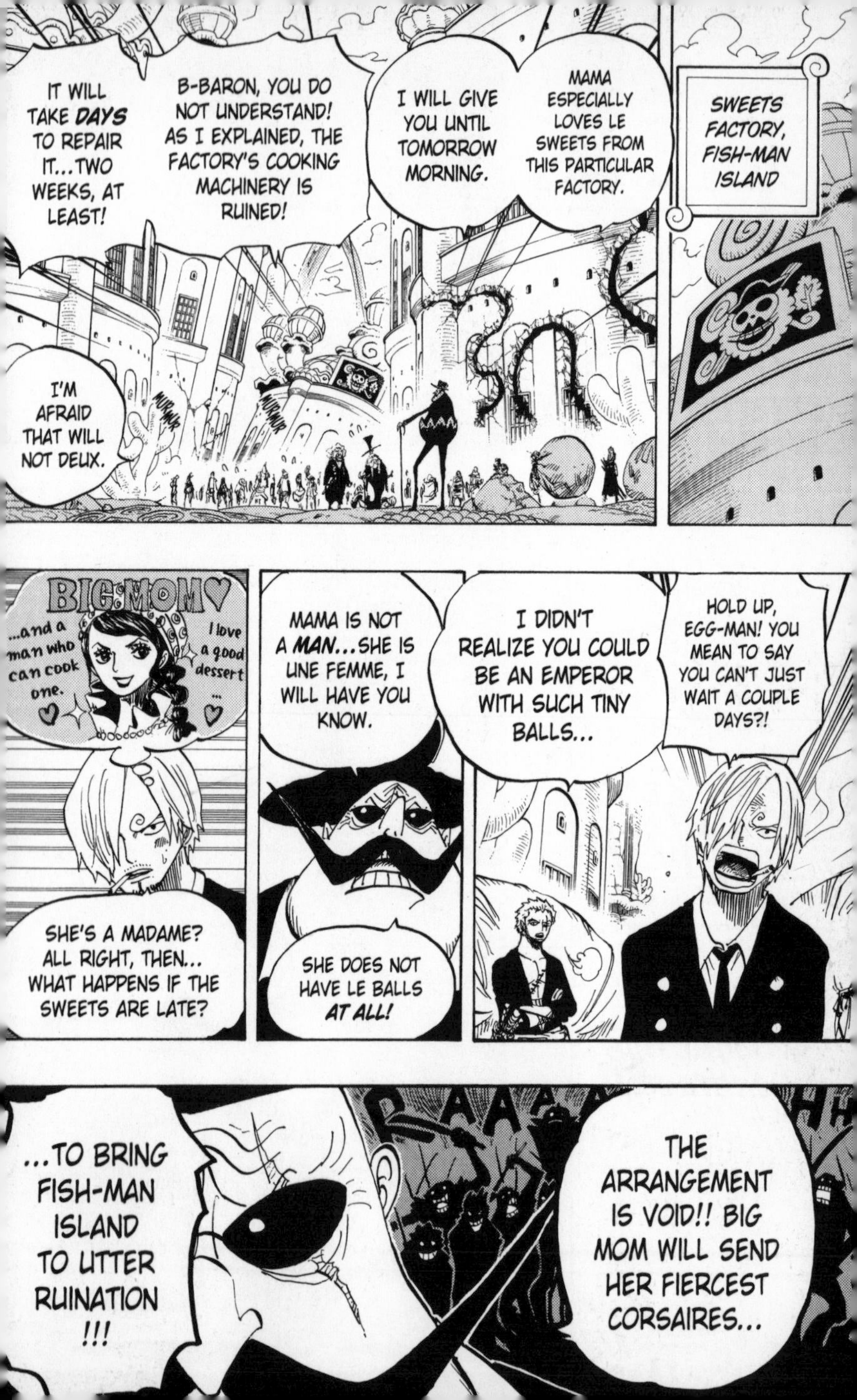

SWEETS FACTORY, FISH-MAN ISLAND
MAMA ESPECIALLY LOVES LE SWEETS FROM THIS PARTICULAR FACTORY.
I WILL GIVE YOU UNTIL TOMORROW MORNING.
B-BARON, YOU DO NOT UNDERSTAND! AS I EXPLAINED, THE FACTORY'S COOKING MACHINERY IS RUINED!
IT WILL TAKE **DAYS** TO REPAIR IT...TWO WEEKS, AT LEAST!
MURMUR
MURMUR
I'M AFRAID THAT WILL NOT DEUX.
HOLD UP, EGG-MAN! YOU MEAN TO SAY YOU CAN'T JUST WAIT A COUPLE DAYS?!
I DIDN'T REALIZE YOU COULD BE AN EMPEROR WITH SUCH TINY BALLS...
MAMA IS NOT A **MAN**...SHE IS UNE FEMME, I WILL HAVE YOU KNOW.
SHE DOES NOT HAVE LE BALLS ***AT ALL!***
BIG MOM♥
I love a good dessert...
...and a man who can cook one.
SHE'S A MADAME? ALL RIGHT, THEN... WHAT HAPPENS IF THE SWEETS ARE LATE?
THE ARRANGEMENT IS VOID!! BIG MOM WILL SEND HER FIERCEST CORSAIRES...
...TO BRING FISH-MAN ISLAND TO UTTER RUINATION!!!

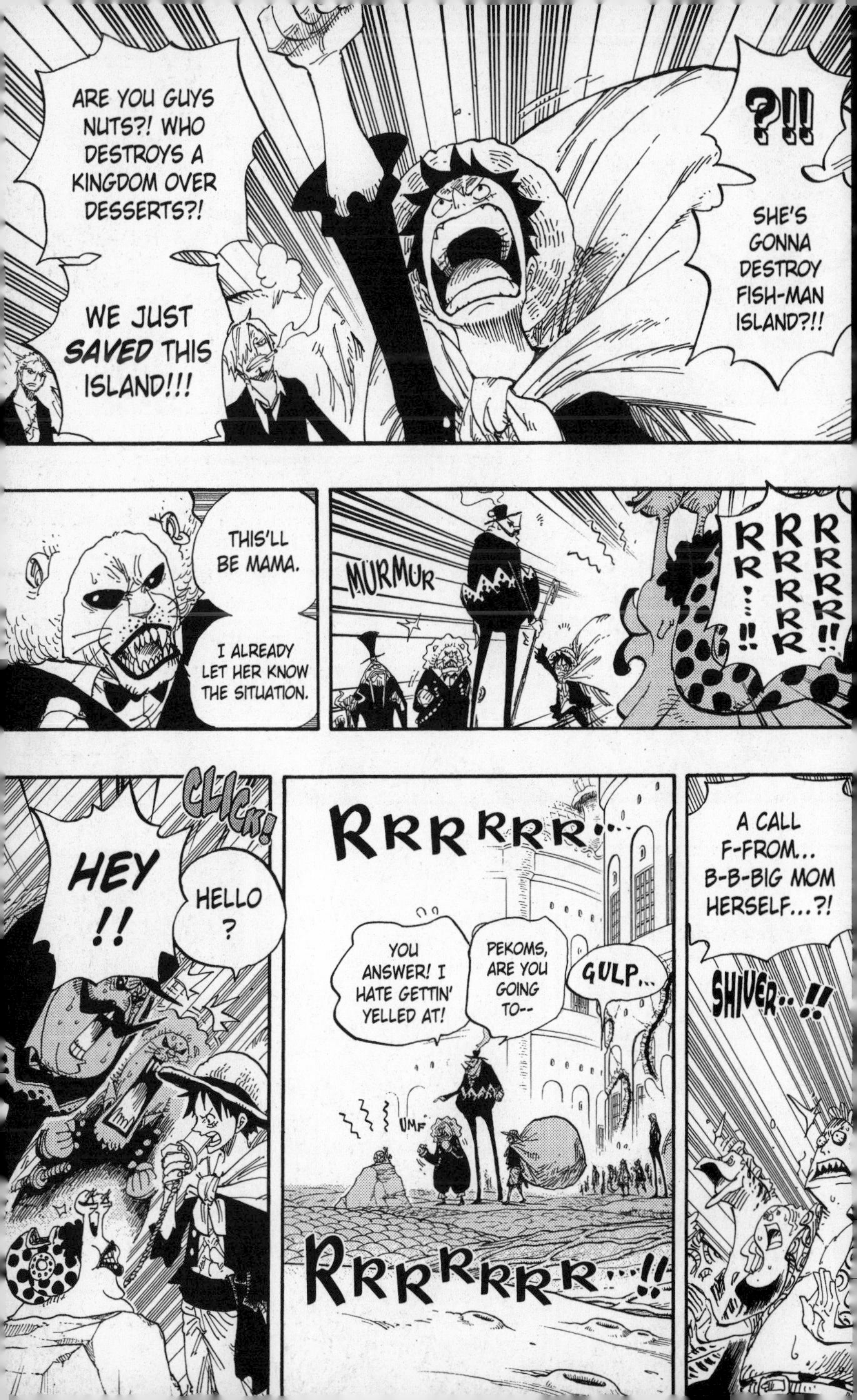

?!!
SHE'S GONNA DESTROY FISH-MAN ISLAND?!!
ARE YOU GUYS NUTS?! WHO DESTROYS A KINGDOM OVER DESSERTS?!
WE JUST SAVED THIS ISLAND!!!
RRRRR!!
RRRRR
RR...!!
MURMUR
THIS'LL BE MAMA.
I ALREADY LET HER KNOW THE SITUATION.
A CALL F-FROM... B-B-BIG MOM HERSELF...?!
SHIVER..!!
RRRRRRR...
GULP...
PEKOMS, ARE YOU GOING TO--
YOU ANSWER! I HATE GETTIN' YELLED AT!
UMF
RRRRRRRR...!!
CLICK!
HEY !!
HELLO ?

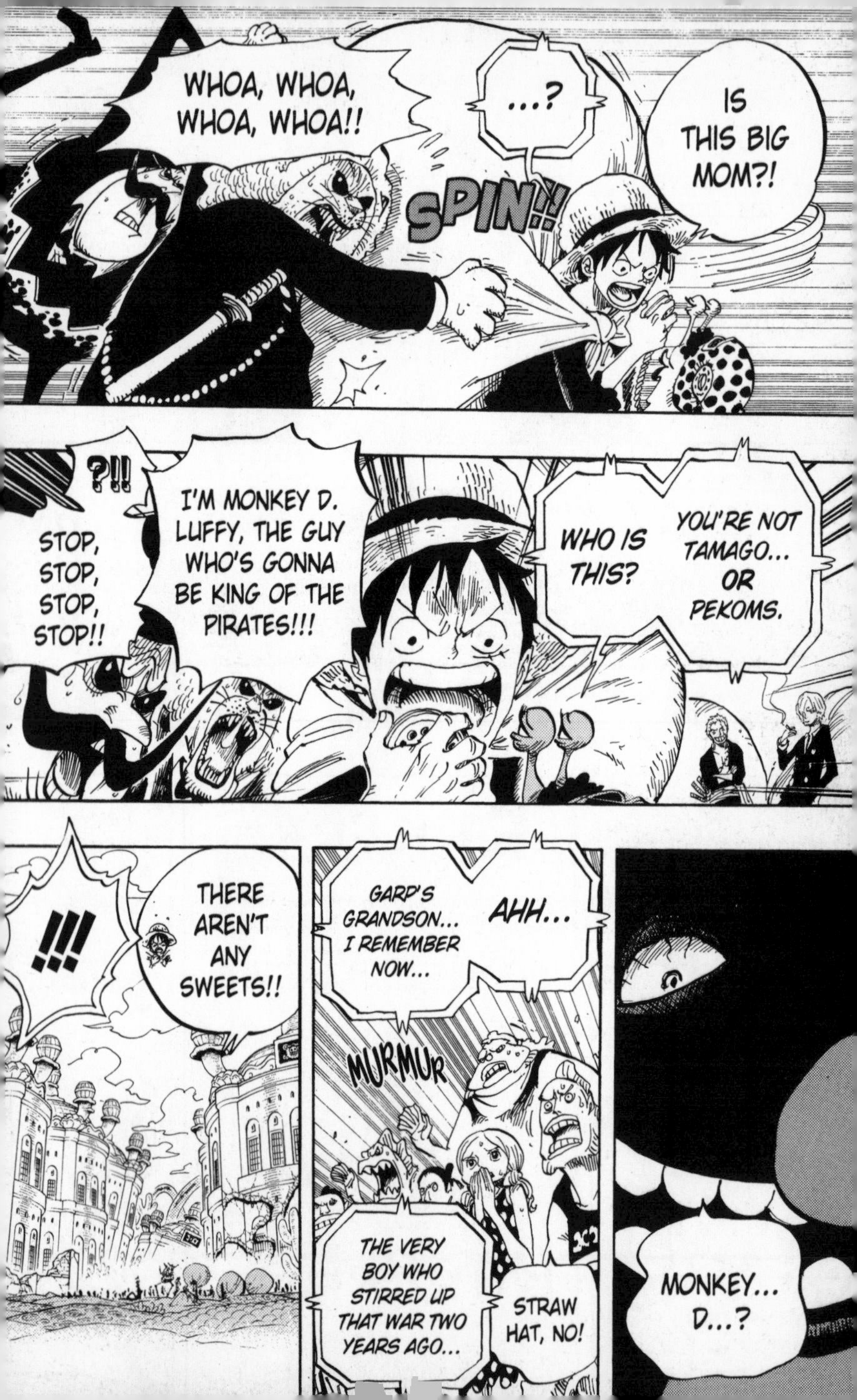
IS THIS BIG MOM?!
...?
SPIN!!
WHOA, WHOA, WHOA, WHOA!!
YOU'RE NOT TAMAGO... OR PEKOMS.
WHO IS THIS?
I'M MONKEY D. LUFFY, THE GUY WHO'S GONNA BE KING OF THE PIRATES!!!
?!!
STOP, STOP, STOP, STOP!!
MONKEY... D...?
AHH...
GARP'S GRANDSON... I REMEMBER NOW...
MURMUR
STRAW HAT, NO!
THE VERY BOY WHO STIRRED UP THAT WAR TWO YEARS AGO...
!!!
THERE AREN'T ANY SWEETS!!

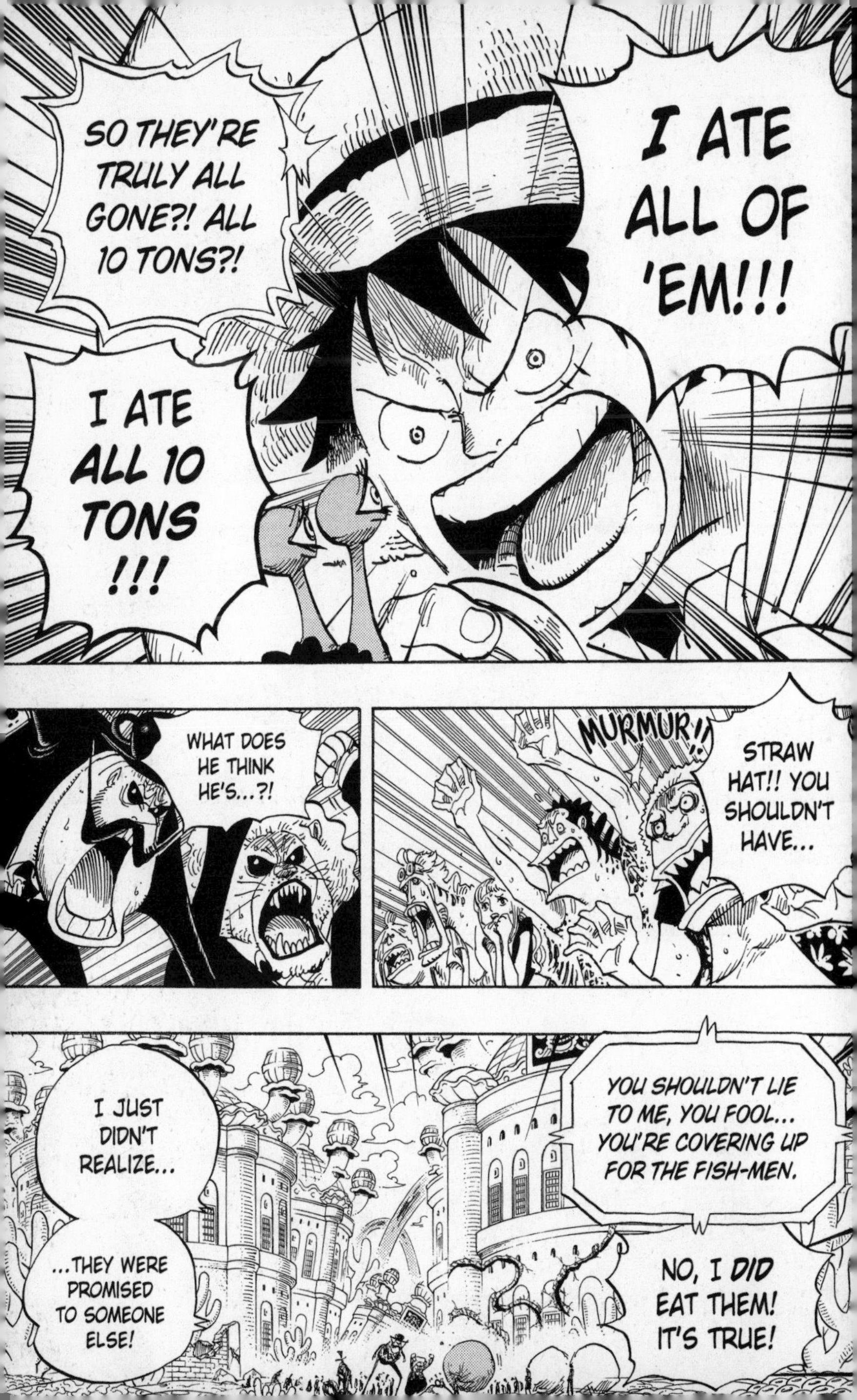
I ATE ALL OF 'EM!!!
SO THEY'RE TRULY ALL GONE?! ALL 10 TONS?!
I ATE ALL 10 TONS!!!
MURMUR!!
STRAW HAT!! YOU SHOULDN'T HAVE...
WHAT DOES HE THINK HE'S...?!
YOU SHOULDN'T LIE TO ME, YOU FOOL... YOU'RE COVERING UP FOR THE FISH-MEN.
NO, I DID EAT THEM! IT'S TRUE!
I JUST DIDN'T REALIZE...
...THEY WERE PROMISED TO SOMEONE ELSE!

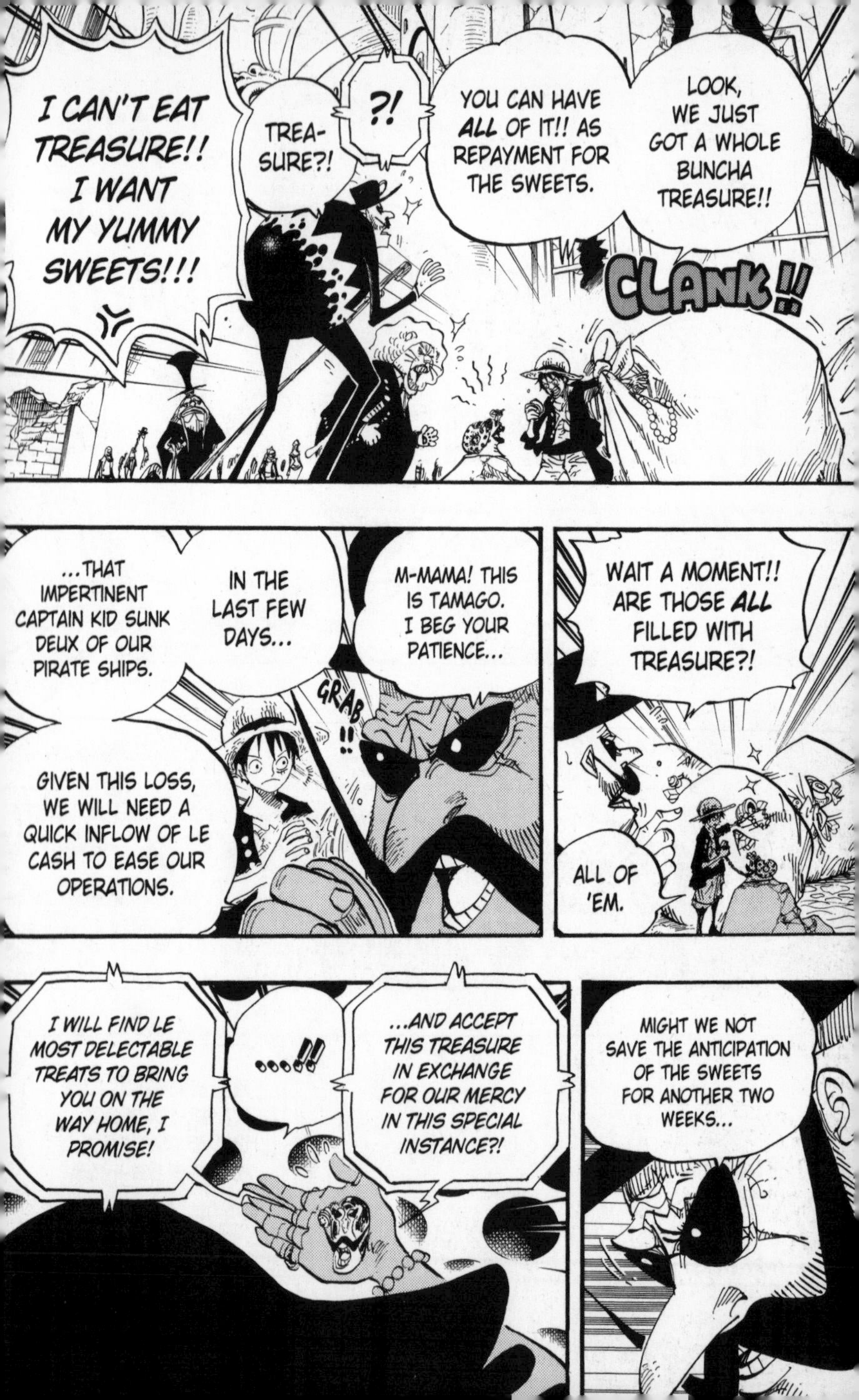
LOOK, WE JUST GOT A WHOLE BUNCHA TREASURE!!
YOU CAN HAVE ALL OF IT!! AS REPAYMENT FOR THE SWEETS.
CLANK!!
?!
TREA-SURE?!
I CAN'T EAT TREASURE!! I WANT MY YUMMY SWEETS!!!
WAIT A MOMENT!! ARE THOSE ALL FILLED WITH TREASURE?!
ALL OF 'EM.
M-MAMA! THIS IS TAMAGO. I BEG YOUR PATIENCE...
GRAB!!
IN THE LAST FEW DAYS...
...THAT IMPERTINENT CAPTAIN KID SUNK DEUX OF OUR PIRATE SHIPS.
GIVEN THIS LOSS, WE WILL NEED A QUICK INFLOW OF LE CASH TO EASE OUR OPERATIONS.
MIGHT WE NOT SAVE THE ANTICIPATION OF THE SWEETS FOR ANOTHER TWO WEEKS...
...AND ACCEPT THIS TREASURE IN EXCHANGE FOR OUR MERCY IN THIS SPECIAL INSTANCE?!
.....!!
I WILL FIND LE MOST DELECTABLE TREATS TO BRING YOU ON THE WAY HOME, I PROMISE!

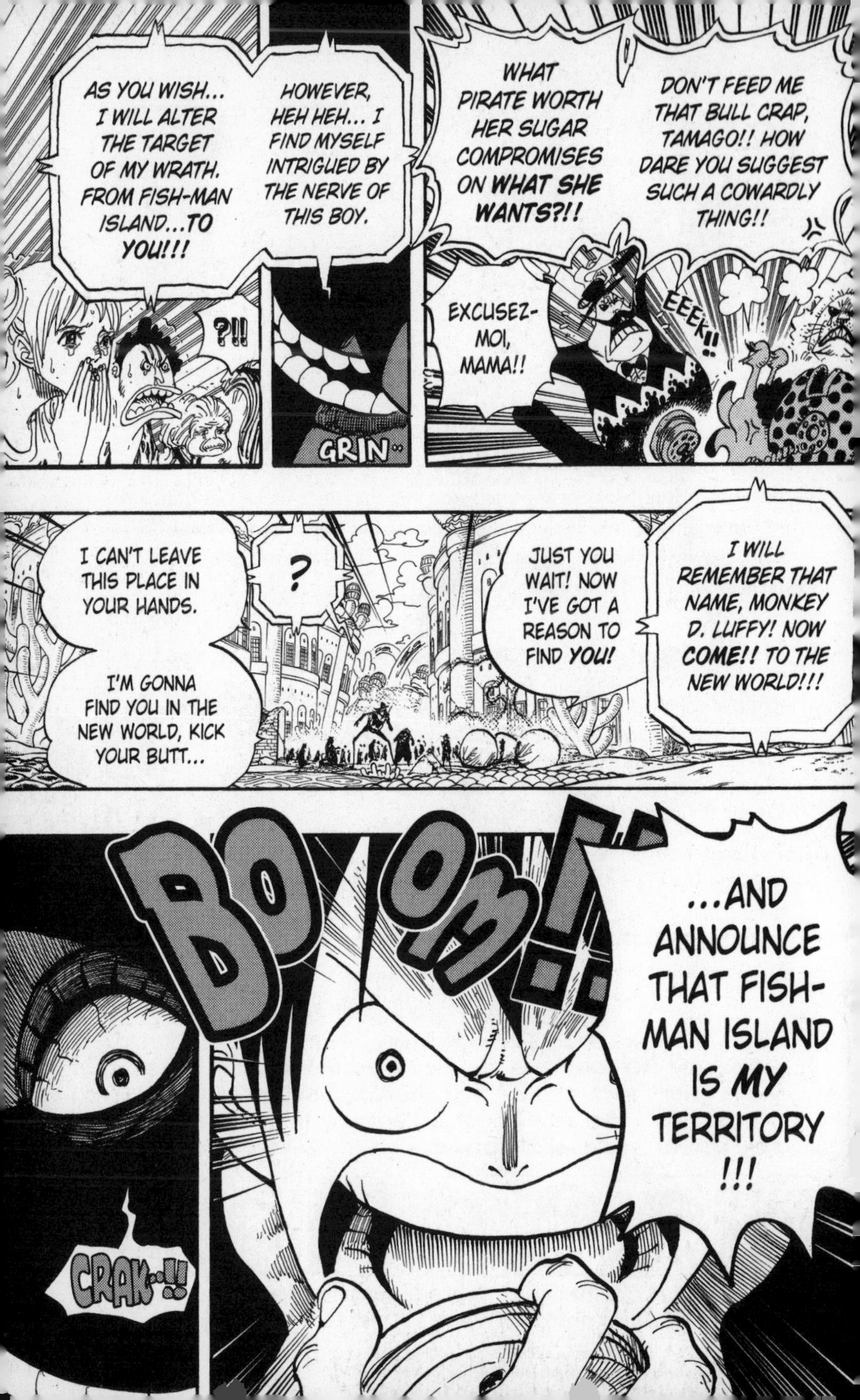
DON'T FEED ME THAT BULL CRAP, TAMAGO!! HOW DARE YOU SUGGEST SUCH A COWARDLY THING!!
WHAT PIRATE WORTH HER SUGAR COMPROMISES ON **WHAT SHE WANTS?!!**
EEEK!!
EXCUSEZ-MOI, MAMA!!
HOWEVER, HEH HEH... I FIND MYSELF INTRIGUED BY THE NERVE OF THIS BOY.
GRIN
AS YOU WISH... I WILL ALTER THE TARGET OF MY WRATH. FROM FISH-MAN ISLAND...TO **YOU!!!**
?!!
I WILL REMEMBER THAT NAME, MONKEY D. LUFFY! NOW **COME!!** TO THE NEW WORLD!!!
JUST YOU WAIT! NOW I'VE GOT A REASON TO FIND **YOU!**
?
I CAN'T LEAVE THIS PLACE IN YOUR HANDS.
I'M GONNA FIND YOU IN THE NEW WORLD, KICK YOUR BUTT...
...AND ANNOUNCE THAT FISH-MAN ISLAND IS *MY* TERRITORY !!!
BOOM!!
CRAK!!

SBS Question Corner

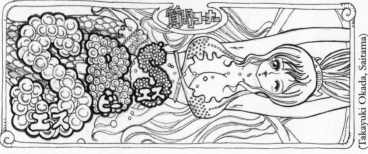

(Takayuki Okada, Saitama)

Q: Odacchi, Odacchi, Odacchi, Odacchi, Odacchi!! There, I called your name five times for no good reason! Hello, here's my question. It's one of the serious ones for once. On pages 198-199 of Volume 64, Chopper says he only needs Rumble Balls for one form, and the other six he can transform into at will. Does this include Guard Point? On page 38 of Volume 62, Chopper ate a Rumble Ball and turned into Guard Point. How come?! Explain it…or I'll stop being your fan!!

--Odacchi Supporter

A: Yes, you're right. In Volume 65, we found out that Chopper can use his monster form safely with a Rumble Ball. Which means that he doesn't need them for the other forms! What does this mean? Take it away, Reader "Escape Is the Best Form of Cowardice"!!

Q: In Chapter 605 of Volume 62, Chopper eats a Rumble Ball-like object before using Guard Point, but with his new training, Chopper shouldn't need it. Of course, I understand he was just eating the popular new Rumble Ball Candy, but I'm sure plenty of readers were tricked into thinking it was an actual Rumble Ball! Stop trying to confuse us, Chopper!!

--Escape Is the Best Form of Cowardice

A: Geez! Thanks a lot for confusing everyone, Chopper! Honestly! Do you have any idea how many readers sent me letters about this? You shouldn't be chowing down on candy on the sea floor! So anyway, let's take a look at Chopper's present forms!

Brain Point	Walk Point	Heavy Point	Guard Point	Kung-fu Point	Horn Point	Monster Point

Can transform into at will (sometimes he likes to eat Rumble Ball candy for fun)

Requires Rumble Ball (three minutes)

Chaper 652:

A PREMONITION OF STORMY SEAS

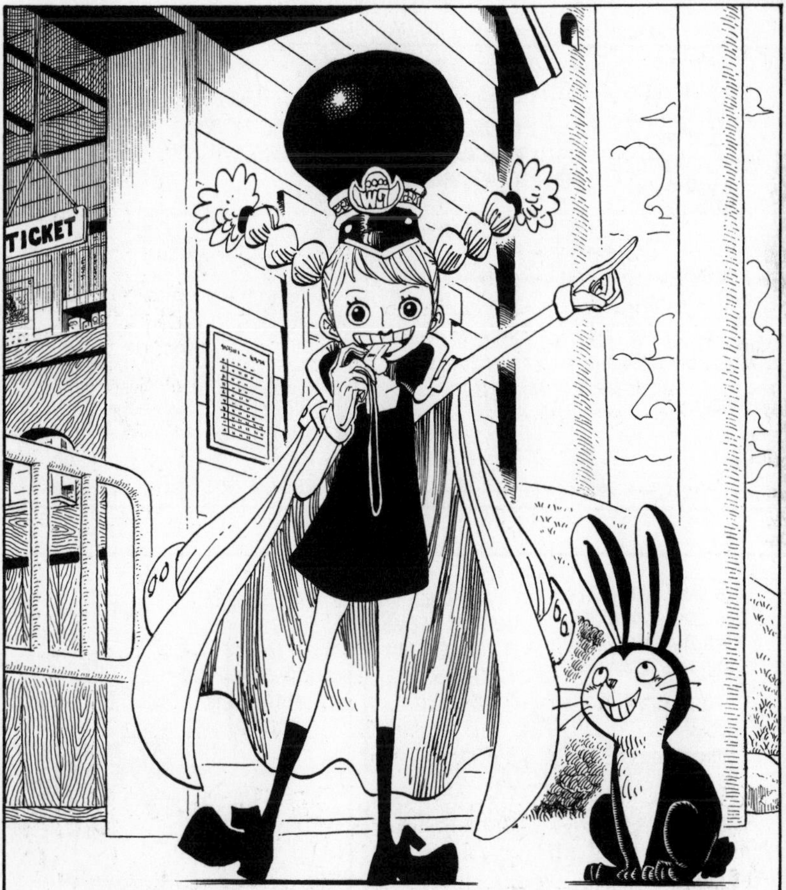
TICKET

DECKS OF THE WORLD, VOL. 34 "SHIFT STATION—
SUNDAY SPECIAL, STATIONMASTER CHIMNEY"

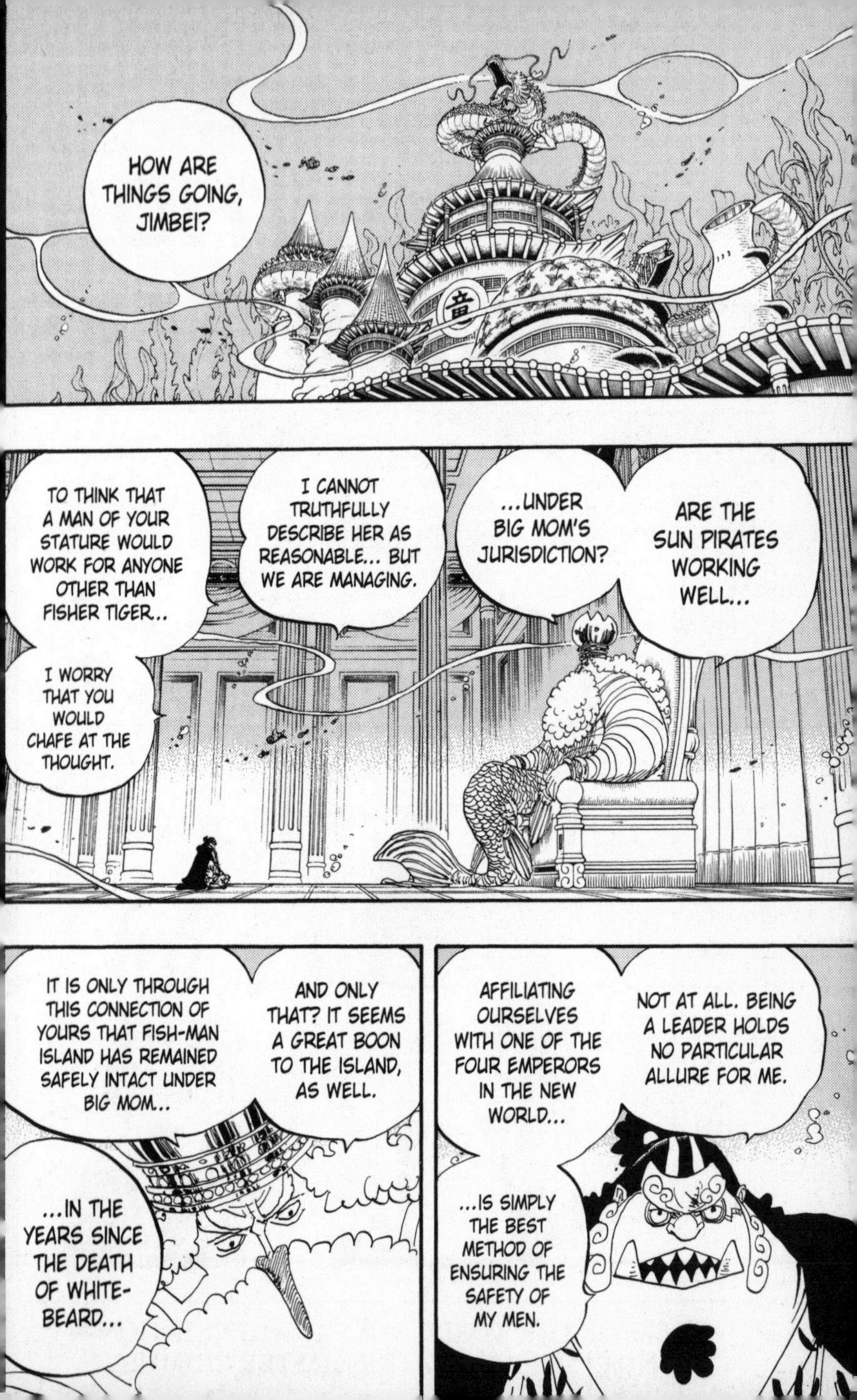
HOW ARE THINGS GOING, JIMBEI?
ARE THE SUN PIRATES WORKING WELL...
...UNDER BIG MOM'S JURISDICTION?
I CANNOT TRUTHFULLY DESCRIBE HER AS REASONABLE... BUT WE ARE MANAGING.
TO THINK THAT A MAN OF YOUR STATURE WOULD WORK FOR ANYONE OTHER THAN FISHER TIGER..
I WORRY THAT YOU WOULD CHAFE AT THE THOUGHT.
NOT AT ALL. BEING A LEADER HOLDS NO PARTICULAR ALLURE FOR ME.
AFFILIATING OURSELVES WITH ONE OF THE FOUR EMPERORS IN THE NEW WORLD...
...IS SIMPLY THE BEST METHOD OF ENSURING THE SAFETY OF MY MEN.
AND ONLY THAT? IT SEEMS A GREAT BOON TO THE ISLAND, AS WELL.
IT IS ONLY THROUGH THIS CONNECTION OF YOURS THAT FISH-MAN ISLAND HAS REMAINED SAFELY INTACT UNDER BIG MOM...
...IN THE YEARS SINCE THE DEATH OF WHITE-BEARD...

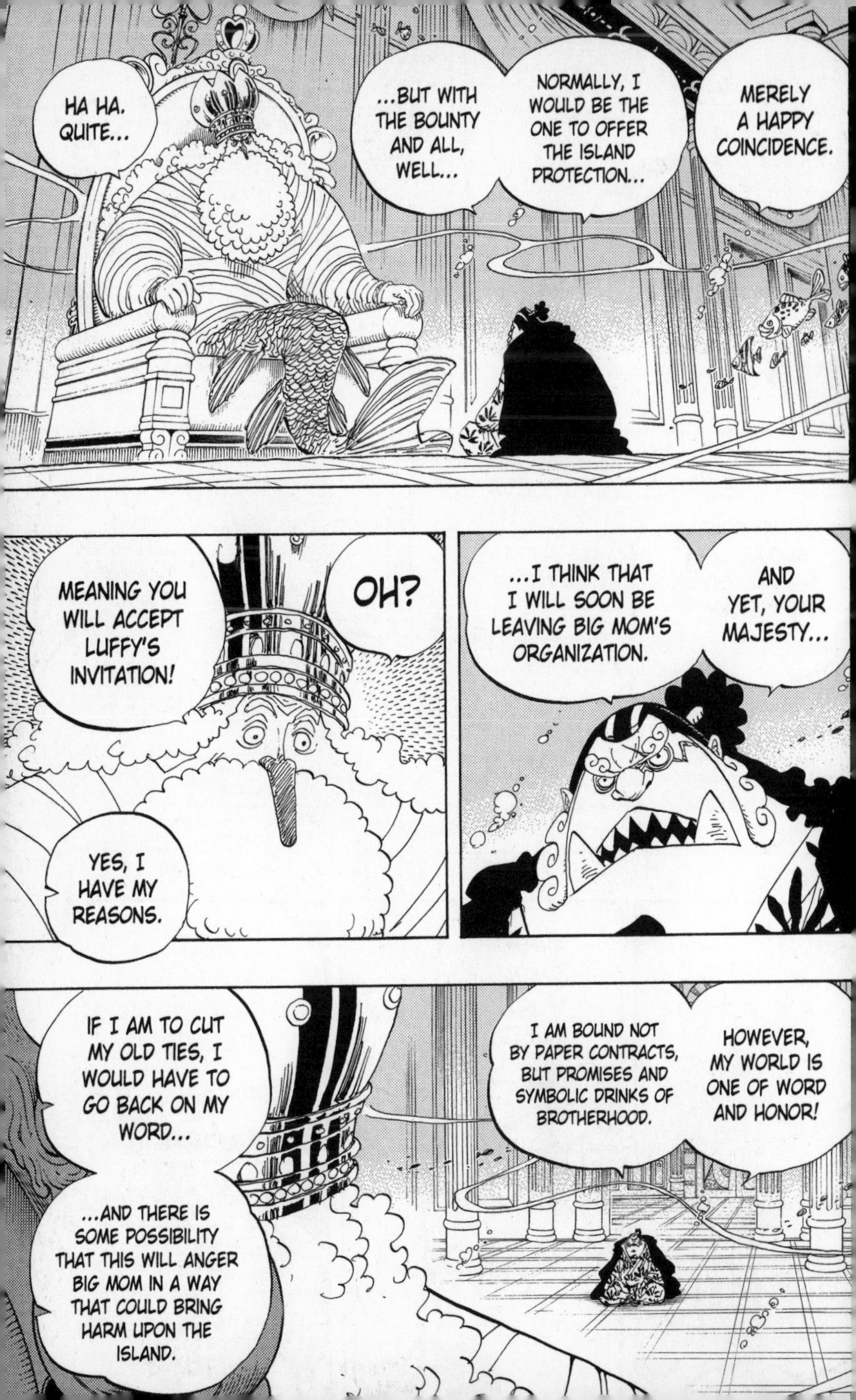
MERELY A HAPPY COINCIDENCE.
NORMALLY, I WOULD BE THE ONE TO OFFER THE ISLAND PROTECTION...
...BUT WITH THE BOUNTY AND ALL, WELL...
HA HA. QUITE...
AND YET, YOUR MAJESTY...
...I THINK THAT I WILL SOON BE LEAVING BIG MOM'S ORGANIZATION.
OH?
MEANING YOU WILL ACCEPT LUFFY'S INVITATION!
YES, I HAVE MY REASONS.
HOWEVER, MY WORLD IS ONE OF WORD AND HONOR!
I AM BOUND NOT BY PAPER CONTRACTS, BUT PROMISES AND SYMBOLIC DRINKS OF BROTHERHOOD.
IF I AM TO CUT MY OLD TIES, I WOULD HAVE TO GO BACK ON MY WORD...
...AND THERE IS SOME POSSIBILITY THAT THIS WILL ANGER BIG MOM IN A WAY THAT COULD BRING HARM UPON THE ISLAND.

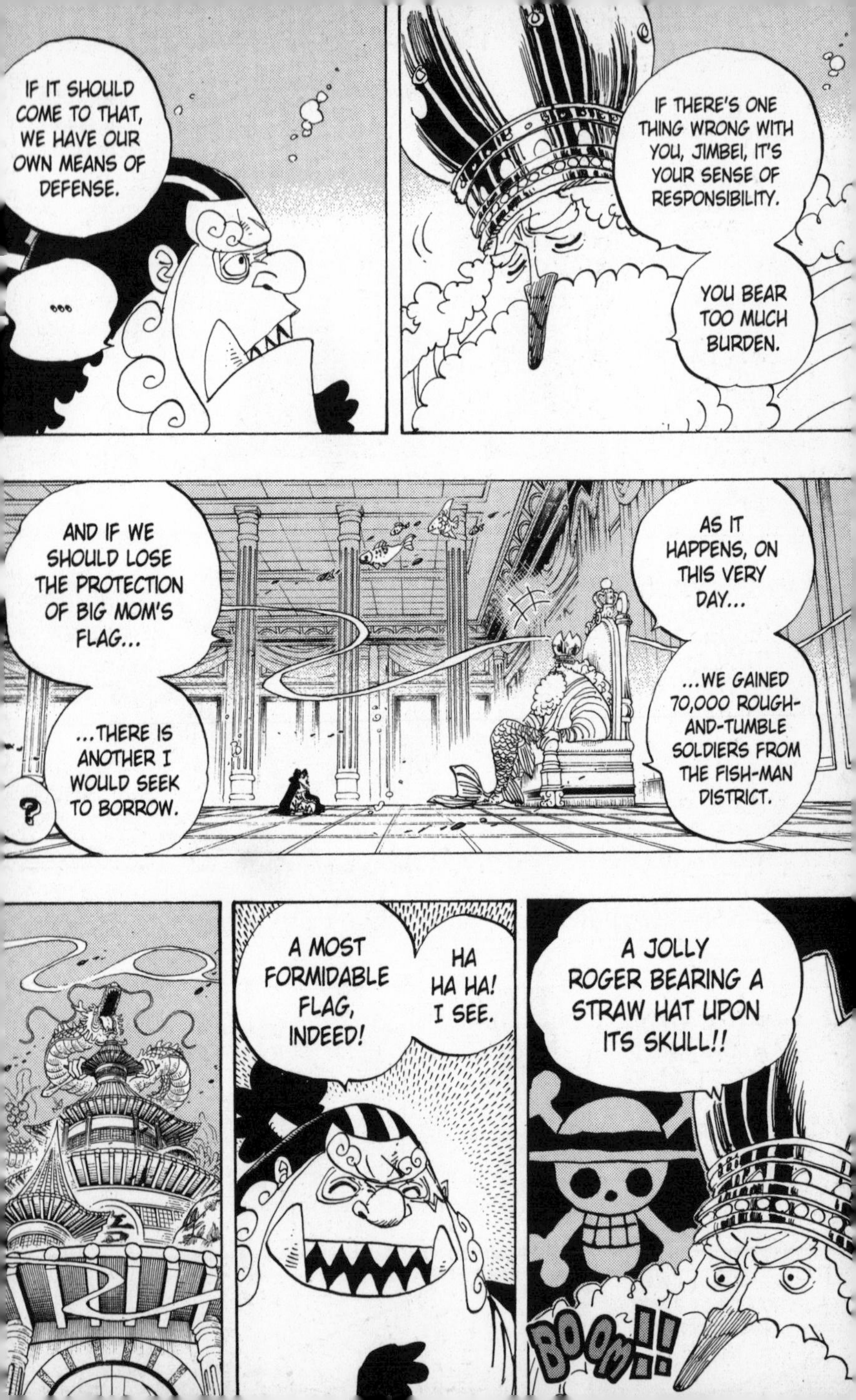
IF THERE'S ONE THING WRONG WITH YOU, JIMBEI, IT'S YOUR SENSE OF RESPONSIBILITY.
YOU BEAR TOO MUCH BURDEN.
IF IT SHOULD COME TO THAT, WE HAVE OUR OWN MEANS OF DEFENSE.
...
AS IT HAPPENS, ON THIS VERY DAY...
...WE GAINED 70,000 ROUGH-AND-TUMBLE SOLDIERS FROM THE FISH-MAN DISTRICT.
AND IF WE SHOULD LOSE THE PROTECTION OF BIG MOM'S FLAG...
...THERE IS ANOTHER I WOULD SEEK TO BORROW.
?
A JOLLY ROGER BEARING A STRAW HAT UPON ITS SKULL!!
BOOM!!
HA HA HA! I SEE.
A MOST FORMIDABLE FLAG, INDEED!

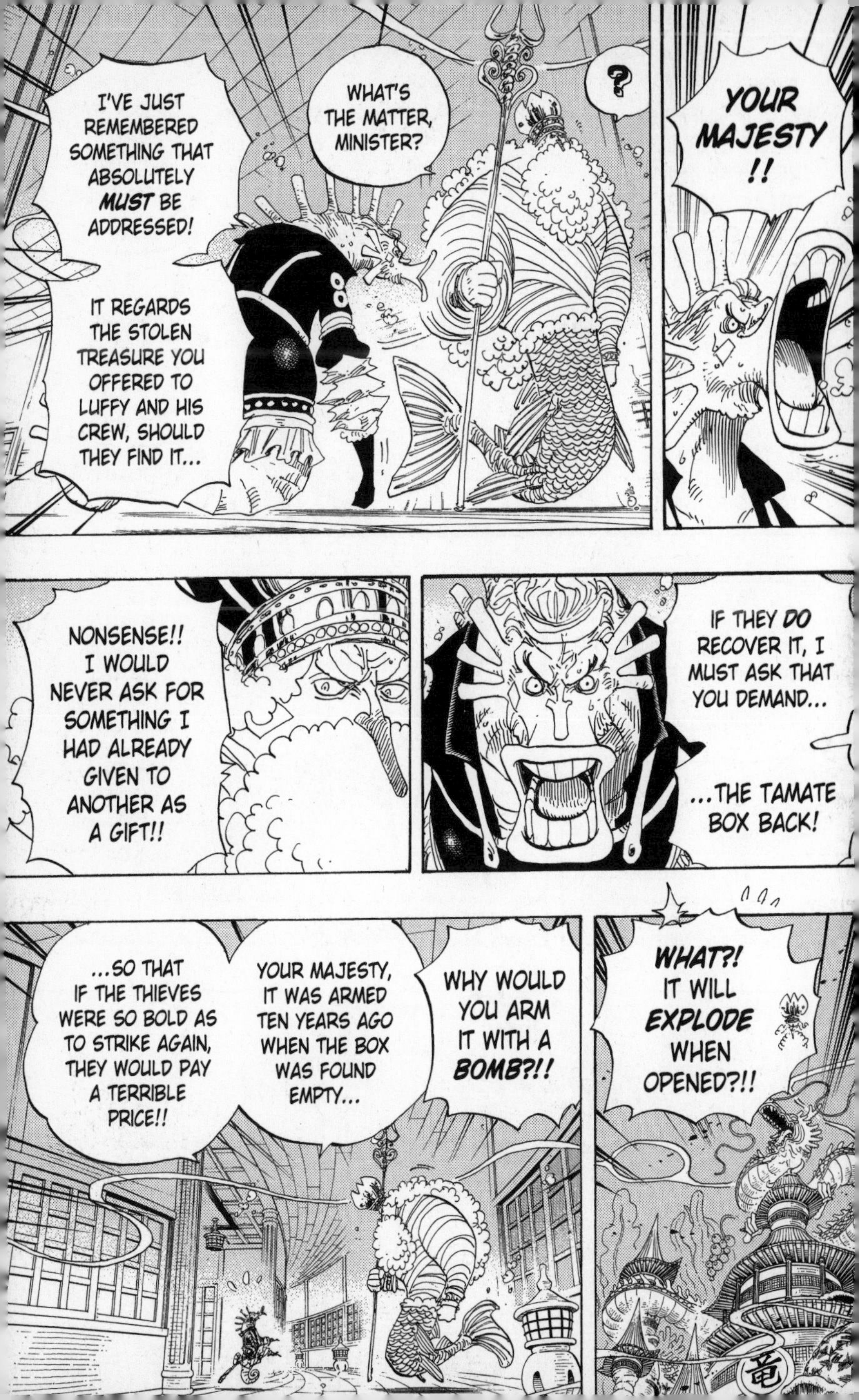
YOUR MAJESTY!!
?
WHAT'S THE MATTER, MINISTER?
I'VE JUST REMEMBERED SOMETHING THAT ABSOLUTELY MUST BE ADDRESSED!
IT REGARDS THE STOLEN TREASURE YOU OFFERED TO LUFFY AND HIS CREW, SHOULD THEY FIND IT...
IF THEY DO RECOVER IT, I MUST ASK THAT YOU DEMAND...
...THE TAMATE BOX BACK!
NONSENSE!! I WOULD NEVER ASK FOR SOMETHING I HAD ALREADY GIVEN TO ANOTHER AS A GIFT!!
WHAT?! IT WILL EXPLODE WHEN OPENED?!!
WHY WOULD YOU ARM IT WITH A BOMB?!!
YOUR MAJESTY, IT WAS ARMED TEN YEARS AGO WHEN THE BOX WAS FOUND EMPTY...
...SO THAT IF THE THIEVES WERE SO BOLD AS TO STRIKE AGAIN, THEY WOULD PAY A TERRIBLE PRICE!!
竜

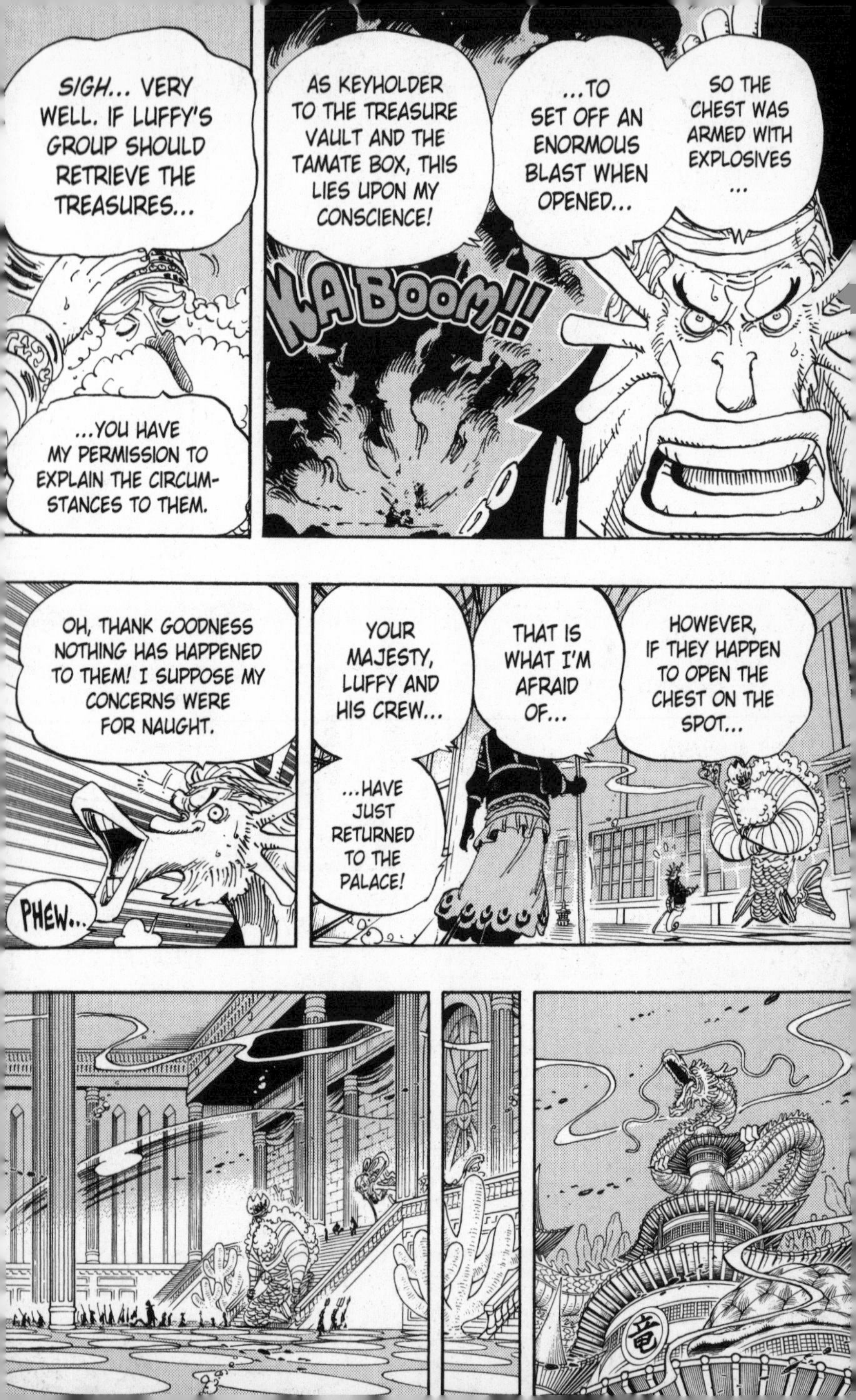
SO THE CHEST WAS ARMED WITH EXPLOSIVES ...
...TO SET OFF AN ENORMOUS BLAST WHEN OPENED...
KA BOOM!!
AS KEYHOLDER TO THE TREASURE VAULT AND THE TAMATE BOX, THIS LIES UPON MY CONSCIENCE!
SIGH... VERY WELL. IF LUFFY'S GROUP SHOULD RETRIEVE THE TREASURES...
...YOU HAVE MY PERMISSION TO EXPLAIN THE CIRCUM-STANCES TO THEM.
HOWEVER, IF THEY HAPPEN TO OPEN THE CHEST ON THE SPOT...
THAT IS WHAT I'M AFRAID OF...
YOUR MAJESTY, LUFFY AND HIS CREW...
...HAVE JUST RETURNED TO THE PALACE!
OH, THANK GOODNESS NOTHING HAS HAPPENED TO THEM! I SUPPOSE MY CONCERNS WERE FOR NAUGHT.
PHEW...

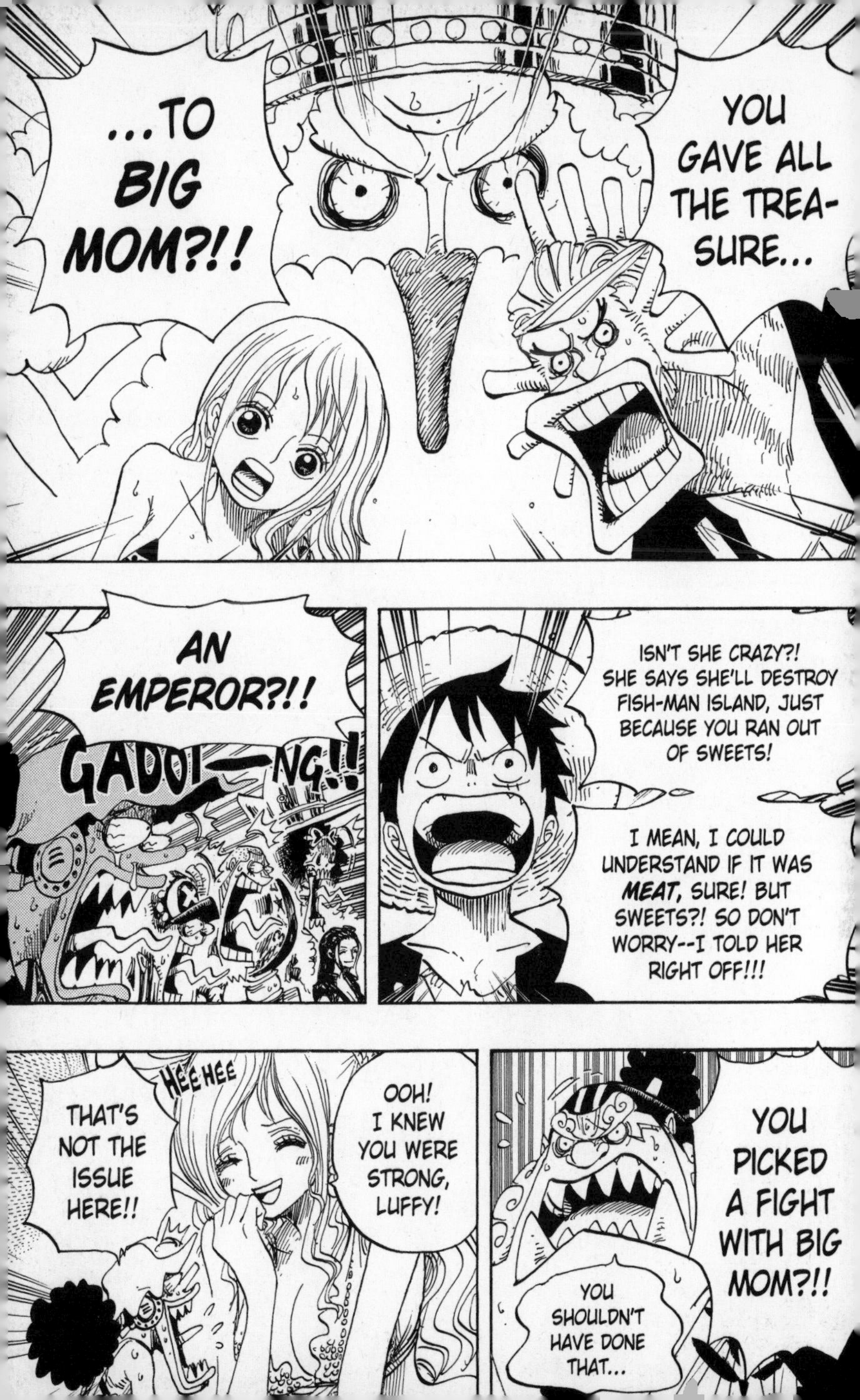
YOU GAVE ALL THE TREA-SURE...
...TO BIG MOM?!!
ISN'T SHE CRAZY?! SHE SAYS SHE'LL DESTROY FISH-MAN ISLAND, JUST BECAUSE YOU RAN OUT OF SWEETS!
I MEAN, I COULD UNDERSTAND IF IT WAS *MEAT*, SURE! BUT SWEETS?! SO DON'T WORRY--I TOLD HER RIGHT OFF!!!
AN EMPEROR?!!
GADOI—NG!!
YOU PICKED A FIGHT WITH BIG MOM?!!
YOU SHOULDN'T HAVE DONE THAT...
OOH! I KNEW YOU WERE STRONG, LUFFY!
HEE HEE
THAT'S NOT THE ISSUE HERE!!

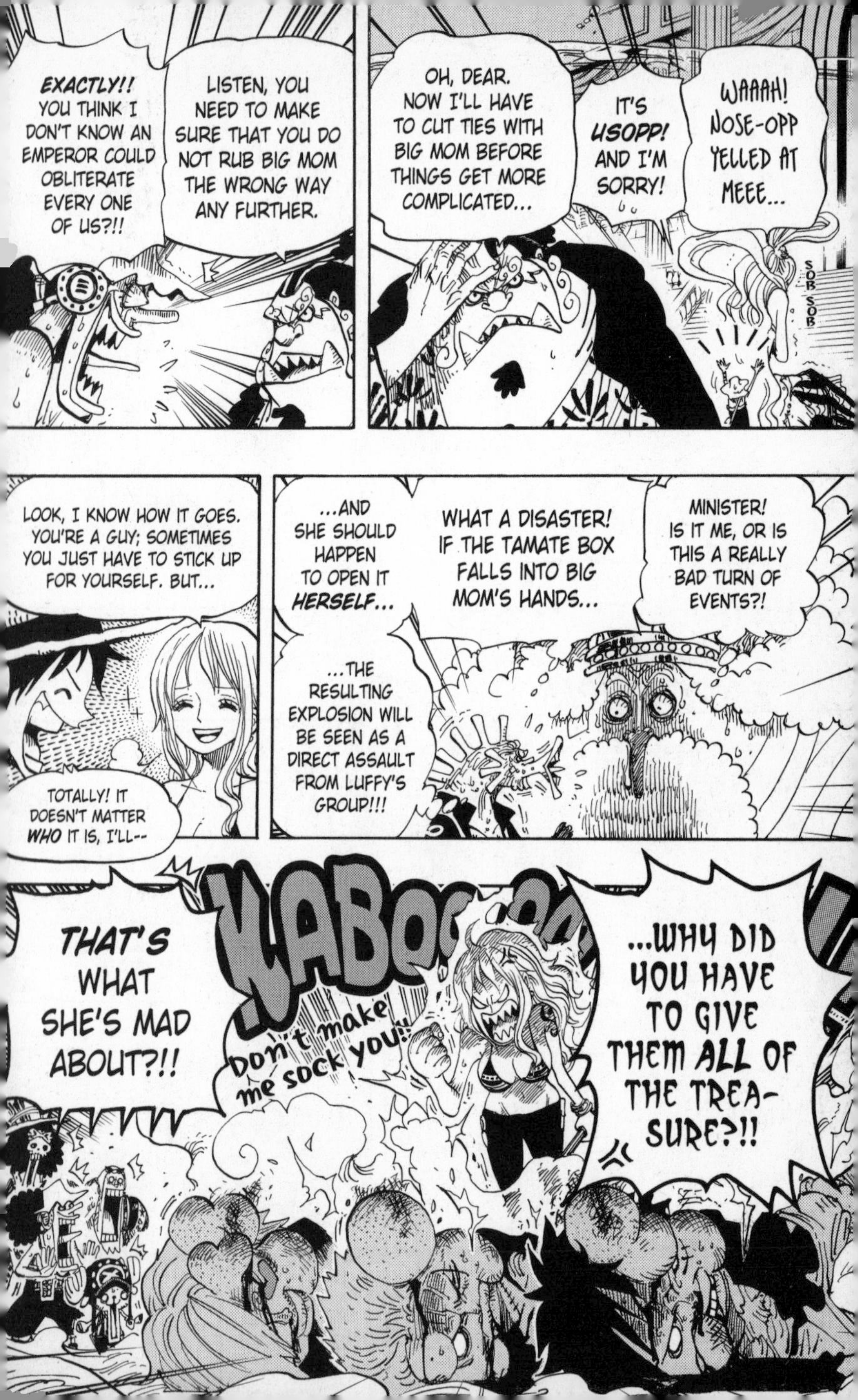
WAAAH! NOSE-OPP YELLED AT MEEE...
SOB SOB
IT'S USOPP! AND I'M SORRY!
OH, DEAR. NOW I'LL HAVE TO CUT TIES WITH BIG MOM BEFORE THINGS GET MORE COMPLICATED...
LISTEN, YOU NEED TO MAKE SURE THAT YOU DO NOT RUB BIG MOM THE WRONG WAY ANY FURTHER.
EXACTLY!! YOU THINK I DON'T KNOW AN EMPEROR COULD OBLITERATE EVERY ONE OF US?!!
MINISTER! IS IT ME, OR IS THIS A REALLY BAD TURN OF EVENTS?!
WHAT A DISASTER! IF THE TAMATE BOX FALLS INTO BIG MOM'S HANDS...
...AND SHE SHOULD HAPPEN TO OPEN IT HERSELF...
...THE RESULTING EXPLOSION WILL BE SEEN AS A DIRECT ASSAULT FROM LUFFY'S GROUP!!!
LOOK, I KNOW HOW IT GOES. YOU'RE A GUY; SOMETIMES YOU JUST HAVE TO STICK UP FOR YOURSELF. BUT...
TOTALLY! IT DOESN'T MATTER WHO IT IS, I'LL--
...WHY DID YOU HAVE TO GIVE THEM ALL OF THE TREA-SURE?!!
KABOO
Don't make me sock you!!
THAT'S WHAT SHE'S MAD ABOUT?!!

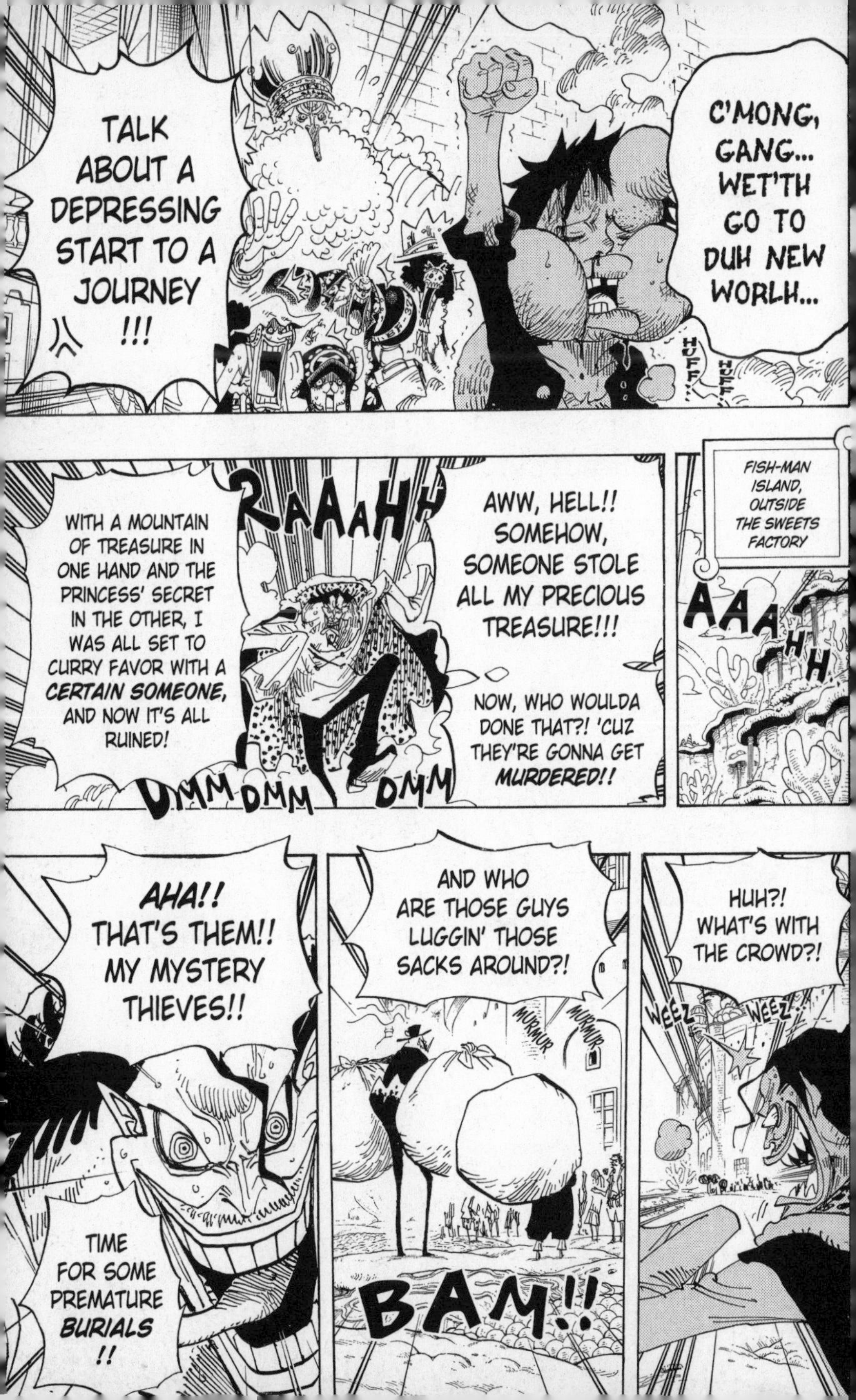
C'MONG, GANG... WET'TH GO TO DUH NEW WORLH...
HUFF... HUFF...
TALK ABOUT A DEPRESSING START TO A JOURNEY !!!
FISH-MAN ISLAND, OUTSIDE THE SWEETS FACTORY
AAAAHH.
AWW, HELL!! SOMEHOW, SOMEONE STOLE ALL MY PRECIOUS TREASURE!!!
RAAAHH
WITH A MOUNTAIN OF TREASURE IN ONE HAND AND THE PRINCESS' SECRET IN THE OTHER, I WAS ALL SET TO CURRY FAVOR WITH A *CERTAIN SOMEONE*, AND NOW IT'S ALL RUINED!
NOW, WHO WOULDA DONE THAT?! 'CUZ THEY'RE GONNA GET *MURDERED!!*
DMM DMM DMM
HUH?! WHAT'S WITH THE CROWD?!
WEEZ WEEZ
AND WHO ARE THOSE GUYS LUGGIN' THOSE SACKS AROUND?!
MURMUR MURMUR
BAM!!
AHA!! THAT'S THEM!! MY MYSTERY THIEVES!!
TIME FOR SOME PREMATURE *BURIALS* !!

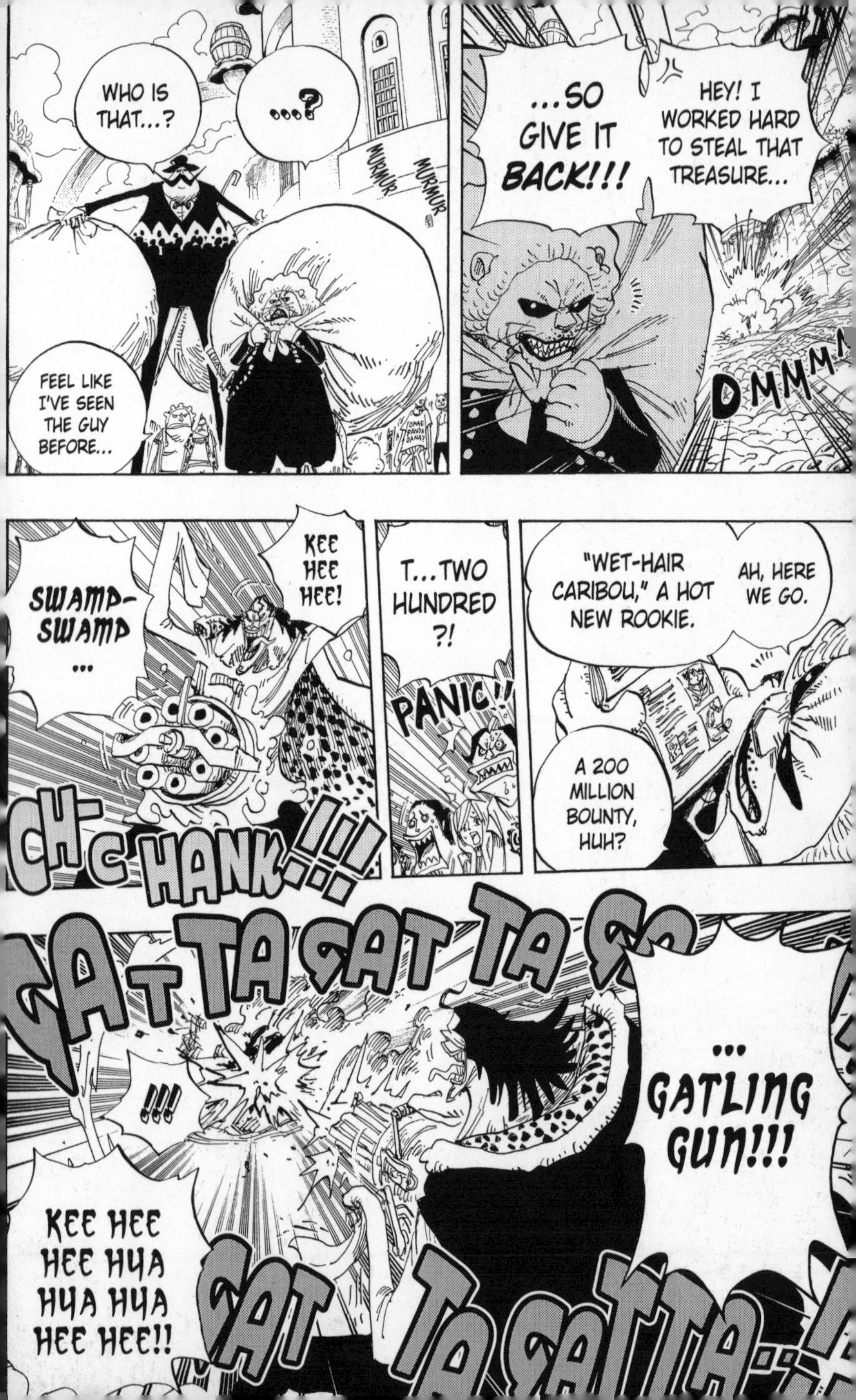
HEY! I WORKED HARD TO STEAL THAT TREASURE...
...SO GIVE IT BACK!!!
DMMM
...?
WHO IS THAT...?
MURMUR
MURMUR
FEEL LIKE I'VE SEEN THE GUY BEFORE...
AH, HERE WE GO.
"WET-HAIR CARIBOU," A HOT NEW ROOKIE.
A 200 MILLION BOUNTY, HUH?
T...TWO HUNDRED ?!
PANIC!!
KEE HEE HEE!
SWAMP-SWAMP ...
CH-CHANK!!!
...GATLING GUN!!!
GAT TA GAT TA GA
!!!
KEE HEE HEE HYA HYA HYA HEE HEE!!
GAT TA GATTA...!!

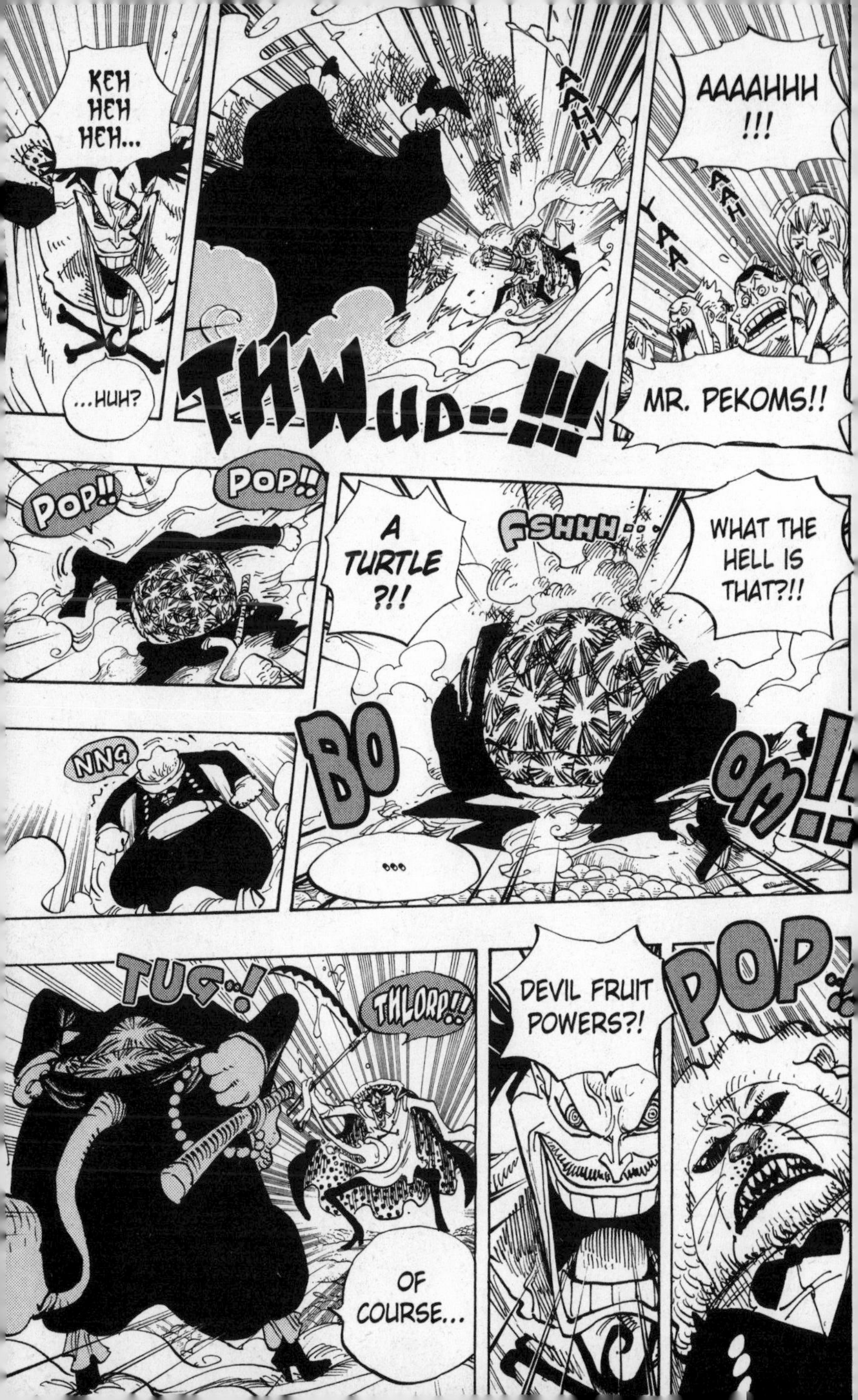
AAAAHHH!!!
AAH
YAA
MR. PEKOMS!!
AAHH
THWUD..!!!
KEH HEH HEH...
...HUH?
WHAT THE HELL IS THAT?!!
FSHHH...
A TURTLE ?!!
BOOM!!
...
POP!!
POP!!
NNG
POP..!
DEVIL FRUIT POWERS?!
THLORP!!
TUG..!
OF COURSE...

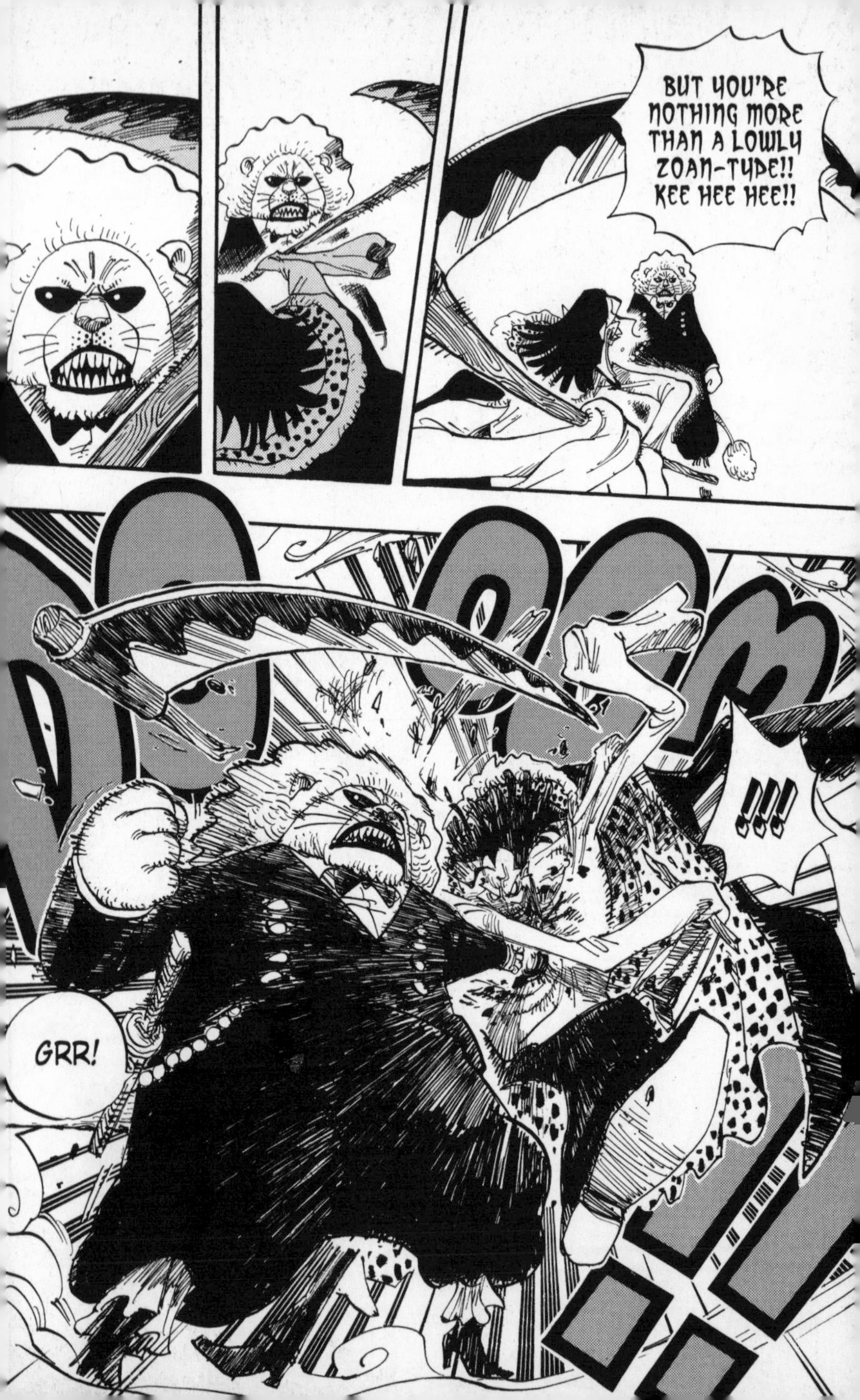
BUT YOU'RE NOTHING MORE THAN A LOWLY ZOAN-TYPE!! KEE HEE HEE!!
!!!
GRR!

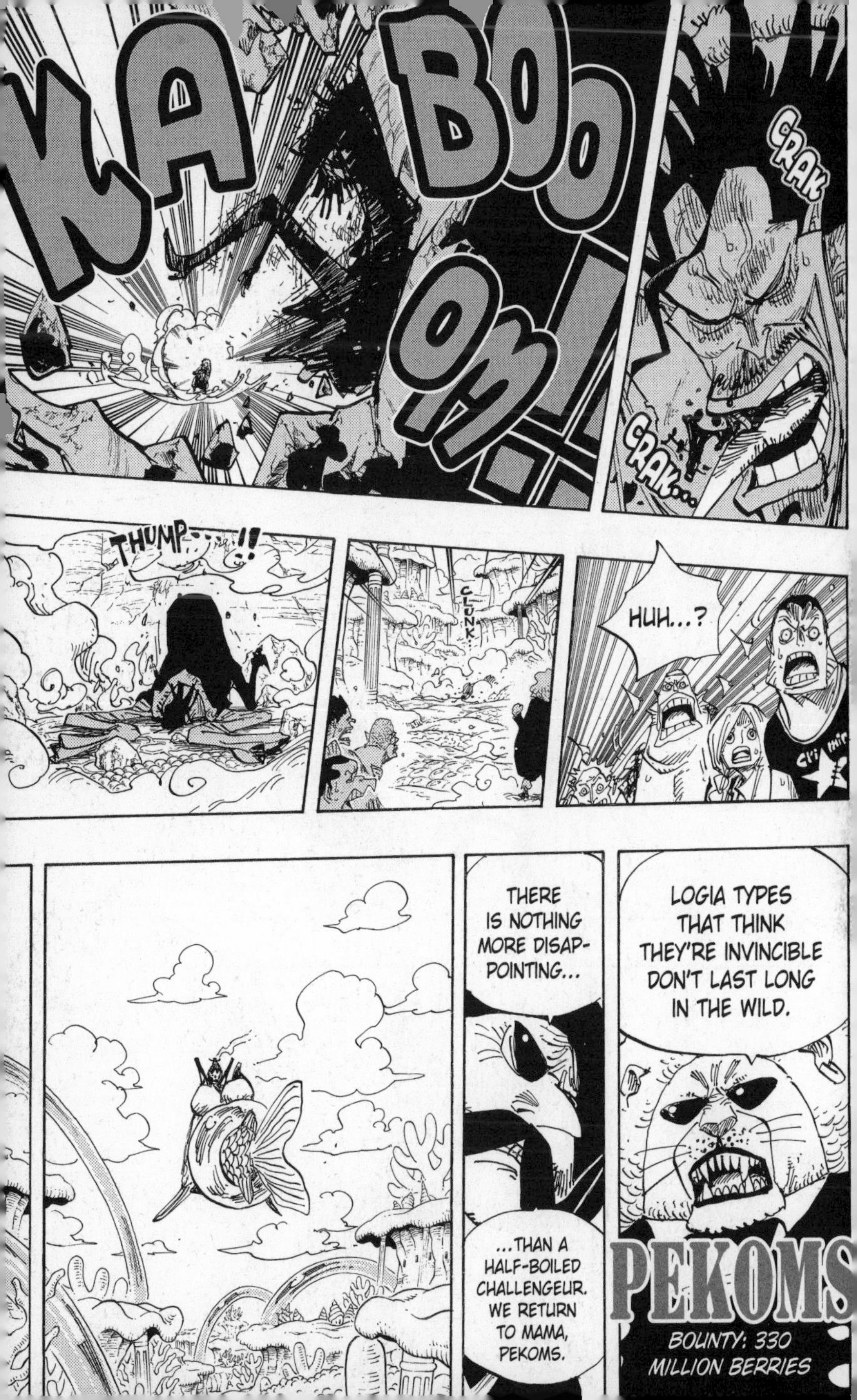
CRAK
CRAK...
KA-BOOM!!
HUH...?
CLUNK
THUMP...!!
LOGIA TYPES THAT THINK THEY'RE INVINCIBLE DON'T LAST LONG IN THE WILD.
PEKOMS
BOUNTY: 330 MILLION BERRIES
THERE IS NOTHING MORE DISAPPOINTING...
...THAN A HALF-BOILED CHALLENGEUR. WE RETURN TO MAMA, PEKOMS.

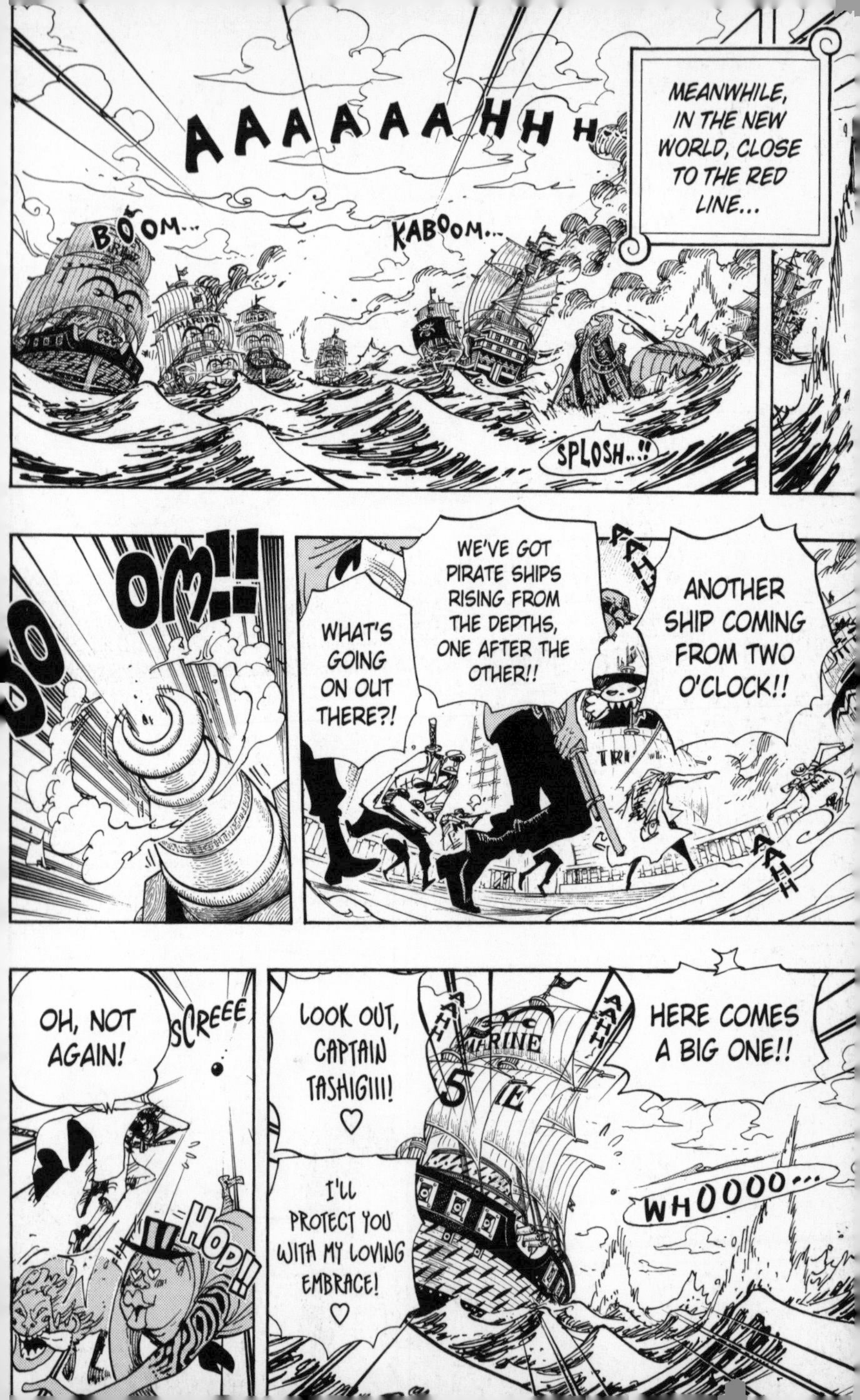
MEANWHILE, IN THE NEW WORLD, CLOSE TO THE RED LINE...
AAAAAAHHH
KABOOM...
BOOM...
SPLOSH..!!
ANOTHER SHIP COMING FROM TWO O'CLOCK!!
AAHH
WE'VE GOT PIRATE SHIPS RISING FROM THE DEPTHS, ONE AFTER THE OTHER!!
WHAT'S GOING ON OUT THERE?!
AAHH
OM!!
HERE COMES A BIG ONE!!
AAHH
AAHH
MARINE
LOOK OUT, CAPTAIN TASHIGIII! ♡
I'LL PROTECT YOU WITH MY LOVING EMBRACE! ♡
WHOOOO...
SCREEE
OH, NOT AGAIN!
HOP!!

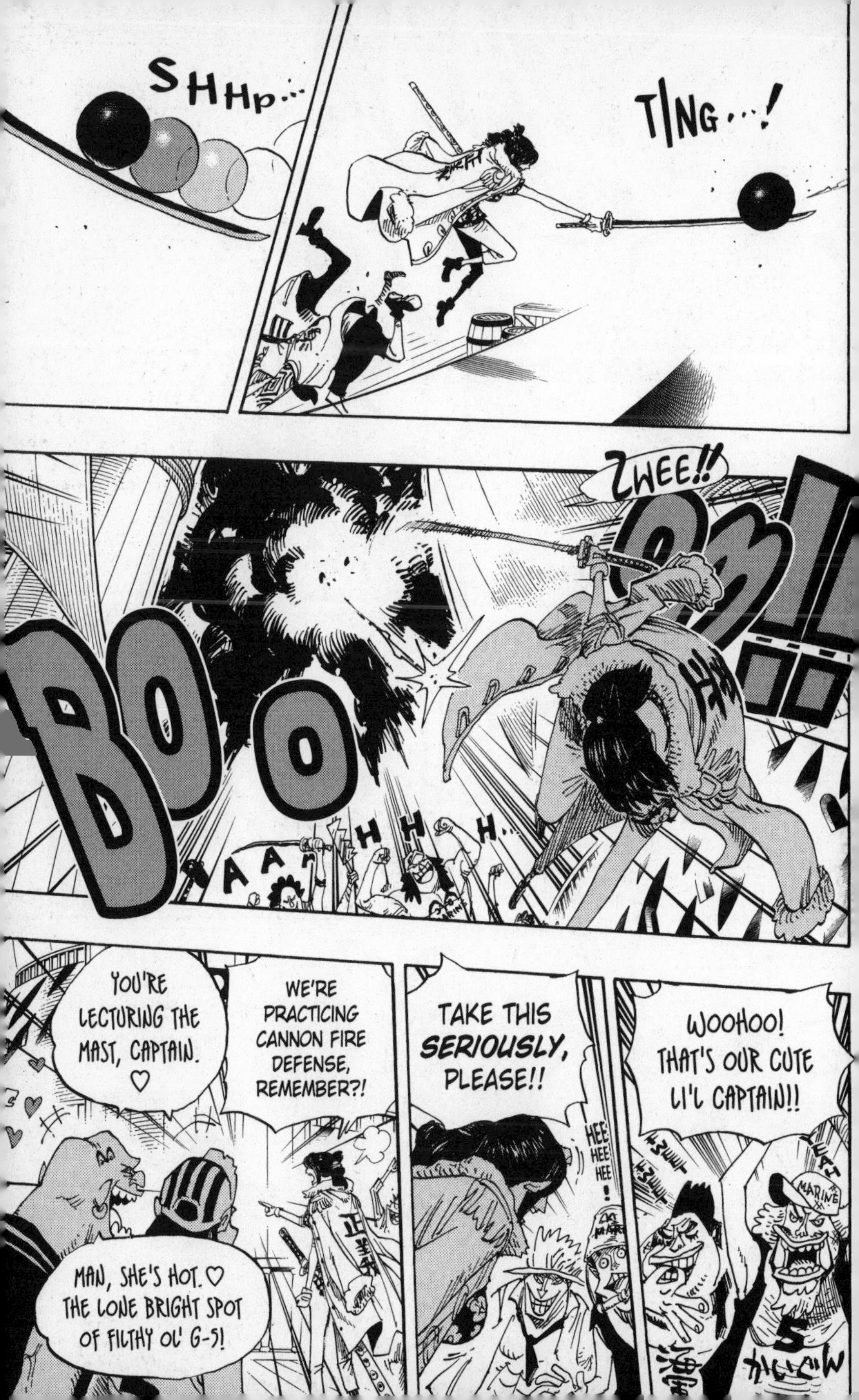
TING...!
SHHP...
ZWEE!!
BOO
AAAHHHH...
WOOHOO! THAT'S OUR CUTE LI'L CAPTAIN!!
TAKE THIS **SERIOUSLY,** PLEASE!!
HEE HEE HEE!
WE'RE PRACTICING CANNON FIRE DEFENSE, REMEMBER?!
YOU'RE LECTURING THE MAST, CAPTAIN. ♡
MAN, SHE'S HOT. ♡ THE LONE BRIGHT SPOT OF FILTHY OL' G-5!

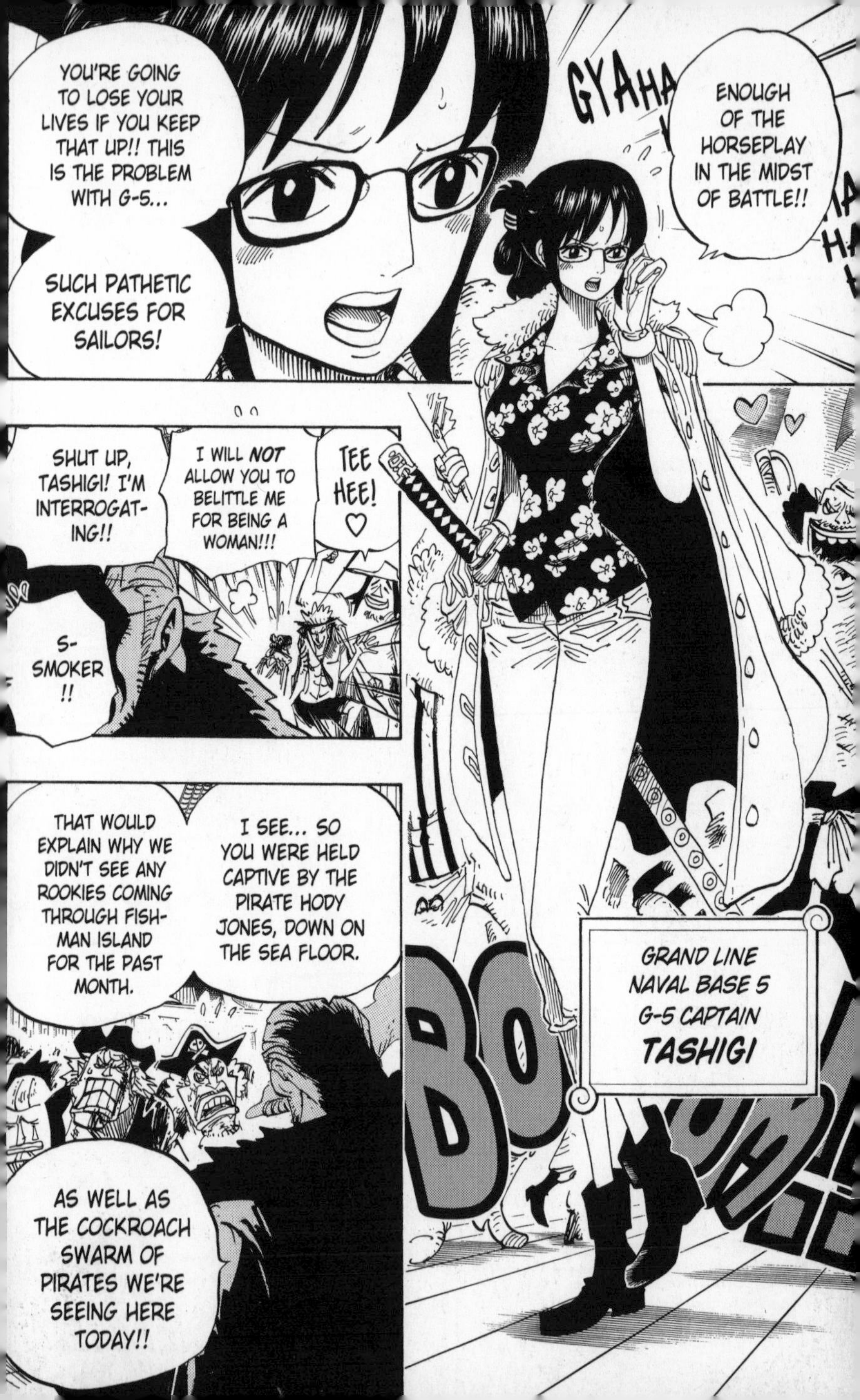
GYAHA
ENOUGH OF THE HORSEPLAY IN THE MIDST OF BATTLE!!
GRAND LINE NAVAL BASE 5 G-5 CAPTAIN ***TASHIGI***
YOU'RE GOING TO LOSE YOUR LIVES IF YOU KEEP THAT UP!! THIS IS THE PROBLEM WITH G-5...
SUCH PATHETIC EXCUSES FOR SAILORS!
TEE HEE! ♡
I WILL ***NOT*** ALLOW YOU TO BELITTLE ME FOR BEING A WOMAN!!!
SHUT UP, TASHIGI! I'M INTERROGATING!!
S-SMOKER!!
I SEE... SO YOU WERE HELD CAPTIVE BY THE PIRATE HODY JONES, DOWN ON THE SEA FLOOR.
THAT WOULD EXPLAIN WHY WE DIDN'T SEE ANY ROOKIES COMING THROUGH FISH-MAN ISLAND FOR THE PAST MONTH.
AS WELL AS THE COCKROACH SWARM OF PIRATES WE'RE SEEING HERE TODAY!!

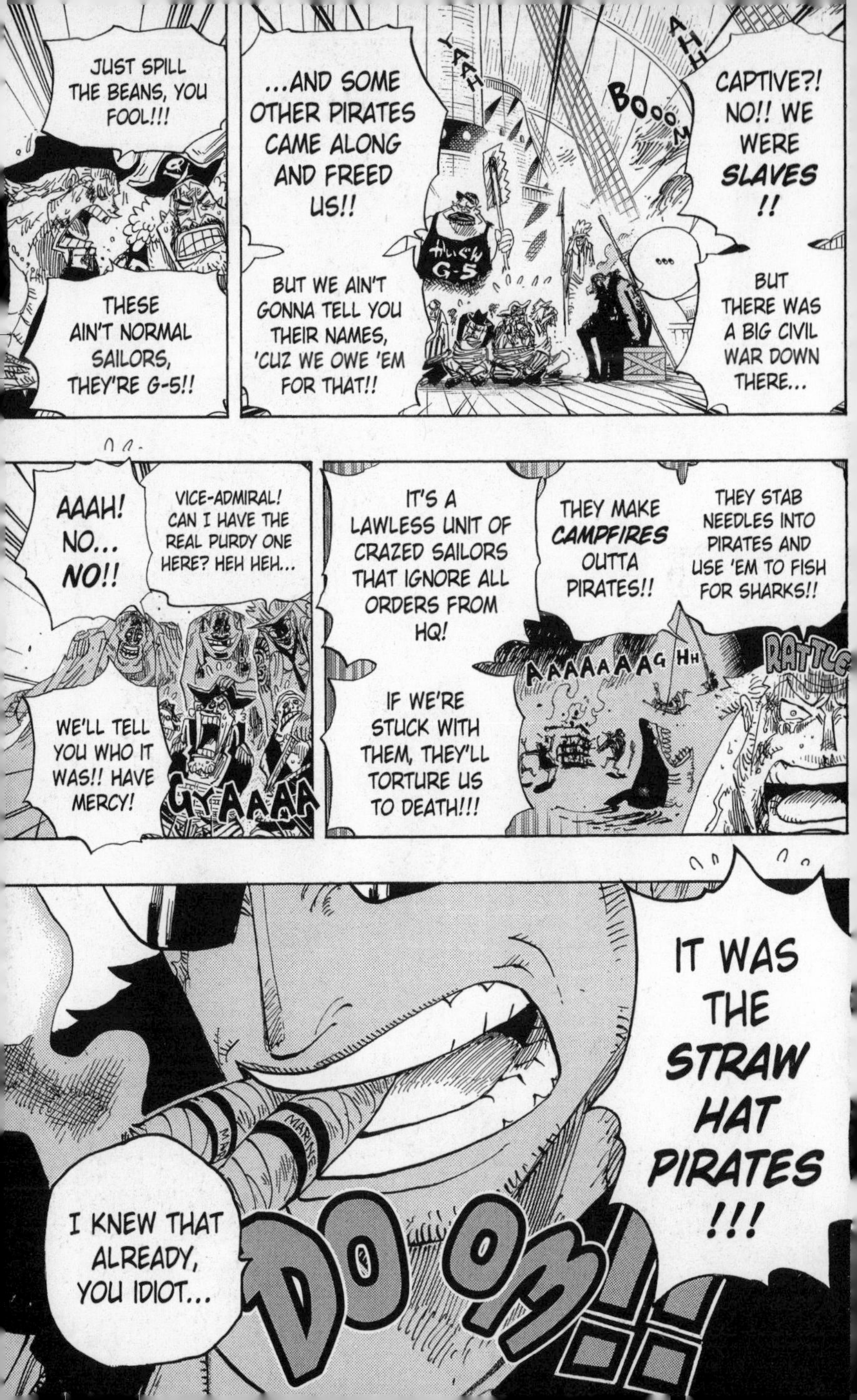
AHH
BOOOM
YAAH
CAPTIVE?! NO!! WE WERE SLAVES!!
...AND SOME OTHER PIRATES CAME ALONG AND FREED US!!
...
BUT THERE WAS A BIG CIVIL WAR DOWN THERE...
BUT WE AIN'T GONNA TELL YOU THEIR NAMES, 'CUZ WE OWE 'EM FOR THAT!!
JUST SPILL THE BEANS, YOU FOOL!!!
THESE AIN'T NORMAL SAILORS, THEY'RE G-5!!
THEY STAB NEEDLES INTO PIRATES AND USE 'EM TO FISH FOR SHARKS!!
THEY MAKE CAMPFIRES OUTTA PIRATES!!
IT'S A LAWLESS UNIT OF CRAZED SAILORS THAT IGNORE ALL ORDERS FROM HQ!
RATTLE
AAAAAAAGHH
IF WE'RE STUCK WITH THEM, THEY'LL TORTURE US TO DEATH!!!
VICE-ADMIRAL! CAN I HAVE THE REAL PURDY ONE HERE? HEH HEH...
AAAH! NO... NO!!
GYAAAA
WE'LL TELL YOU WHO IT WAS!! HAVE MERCY!
IT WAS THE STRAW HAT PIRATES!!!
DOOM!!
I KNEW THAT ALREADY, YOU IDIOT...

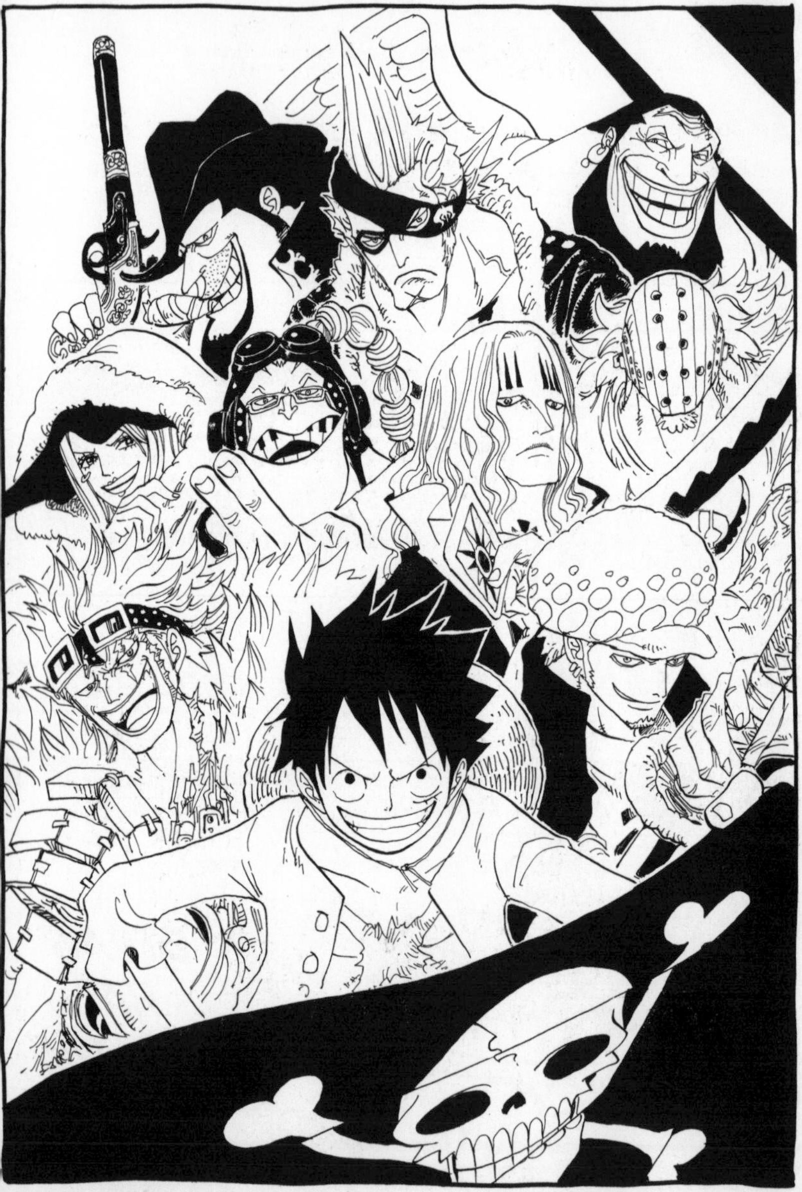

Chaper 653:
THE HERO HAT

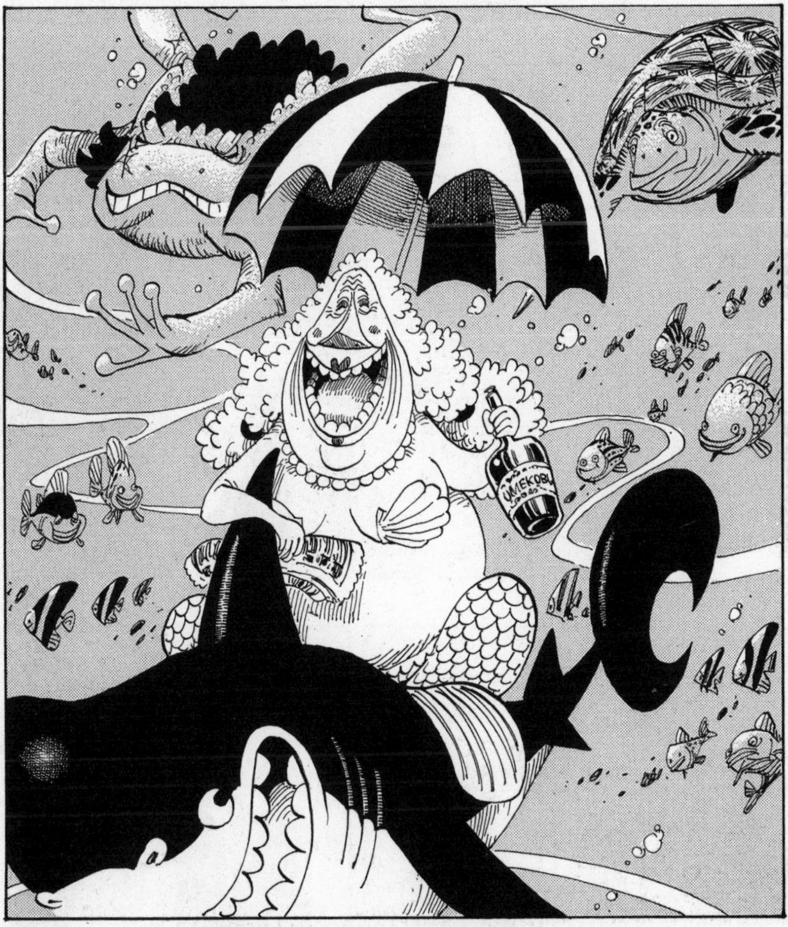
UMEKOBU

DECKS OF THE WORLD, VOL. 35
"ICEFISH MERMAID KOKORO'S ELEGANT DAY OFF"

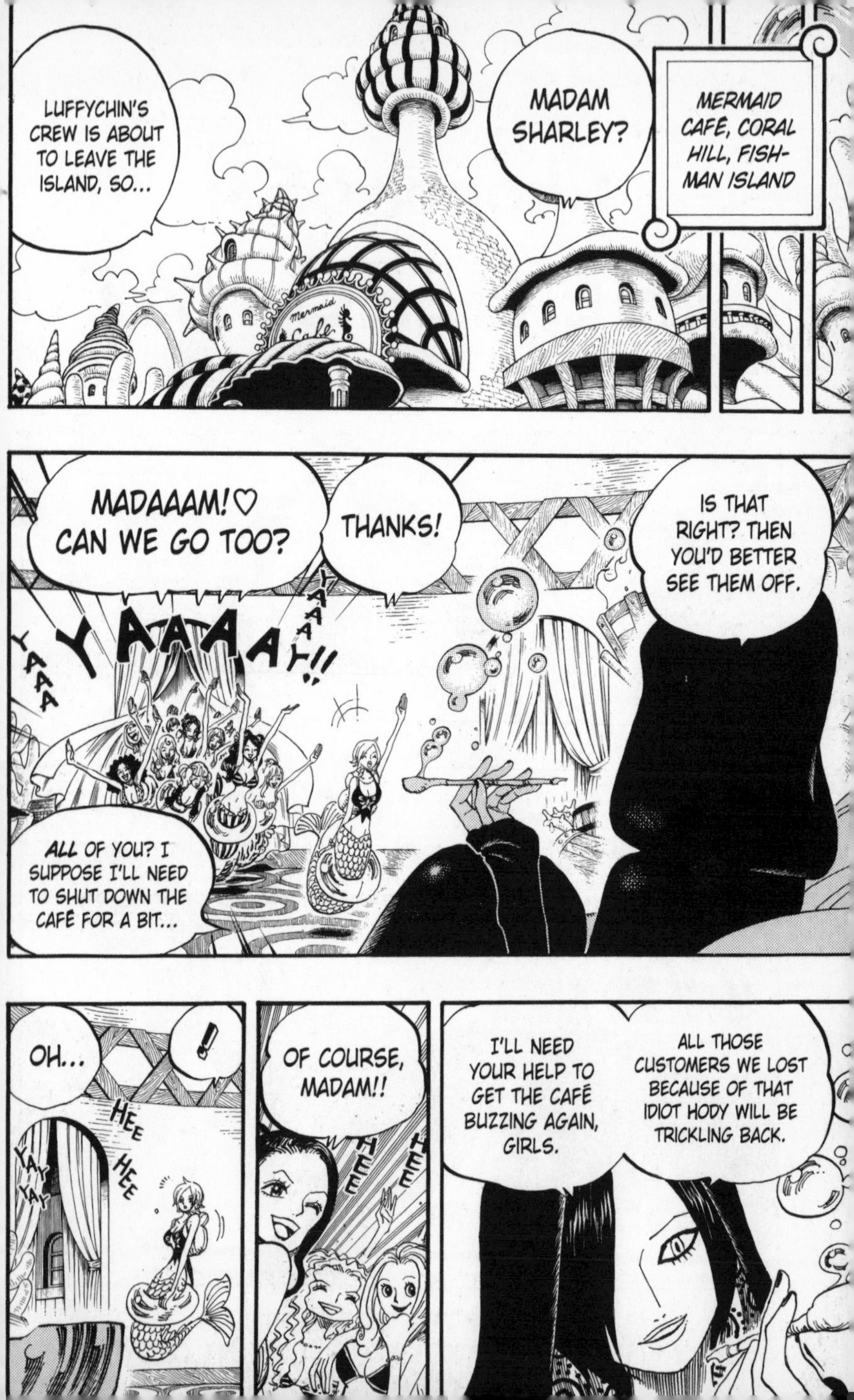
MERMAID CAFÉ, CORAL HILL, FISH-MAN ISLAND
MADAM SHARLEY?
LUFFYCHIN'S CREW IS ABOUT TO LEAVE THE ISLAND, SO...
Mermaid Cafe
IS THAT RIGHT? THEN YOU'D BETTER SEE THEM OFF.
THANKS!
MADAAAM! ♡ CAN WE GO TOO?
YAAAA
YAAAAY!!
YAAA
ALL OF YOU? I SUPPOSE I'LL NEED TO SHUT DOWN THE CAFÉ FOR A BIT...
ALL THOSE CUSTOMERS WE LOST BECAUSE OF THAT IDIOT HODY WILL BE TRICKLING BACK.
I'LL NEED YOUR HELP TO GET THE CAFÉ BUZZING AGAIN, GIRLS.
OF COURSE, MADAM!!
HEE
HEE
!
OH...
HEE
HEE
YAY
YAY

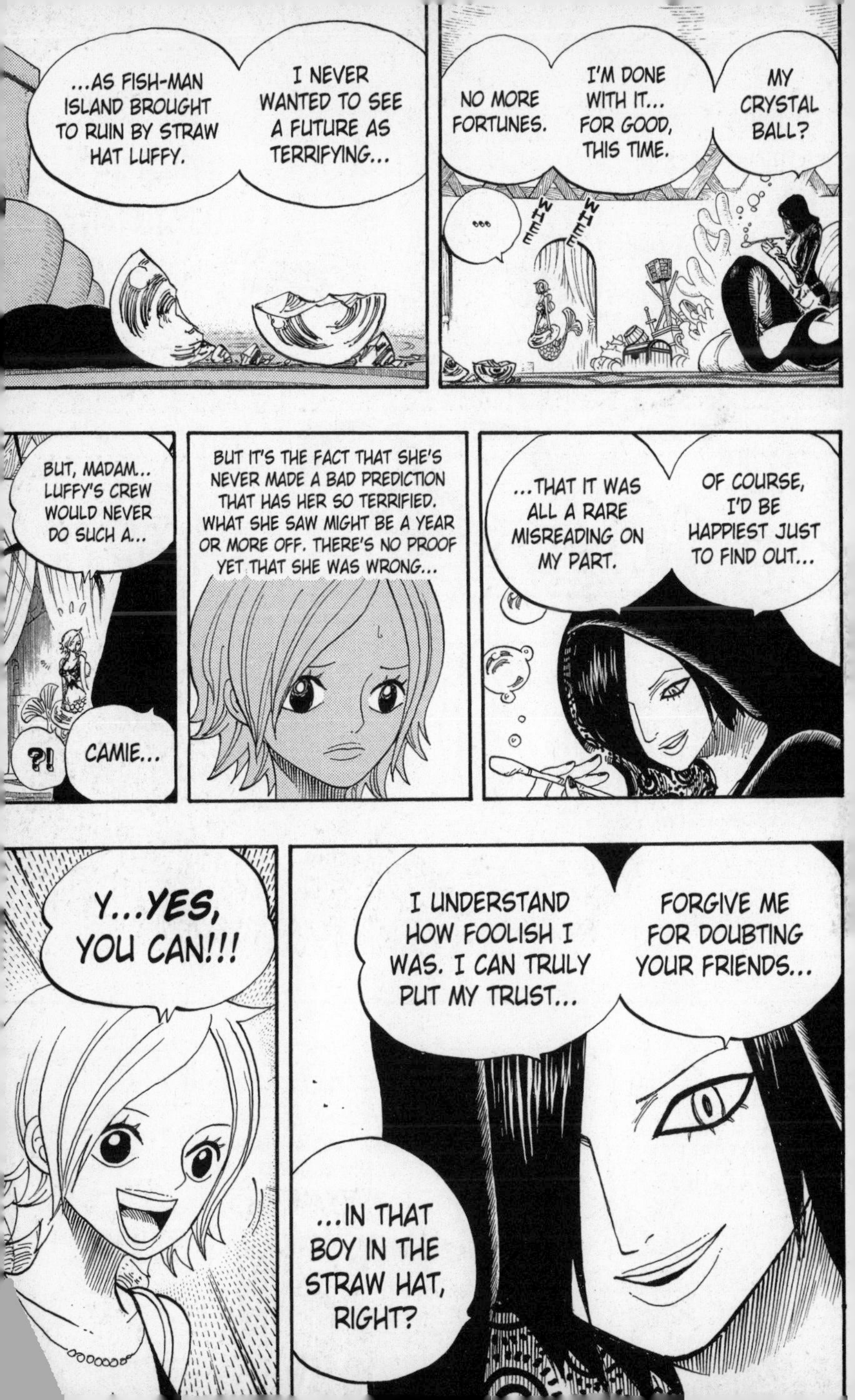
MY CRYSTAL BALL?
I'M DONE WITH IT... FOR GOOD, THIS TIME.
NO MORE FORTUNES.
...
WHEE
WHEE
I NEVER WANTED TO SEE A FUTURE AS TERRIFYING...
...AS FISH-MAN ISLAND BROUGHT TO RUIN BY STRAW HAT LUFFY.
OF COURSE, I'D BE HAPPIEST JUST TO FIND OUT...
...THAT IT WAS ALL A RARE MISREADING ON MY PART.
BUT IT'S THE FACT THAT SHE'S NEVER MADE A BAD PREDICTION THAT HAS HER SO TERRIFIED. WHAT SHE SAW MIGHT BE A YEAR OR MORE OFF. THERE'S NO PROOF YET THAT SHE WAS WRONG...
BUT, MADAM... LUFFY'S CREW WOULD NEVER DO SUCH A...
CAMIE...
?!
FORGIVE ME FOR DOUBTING YOUR FRIENDS...
I UNDERSTAND HOW FOOLISH I WAS. I CAN TRULY PUT MY TRUST...
...IN THAT BOY IN THE STRAW HAT, RIGHT?
Y...YES, YOU CAN!!!

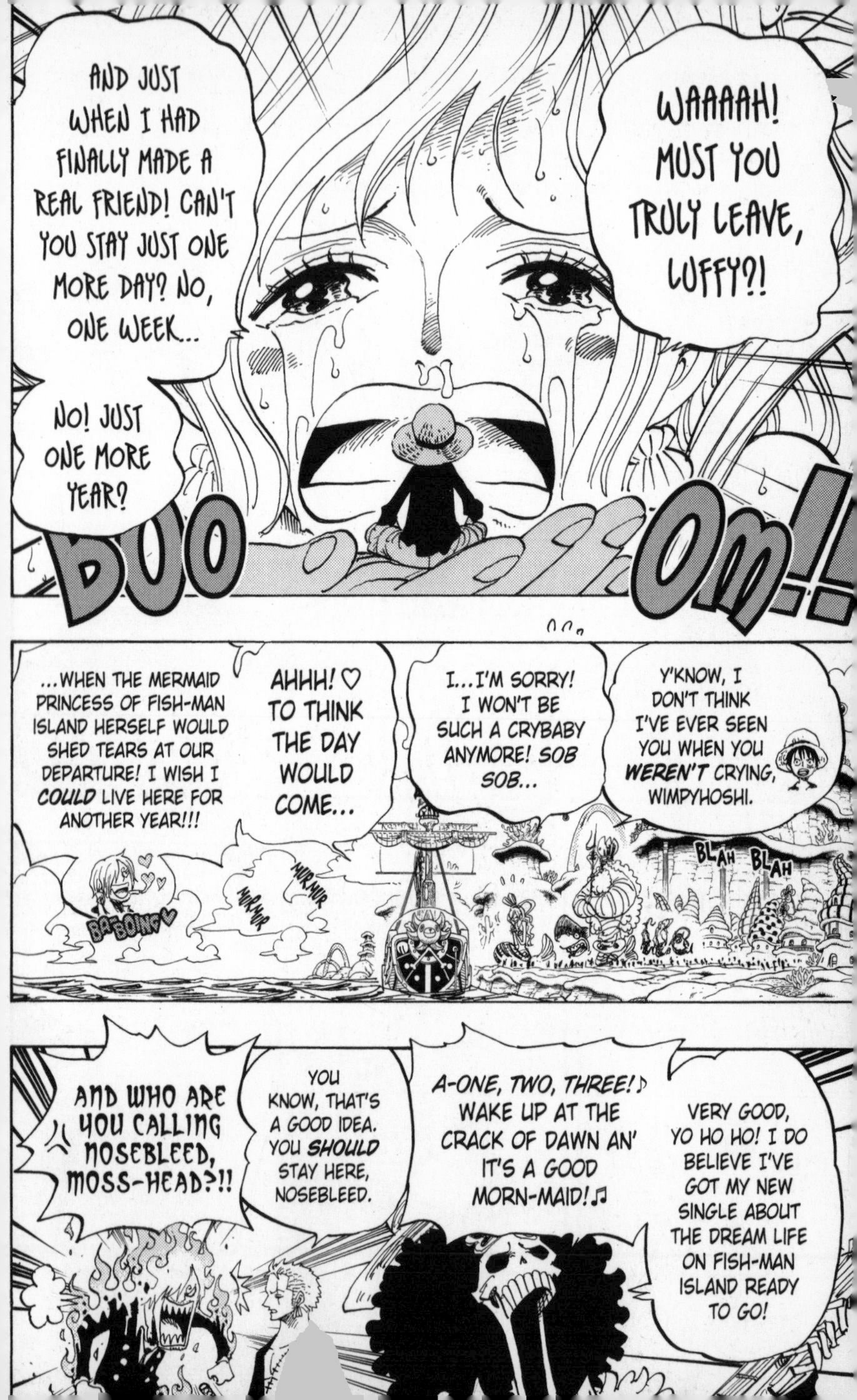
WAAAAH! MUST YOU TRULY LEAVE, LUFFY?!
AND JUST WHEN I HAD FINALLY MADE A REAL FRIEND! CAN'T YOU STAY JUST ONE MORE DAY? NO, ONE WEEK...
NO! JUST ONE MORE YEAR?
BOOOM!!
Y'KNOW, I DON'T THINK I'VE EVER SEEN YOU WHEN YOU WEREN'T CRYING, WIMPYHOSHI.
I...I'M SORRY! I WON'T BE SUCH A CRYBABY ANYMORE! SOB SOB...
BLAH BLAH
AHHH! ♡ TO THINK THE DAY WOULD COME...
...WHEN THE MERMAID PRINCESS OF FISH-MAN ISLAND HERSELF WOULD SHED TEARS AT OUR DEPARTURE! I WISH I COULD LIVE HERE FOR ANOTHER YEAR!!!
MURMUR
MURMUR
BA-BOING♡
VERY GOOD, YO HO HO! I DO BELIEVE I'VE GOT MY NEW SINGLE ABOUT THE DREAM LIFE ON FISH-MAN ISLAND READY TO GO!
A-ONE, TWO, THREE!♪ WAKE UP AT THE CRACK OF DAWN AN' IT'S A GOOD MORN-MAID!♫
YOU KNOW, THAT'S A GOOD IDEA. YOU SHOULD STAY HERE, NOSEBLEED.
AND WHO ARE YOU CALLING NOSEBLEED, MOSS-HEAD?!!

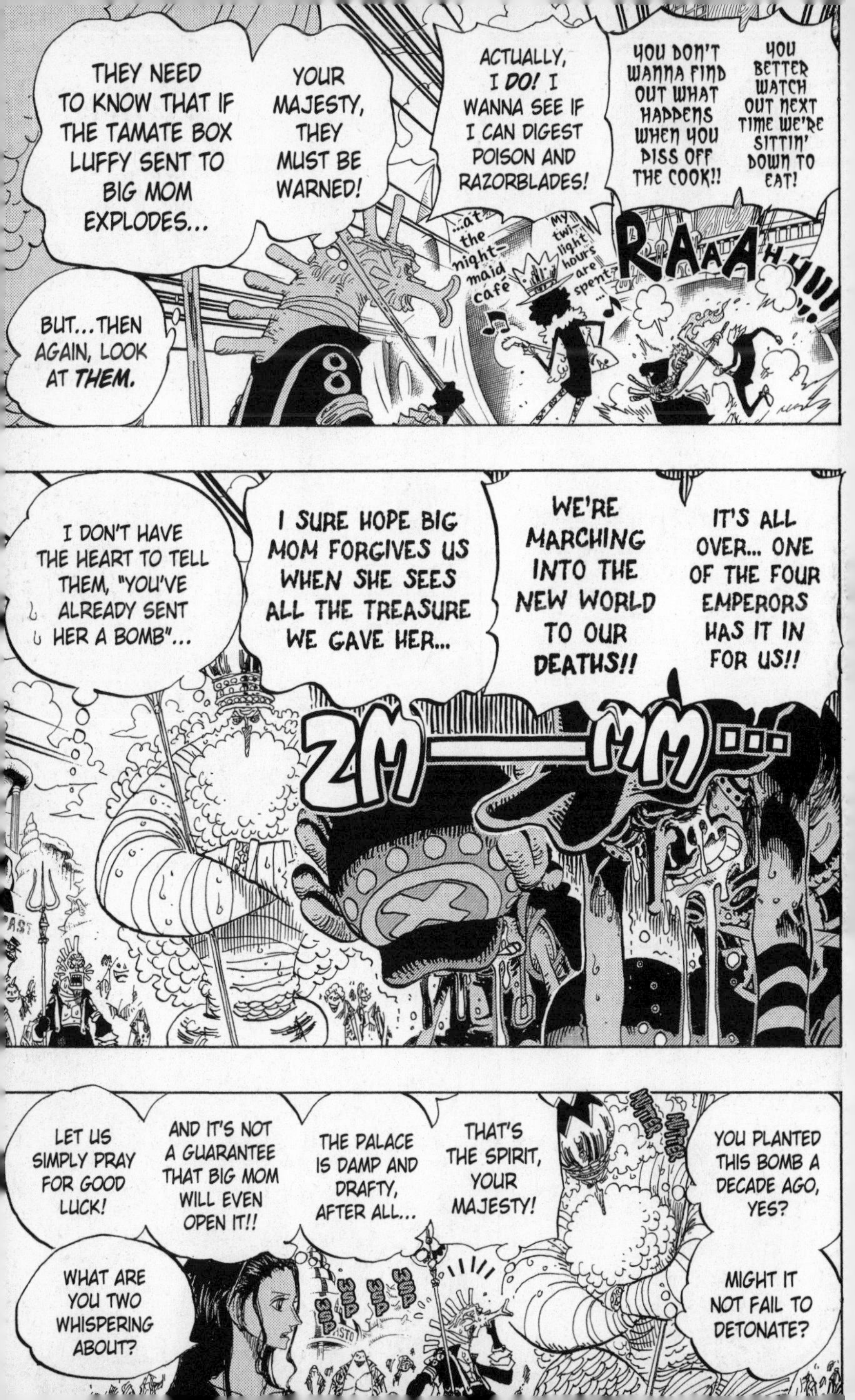
YOU BETTER WATCH OUT NEXT TIME WE'RE SITTIN' DOWN TO EAT!
YOU DON'T WANNA FIND OUT WHAT HAPPENS WHEN YOU PISS OFF THE COOK!!
RAAAHHH!!!
ACTUALLY, I DO! I WANNA SEE IF I CAN DIGEST POISON AND RAZORBLADES!
My twilight hours are spent...
...at the night-maid café
YOUR MAJESTY, THEY MUST BE WARNED!
THEY NEED TO KNOW THAT IF THE TAMATE BOX LUFFY SENT TO BIG MOM EXPLODES...
BUT...THEN AGAIN, LOOK AT THEM.
IT'S ALL OVER... ONE OF THE FOUR EMPERORS HAS IT IN FOR US!!
WE'RE MARCHING INTO THE NEW WORLD TO OUR DEATHS!!
I SURE HOPE BIG MOM FORGIVES US WHEN SHE SEES ALL THE TREASURE WE GAVE HER...
I DON'T HAVE THE HEART TO TELL THEM, "YOU'VE ALREADY SENT HER A BOMB"...
ZM——MM...
YOU PLANTED THIS BOMB A DECADE AGO, YES?
MIGHT IT NOT FAIL TO DETONATE?
WHISPER WHISPER
THAT'S THE SPIRIT, YOUR MAJESTY!
THE PALACE IS DAMP AND DRAFTY, AFTER ALL...
AND IT'S NOT A GUARANTEE THAT BIG MOM WILL EVEN OPEN IT!!
LET US SIMPLY PRAY FOR GOOD LUCK!
WHAT ARE YOU TWO WHISPERING ABOUT?

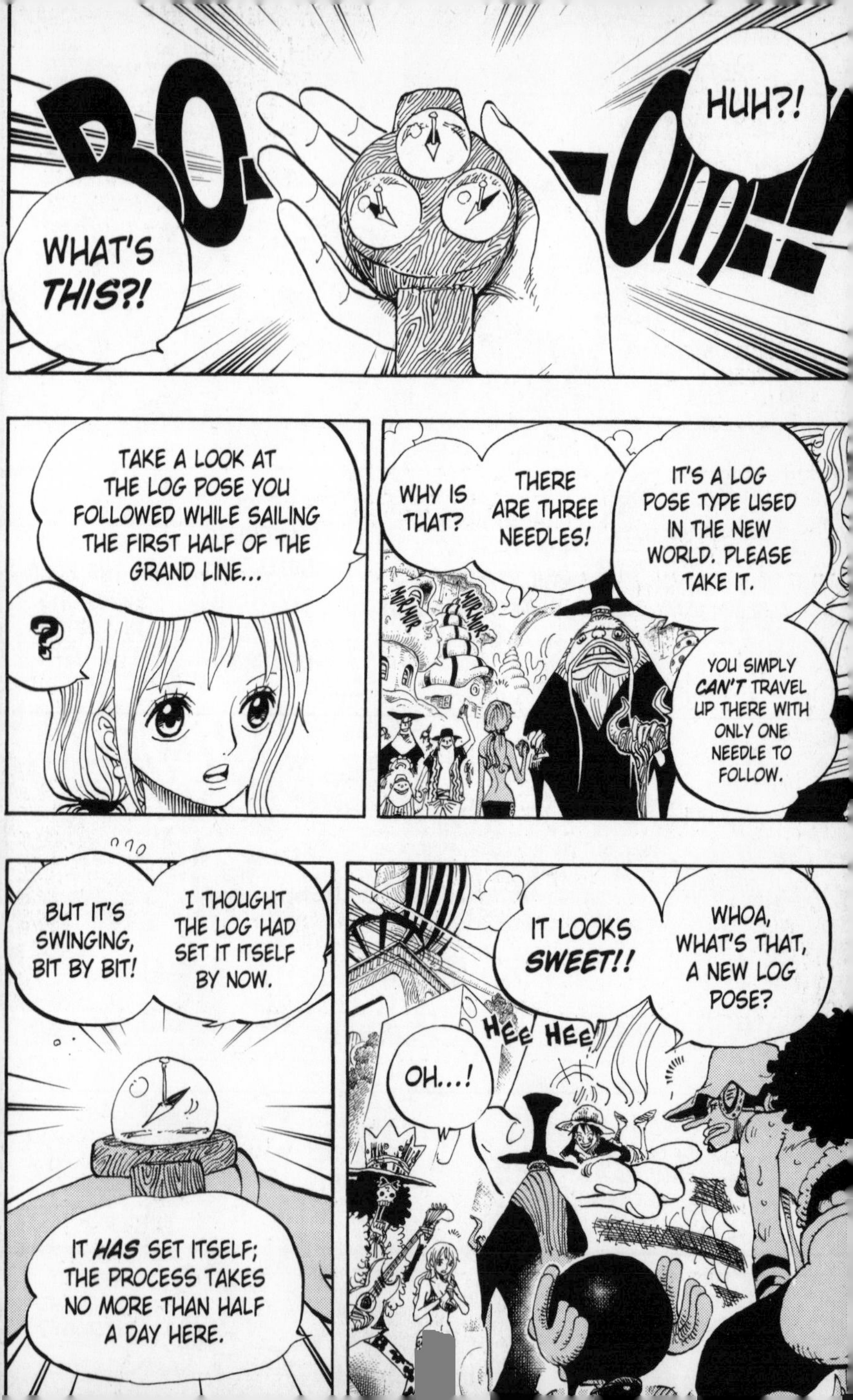
HUH?!
BO-OM!!
WHAT'S *THIS?!*
IT'S A LOG POSE TYPE USED IN THE NEW WORLD. PLEASE TAKE IT.
THERE ARE THREE NEEDLES!
WHY IS THAT?
YOU SIMPLY *CAN'T* TRAVEL UP THERE WITH ONLY ONE NEEDLE TO FOLLOW.
MURMUR
MURMUR
TAKE A LOOK AT THE LOG POSE YOU FOLLOWED WHILE SAILING THE FIRST HALF OF THE GRAND LINE...
?
WHOA, WHAT'S THAT, A NEW LOG POSE?
IT LOOKS *SWEET!!*
HEE HEE
OH...!
I THOUGHT THE LOG HAD SET IT ITSELF BY NOW.
BUT IT'S SWINGING, BIT BY BIT!
IT *HAS* SET ITSELF; THE PROCESS TAKES NO MORE THAN HALF A DAY HERE.

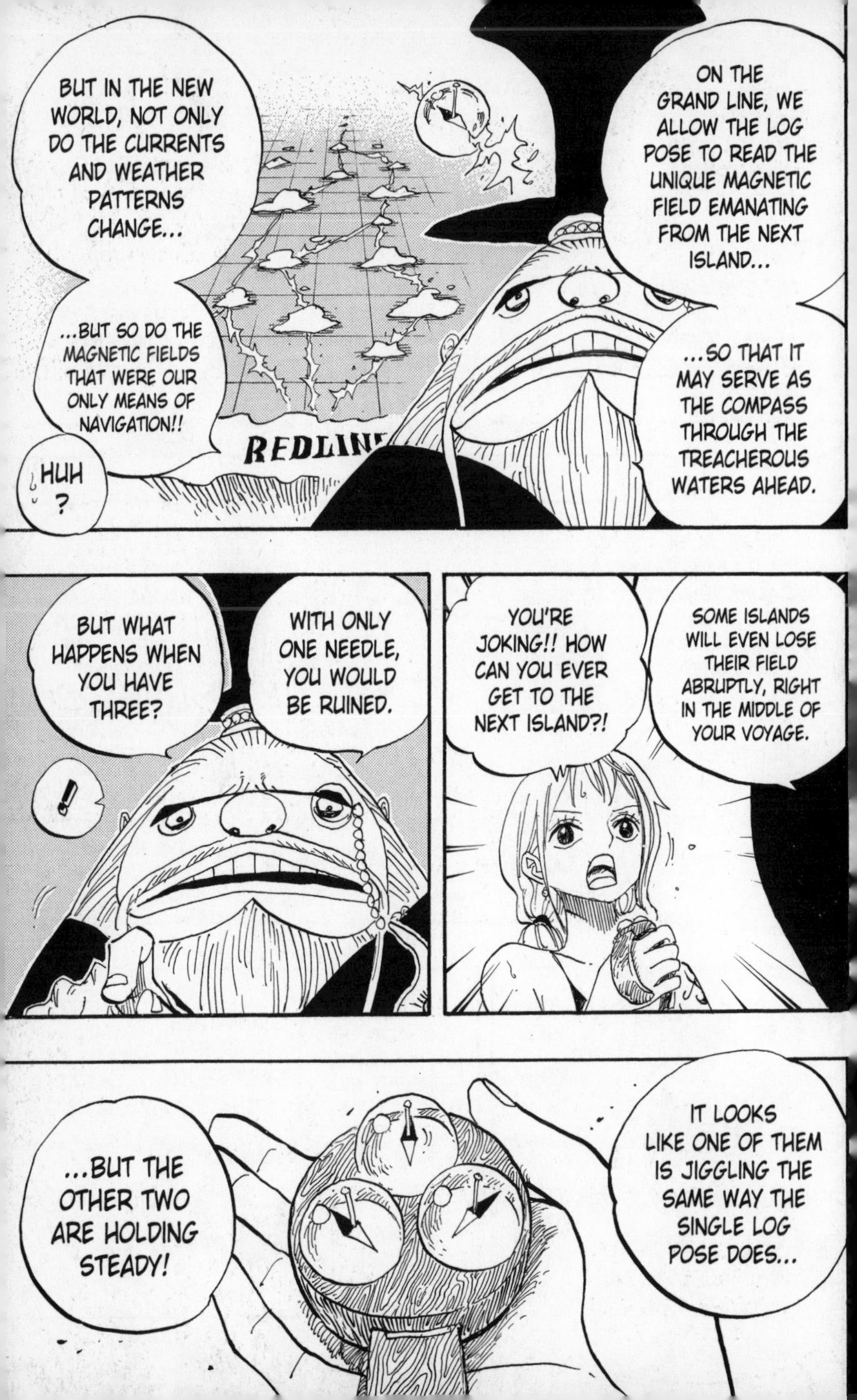
ON THE GRAND LINE, WE ALLOW THE LOG POSE TO READ THE UNIQUE MAGNETIC FIELD EMANATING FROM THE NEXT ISLAND...
...SO THAT IT MAY SERVE AS THE COMPASS THROUGH THE TREACHEROUS WATERS AHEAD.
BUT IN THE NEW WORLD, NOT ONLY DO THE CURRENTS AND WEATHER PATTERNS CHANGE...
...BUT SO DO THE MAGNETIC FIELDS THAT WERE OUR ONLY MEANS OF NAVIGATION!!
REDLIN
HUH ?
SOME ISLANDS WILL EVEN LOSE THEIR FIELD ABRUPTLY, RIGHT IN THE MIDDLE OF YOUR VOYAGE.
YOU'RE JOKING!! HOW CAN YOU EVER GET TO THE NEXT ISLAND?!
WITH ONLY ONE NEEDLE, YOU WOULD BE RUINED.
BUT WHAT HAPPENS WHEN YOU HAVE THREE?
!
IT LOOKS LIKE ONE OF THEM IS JIGGLING THE SAME WAY THE SINGLE LOG POSE DOES...
...BUT THE OTHER TWO ARE HOLDING STEADY!

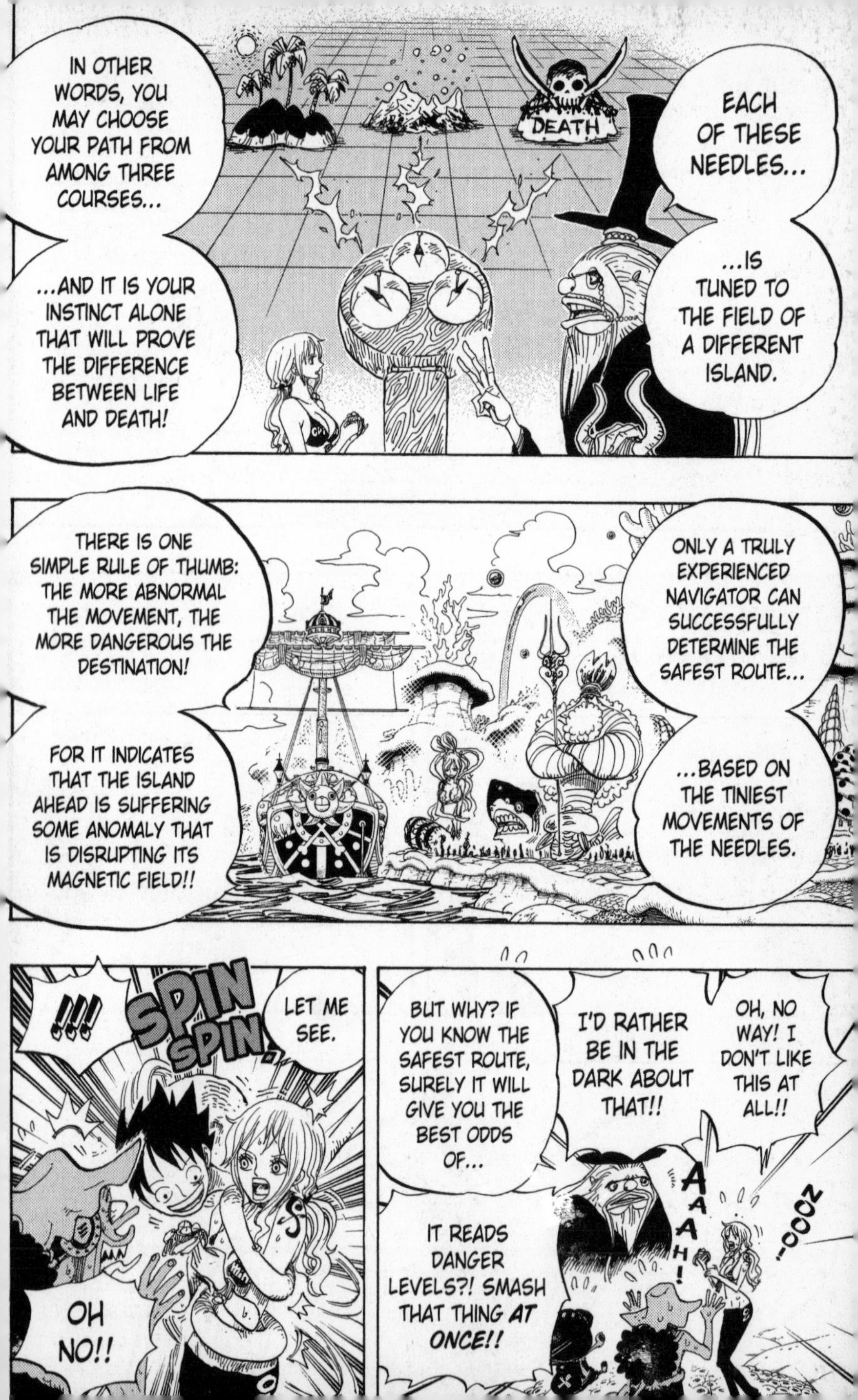
EACH OF THESE NEEDLES...
...IS TUNED TO THE FIELD OF A DIFFERENT ISLAND.
DEATH
IN OTHER WORDS, YOU MAY CHOOSE YOUR PATH FROM AMONG THREE COURSES...
...AND IT IS YOUR INSTINCT ALONE THAT WILL PROVE THE DIFFERENCE BETWEEN LIFE AND DEATH!
ONLY A TRULY EXPERIENCED NAVIGATOR CAN SUCCESSFULLY DETERMINE THE SAFEST ROUTE...
...BASED ON THE TINIEST MOVEMENTS OF THE NEEDLES.
THERE IS ONE SIMPLE RULE OF THUMB: THE MORE ABNORMAL THE MOVEMENT, THE MORE DANGEROUS THE DESTINATION!
FOR IT INDICATES THAT THE ISLAND AHEAD IS SUFFERING SOME ANOMALY THAT IS DISRUPTING ITS MAGNETIC FIELD!!
OH, NO WAY! I DON'T LIKE THIS AT ALL!!
I'D RATHER BE IN THE DARK ABOUT THAT!!
BUT WHY? IF YOU KNOW THE SAFEST ROUTE, SURELY IT WILL GIVE YOU THE BEST ODDS OF...
ZOOO...
AAAH!
IT READS DANGER LEVELS?! SMASH THAT THING AT ONCE!!
LET ME SEE.
SPIN SPIN
!!!
OH NO!!

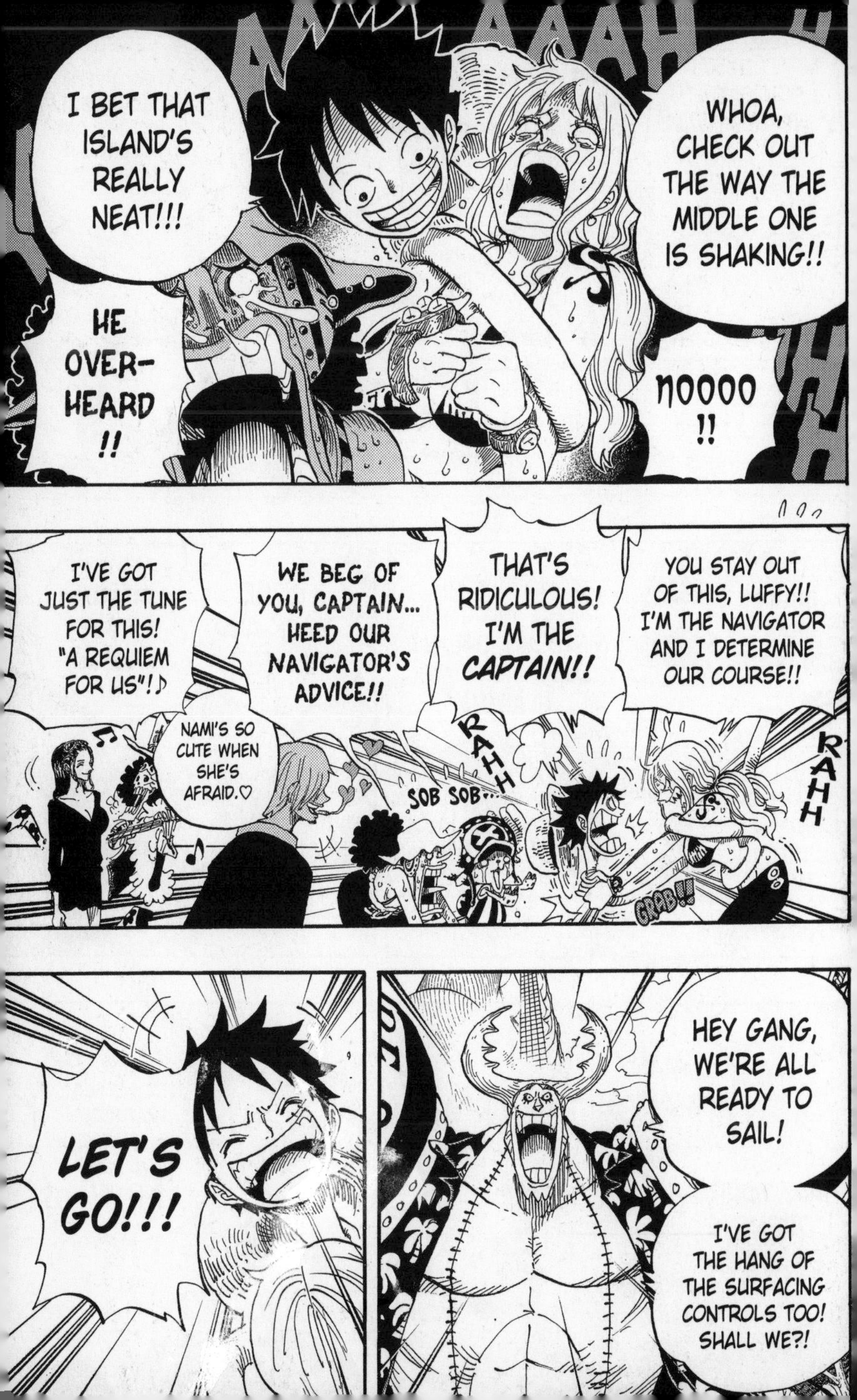
AAAH
WHOA, CHECK OUT THE WAY THE MIDDLE ONE IS SHAKING!!
nOOOO !!
I BET THAT ISLAND'S REALLY NEAT!!!
HE OVER-HEARD!!
YOU STAY OUT OF THIS, LUFFY!! I'M THE NAVIGATOR AND I DETERMINE OUR COURSE!!
THAT'S RIDICULOUS! I'M THE CAPTAIN!!
WE BEG OF YOU, CAPTAIN... HEED OUR NAVIGATOR'S ADVICE!!
I'VE GOT JUST THE TUNE FOR THIS! "A REQUIEM FOR US"!♪
RAHH
RAHH
SOB SOB...
NAMI'S SO CUTE WHEN SHE'S AFRAID.♡
GRAB!!
HEY GANG, WE'RE ALL READY TO SAIL!
I'VE GOT THE HANG OF THE SURFACING CONTROLS TOO! SHALL WE?!
LET'S GO!!!

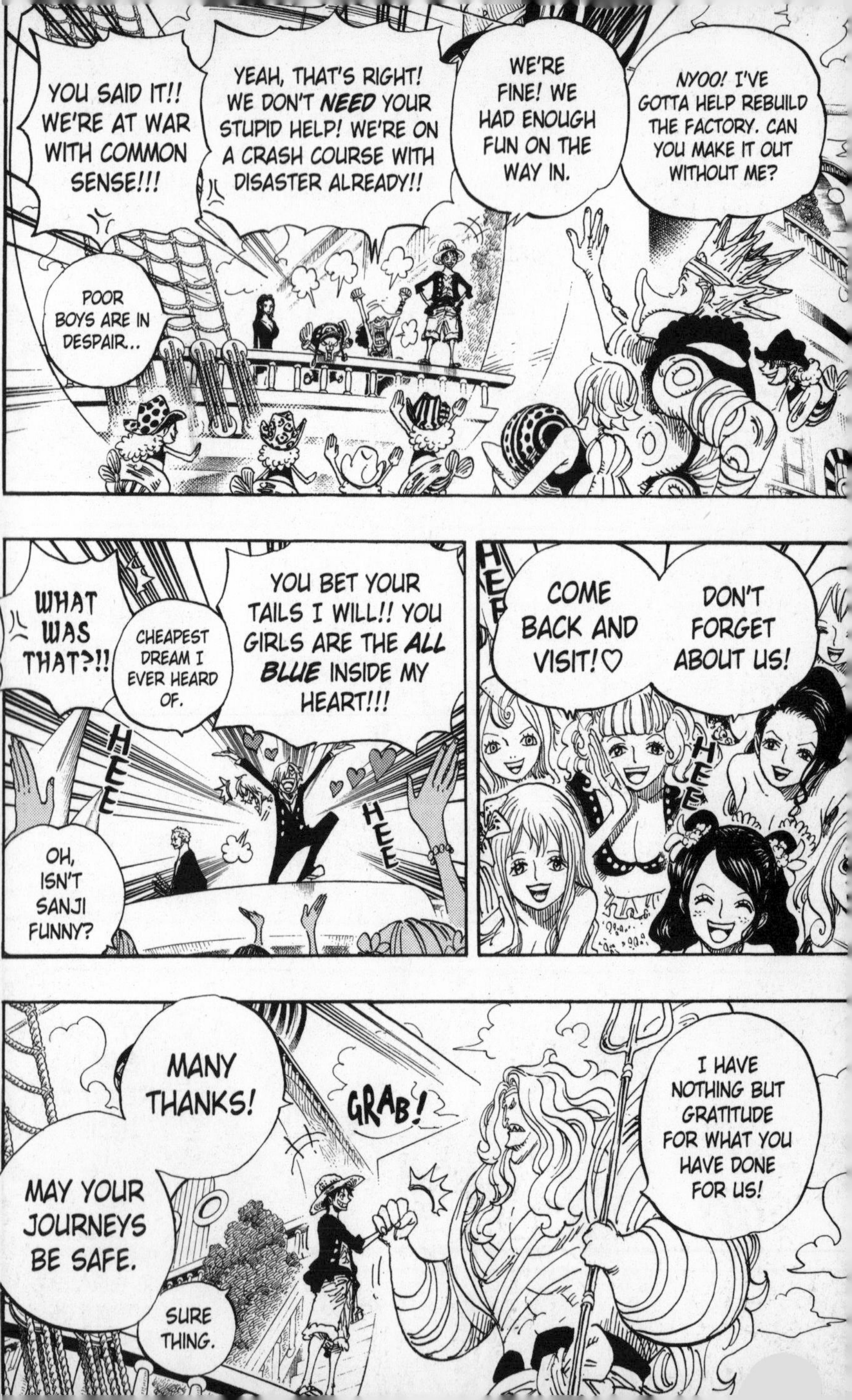
NYOO! I'VE GOTTA HELP REBUILD THE FACTORY. CAN YOU MAKE IT OUT WITHOUT ME?
WE'RE FINE! WE HAD ENOUGH FUN ON THE WAY IN.
YEAH, THAT'S RIGHT! WE DON'T *NEED* YOUR STUPID HELP! WE'RE ON A CRASH COURSE WITH DISASTER ALREADY!!
YOU SAID IT!! WE'RE AT WAR WITH COMMON SENSE!!!
POOR BOYS ARE IN DESPAIR...
DON'T FORGET ABOUT US!
COME BACK AND VISIT!♡
HEE
HEE
HEE
YOU BET YOUR TAILS I WILL!! YOU GIRLS ARE THE ***ALL BLUE*** INSIDE MY HEART!!!
CHEAPEST DREAM I EVER HEARD OF.
WHAT WAS THAT?!!
HEE
HEE
OH, ISN'T SANJI FUNNY?
I HAVE NOTHING BUT GRATITUDE FOR WHAT YOU HAVE DONE FOR US!
GRAB!
MANY THANKS!
MAY YOUR JOURNEYS BE SAFE.
SURE THING.

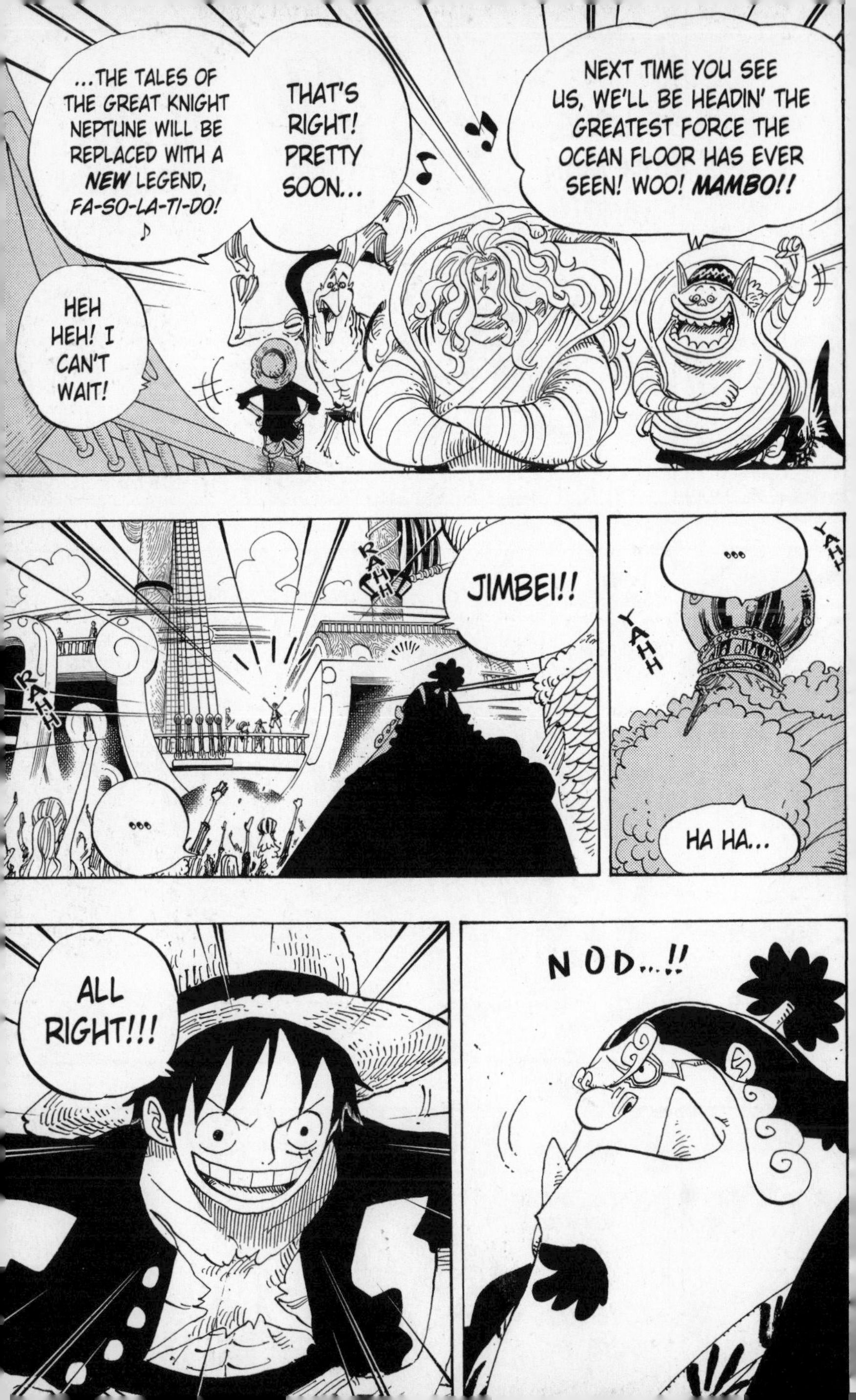
NEXT TIME YOU SEE US, WE'LL BE HEADIN' THE GREATEST FORCE THE OCEAN FLOOR HAS EVER SEEN! WOO! MAMBO!!
THAT'S RIGHT! PRETTY SOON...
...THE TALES OF THE GREAT KNIGHT NEPTUNE WILL BE REPLACED WITH A NEW LEGEND, FA-SO-LA-TI-DO! ♪
HEH HEH! I CAN'T WAIT!
YAHH
...
YAHH
HA HA...
RAHH
JIMBEI!!
RAHH
...
NOD...!!
ALL RIGHT!!!

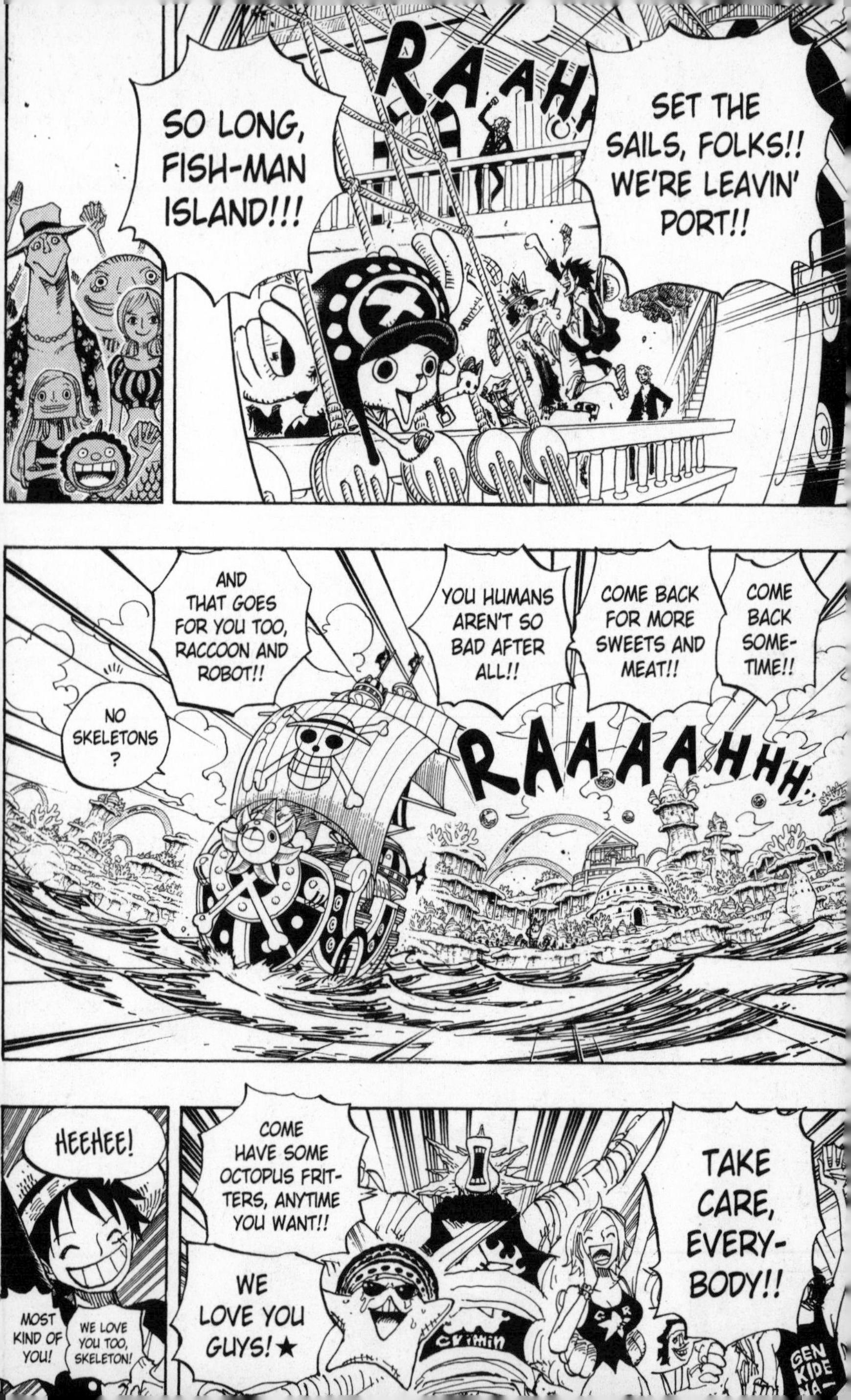
SET THE SAILS, FOLKS!! WE'RE LEAVIN' PORT!!
RAAHH
SO LONG, FISH-MAN ISLAND!!!
COME BACK SOME-TIME!!
COME BACK FOR MORE SWEETS AND MEAT!!
YOU HUMANS AREN'T SO BAD AFTER ALL!!
AND THAT GOES FOR YOU TOO, RACCOON AND ROBOT!!
NO SKELETONS ?
RAAAAHHH
TAKE CARE, EVERY-BODY!!
COME HAVE SOME OCTOPUS FRIT-TERS, ANYTIME YOU WANT!!
WE LOVE YOU GUYS!★
HEEHEE!
WE LOVE YOU TOO, SKELETON!
MOST KIND OF YOU!

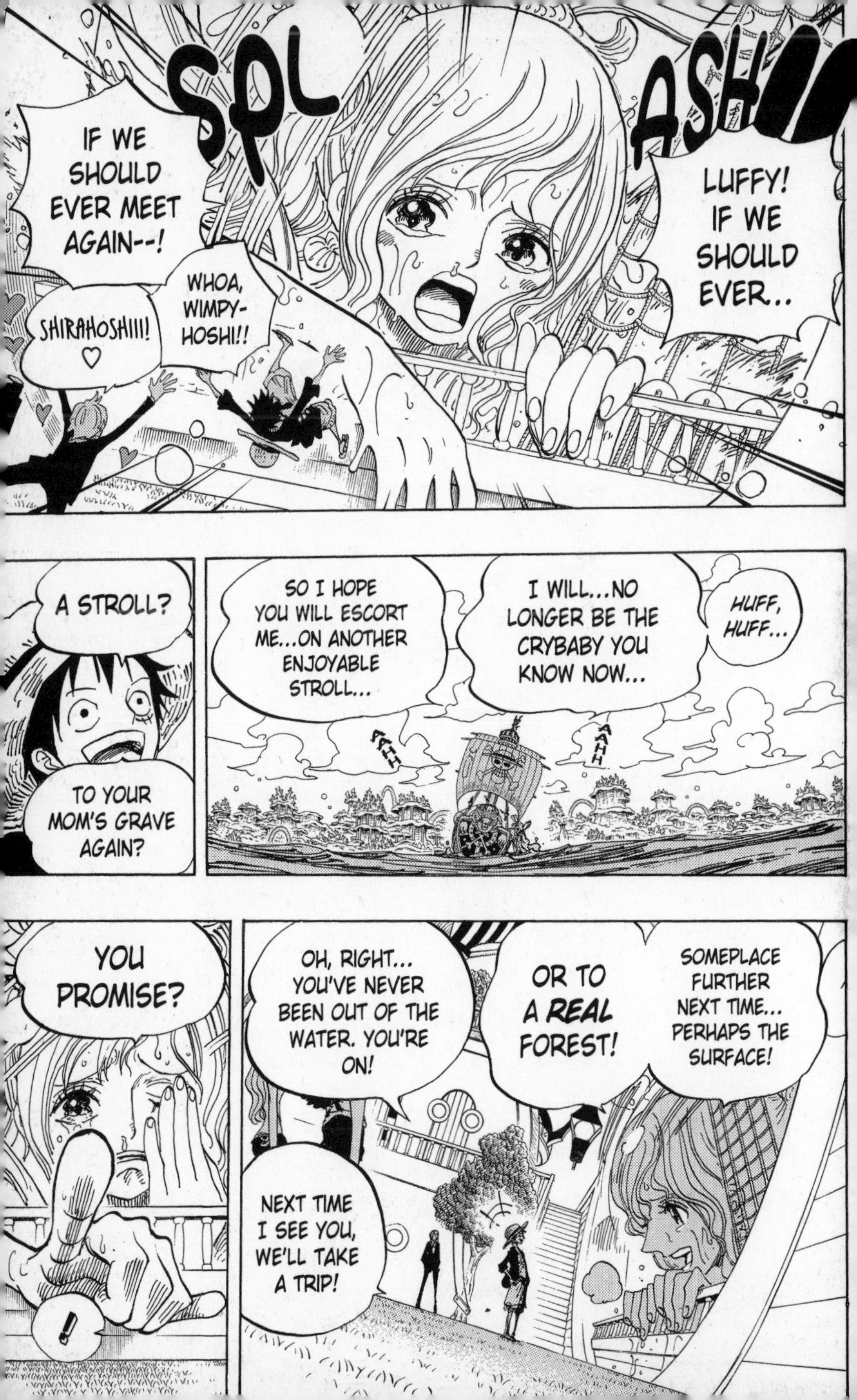

SPL
ASH
LUFFY! IF WE SHOULD EVER...
IF WE SHOULD EVER MEET AGAIN--!
WHOA, WIMPY-HOSHI!!
SHIRAHOSHIIII! ♡
HUFF, HUFF...
I WILL...NO LONGER BE THE CRYBABY YOU KNOW NOW...
SO I HOPE YOU WILL ESCORT ME...ON ANOTHER ENJOYABLE STROLL...
AAHH
AAHH
A STROLL?
TO YOUR MOM'S GRAVE AGAIN?
SOMEPLACE FURTHER NEXT TIME... PERHAPS THE SURFACE!
OR TO A *REAL* FOREST!
OH, RIGHT... YOU'VE NEVER BEEN OUT OF THE WATER. YOU'RE ON!
NEXT TIME I SEE YOU, WE'LL TAKE A TRIP!
YOU PROMISE?
!

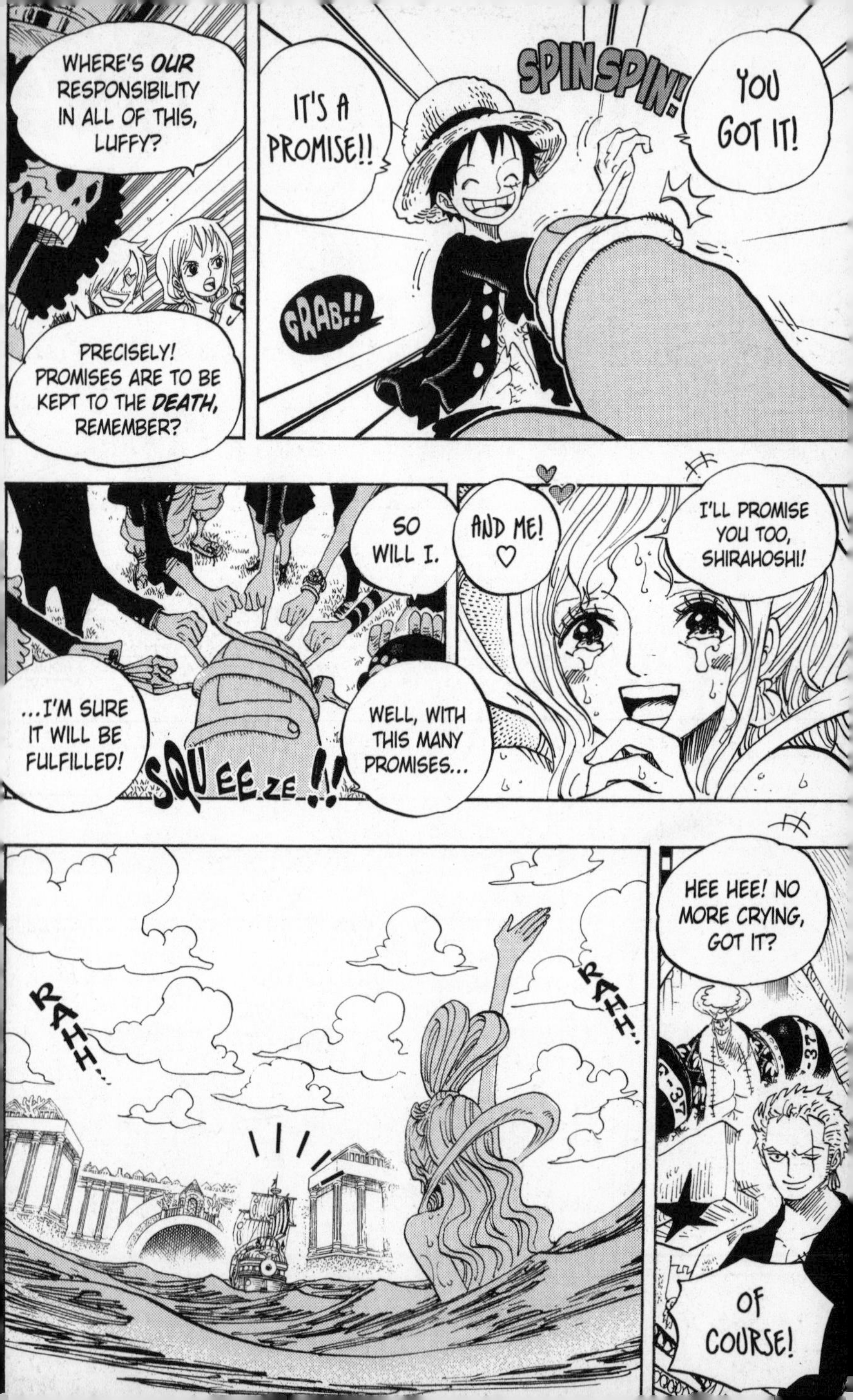
YOU GOT IT!
SPINSPIN!
IT'S A PROMISE!!
GRAB!!
WHERE'S OUR RESPONSIBILITY IN ALL OF THIS, LUFFY?
PRECISELY! PROMISES ARE TO BE KEPT TO THE DEATH, REMEMBER?
I'LL PROMISE YOU TOO, SHIRAHOSHI!
AND ME! ♡
SO WILL I.
WELL, WITH THIS MANY PROMISES...
...I'M SURE IT WILL BE FULFILLED!
SQUEEZE!!
HEE HEE! NO MORE CRYING, GOT IT?
OF COURSE!
RAHH...
RAHH...

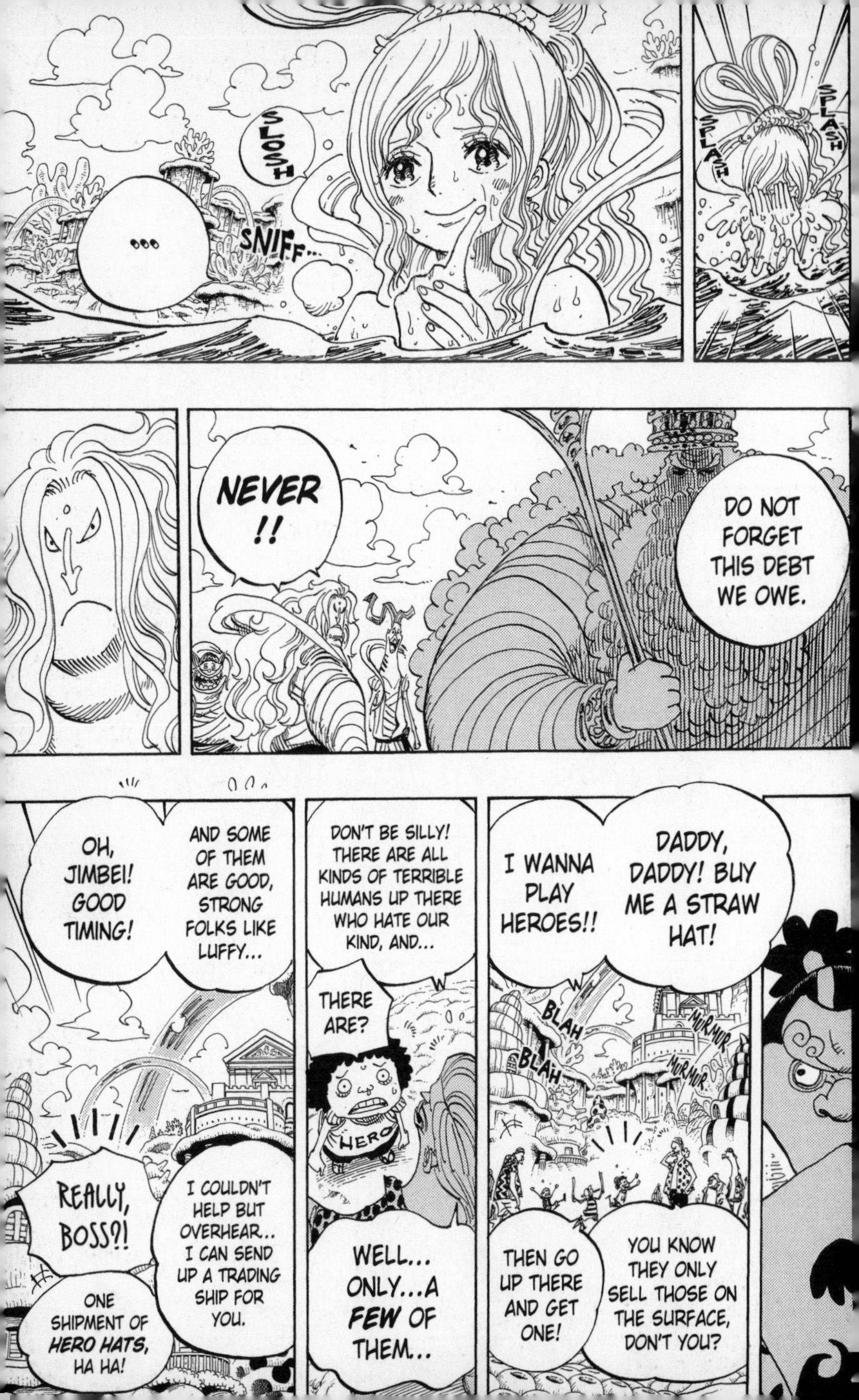
SPLASH
SPLASH
SLOSH
...
SNIFF...
DO NOT FORGET THIS DEBT WE OWE.
NEVER!!
DADDY, DADDY! BUY ME A STRAW HAT!
I WANNA PLAY HEROES!!
MURMUR
MURMUR
BLAH
BLAH
YOU KNOW THEY ONLY SELL THOSE ON THE SURFACE, DON'T YOU?
THEN GO UP THERE AND GET ONE!
DON'T BE SILLY! THERE ARE ALL KINDS OF TERRIBLE HUMANS UP THERE WHO HATE OUR KIND, AND...
THERE ARE?
HERO
WELL... ONLY...A FEW OF THEM...
AND SOME OF THEM ARE GOOD, STRONG FOLKS LIKE LUFFY...
OH, JIMBEI! GOOD TIMING!
REALLY, BOSS?!
I COULDN'T HELP BUT OVERHEAR... I CAN SEND UP A TRADING SHIP FOR YOU.
ONE SHIPMENT OF HERO HATS, HA HA!

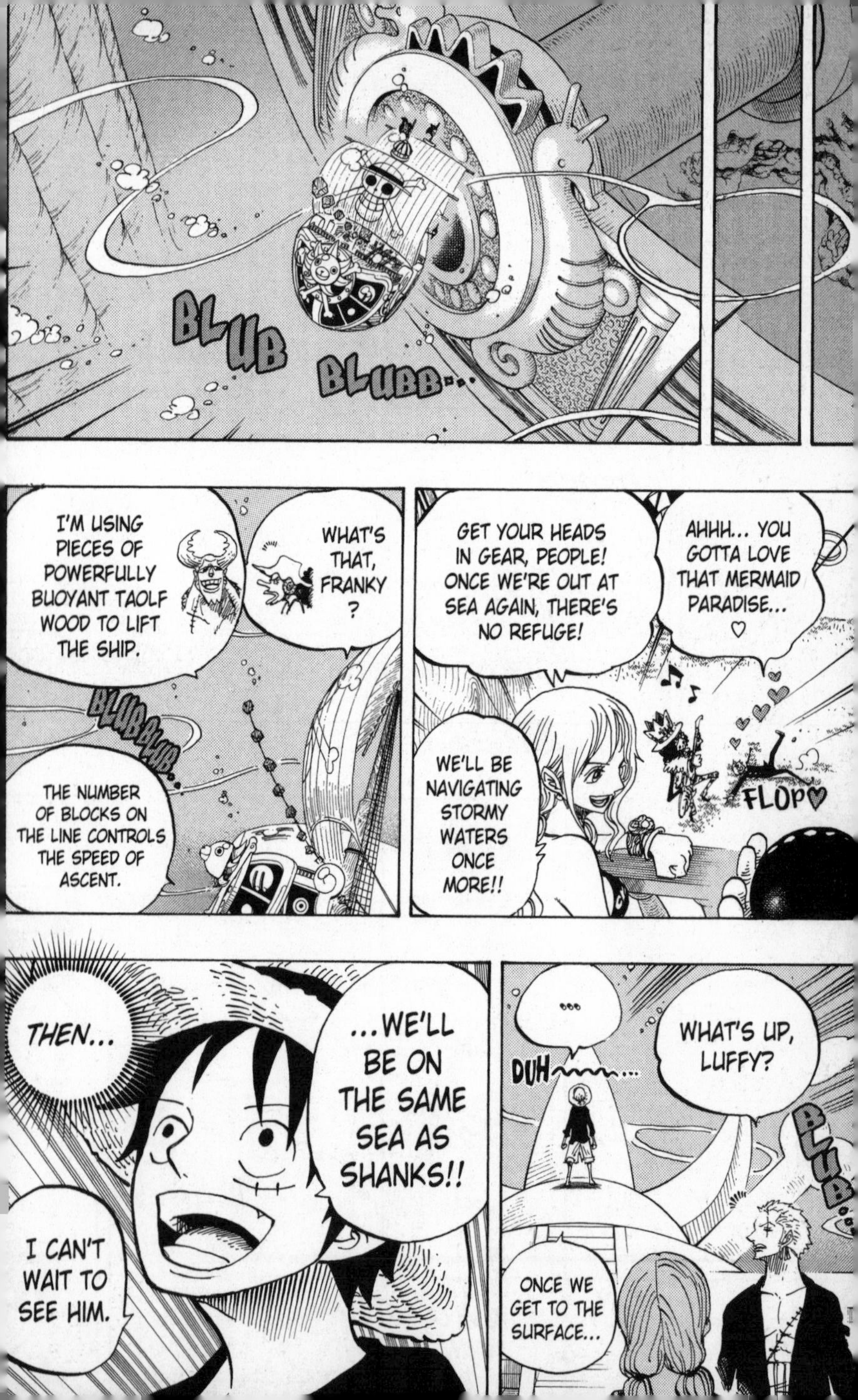
BLUB
BLUBB...
AHHH... YOU GOTTA LOVE THAT MERMAID PARADISE... ♡
GET YOUR HEADS IN GEAR, PEOPLE! ONCE WE'RE OUT AT SEA AGAIN, THERE'S NO REFUGE!
FLOP♡
WE'LL BE NAVIGATING STORMY WATERS ONCE MORE!!
WHAT'S THAT, FRANKY?
I'M USING PIECES OF POWERFULLY BUOYANT TAOLF WOOD TO LIFT THE SHIP.
BLUBBLUB...
THE NUMBER OF BLOCKS ON THE LINE CONTROLS THE SPEED OF ASCENT.
...
WHAT'S UP, LUFFY?
DUH...
BLUB...
ONCE WE GET TO THE SURFACE...
THEN...
...WE'LL BE ON THE SAME SEA AS SHANKS!!
I CAN'T WAIT TO SEE HIM.

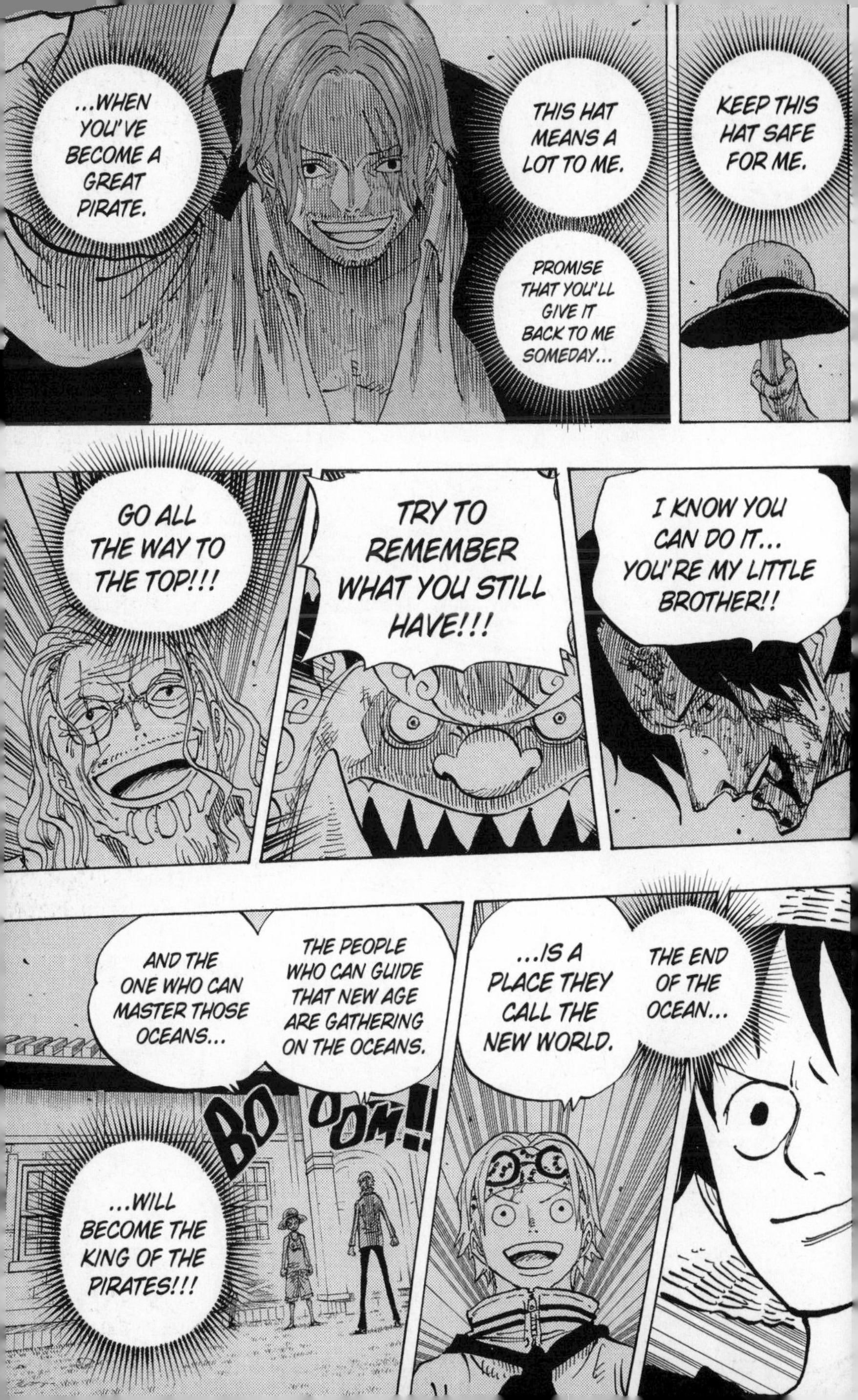
KEEP THIS HAT SAFE FOR ME.
THIS HAT MEANS A LOT TO ME.
PROMISE THAT YOU'LL GIVE IT BACK TO ME SOMEDAY...
...WHEN YOU'VE BECOME A GREAT PIRATE.
I KNOW YOU CAN DO IT... YOU'RE MY LITTLE BROTHER!!
TRY TO REMEMBER WHAT YOU STILL HAVE!!!
GO ALL THE WAY TO THE TOP!!!
THE END OF THE OCEAN...
...IS A PLACE THEY CALL THE NEW WORLD.
THE PEOPLE WHO CAN GUIDE THAT NEW AGE ARE GATHERING ON THE OCEANS.
AND THE ONE WHO CAN MASTER THOSE OCEANS...
BOOOOM!!
...WILL BECOME THE KING OF THE PIRATES!!!

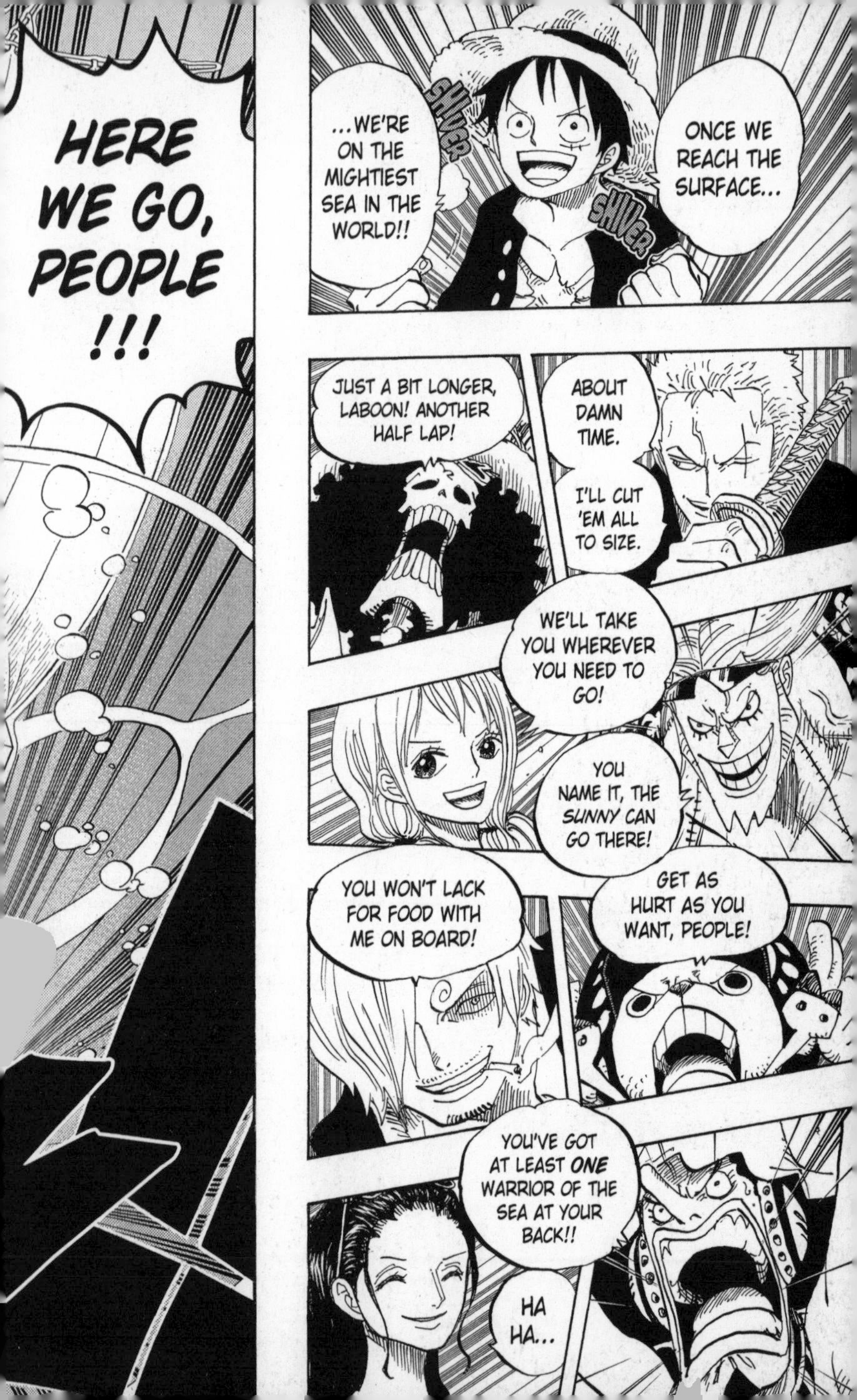
ONCE WE REACH THE SURFACE...
SHIVER
SHIVER
...WE'RE ON THE MIGHTIEST SEA IN THE WORLD!!
ABOUT DAMN TIME.
I'LL CUT 'EM ALL TO SIZE.
JUST A BIT LONGER, LABOON! ANOTHER HALF LAP!
WE'LL TAKE YOU WHEREVER YOU NEED TO GO!
YOU NAME IT, THE *SUNNY* CAN GO THERE!
GET AS HURT AS YOU WANT, PEOPLE!
YOU WON'T LACK FOR FOOD WITH ME ON BOARD!
YOU'VE GOT AT LEAST *ONE* WARRIOR OF THE SEA AT YOUR BACK!!
HA HA...
HERE WE GO, PEOPLE!!!

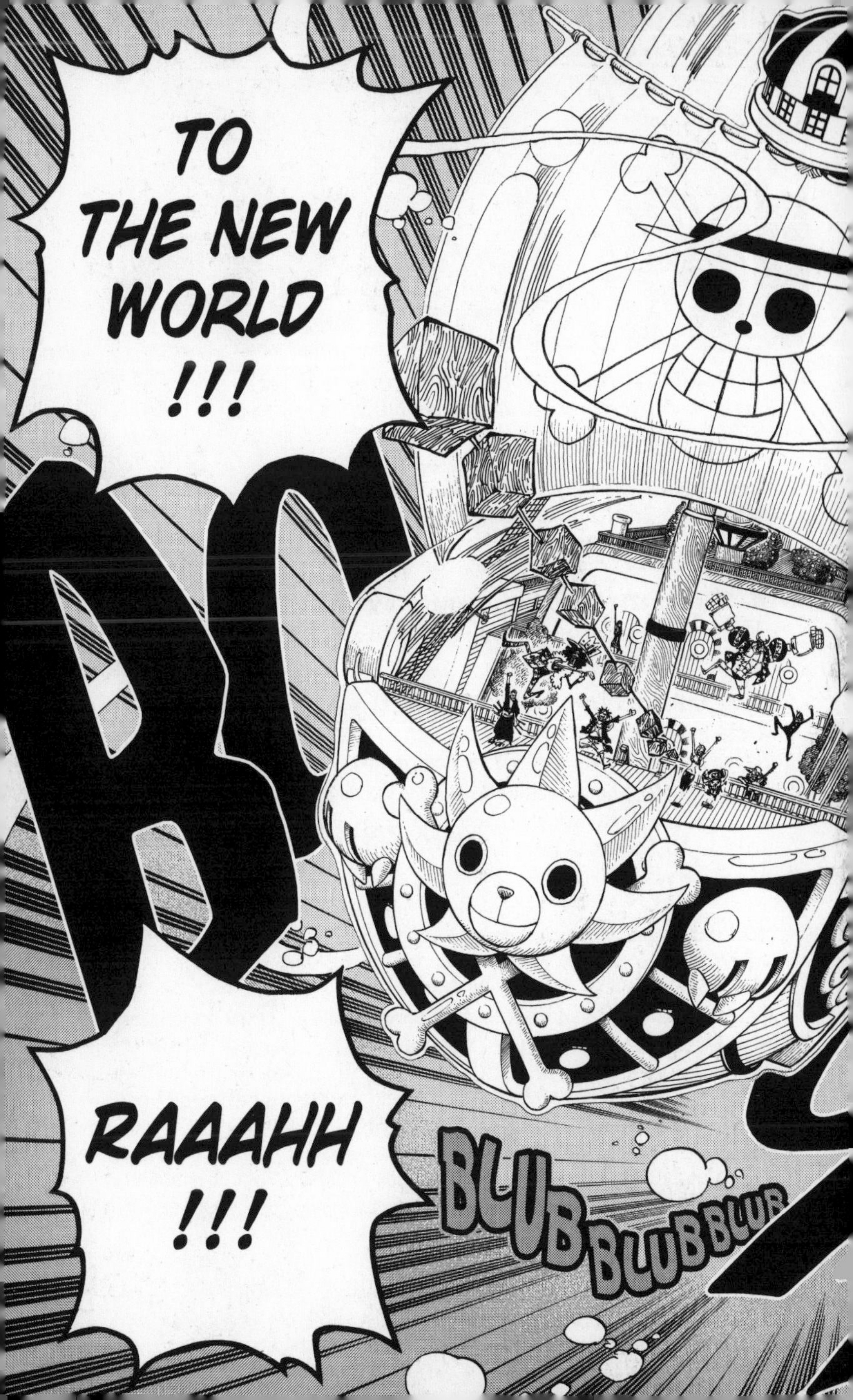
TO THE NEW WORLD !!!
BO
RAAAHH !!!
BLUB BLUB BLUB

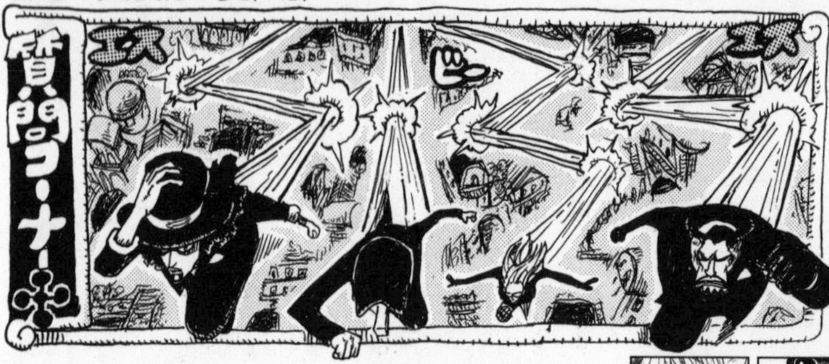
質問コーナー

(Ponio, Aichi)

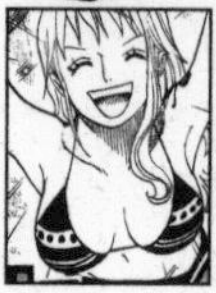

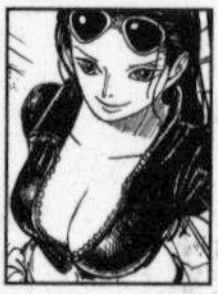

Q: Mr. Odacchi!! You once claimed Nami was an I-cup… Has her bust size changed in the New World? What cup is she now?? Tell us!

--♡Riko♡Emi♡Nanami♡

A: Trust me, I've been getting this question from the moment we came back from the time-skip. It's time to bring an end to this. There's only one man for the job: Sanjiiii!

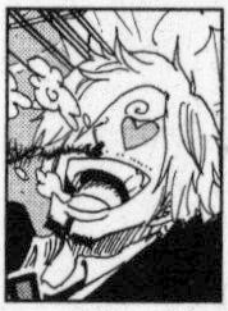

Sanji: You rang?! What's up, you need my bust scope? Okay, time to lock on! Nami and Robin's...Squirt!!♡

A: Sanjiiiiiii!!!

Okay, what cup size do you think Nami and Robin's busts are?

Send me your ideas(^^)!! (←Gave up)

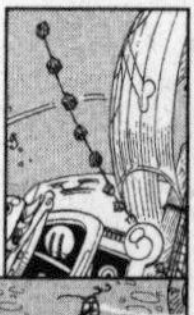

Q: In Chapter 653, Franky mentions special wood that floats really well. It occurred to me, is this related to the incredible floating wood that kept Mr. 3 afloat in water in Chapter 175, back in Alabasta?!✧ What's the answer?!

--Daicha

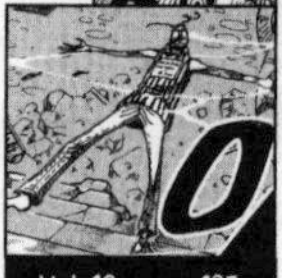

Vol. 19, page 185

A: You noticed? Excellent! In the SBS Corner of Volume 25, I revealed the truth behind Mr. 3's incredible buoyancy despite his Devil Fruit Powers, and this is the same thing. This is what I was talking about back then!! Let me guess...you all thought I was just making it up back then to cover up a mistake, right? Wrong! I already had this entirely...planned out... No, really! Y-y-you gotta believe me!

Q: I've noticed that pretty much all the women in One Piece are well endowed, while the men are all ripped with huge six-packs. My mom says this is the manifestation of the ideal body you wish to have, Mr. Oda. Is that right?

--I Love Marco!!

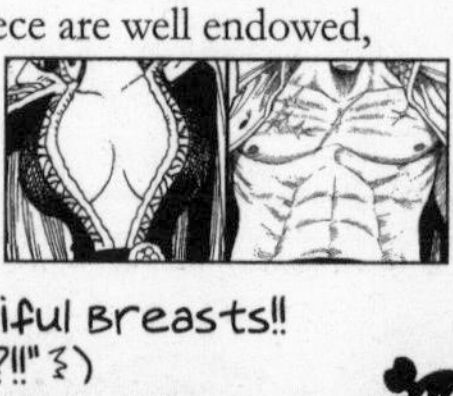

A: That's right. I want to have huge, beautiful breasts!! (Correct reaction: "Not the other kind?!!")

Chaper 654:
A GAM OF WHALES

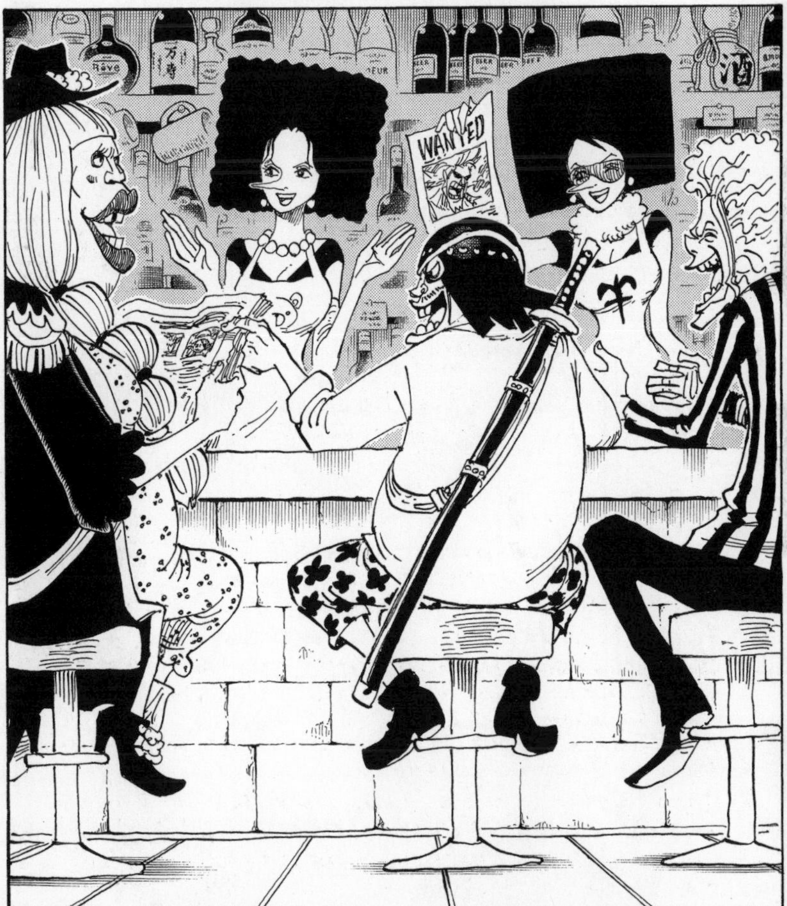
Rêve
WANTED
酒

DECKS OF THE WORLD, VOL. 36
"WATER SEVEN—MOZU AND KIWI'S BAR"

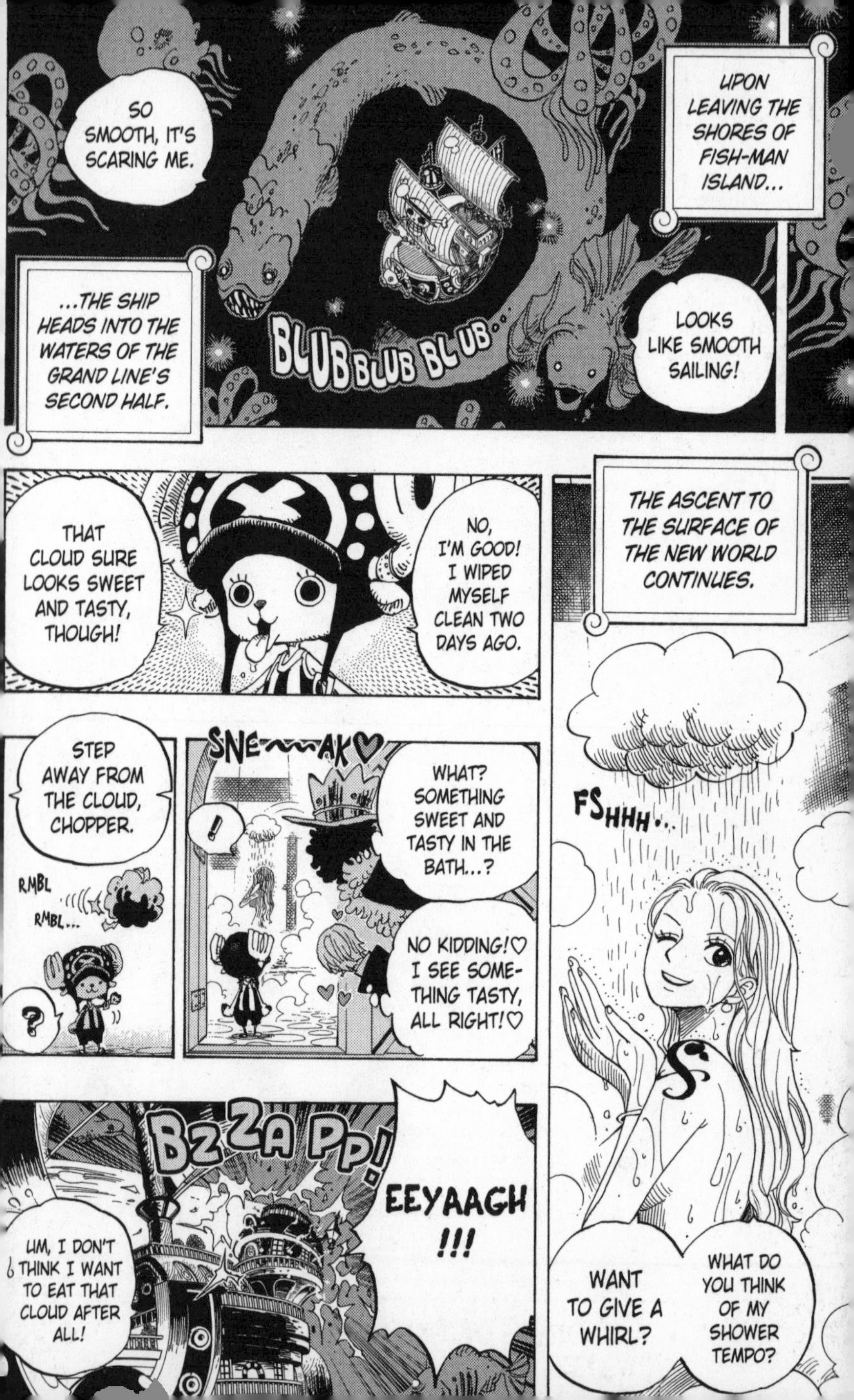
UPON LEAVING THE SHORES OF FISH-MAN ISLAND...
...THE SHIP HEADS INTO THE WATERS OF THE GRAND LINE'S SECOND HALF.
BLUB BLUB BLUB
LOOKS LIKE SMOOTH SAILING!
SO SMOOTH, IT'S SCARING ME.
THE ASCENT TO THE SURFACE OF THE NEW WORLD CONTINUES.
FSHHH...
WHAT DO YOU THINK OF MY SHOWER TEMPO?
WANT TO GIVE A WHIRL?
NO, I'M GOOD! I WIPED MYSELF CLEAN TWO DAYS AGO.
THAT CLOUD SURE LOOKS SWEET AND TASTY, THOUGH!
SNE~~~AK♡
WHAT? SOMETHING SWEET AND TASTY IN THE BATH...?
!
NO KIDDING!♡ I SEE SOMETHING TASTY, ALL RIGHT!♡
STEP AWAY FROM THE CLOUD, CHOPPER.
RMBL
RMBL...
?
EEYAAGH!!!
BZZAPP!
UM, I DON'T THINK I WANT TO EAT THAT CLOUD AFTER ALL!

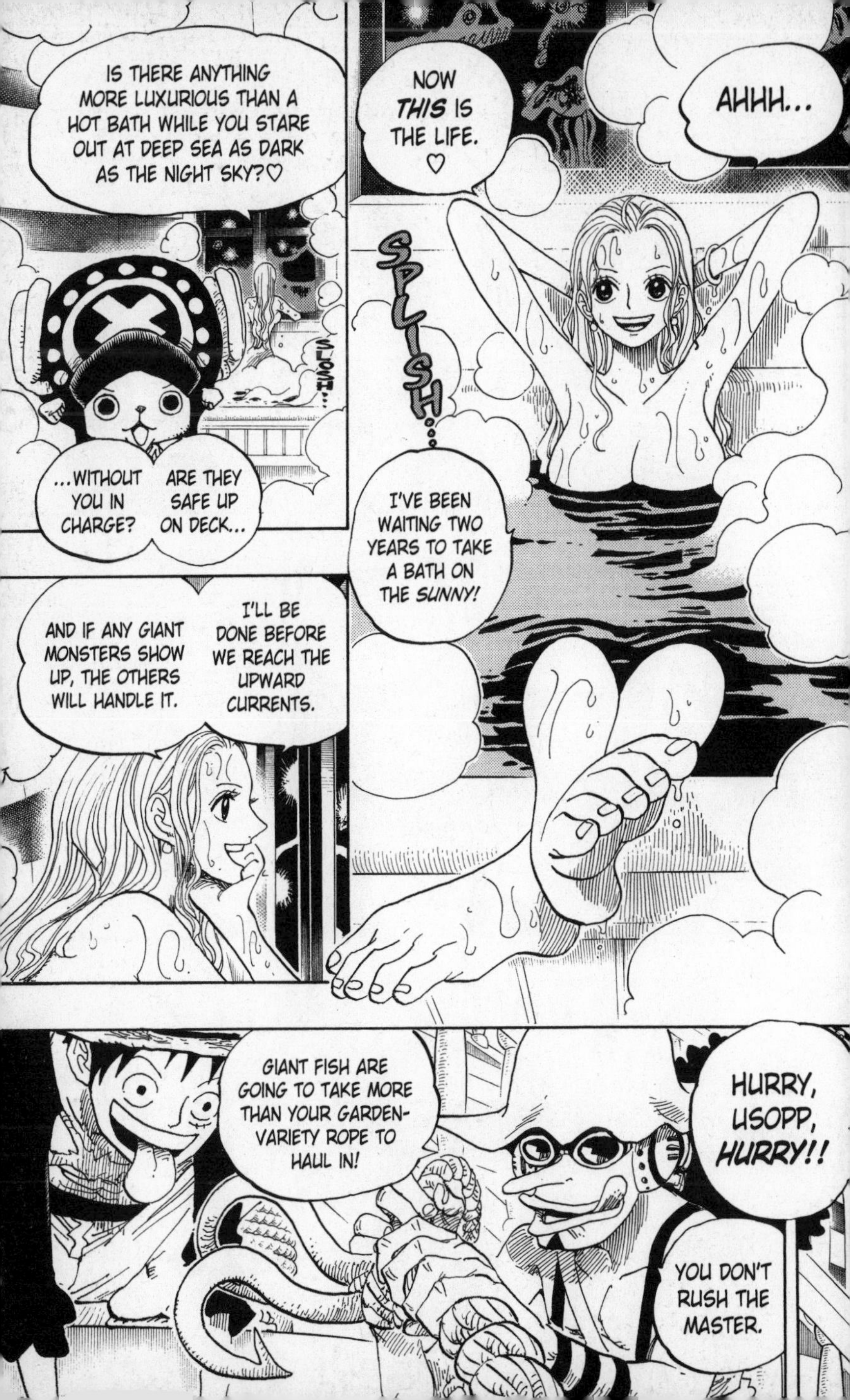
AHHH...
NOW *THIS* IS THE LIFE. ♡
SPLISH...
I'VE BEEN WAITING TWO YEARS TO TAKE A BATH ON THE *SUNNY*!
IS THERE ANYTHING MORE LUXURIOUS THAN A HOT BATH WHILE YOU STARE OUT AT DEEP SEA AS DARK AS THE NIGHT SKY?♡
SLOSH!
ARE THEY SAFE UP ON DECK...
...WITHOUT YOU IN CHARGE?
I'LL BE DONE BEFORE WE REACH THE UPWARD CURRENTS.
AND IF ANY GIANT MONSTERS SHOW UP, THE OTHERS WILL HANDLE IT.
HURRY, USOPP, *HURRY!!*
GIANT FISH ARE GOING TO TAKE MORE THAN YOUR GARDEN-VARIETY ROPE TO HAUL IN!
YOU DON'T RUSH THE MASTER.

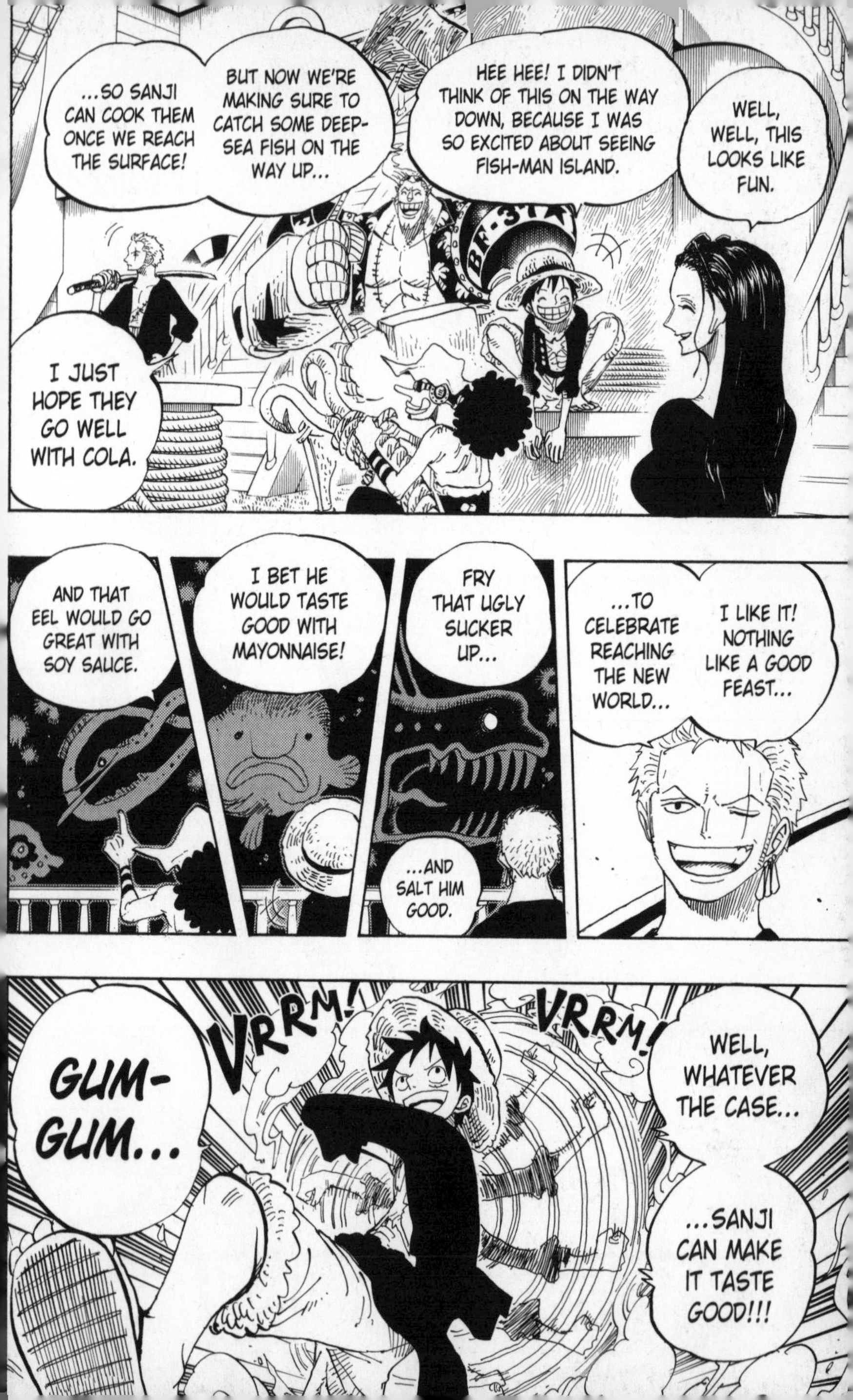
WELL, WELL, THIS LOOKS LIKE FUN.
HEE HEE! I DIDN'T THINK OF THIS ON THE WAY DOWN, BECAUSE I WAS SO EXCITED ABOUT SEEING FISH-MAN ISLAND.
BUT NOW WE'RE MAKING SURE TO CATCH SOME DEEP-SEA FISH ON THE WAY UP...
...SO SANJI CAN COOK THEM ONCE WE REACH THE SURFACE!
I JUST HOPE THEY GO WELL WITH COLA.
I LIKE IT! NOTHING LIKE A GOOD FEAST...
...TO CELEBRATE REACHING THE NEW WORLD...
FRY THAT UGLY SUCKER UP...
...AND SALT HIM GOOD.
I BET HE WOULD TASTE GOOD WITH MAYONNAISE!
AND THAT EEL WOULD GO GREAT WITH SOY SAUCE.
WELL, WHATEVER THE CASE...
...SANJI CAN MAKE IT TASTE GOOD!!!
VRRM!
VRRM!
GUM-GUM...

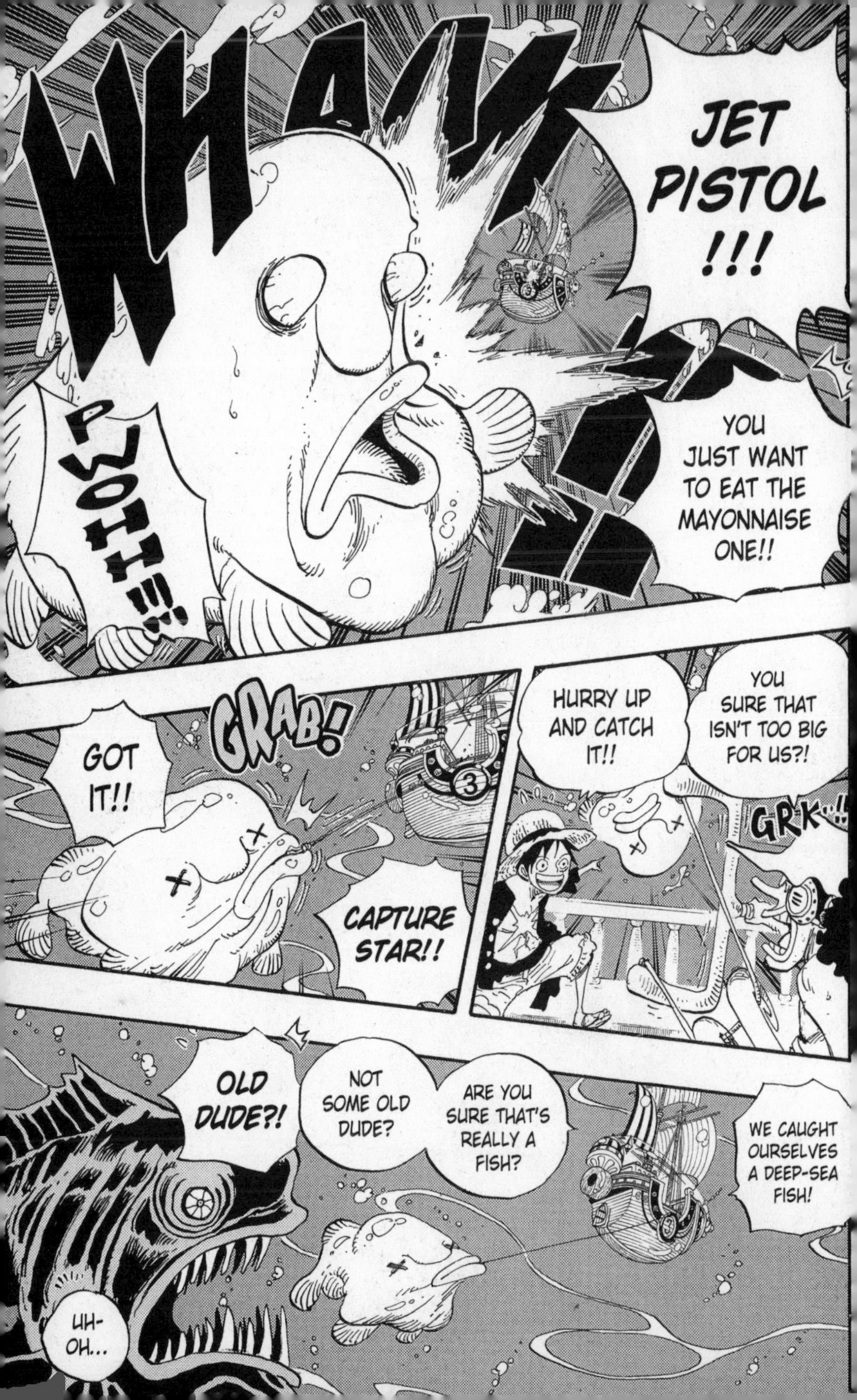
JET PISTOL!!!
WHAM
YOU JUST WANT TO EAT THE MAYONNAISE ONE!!
PWOHH!!!
YOU SURE THAT ISN'T TOO BIG FOR US?!
HURRY UP AND CATCH IT!!
GRK..!!
GRAB!
GOT IT!!
CAPTURE STAR!!
WE CAUGHT OURSELVES A DEEP-SEA FISH!
ARE YOU SURE THAT'S REALLY A FISH?
NOT SOME OLD DUDE?
OLD DUDE?!
UH-OH...

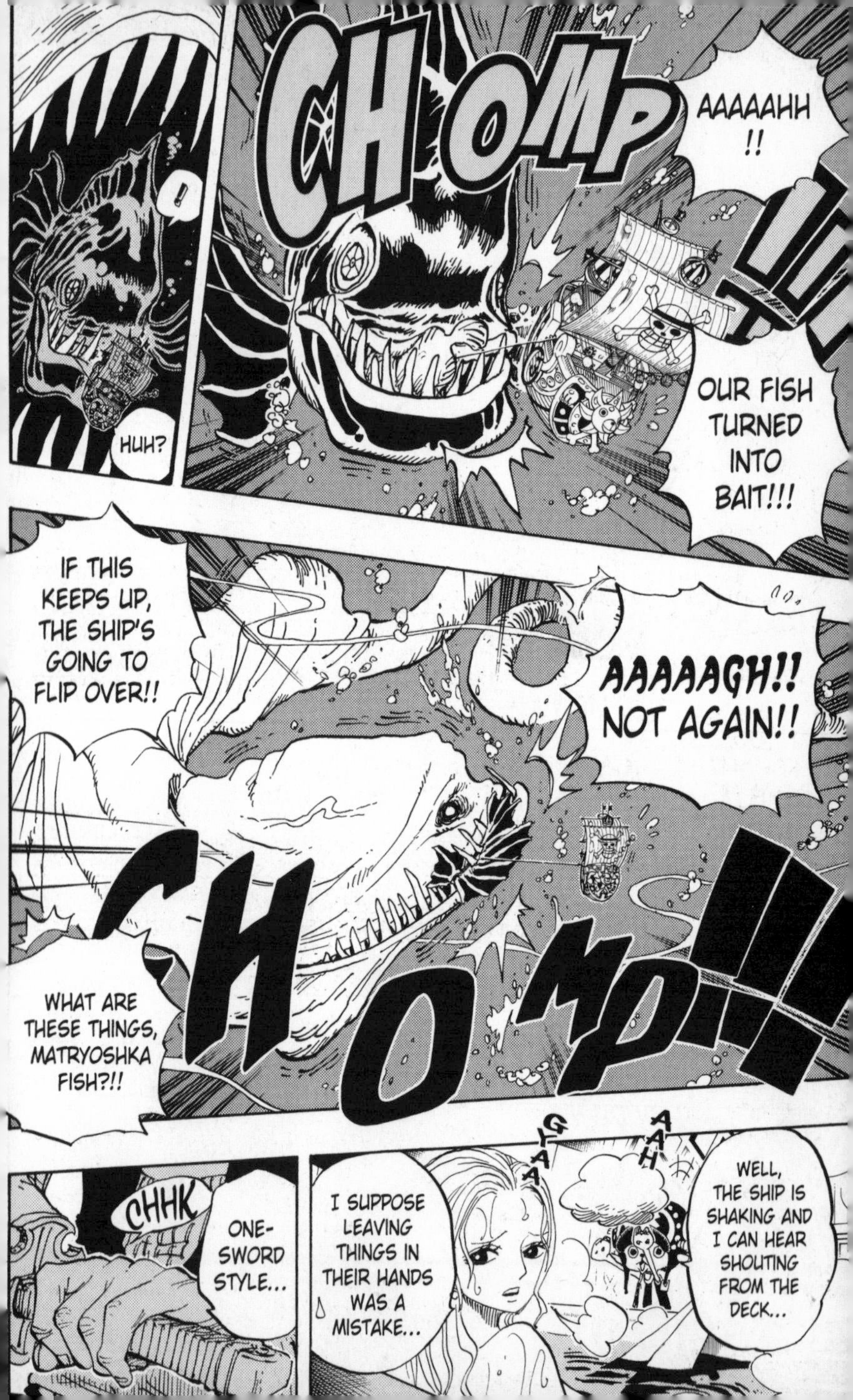
AAAAAHH !!
CHOMP
OUR FISH TURNED INTO BAIT!!!
!
HUH?
AAAAAGH!! NOT AGAIN!!
IF THIS KEEPS UP, THE SHIP'S GOING TO FLIP OVER!!
CHOMP!!
WHAT ARE THESE THINGS, MATRYOSHKA FISH?!!
WELL, THE SHIP IS SHAKING AND I CAN HEAR SHOUTING FROM THE DECK...
AAAH
GYAAA
I SUPPOSE LEAVING THINGS IN THEIR HANDS WAS A MISTAKE...
CHHK
ONE-SWORD STYLE...

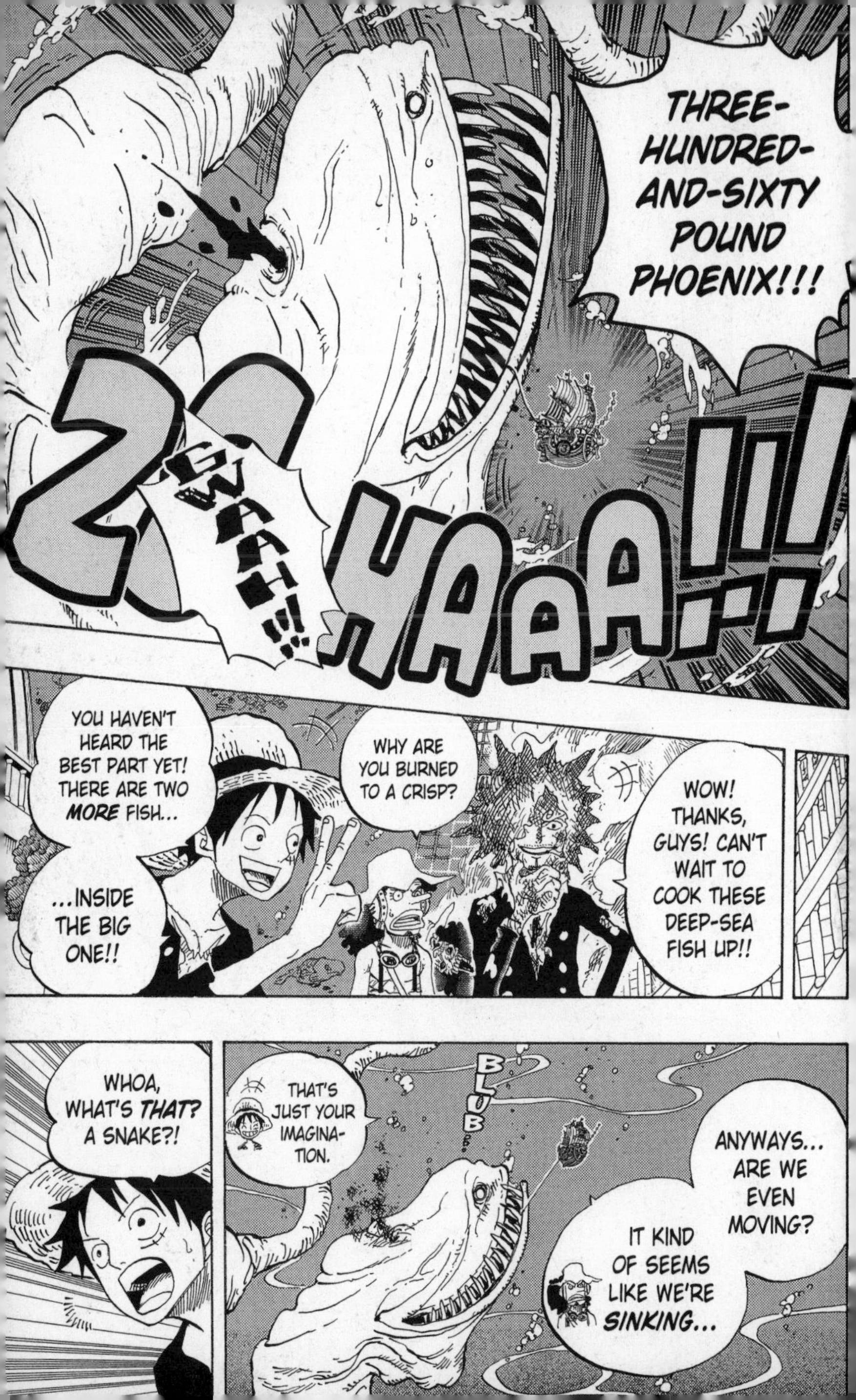
THREE-HUNDRED-AND-SIXTY POUND PHOENIX!!!
GWAAAH!!!
Z HAAA!!!
WOW! THANKS, GUYS! CAN'T WAIT TO COOK THESE DEEP-SEA FISH UP!!
WHY ARE YOU BURNED TO A CRISP?
YOU HAVEN'T HEARD THE BEST PART YET! THERE ARE TWO *MORE* FISH...
...INSIDE THE BIG ONE!!
BLUB...
ANYWAYS... ARE WE EVEN MOVING?
IT KIND OF SEEMS LIKE WE'RE *SINKING*...
THAT'S JUST YOUR IMAGINATION.
WHOA, WHAT'S *THAT*? A SNAKE?!

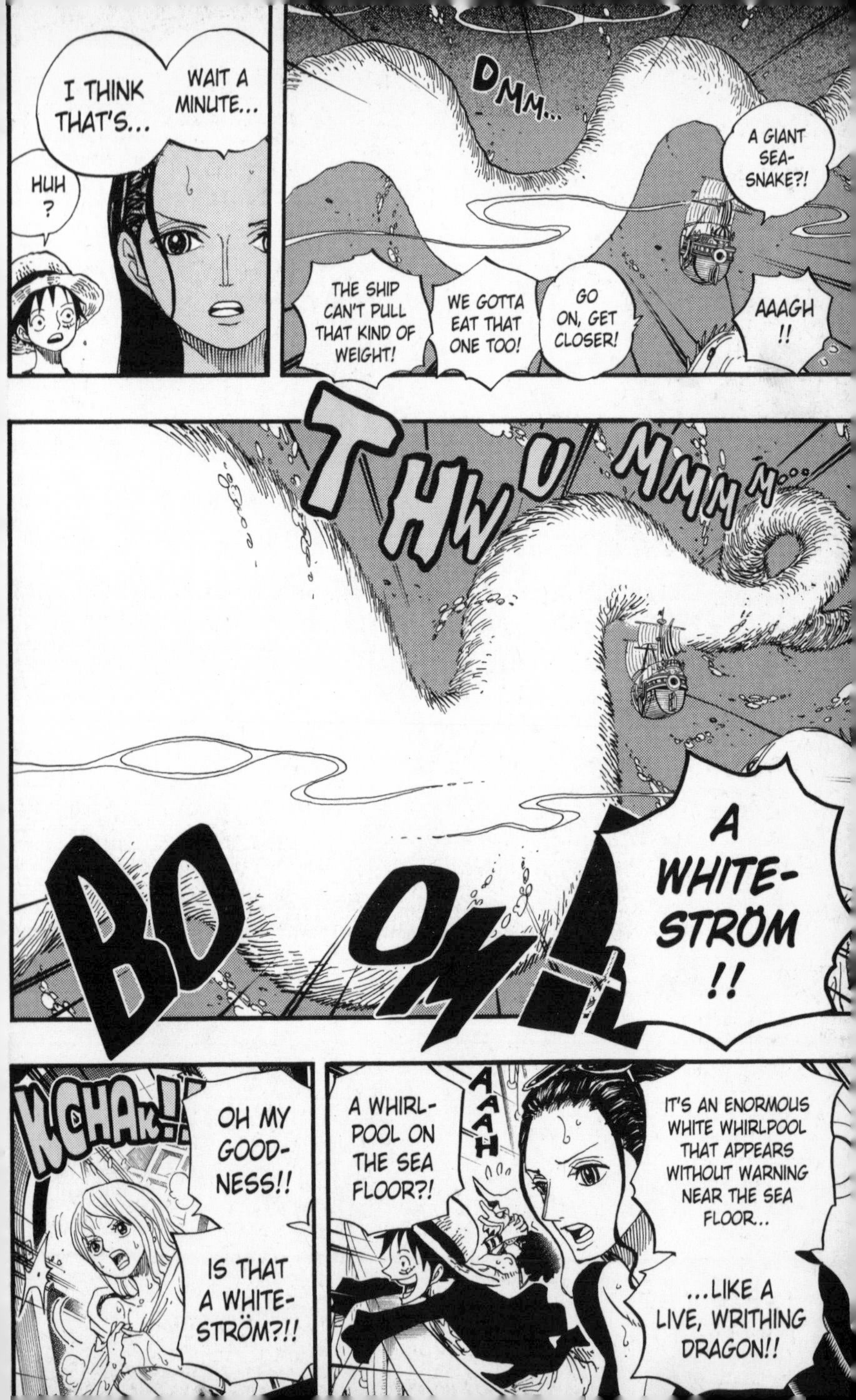
DMM...
A GIANT SEA-SNAKE?!
AAAGH!!
GO ON, GET CLOSER!
WE GOTTA EAT THAT ONE TOO!
THE SHIP CAN'T PULL THAT KIND OF WEIGHT!
WAIT A MINUTE...
I THINK THAT'S...
HUH?
THWUMMMM...
A WHITE-STRÖM!!
BOOM
IT'S AN ENORMOUS WHITE WHIRLPOOL THAT APPEARS WITHOUT WARNING NEAR THE SEA FLOOR...
...LIKE A LIVE, WRITHING DRAGON!!
AAAH
A WHIRL-POOL ON THE SEA FLOOR?!
KCHAK!!
OH MY GOOD-NESS!!
IS THAT A WHITE-STRÖM?!!

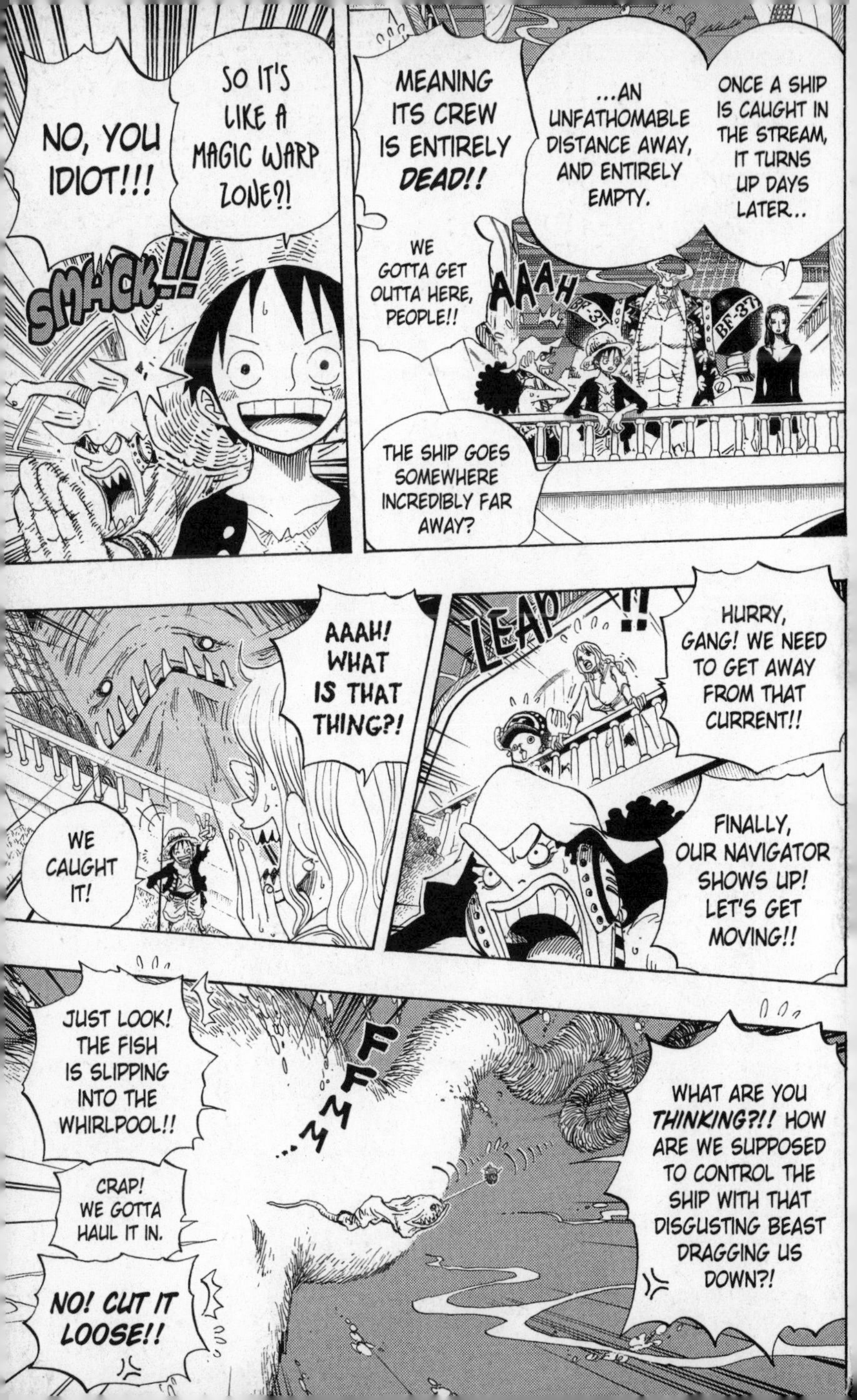
ONCE A SHIP IS CAUGHT IN THE STREAM, IT TURNS UP DAYS LATER...
...AN UNFATHOMABLE DISTANCE AWAY, AND ENTIRELY EMPTY.
MEANING ITS CREW IS ENTIRELY *DEAD!!*
AAAH
WE GOTTA GET OUTTA HERE, PEOPLE!!
THE SHIP GOES SOMEWHERE INCREDIBLY FAR AWAY?
SO IT'S LIKE A MAGIC WARP ZONE?!
NO, YOU IDIOT!!!
SMACK!!
HURRY, GANG! WE NEED TO GET AWAY FROM THAT CURRENT!!
LEAP!!
FINALLY, OUR NAVIGATOR SHOWS UP! LET'S GET MOVING!!
AAAH! WHAT **IS** THAT THING?!
WE CAUGHT IT!
WHAT ARE YOU *THINKING?!!* HOW ARE WE SUPPOSED TO CONTROL THE SHIP WITH THAT DISGUSTING BEAST DRAGGING US DOWN?!
...FFMM
JUST LOOK! THE FISH IS SLIPPING INTO THE WHIRLPOOL!!
CRAP! WE GOTTA HAUL IT IN.
NO! CUT IT LOOSE!!

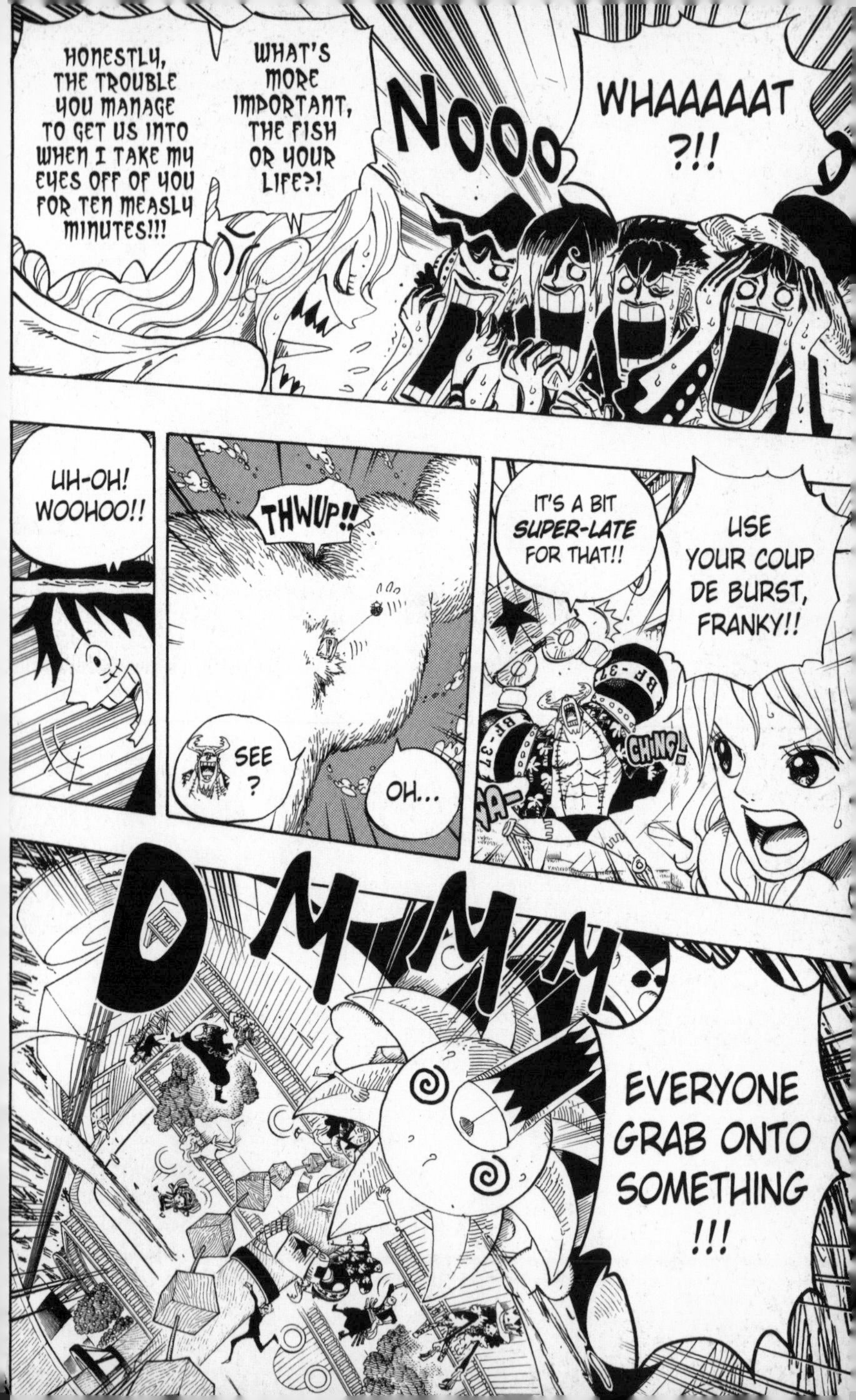
WHAAAAAT ?!!
NOOO
WHAT'S MORE IMPORTANT, THE FISH OR YOUR LIFE?!
HONESTLY, THE TROUBLE YOU MANAGE TO GET US INTO WHEN I TAKE MY EYES OFF OF YOU FOR TEN MEASLY MINUTES!!!
USE YOUR COUP DE BURST, FRANKY!!
IT'S A BIT SUPER-LATE FOR THAT!!
CHING!
GA-
THWUP!!
OH...
SEE ?
UH-OH! WOOHOO!!
DMMM
EVERYONE GRAB ONTO SOMETHING !!!

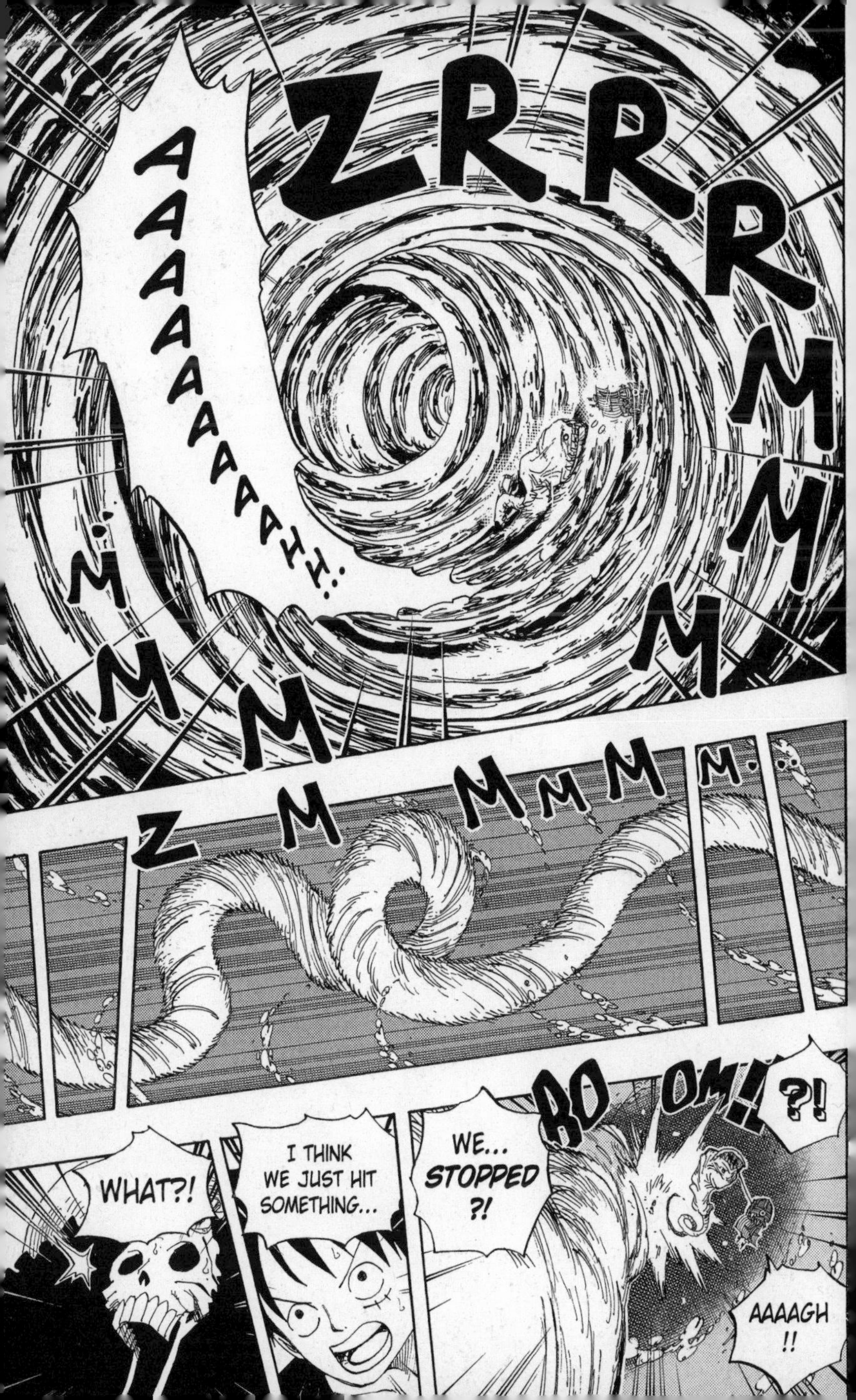
ZRRRRMMMMMM
AAAAAAAAAAAH!!
ZMMMMMM
?!
BOOM!!
AAAAGH !!
WE... STOPPED ?!
I THINK WE JUST HIT SOMETHING...
WHAT?!

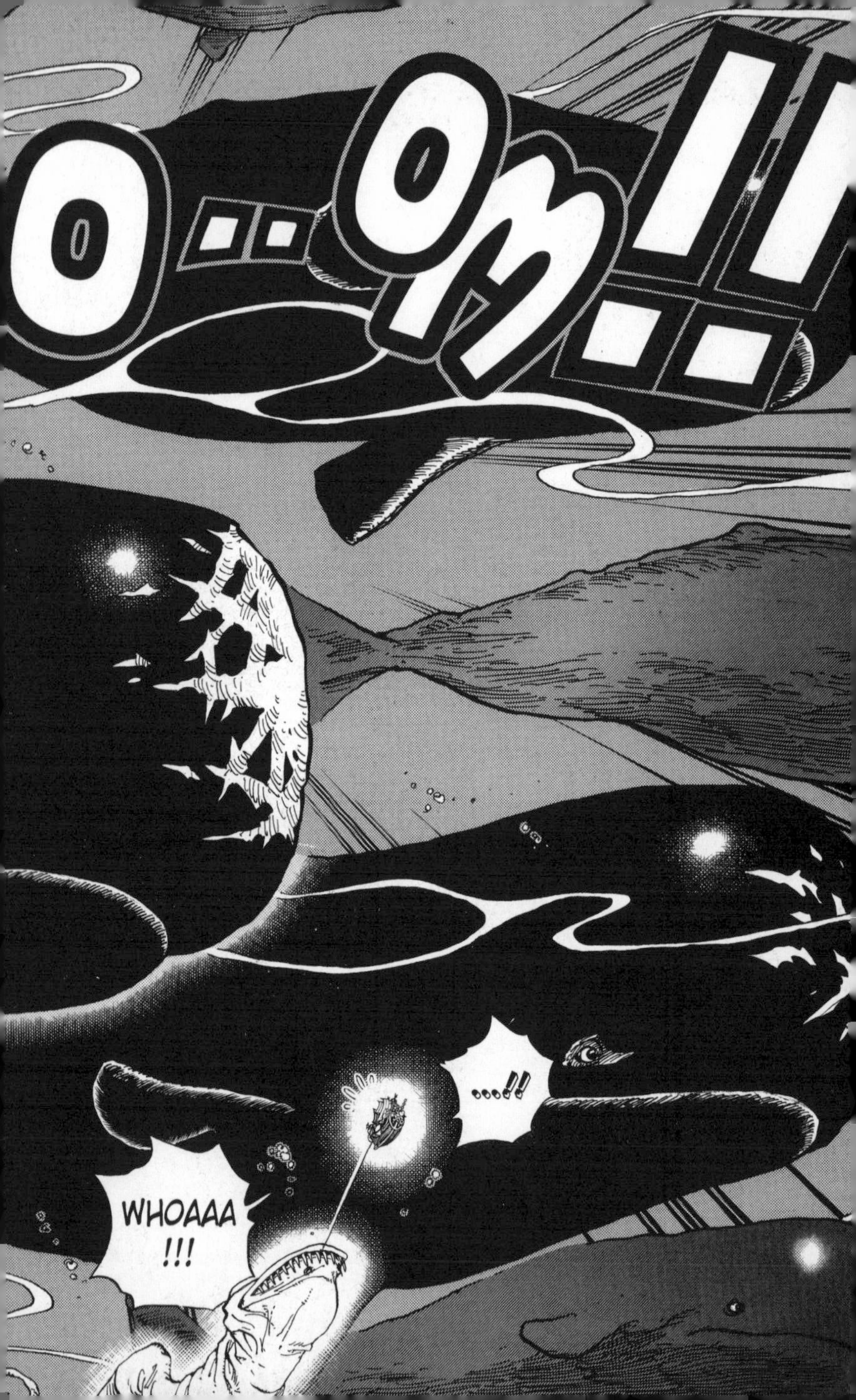
O..OM!!
...!!
WHOAAA !!!

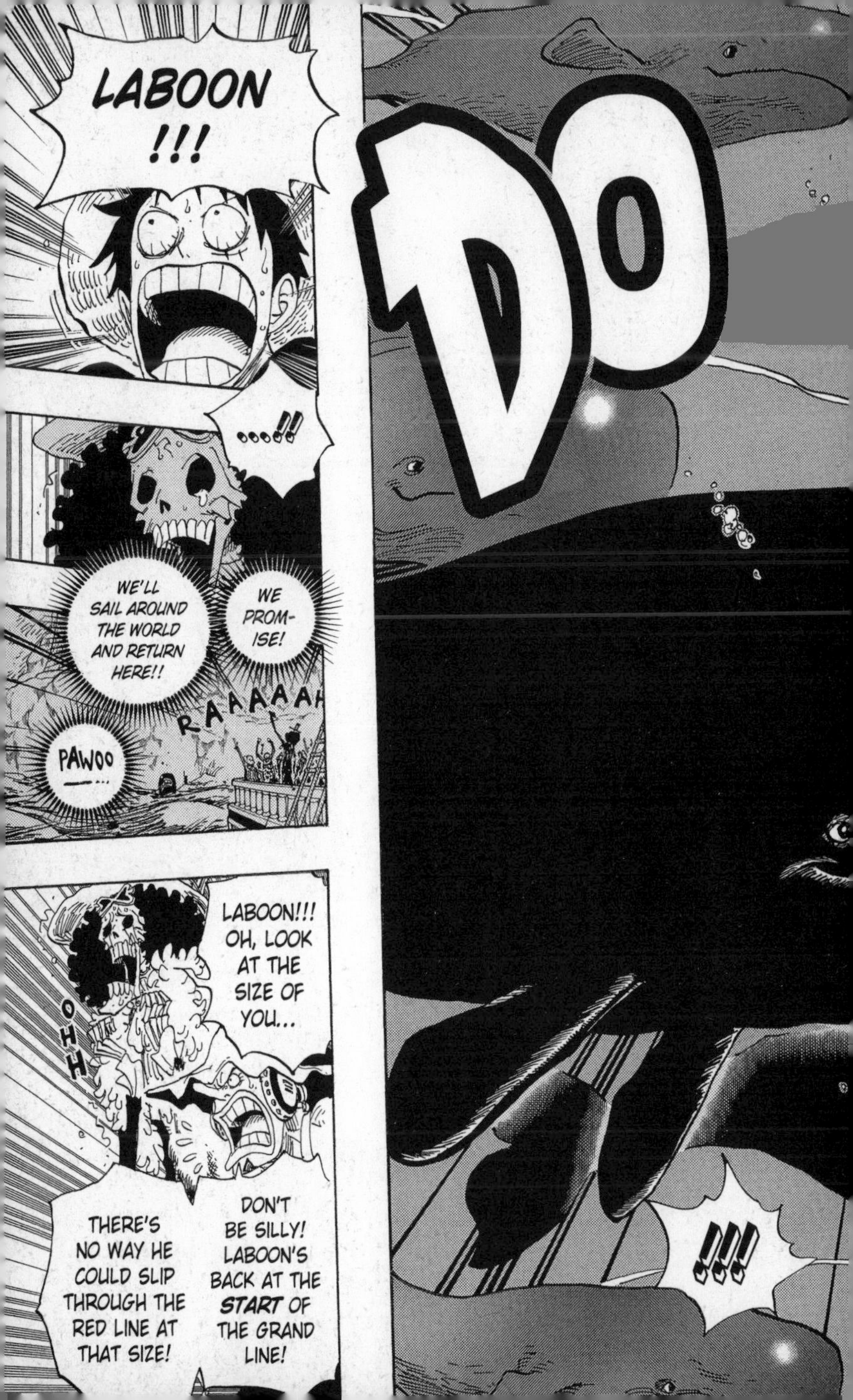
DO
!!!
LABOON !!!
....!!
WE PROMISE!
WE'LL SAIL AROUND THE WORLD AND RETURN HERE!!
RAAAAAH
PAWOO —...
LABOON!!! OH, LOOK AT THE SIZE OF YOU...
OHH
DON'T BE SILLY! LABOON'S BACK AT THE START OF THE GRAND LINE!
THERE'S NO WAY HE COULD SLIP THROUGH THE RED LINE AT THAT SIZE!

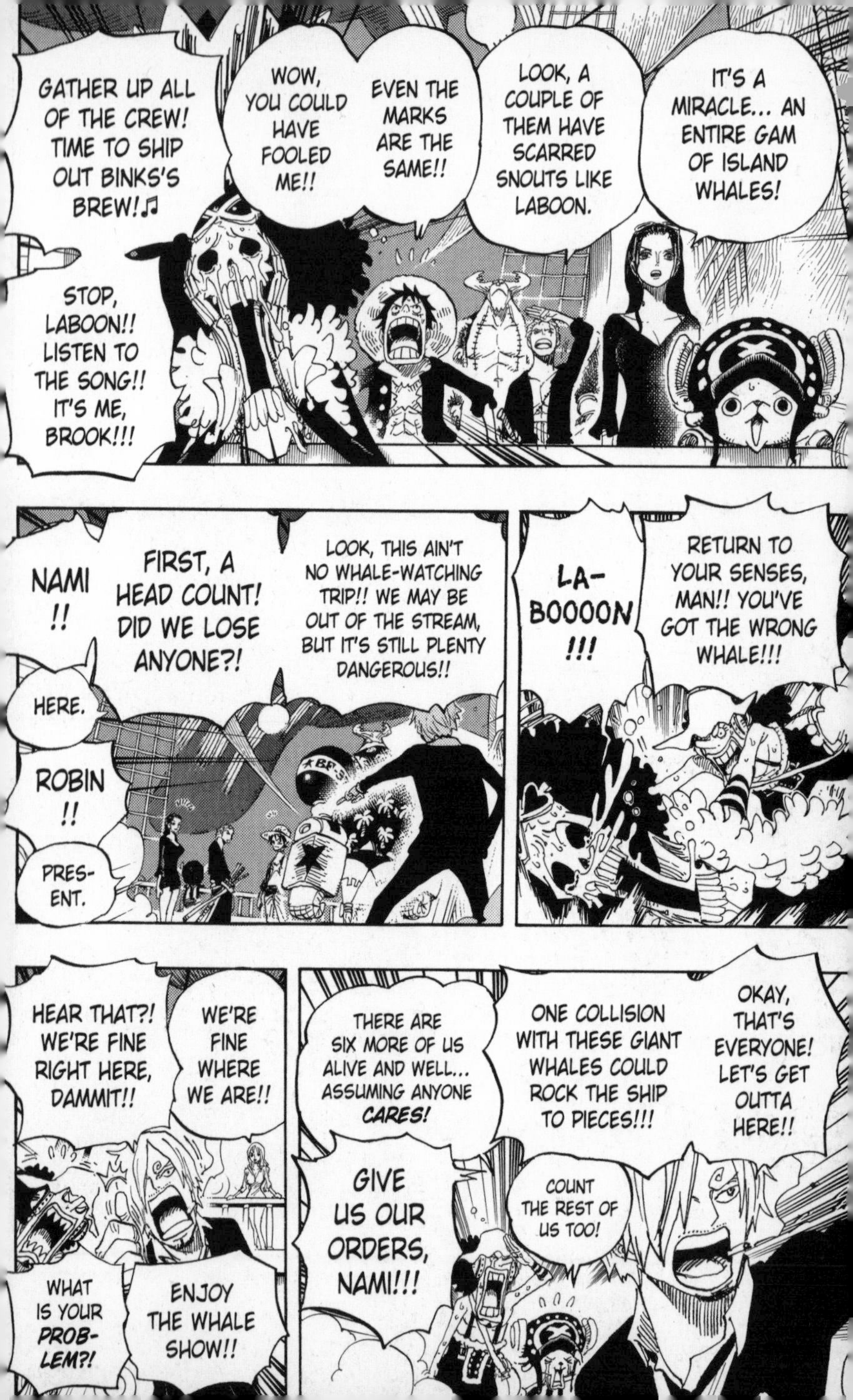
IT'S A MIRACLE... AN ENTIRE GAM OF ISLAND WHALES!
LOOK, A COUPLE OF THEM HAVE SCARRED SNOUTS LIKE LABOON.
EVEN THE MARKS ARE THE SAME!!
WOW, YOU COULD HAVE FOOLED ME!!
GATHER UP ALL OF THE CREW! TIME TO SHIP OUT BINKS'S BREW!♫
STOP, LABOON!! LISTEN TO THE SONG!! IT'S ME, BROOK!!!
RETURN TO YOUR SENSES, MAN!! YOU'VE GOT THE WRONG WHALE!!!
LA-BOOOON!!!
LOOK, THIS AIN'T NO WHALE-WATCHING TRIP!! WE MAY BE OUT OF THE STREAM, BUT IT'S STILL PLENTY DANGEROUS!!
FIRST, A HEAD COUNT! DID WE LOSE ANYONE?!
NAMI!!
HERE.
ROBIN!!
PRESENT.
OKAY, THAT'S EVERYONE! LET'S GET OUTTA HERE!!
ONE COLLISION WITH THESE GIANT WHALES COULD ROCK THE SHIP TO PIECES!!!
THERE ARE SIX MORE OF US ALIVE AND WELL... ASSUMING ANYONE *CARES!*
COUNT THE REST OF US TOO!
GIVE US OUR ORDERS, NAMI!!!
WE'RE FINE WHERE WE ARE!!
HEAR THAT?! WE'RE FINE RIGHT HERE, DAMMIT!!
ENJOY THE WHALE SHOW!!
WHAT IS YOUR *PROBLEM?!*

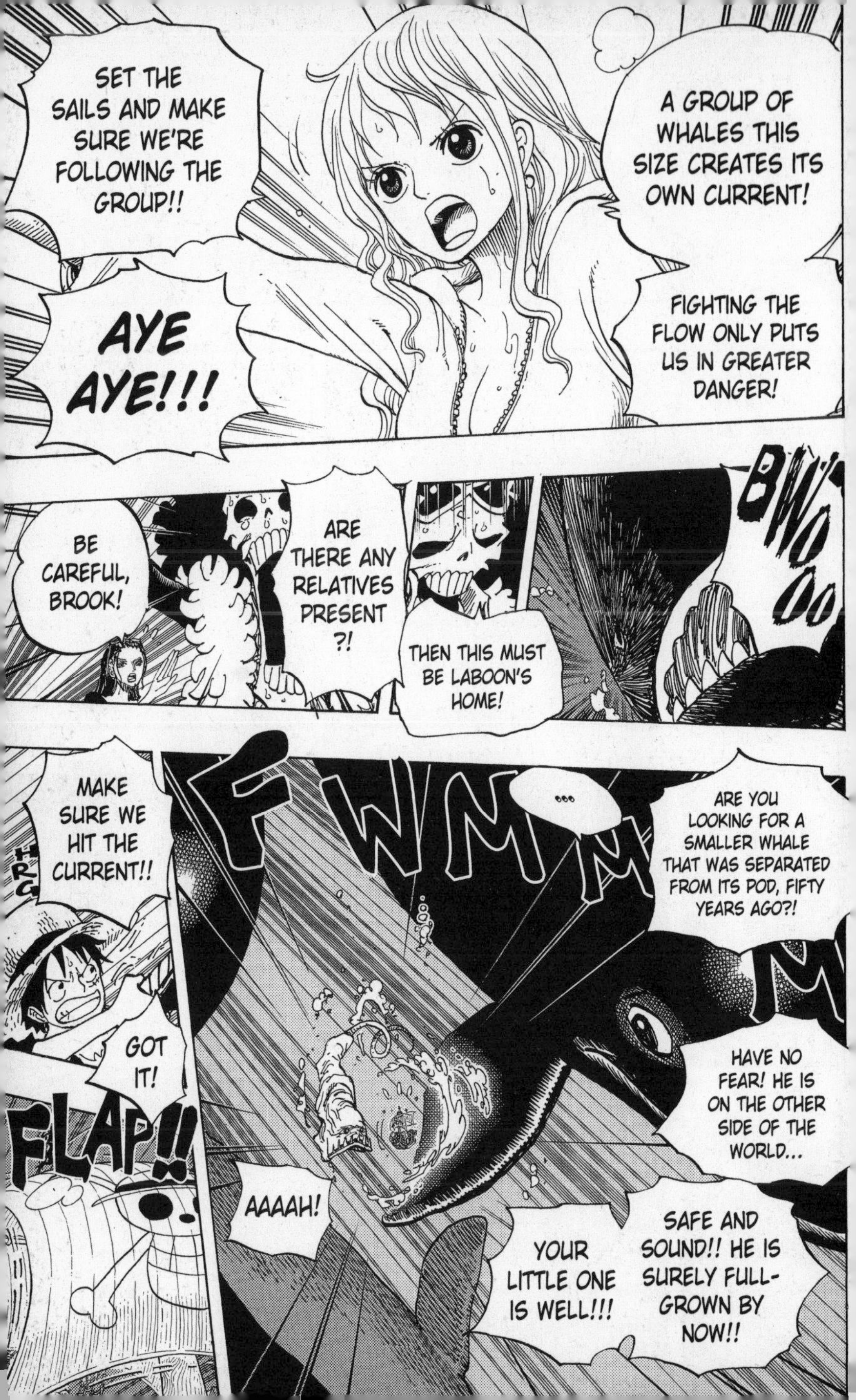
A GROUP OF WHALES THIS SIZE CREATES ITS OWN CURRENT!
FIGHTING THE FLOW ONLY PUTS US IN GREATER DANGER!
SET THE SAILS AND MAKE SURE WE'RE FOLLOWING THE GROUP!!
AYE AYE!!!
BWOOOO
THEN THIS MUST BE LABOON'S HOME!
ARE THERE ANY RELATIVES PRESENT ?!
BE CAREFUL, BROOK!
...
ARE YOU LOOKING FOR A SMALLER WHALE THAT WAS SEPARATED FROM ITS POD, FIFTY YEARS AGO?!
FWMMM
HAVE NO FEAR! HE IS ON THE OTHER SIDE OF THE WORLD...
SAFE AND SOUND!! HE IS SURELY FULL-GROWN BY NOW!!
YOUR LITTLE ONE IS WELL!!!
AAAAH!
MAKE SURE WE HIT THE CURRENT!!
GOT IT!
FLAP!!

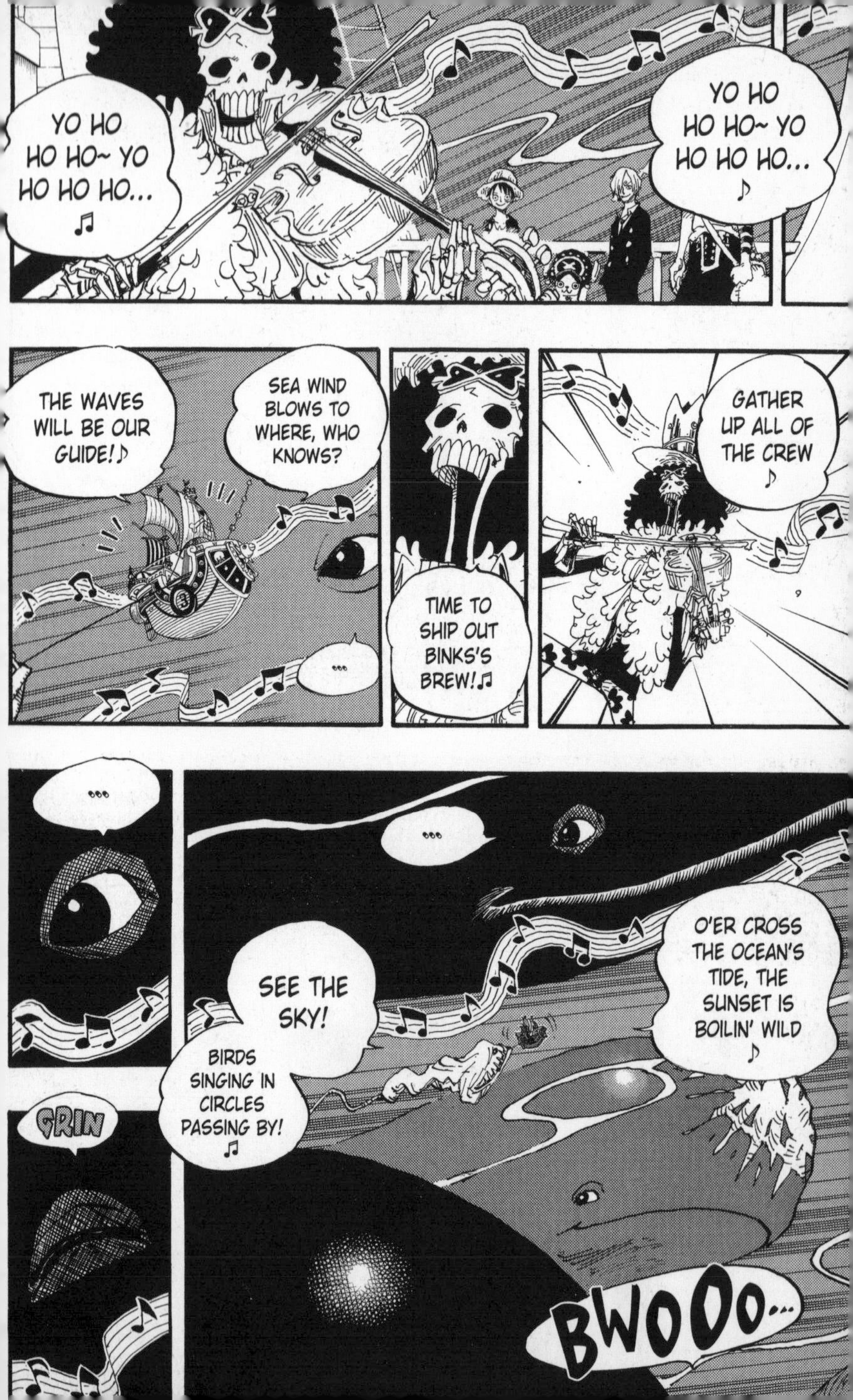
YO HO HO HO~ YO HO HO HO... ♪
YO HO HO HO~ YO HO HO HO... ♫
GATHER UP ALL OF THE CREW ♪
TIME TO SHIP OUT BINKS'S BREW!♫
SEA WIND BLOWS TO WHERE, WHO KNOWS?
THE WAVES WILL BE OUR GUIDE!♪
...
...
O'ER CROSS THE OCEAN'S TIDE, THE SUNSET IS BOILIN' WILD ♪
SEE THE SKY!
BIRDS SINGING IN CIRCLES PASSING BY! ♫
BWOOO...
...
GRIN

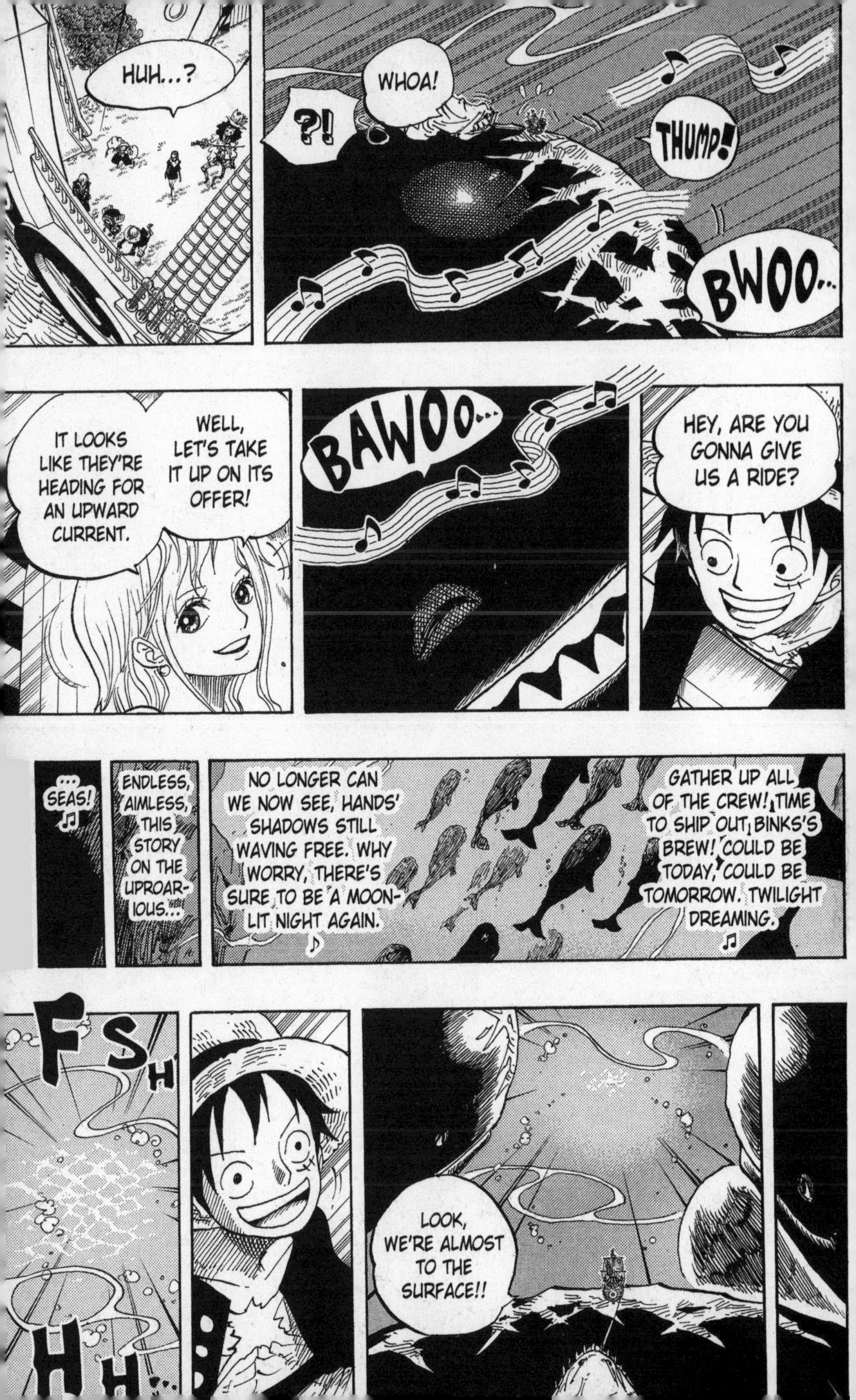
WHOA!
?!
THUMP!
BWOO...
HUH...?
HEY, ARE YOU GONNA GIVE US A RIDE?
BAWOO...
WELL, LET'S TAKE IT UP ON ITS OFFER!
IT LOOKS LIKE THEY'RE HEADING FOR AN UPWARD CURRENT.
GATHER UP ALL OF THE CREW! TIME TO SHIP OUT BINKS'S BREW! COULD BE TODAY, COULD BE TOMORROW. TWILIGHT DREAMING. ♫
NO LONGER CAN WE NOW SEE, HANDS' SHADOWS STILL WAVING FREE. WHY WORRY, THERE'S SURE TO BE A MOON-LIT NIGHT AGAIN. ♪
ENDLESS, AIMLESS, THIS STORY ON THE UPROAR-IOUS...
...SEAS! ♫
LOOK, WE'RE ALMOST TO THE SURFACE!!
FSH
HH...

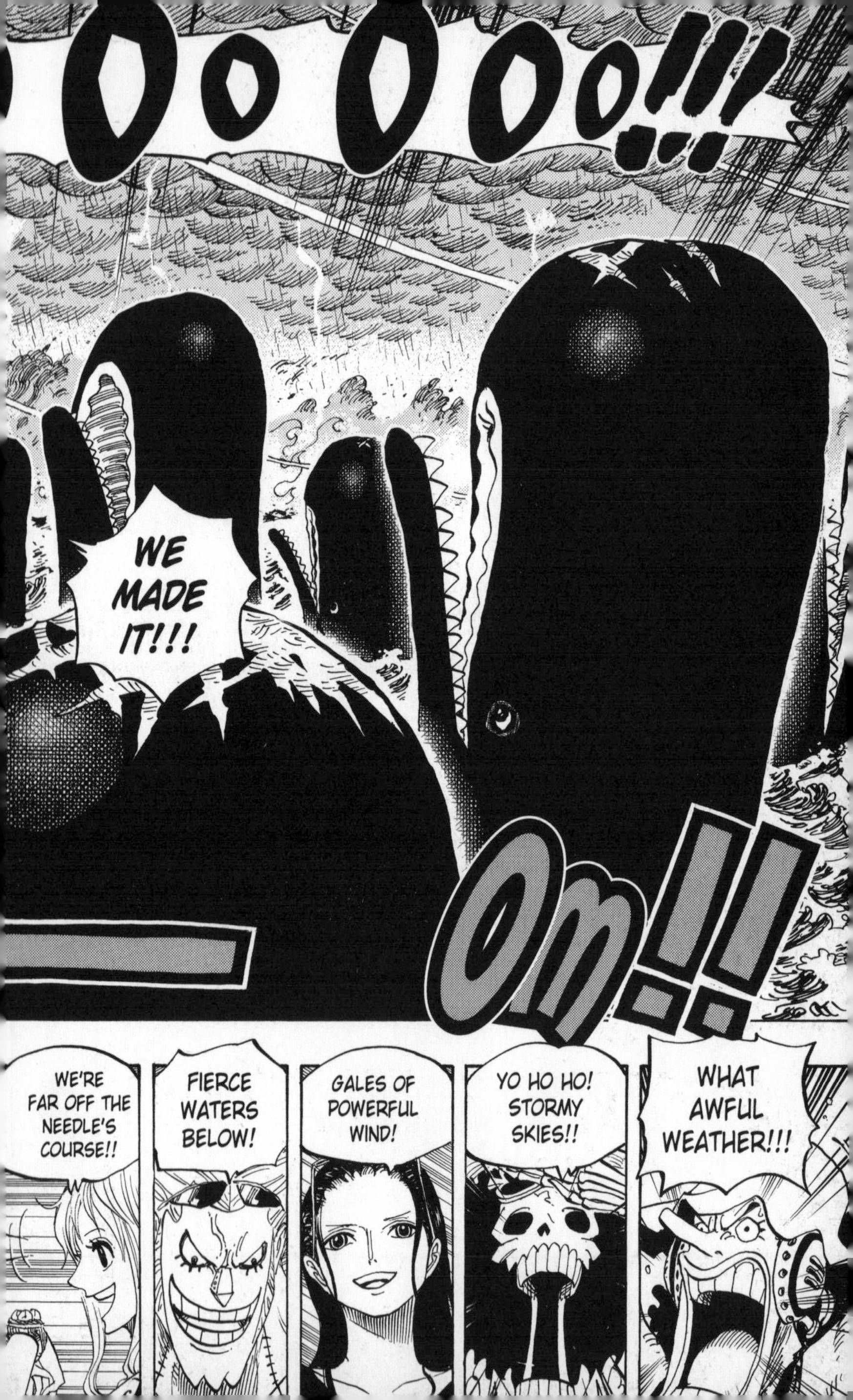

OOOOO!!!
WE MADE IT!!!
—OM!!
WHAT AWFUL WEATHER!!!
YO HO HO! STORMY SKIES!!
GALES OF POWERFUL WIND!
FIERCE WATERS BELOW!
WE'RE FAR OFF THE NEEDLE'S COURSE!!

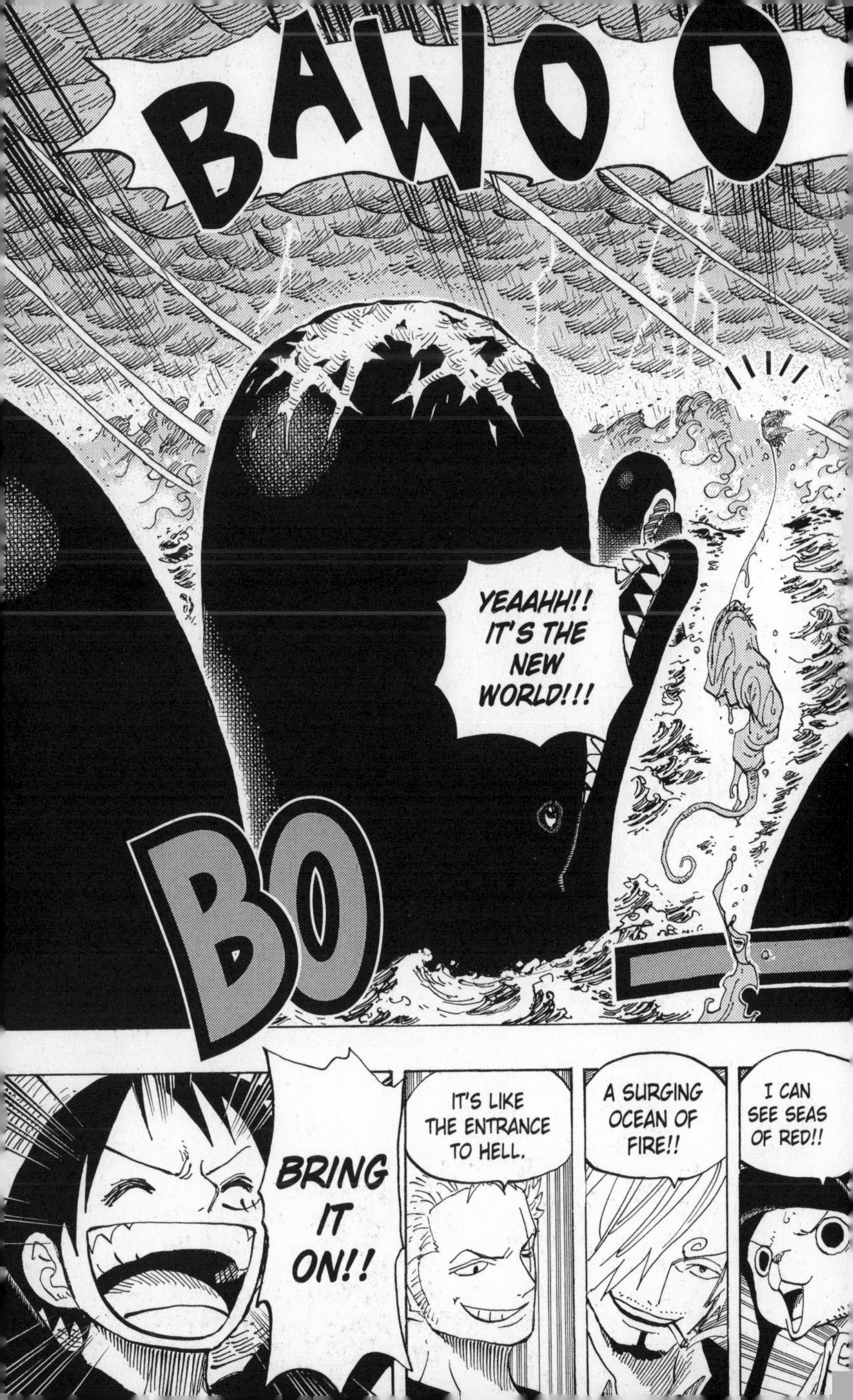
BAWO O
YEAAHH!! IT'S THE NEW WORLD!!!
BO
I CAN SEE SEAS OF RED!!
A SURGING OCEAN OF FIRE!!
IT'S LIKE THE ENTRANCE TO HELL.
BRING IT ON!!

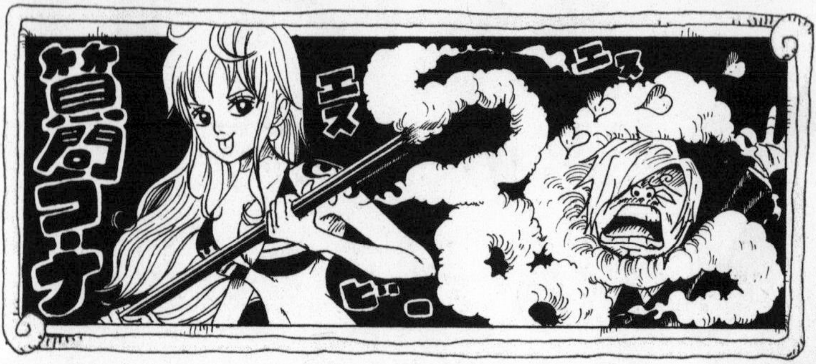
質問コーナー
エス

(Michi Nakahara, Tottori)

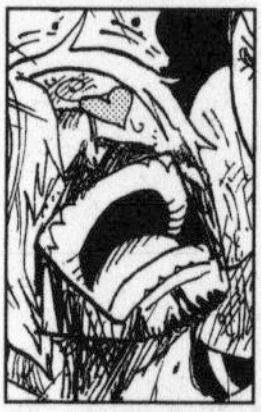

Q: Hello, Mr. Oda! When Sanji met the mermaids in Volume 62 and had a huge nosebleed, Chopper claimed he had "type-S" blood. Isn't that kinda weird? What other blood types are there? Give us the blood types of the entire crew while you're at it!

--Bepo

A: Okay, here.

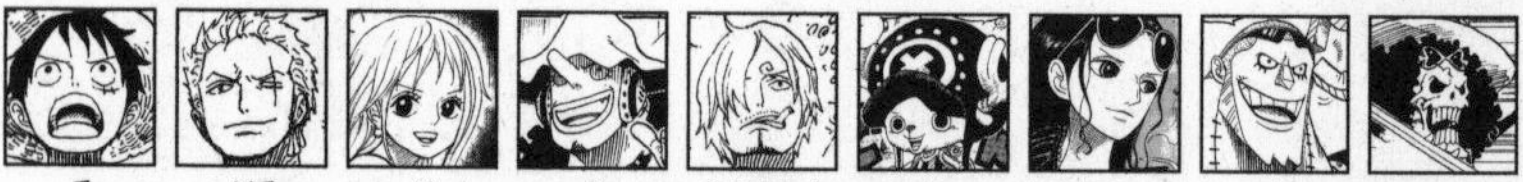

F XF X S S (RH-) X S XF X

They're mostly split between F, S, X and XF. But elsewhere around the world, blood types are known by different designations, so in some places they'd be considered types A, B, C, and so on.

Q: Odacchi!!!! Question!! Is this guy [➘] on p.55 of Volume 62 the same as this guy? [➡]

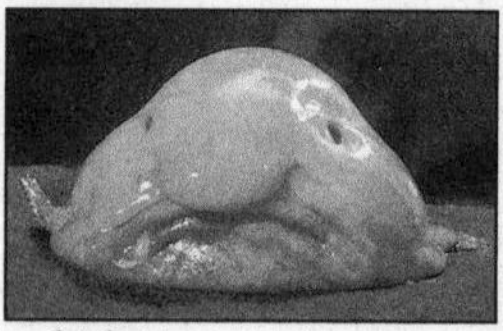

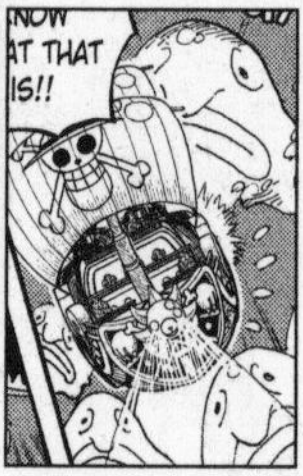
AT THAT

It is, isn't it?! When I looked up "hideous creatures," it turned up a picture of this guy ([➡])!!!!! How did you find it, Odacchi? Were you looking up hideous creatures too? You must have a lot of free time...

--Now In Class

A: Yes, that's it. The very same. But I don't type in weird searches like that. Mine are way weirder. This creature is known as a blobfish, and you'll always see a picture of one in any book on deep-sea fish. (Because it's so weird) Of course, they're not the size of ships, as they are in the story. It's a real deep-sea fish that grows to about a foot in length. It's also the same fish Luffy wanted to eat with mayonnaise just now in Chapter 654.

Chaper 655:
PUNK HAZARD

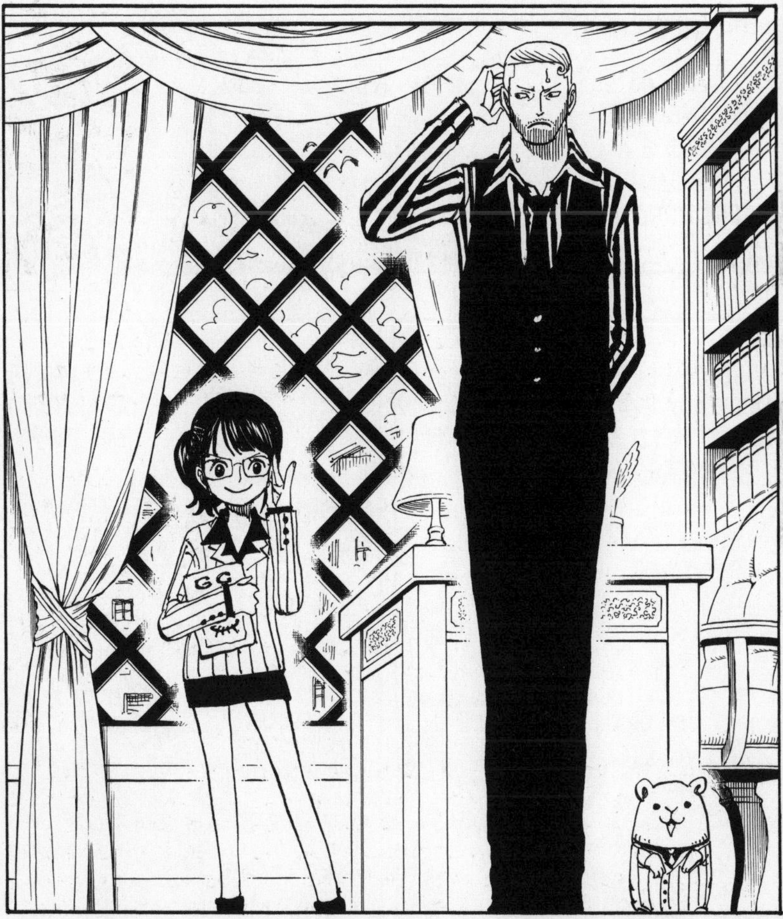

DECKS OF THE WORLD, VOL. 37 "WATER SEVEN—
GALLEY-LA COMPANY'S GENIUS 10-YEAR-OLD SECRETARY"

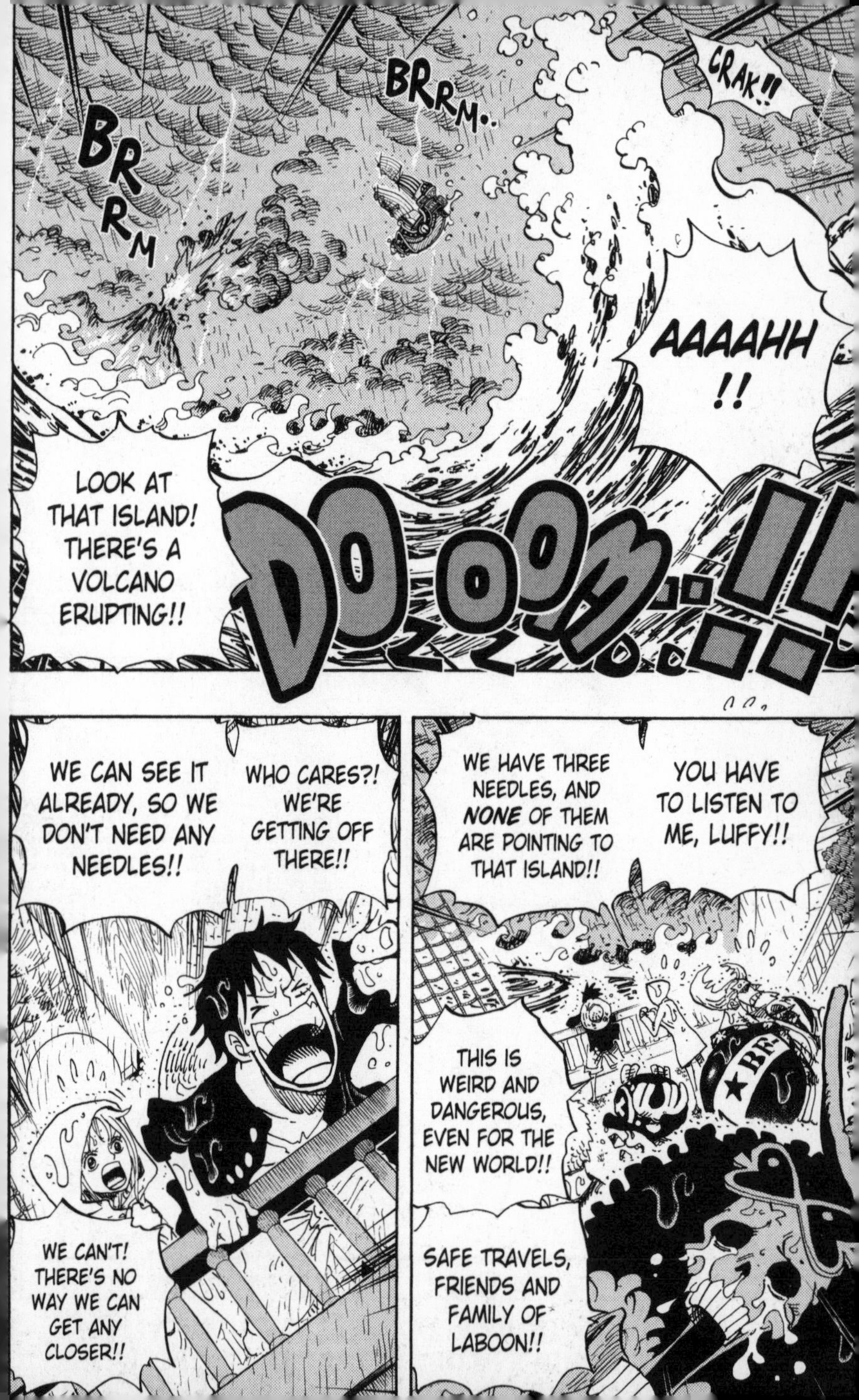
CRAK!!
AAAAHH!!
BRRRM..
BRRRM
LOOK AT THAT ISLAND! THERE'S A VOLCANO ERUPTING!!
DOOOM!!
YOU HAVE TO LISTEN TO ME, LUFFY!!
WE HAVE THREE NEEDLES, AND *NONE* OF THEM ARE POINTING TO THAT ISLAND!!
THIS IS WEIRD AND DANGEROUS, EVEN FOR THE NEW WORLD!!
SAFE TRAVELS, FRIENDS AND FAMILY OF LABOON!!
WHO CARES?! WE'RE GETTING OFF THERE!!
WE CAN SEE IT ALREADY, SO WE DON'T NEED ANY NEEDLES!!
WE CAN'T! THERE'S NO WAY WE CAN GET ANY CLOSER!!

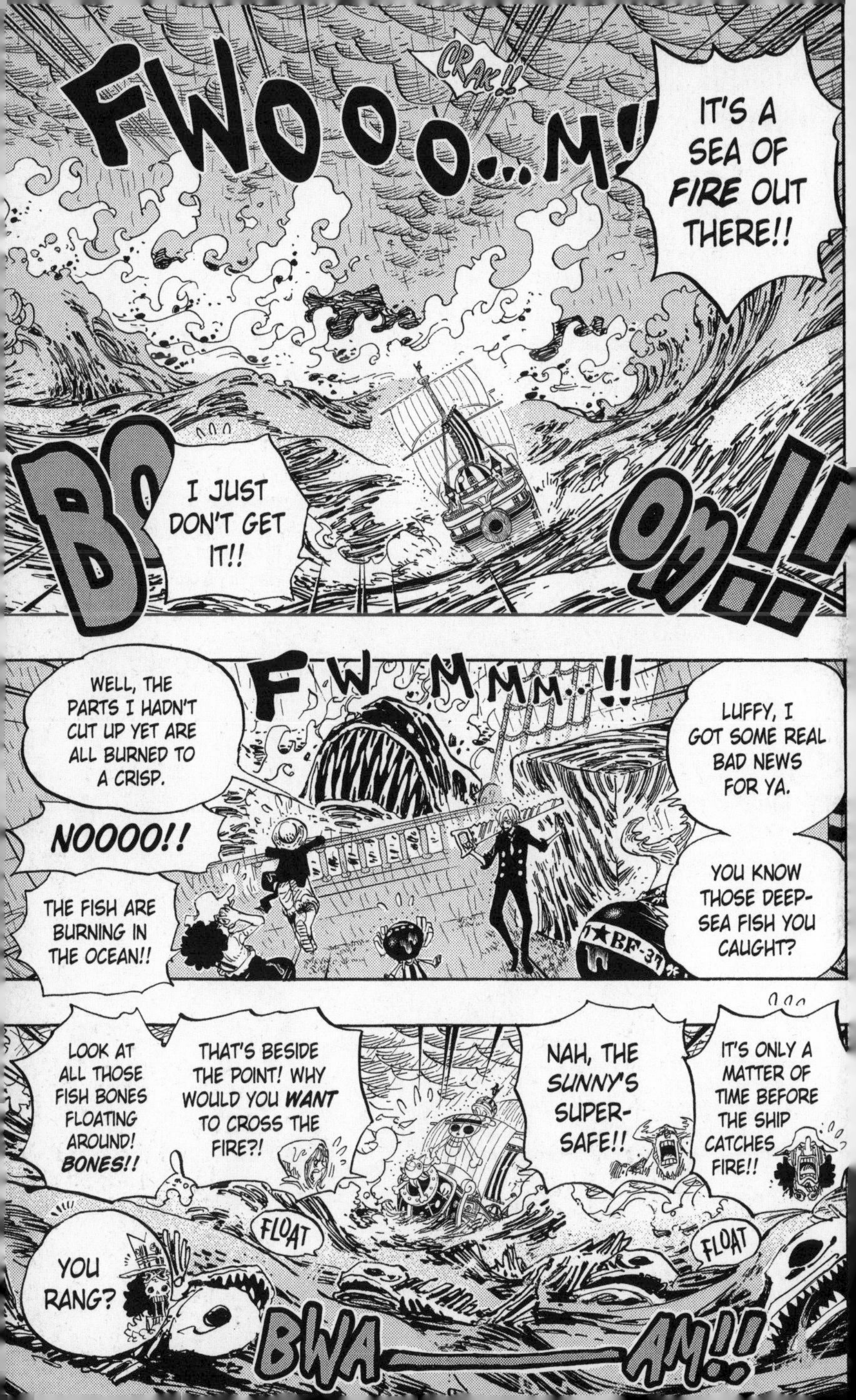
CRAK!!
IT'S A SEA OF FIRE OUT THERE!!
FWOOO...M!!
BOOM!!
I JUST DON'T GET IT!!
LUFFY, I GOT SOME REAL BAD NEWS FOR YA.
YOU KNOW THOSE DEEP-SEA FISH YOU CAUGHT?
FWMMM!!
WELL, THE PARTS I HADN'T CUT UP YET ARE ALL BURNED TO A CRISP.
NOOOO!!
THE FISH ARE BURNING IN THE OCEAN!!
IT'S ONLY A MATTER OF TIME BEFORE THE SHIP CATCHES FIRE!!
NAH, THE SUNNY'S SUPER-SAFE!!
THAT'S BESIDE THE POINT! WHY WOULD YOU WANT TO CROSS THE FIRE?!
LOOK AT ALL THOSE FISH BONES FLOATING AROUND! BONES!!
FLOAT
FLOAT
YOU RANG?
BWA—AM!!

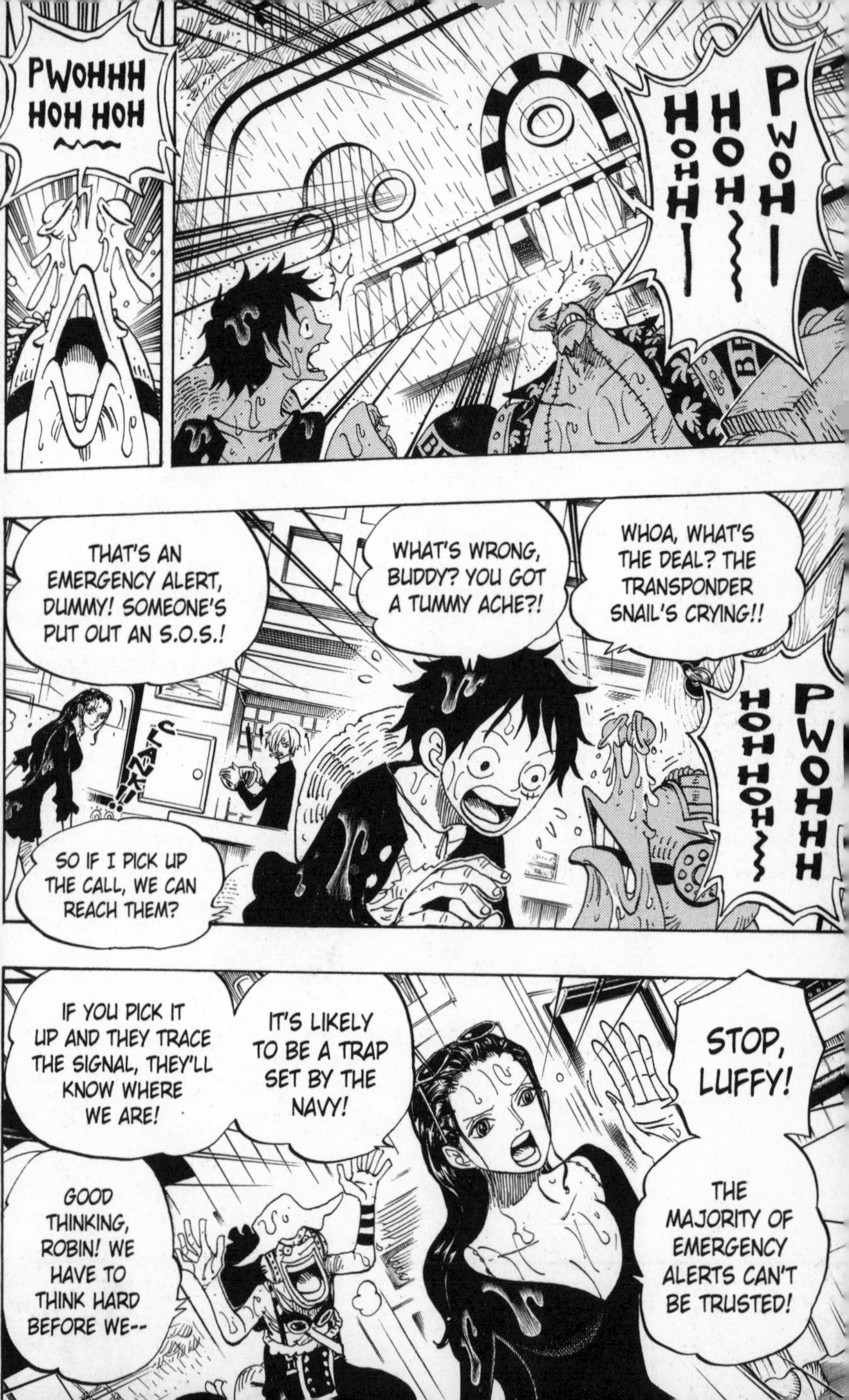
PWOH— HOH~ HOH—
PWOHHH HOH HOH ~
PWOHHH HOHHOH~
WHOA, WHAT'S THE DEAL? THE TRANSPONDER SNAIL'S CRYING!!
WHAT'S WRONG, BUDDY? YOU GOT A TUMMY ACHE?!
THAT'S AN EMERGENCY ALERT, DUMMY! SOMEONE'S PUT OUT AN S.O.S.!
CLANK!!
SO IF I PICK UP THE CALL, WE CAN REACH THEM?
STOP, LUFFY!
THE MAJORITY OF EMERGENCY ALERTS CAN'T BE TRUSTED!
IT'S LIKELY TO BE A TRAP SET BY THE NAVY!
IF YOU PICK IT UP AND THEY TRACE THE SIGNAL, THEY'LL KNOW WHERE WE ARE!
GOOD THINKING, ROBIN! WE HAVE TO THINK HARD BEFORE WE--

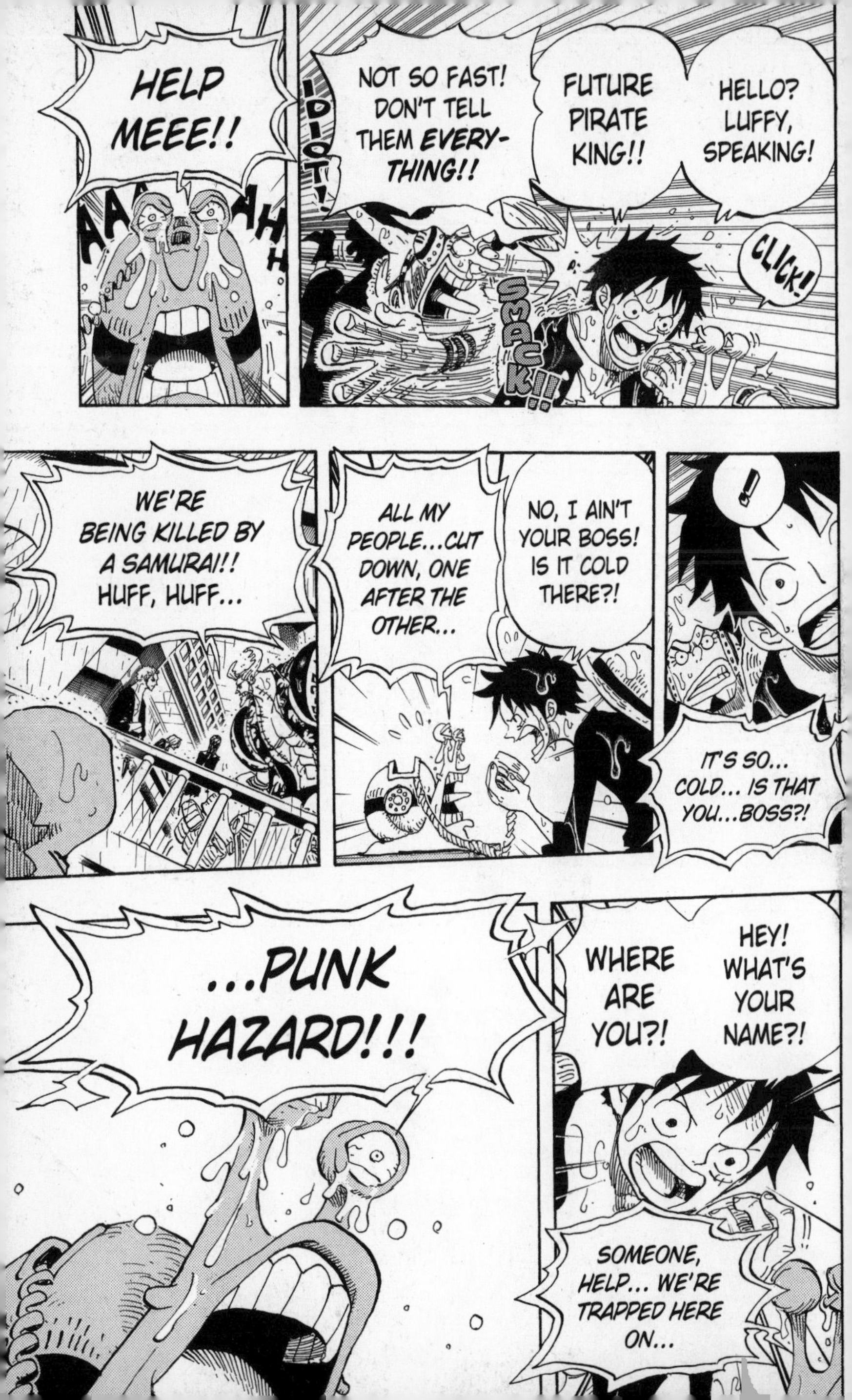
HELLO? LUFFY, SPEAKING!
FUTURE PIRATE KING!!
CLICK!
NOT SO FAST! DON'T TELL THEM EVERY-THING!!
IDIOT!
SMACK!!
HELP MEEE!!
AAAAHH
!
IT'S SO... COLD... IS THAT YOU...BOSS?!
NO, I AIN'T YOUR BOSS! IS IT COLD THERE?!
ALL MY PEOPLE...CUT DOWN, ONE AFTER THE OTHER...
WE'RE BEING KILLED BY A SAMURAI!! HUFF, HUFF...
HEY! WHAT'S YOUR NAME?!
WHERE ARE YOU?!
SOMEONE, HELP... WE'RE TRAPPED HERE ON...
...PUNK HAZARD!!!

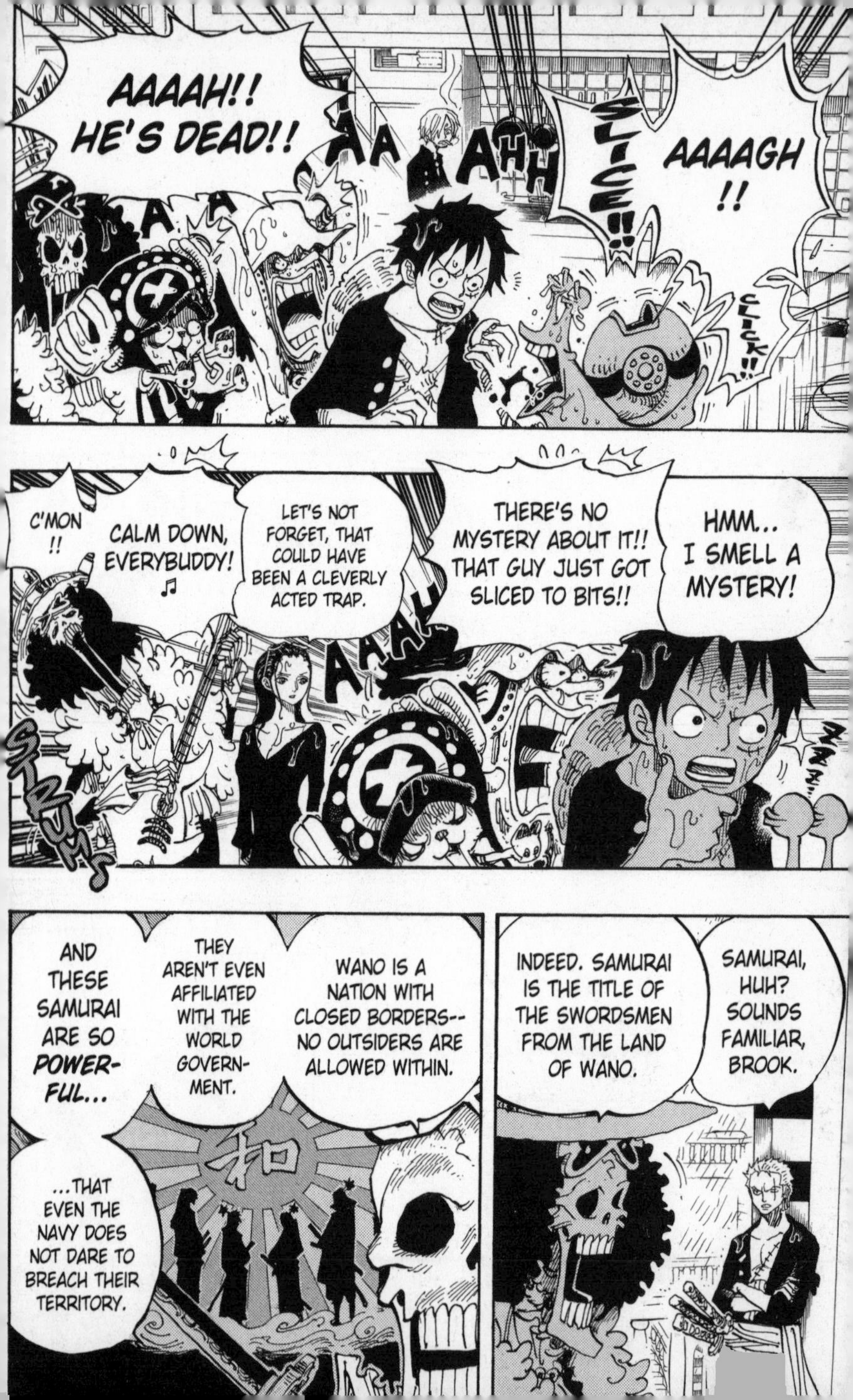
AAAAGH !!
SLICE!!
CLICK!!
AHH
AA
AAAAH!! HE'S DEAD!!
A A
HMM... I SMELL A MYSTERY!
THERE'S NO MYSTERY ABOUT IT!! THAT GUY JUST GOT SLICED TO BITS!!
LET'S NOT FORGET, THAT COULD HAVE BEEN A CLEVERLY ACTED TRAP.
CALM DOWN, EVERYBUDDY! ♪
C'MON !!
SAMURAI, HUH? SOUNDS FAMILIAR, BROOK.
INDEED. SAMURAI IS THE TITLE OF THE SWORDSMEN FROM THE LAND OF WANO.
WANO IS A NATION WITH CLOSED BORDERS-- NO OUTSIDERS ARE ALLOWED WITHIN.
THEY AREN'T EVEN AFFILIATED WITH THE WORLD GOVERN-MENT.
AND THESE SAMURAI ARE SO POWER-FUL...
...THAT EVEN THE NAVY DOES NOT DARE TO BREACH THEIR TERRITORY.

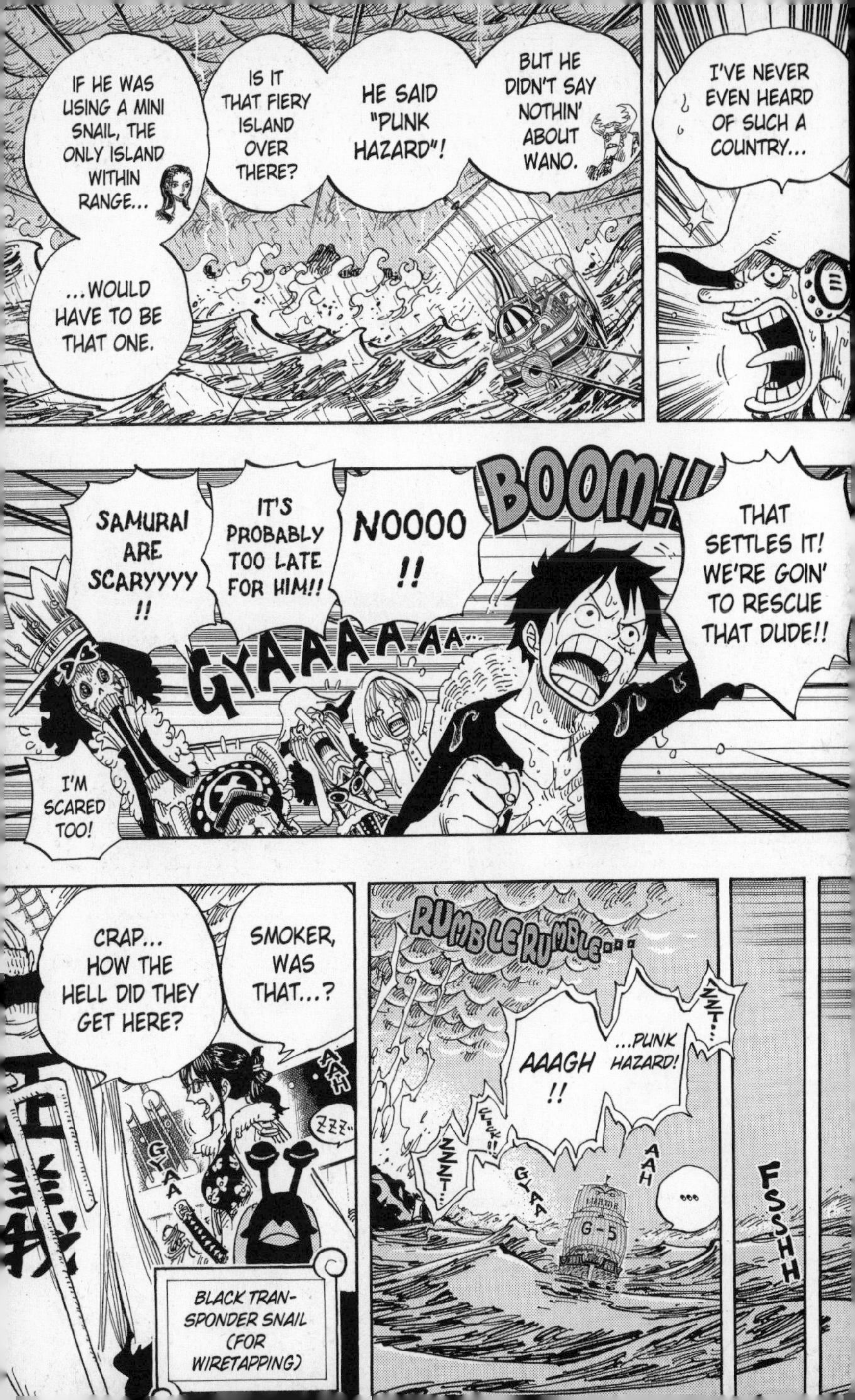
I'VE NEVER EVEN HEARD OF SUCH A COUNTRY...
BUT HE DIDN'T SAY NOTHIN' ABOUT WANO.
HE SAID "PUNK HAZARD"!
IS IT THAT FIERY ISLAND OVER THERE?
IF HE WAS USING A MINI SNAIL, THE ONLY ISLAND WITHIN RANGE...
...WOULD HAVE TO BE THAT ONE.
BOOM!!
THAT SETTLES IT! WE'RE GOIN' TO RESCUE THAT DUDE!!
NOOOO!!
IT'S PROBABLY TOO LATE FOR HIM!!
SAMURAI ARE SCARYYYY!!
GYAAAAAAA...
I'M SCARED TOO!
RUMBLE RUMBLE...
ZZZT...
...PUNK HAZARD!
AAAGH!!
CLICK!!
ZZZT...
AAH
GYAA
...
FSSHH
SMOKER, WAS THAT...?
CRAP... HOW THE HELL DID THEY GET HERE?
AAH
ZZZ...
GYAA
BLACK TRANSPONDER SNAIL (FOR WIRETAPPING)

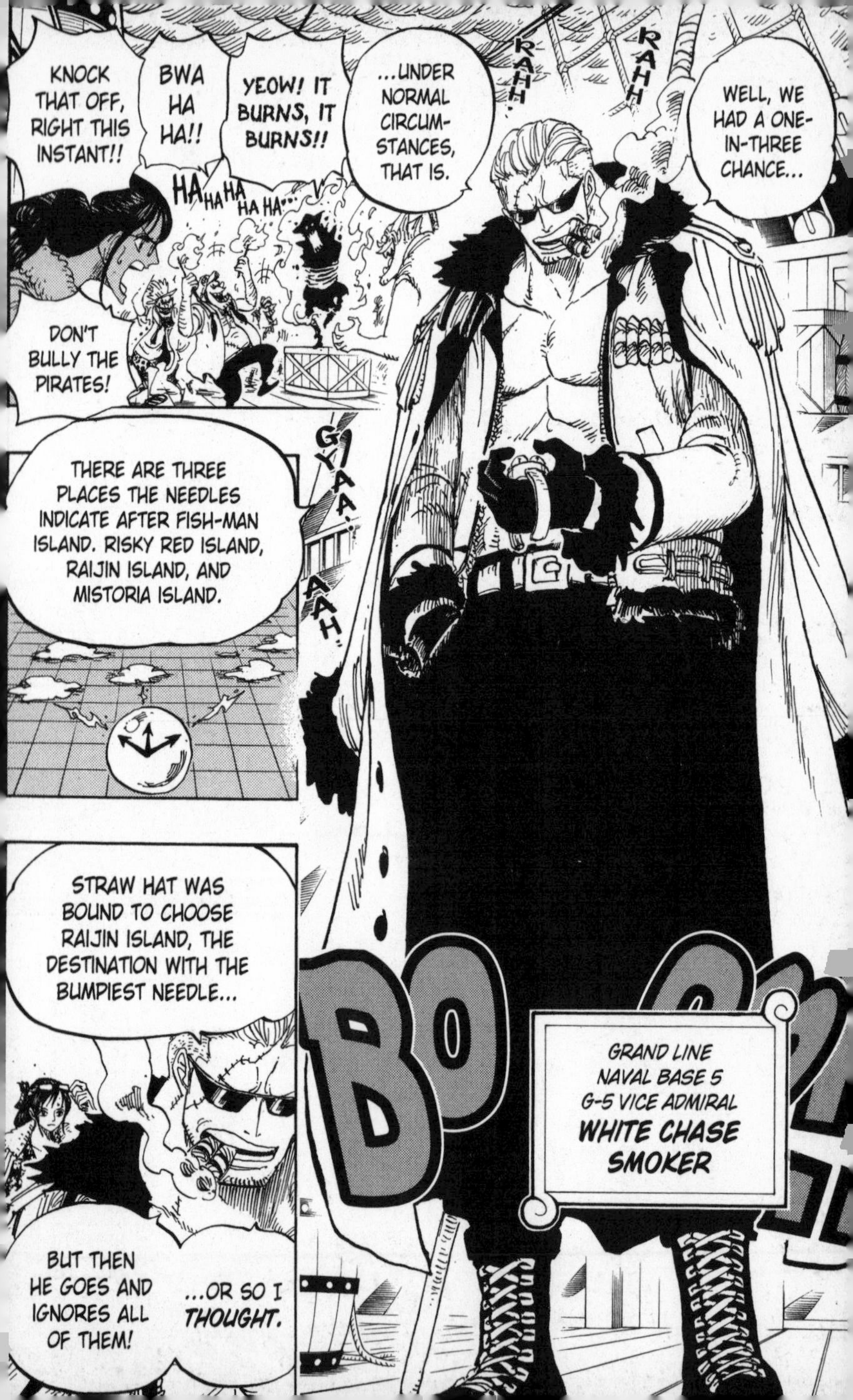
RAHH
RAHH
WELL, WE HAD A ONE-IN-THREE CHANCE...
...UNDER NORMAL CIRCUMSTANCES, THAT IS.
GYAAA
AAH
GRAND LINE NAVAL BASE 5 G-5 VICE ADMIRAL WHITE CHASE SMOKER
YEOW! IT BURNS, IT BURNS!!
BWA HA HA!!
KNOCK THAT OFF, RIGHT THIS INSTANT!!
HA HA HA HA HA...
DON'T BULLY THE PIRATES!
THERE ARE THREE PLACES THE NEEDLES INDICATE AFTER FISH-MAN ISLAND. RISKY RED ISLAND, RAIJIN ISLAND, AND MISTORIA ISLAND.
STRAW HAT WAS BOUND TO CHOOSE RAIJIN ISLAND, THE DESTINATION WITH THE BUMPIEST NEEDLE...
...OR SO I THOUGHT.
BUT THEN HE GOES AND IGNORES ALL OF THEM!

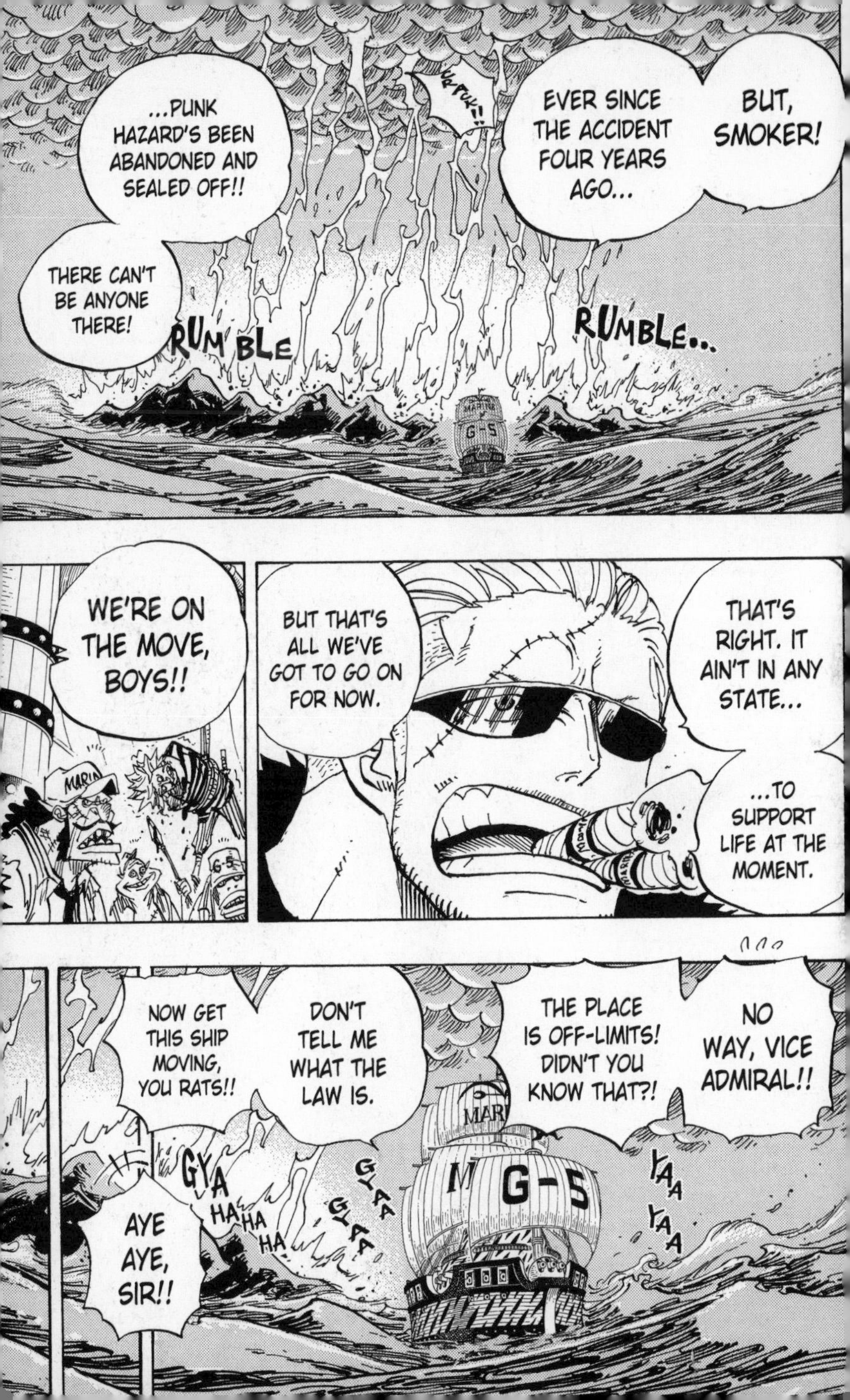
BUT, SMOKER!
EVER SINCE THE ACCIDENT FOUR YEARS AGO...
...PUNK HAZARD'S BEEN ABANDONED AND SEALED OFF!!
THERE CAN'T BE ANYONE THERE!
RUMBLE...
RUMBLE
THAT'S RIGHT. IT AIN'T IN ANY STATE...
...TO SUPPORT LIFE AT THE MOMENT.
BUT THAT'S ALL WE'VE GOT TO GO ON FOR NOW.
WE'RE ON THE MOVE, BOYS!!
NO WAY, VICE ADMIRAL!!
THE PLACE IS OFF-LIMITS! DIDN'T YOU KNOW THAT?!
DON'T TELL ME WHAT THE LAW IS.
NOW GET THIS SHIP MOVING, YOU RATS!!
YAAA YAAA
GYAA GYAA
GYA HA HA HA
AYE AYE, SIR!!

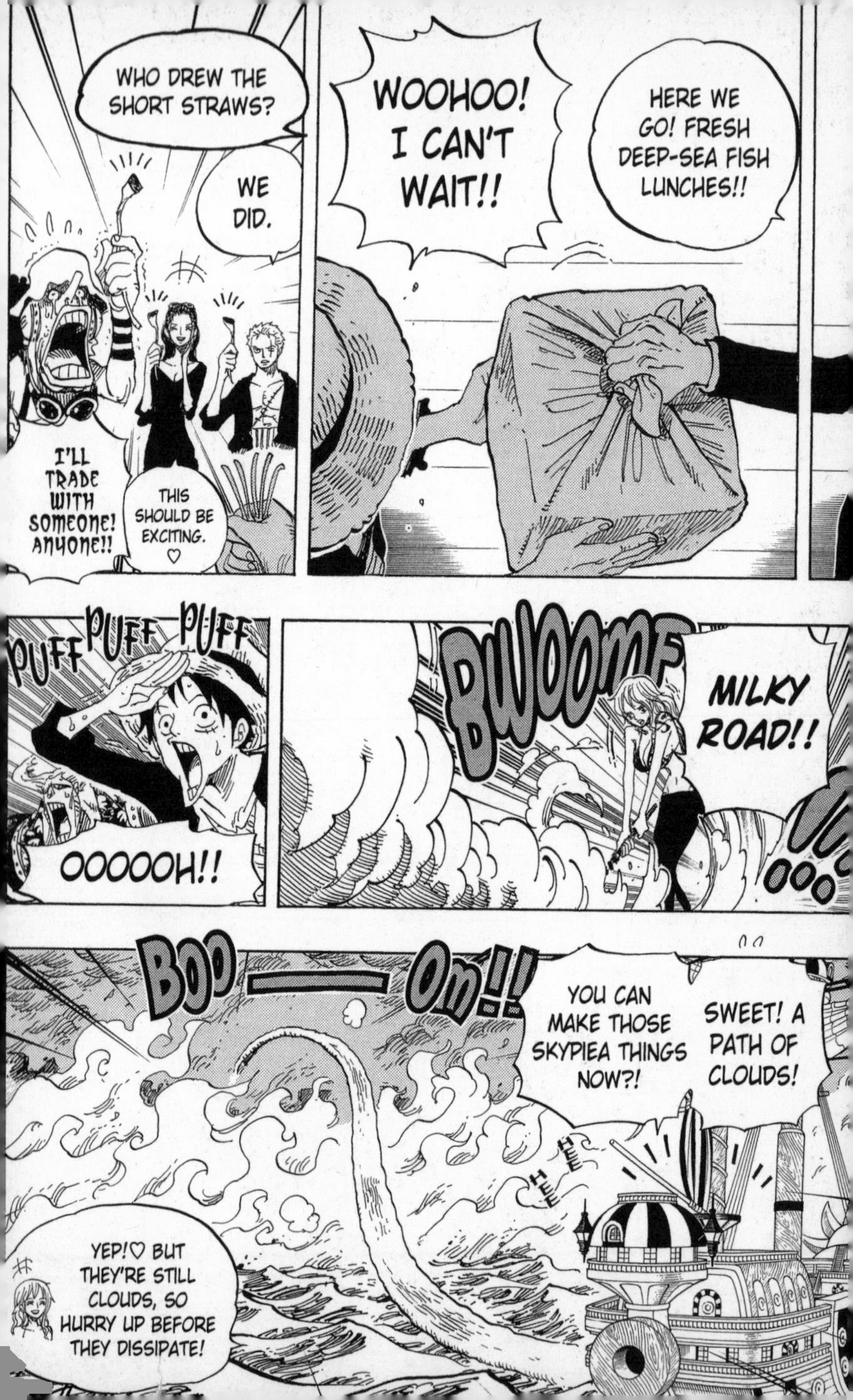
HERE WE GO! FRESH DEEP-SEA FISH LUNCHES!!
WOOHOO! I CAN'T WAIT!!
WHO DREW THE SHORT STRAWS?
WE DID.
THIS SHOULD BE EXCITING. ♡
I'LL TRADE WITH SOMEONE! ANYONE!!
MILKY ROAD!!
BWOOMF
PUFF PUFF PUFF
OOOOOH!!
BOO—OM!!
SWEET! A PATH OF CLOUDS!
YOU CAN MAKE THOSE SKYPIEA THINGS NOW?!
HEHE
YEP!♡ BUT THEY'RE STILL CLOUDS, SO HURRY UP BEFORE THEY DISSIPATE!

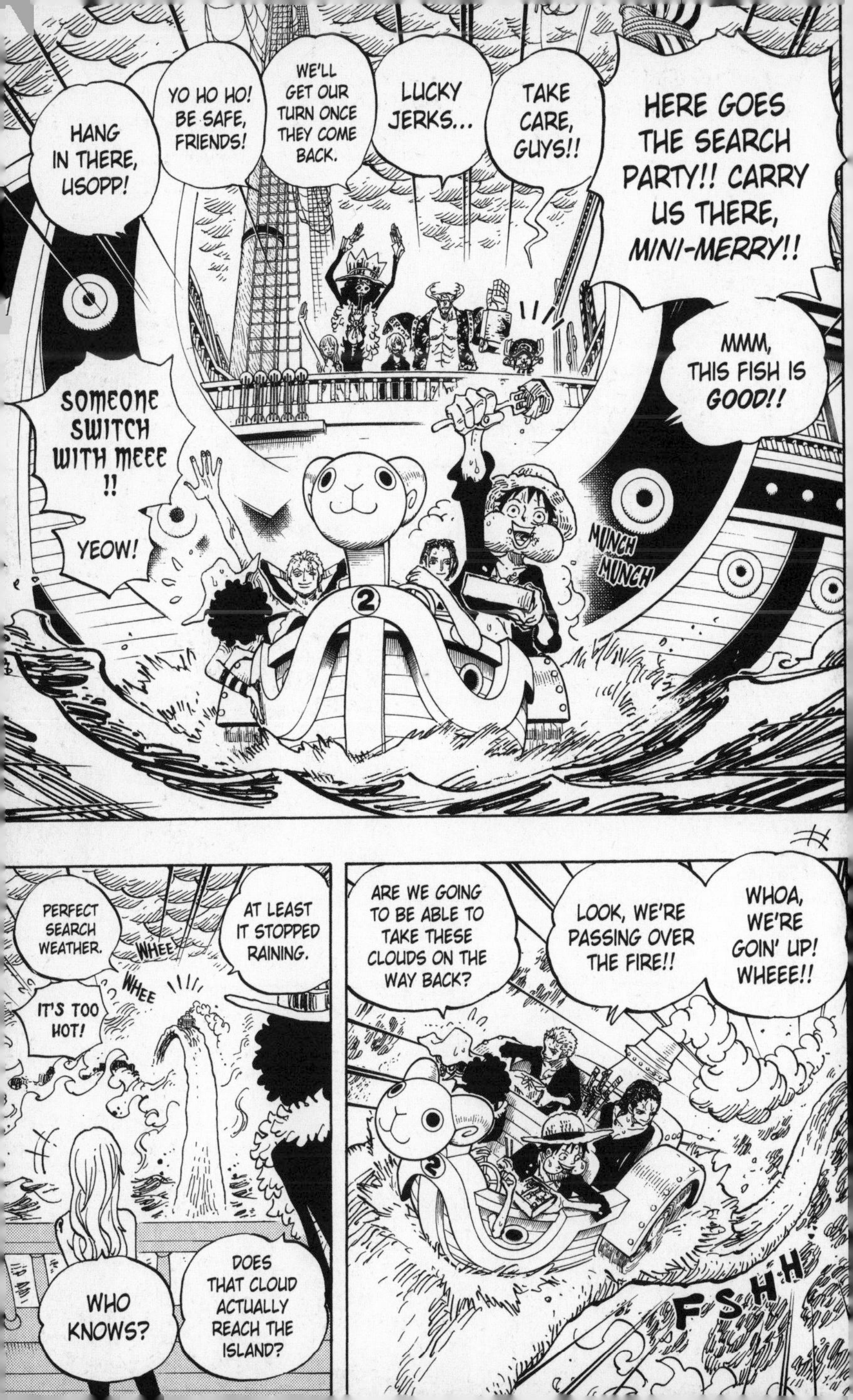
HERE GOES THE SEARCH PARTY!! CARRY US THERE, *MINI-MERRY*!!
TAKE CARE, GUYS!!
LUCKY JERKS...
WE'LL GET OUR TURN ONCE THEY COME BACK.
YO HO HO! BE SAFE, FRIENDS!
HANG IN THERE, USOPP!
MMM, THIS FISH IS *GOOD*!!
MUNCH MUNCH
SOMEONE SWITCH WITH MEEE !!
YEOW!
WHOA, WE'RE GOIN' UP! WHEEE!!
LOOK, WE'RE PASSING OVER THE FIRE!!
ARE WE GOING TO BE ABLE TO TAKE THESE CLOUDS ON THE WAY BACK?
FSHH
AT LEAST IT STOPPED RAINING.
PERFECT SEARCH WEATHER.
WHEE
WHEE
IT'S TOO HOT!
DOES THAT CLOUD ACTUALLY REACH THE ISLAND?
WHO KNOWS?

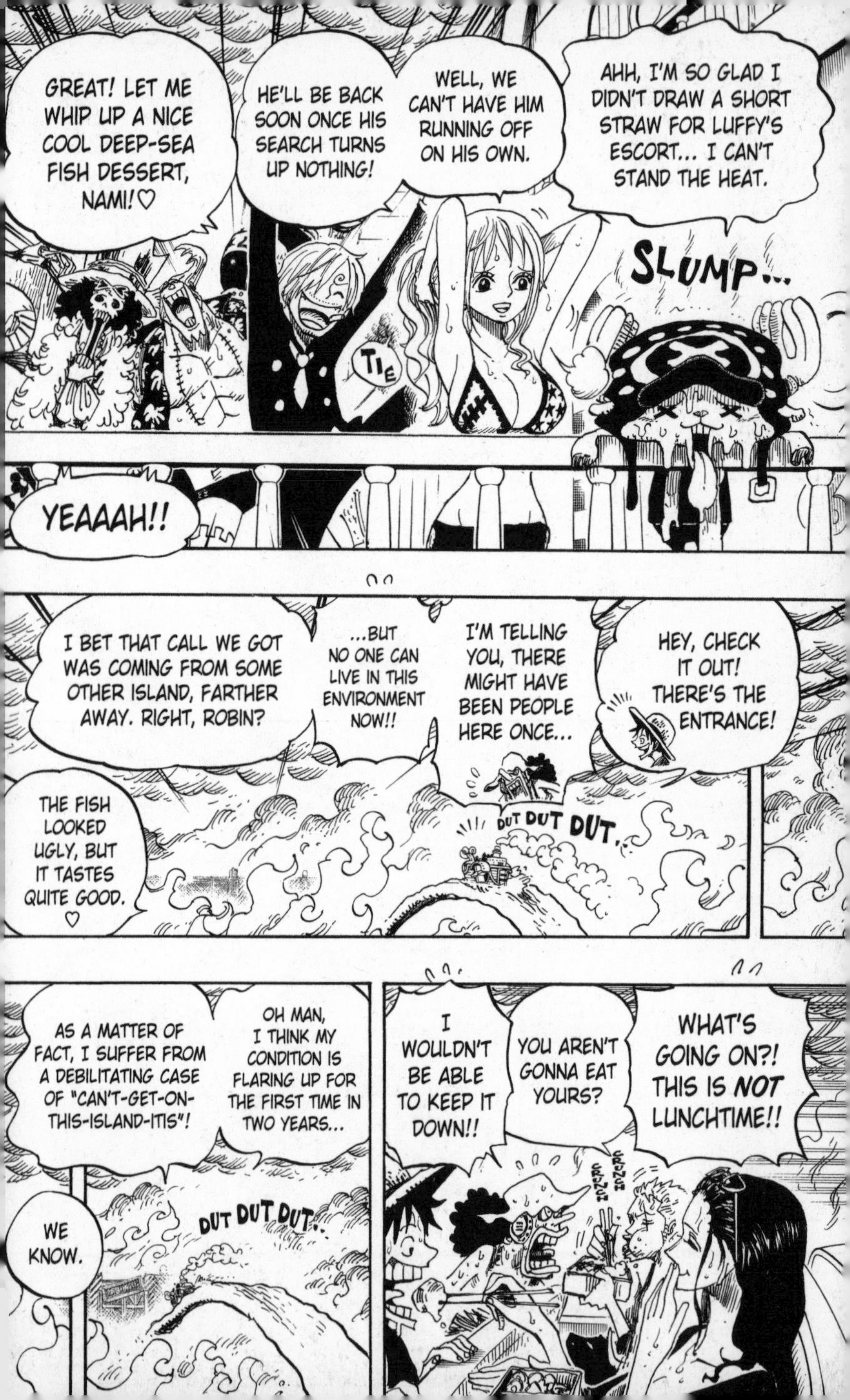

AHH, I'M SO GLAD I DIDN'T DRAW A SHORT STRAW FOR LUFFY'S ESCORT... I CAN'T STAND THE HEAT.
SLUMP...
WELL, WE CAN'T HAVE HIM RUNNING OFF ON HIS OWN.
HE'LL BE BACK SOON ONCE HIS SEARCH TURNS UP NOTHING!
TIE
GREAT! LET ME WHIP UP A NICE COOL DEEP-SEA FISH DESSERT, NAMI!♡
YEAAAH!!
HEY, CHECK IT OUT! THERE'S THE ENTRANCE!
I'M TELLING YOU, THERE MIGHT HAVE BEEN PEOPLE HERE ONCE...
...BUT NO ONE CAN LIVE IN THIS ENVIRONMENT NOW!!
I BET THAT CALL WE GOT WAS COMING FROM SOME OTHER ISLAND, FARTHER AWAY. RIGHT, ROBIN?
DUT DUT DUT.
THE FISH LOOKED UGLY, BUT IT TASTES QUITE GOOD. ♡
WHAT'S GOING ON?! THIS IS NOT LUNCHTIME!!
YOU AREN'T GONNA EAT YOURS?
I WOULDN'T BE ABLE TO KEEP IT DOWN!!
CRUNCH CRUNCH
OH MAN, I THINK MY CONDITION IS FLARING UP FOR THE FIRST TIME IN TWO YEARS...
AS A MATTER OF FACT, I SUFFER FROM A DEBILITATING CASE OF "CAN'T-GET-ON-THIS-ISLAND-ITIS"!
DUT DUT DUT..
WE KNOW.

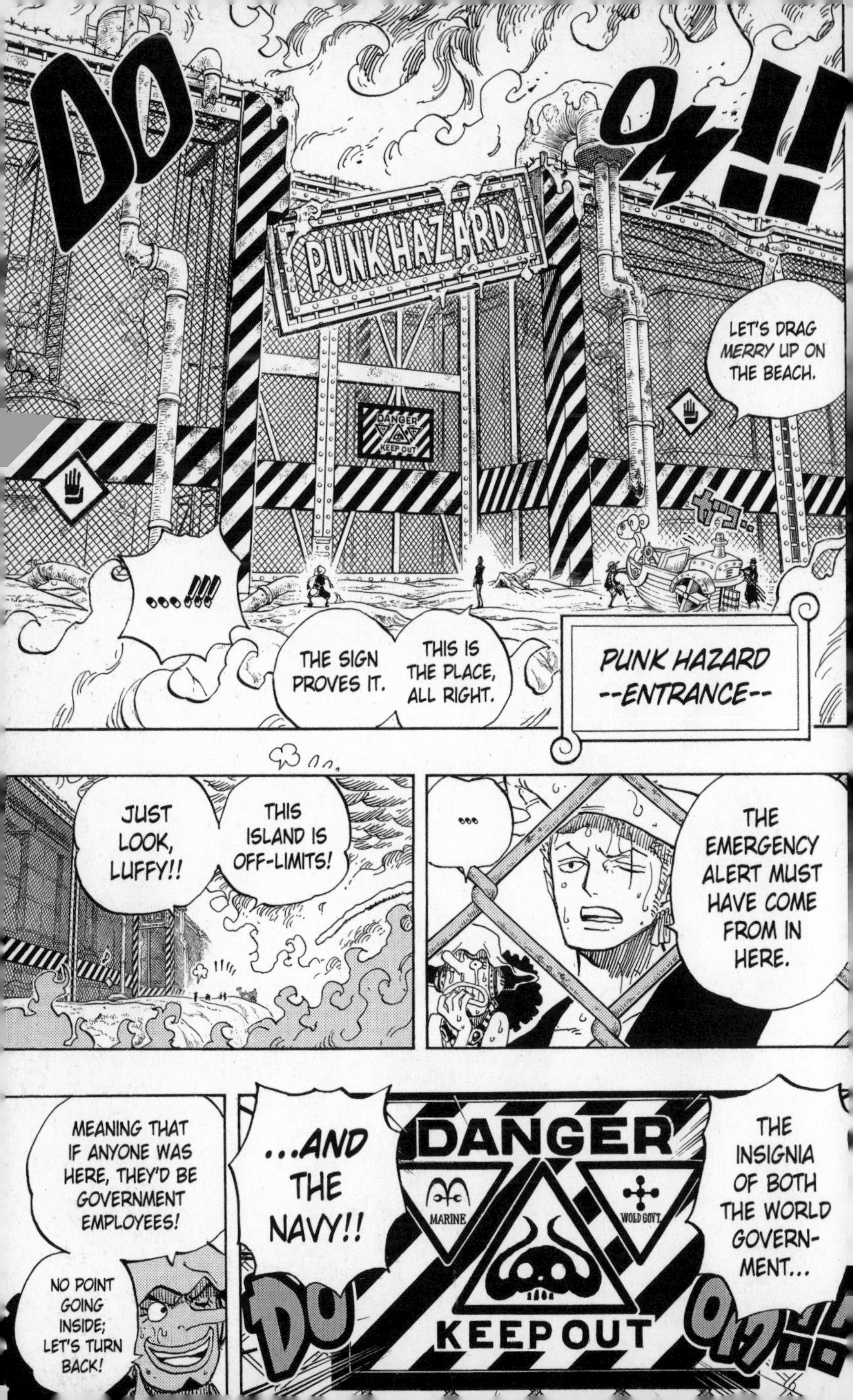
DO
OM!!
PUNK HAZARD
DANGER
KEEP OUT
LET'S DRAG MERRY UP ON THE BEACH.
PUNK HAZARD --ENTRANCE--
THIS IS THE PLACE, ALL RIGHT.
THE SIGN PROVES IT.
...!!!
THE EMERGENCY ALERT MUST HAVE COME FROM IN HERE.
...
THIS ISLAND IS OFF-LIMITS!
JUST LOOK, LUFFY!!
THE INSIGNIA OF BOTH THE WORLD GOVERN-MENT...
DANGER
MARINE
WOLD GOVT
KEEP OUT
...AND THE NAVY!!
MEANING THAT IF ANYONE WAS HERE, THEY'D BE GOVERNMENT EMPLOYEES!
NO POINT GOING INSIDE; LET'S TURN BACK!

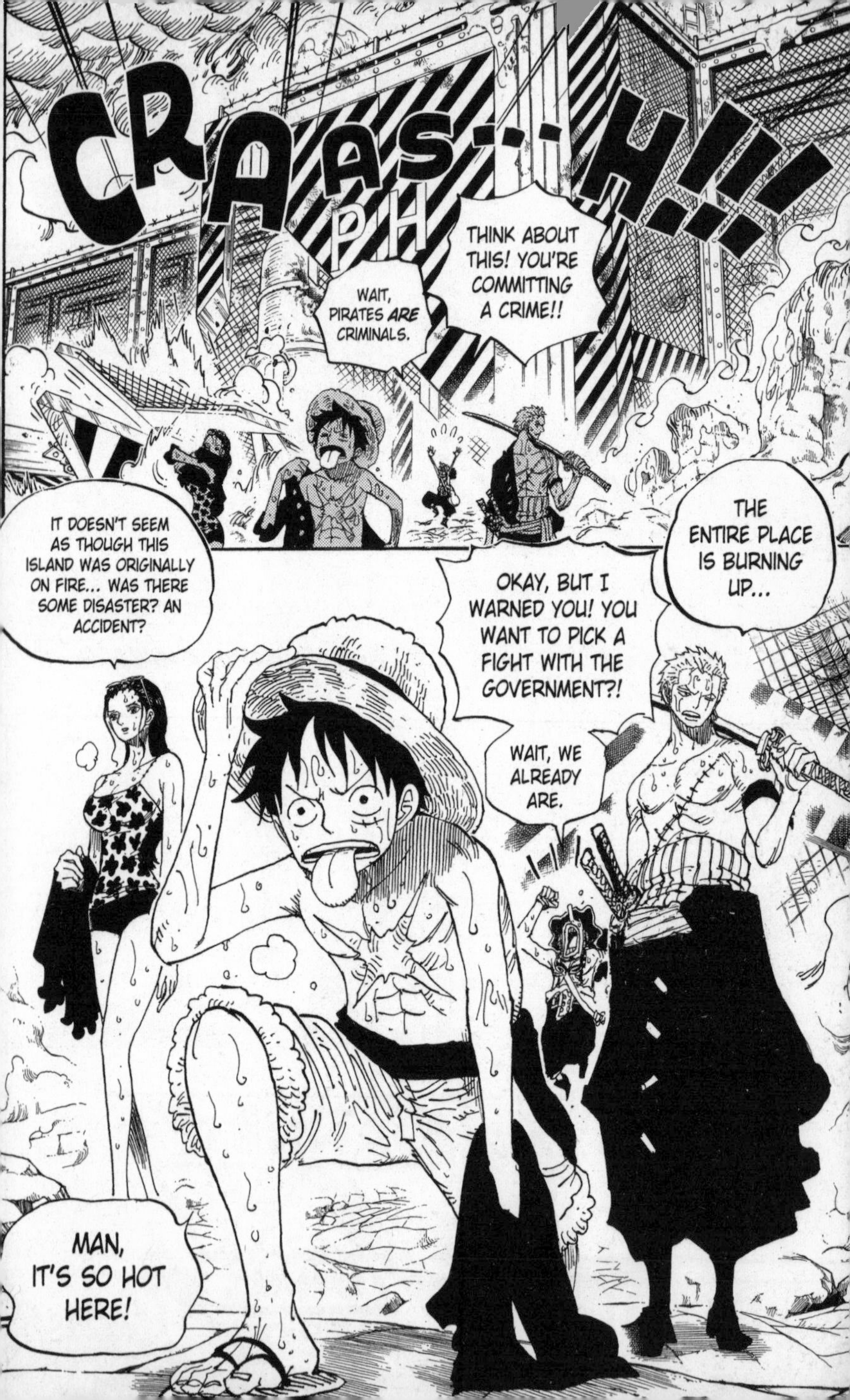
CRAAS--H!!!
PH
THINK ABOUT THIS! YOU'RE COMMITTING A CRIME!!
WAIT, PIRATES *ARE* CRIMINALS.
THE ENTIRE PLACE IS BURNING UP...
OKAY, BUT I WARNED YOU! YOU WANT TO PICK A FIGHT WITH THE GOVERNMENT?!
WAIT, WE ALREADY ARE.
IT DOESN'T SEEM AS THOUGH THIS ISLAND WAS ORIGINALLY ON FIRE... WAS THERE SOME DISASTER? AN ACCIDENT?
MAN, IT'S SO HOT HERE!

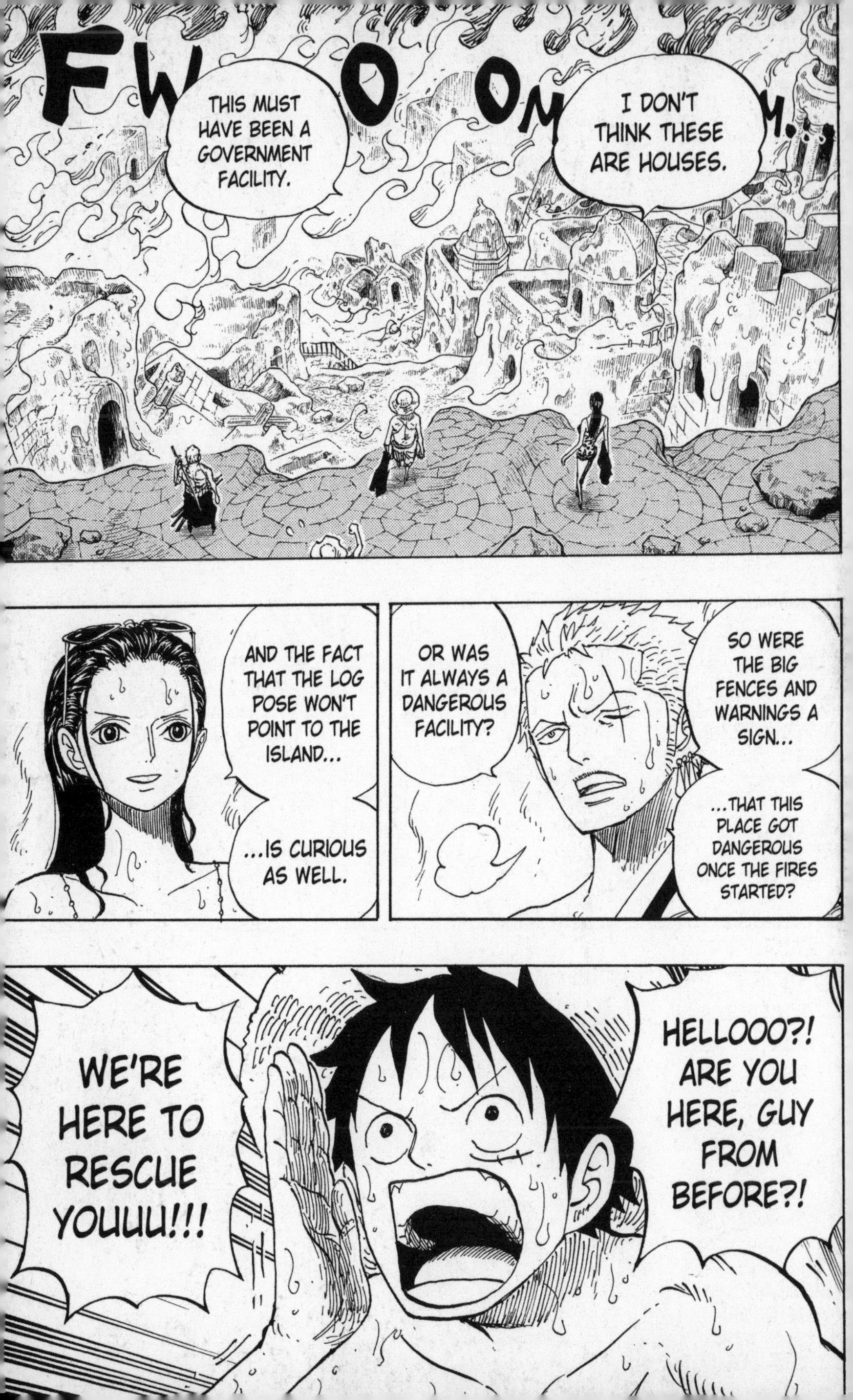
FW O OM M...
I DON'T THINK THESE ARE HOUSES.
THIS MUST HAVE BEEN A GOVERNMENT FACILITY.
SO WERE THE BIG FENCES AND WARNINGS A SIGN...
...THAT THIS PLACE GOT DANGEROUS ONCE THE FIRES STARTED?
OR WAS IT ALWAYS A DANGEROUS FACILITY?
AND THE FACT THAT THE LOG POSE WON'T POINT TO THE ISLAND...
...IS CURIOUS AS WELL.
HELLOOO?! ARE YOU HERE, GUY FROM BEFORE?!
WE'RE HERE TO RESCUE YOUUU!!!

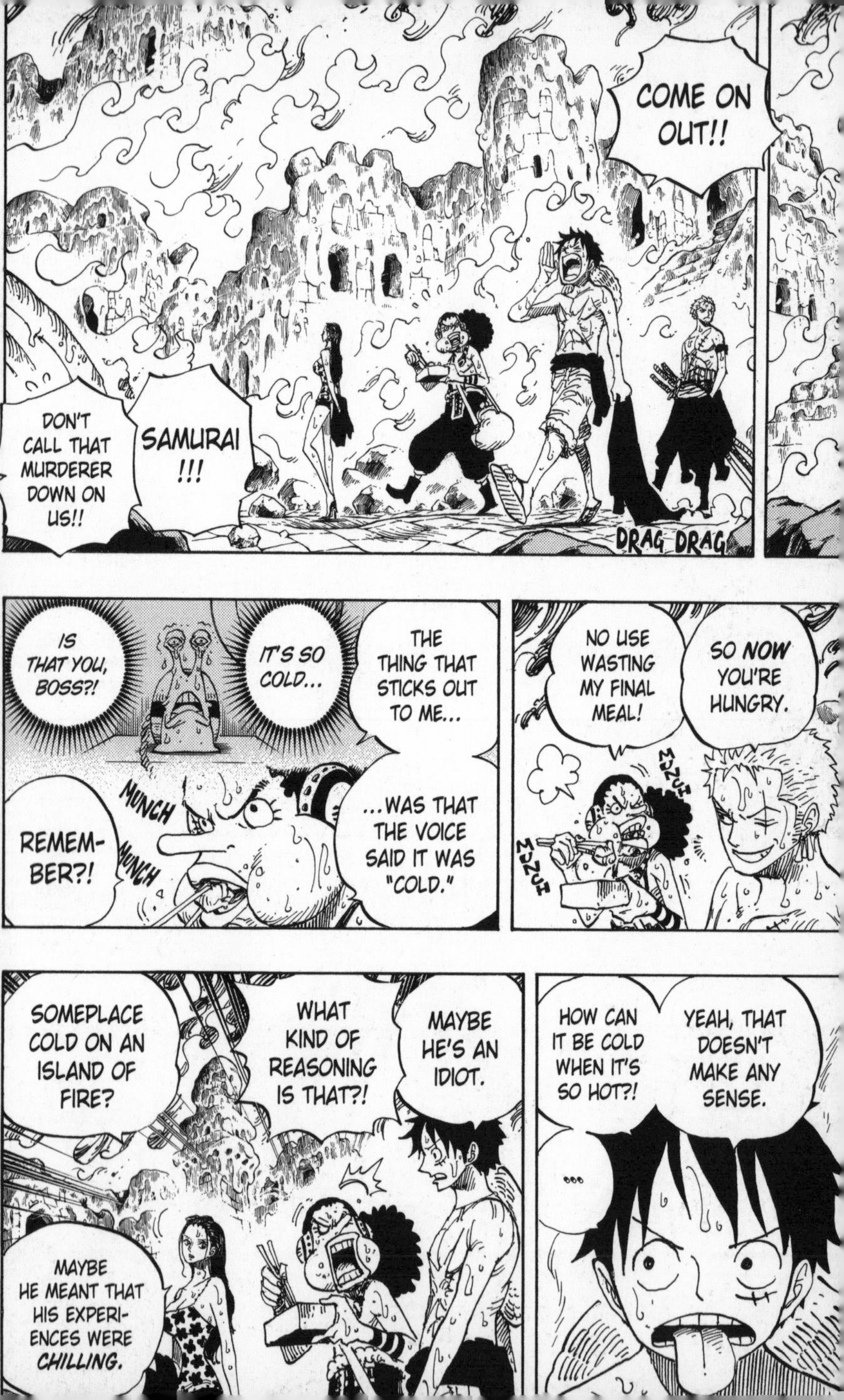
COME ON OUT!!
SAMURAI !!!
DON'T CALL THAT MURDERER DOWN ON US!!
DRAG DRAG
SO NOW YOU'RE HUNGRY.
NO USE WASTING MY FINAL MEAL!
MUNCH
MUNCH
THE THING THAT STICKS OUT TO ME...
...WAS THAT THE VOICE SAID IT WAS "COLD."
IT'S SO COLD...
IS THAT YOU, BOSS?!
MUNCH
MUNCH
REMEMBER?!
YEAH, THAT DOESN'T MAKE ANY SENSE.
HOW CAN IT BE COLD WHEN IT'S SO HOT?!
...
MAYBE HE'S AN IDIOT.
WHAT KIND OF REASONING IS THAT?!
SOMEPLACE COLD ON AN ISLAND OF FIRE?
MAYBE HE MEANT THAT HIS EXPERIENCES WERE CHILLING.

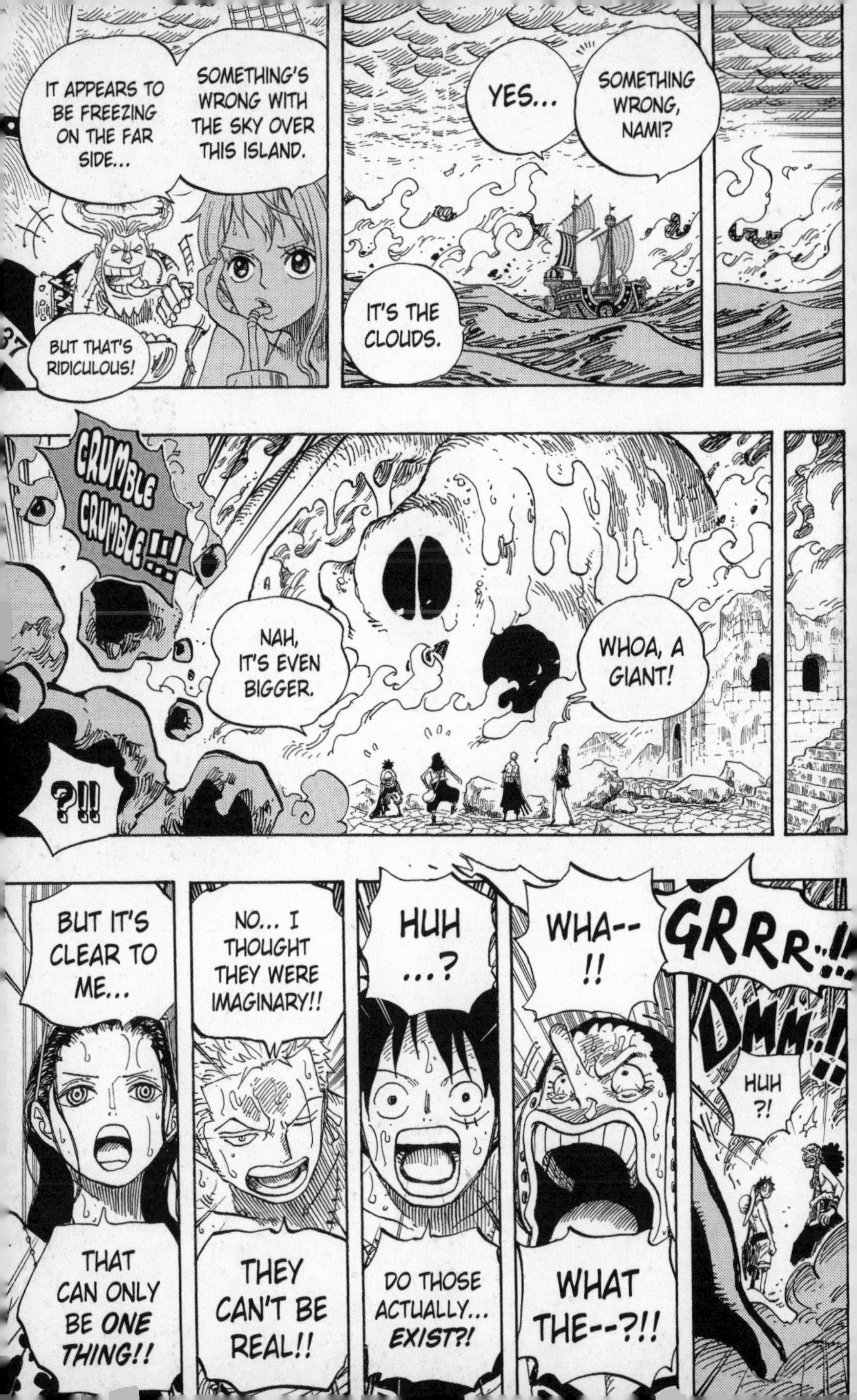
SOMETHING WRONG, NAMI?
YES...
IT'S THE CLOUDS.
SOMETHING'S WRONG WITH THE SKY OVER THIS ISLAND.
IT APPEARS TO BE FREEZING ON THE FAR SIDE...
BUT THAT'S RIDICULOUS!
WHOA, A GIANT!
NAH, IT'S EVEN BIGGER.
CRUMBLE CRUMBLE!!!
?!!
GRRRR..!!!
DMM..!!
HUH ?!
WHA-- !!
WHAT THE--?!!
HUH ...?
DO THOSE ACTUALLY... EXIST?!
NO... I THOUGHT THEY WERE IMAGINARY!!
THEY CAN'T BE REAL!!
BUT IT'S CLEAR TO ME...
THAT CAN ONLY BE ONE THING!!

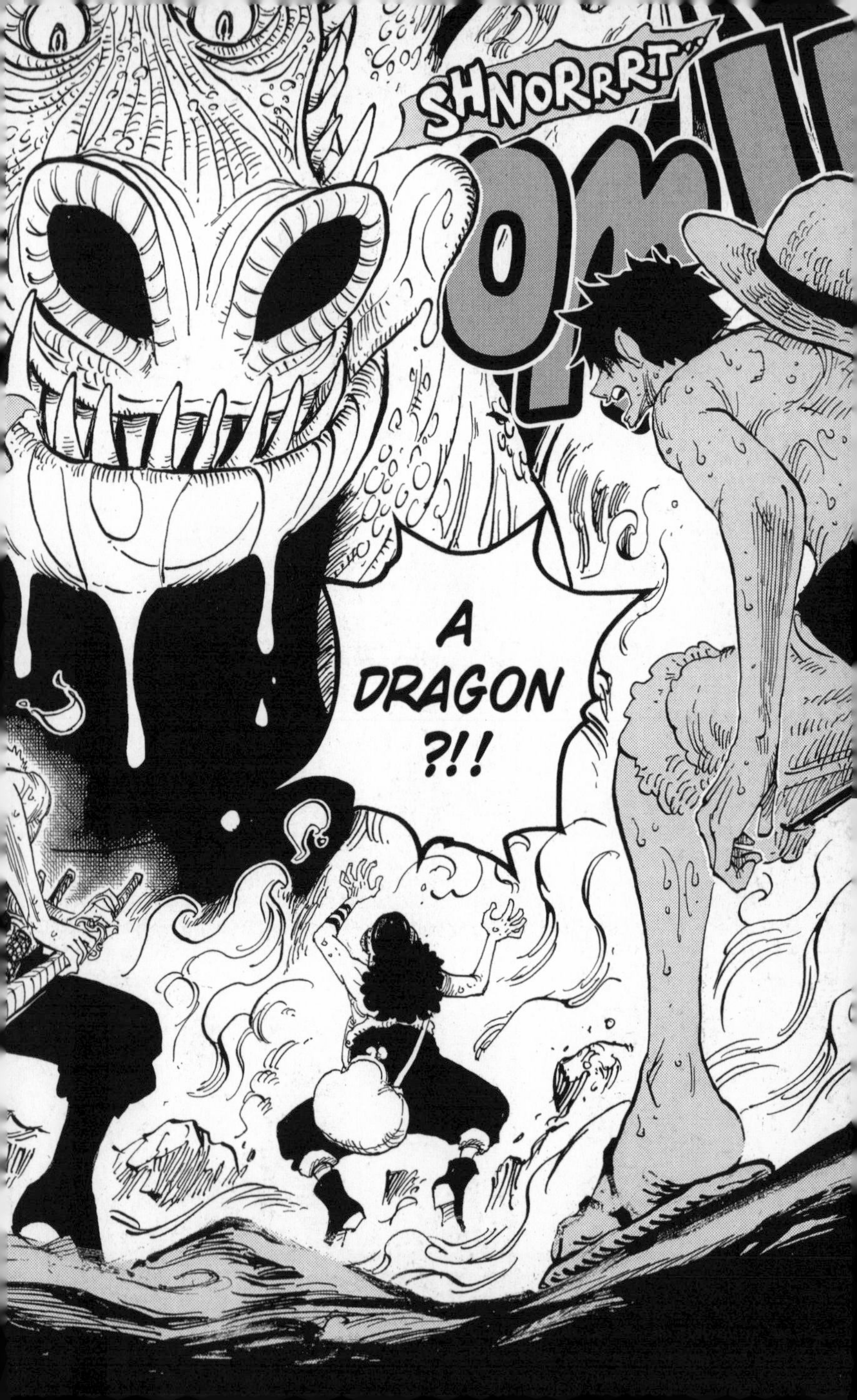
SHNORRRT
A DRAGON ?!!

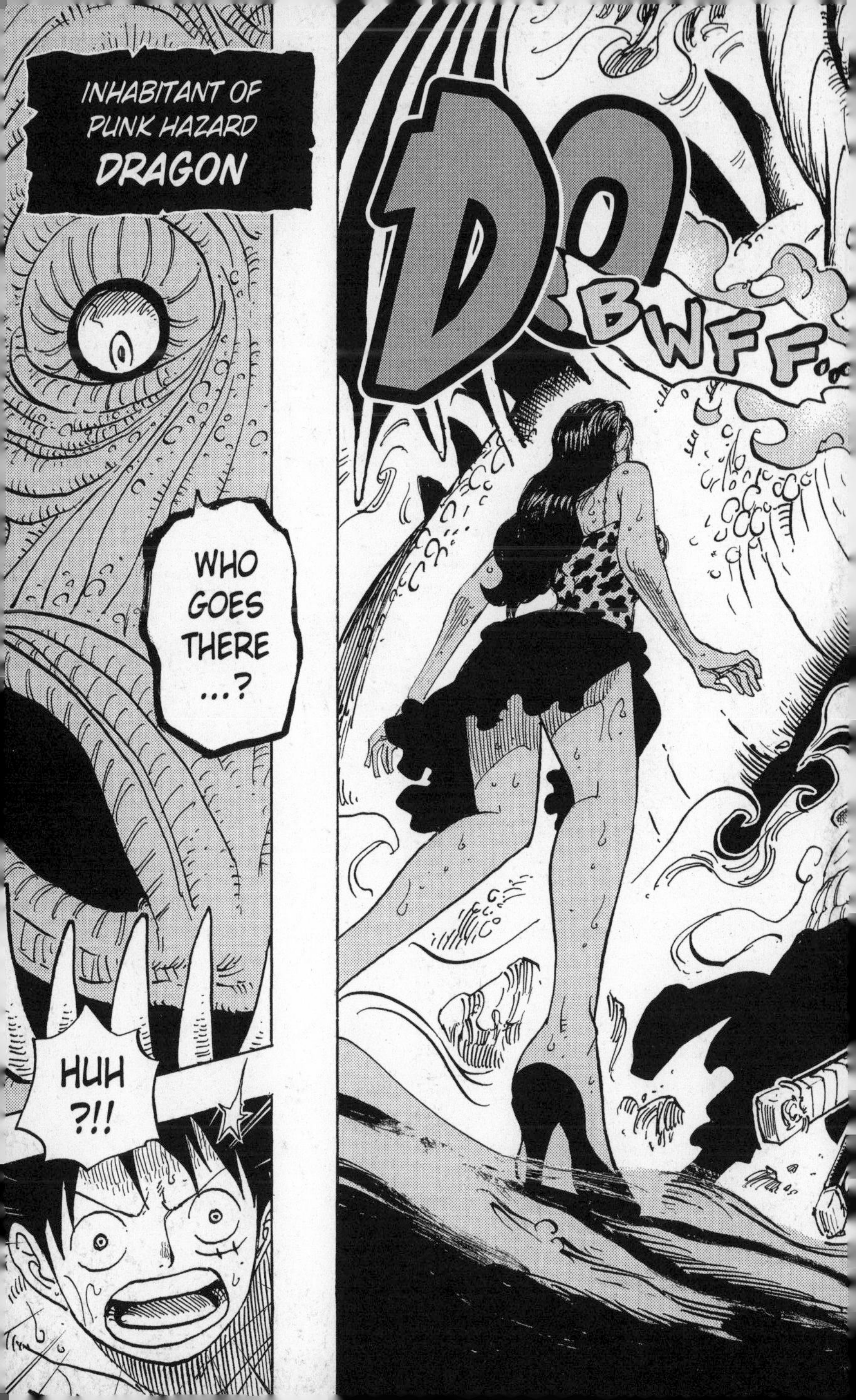
DO
BWFF...
INHABITANT OF PUNK HAZARD DRAGON
WHO GOES THERE ...?
HUH ?!!

SBS Question Corner

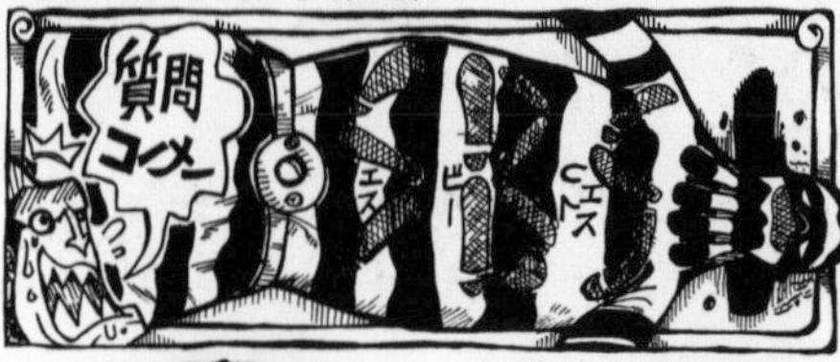

(Michi Nakahara, Tottori)

Q: By the way, I've noticed that you're drawing lots of "when they were kids" portraits, so I wondered if you might draw Perona. Would you mind doing that? (Plus Absalom, Hogback and Cindry.)

--Witch Princess Eustass Luna

A: Okay.

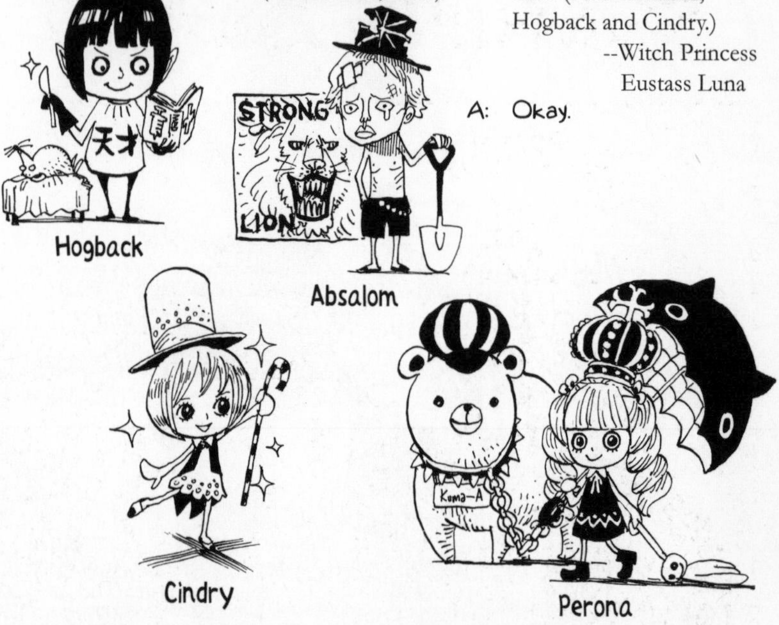

天才
Hogback
STRONG
LION
Absalom
Cindry
Koma-A
Perona

Q: Hello, Mr. Oda! All the young mermaids at the mermaid inlet are so beautiful. So I was wondering, what was old lady Kokoro like when she was young? Draw her for us!!

A: Okay. This is the end for the questions this volume. See you next time!

Before

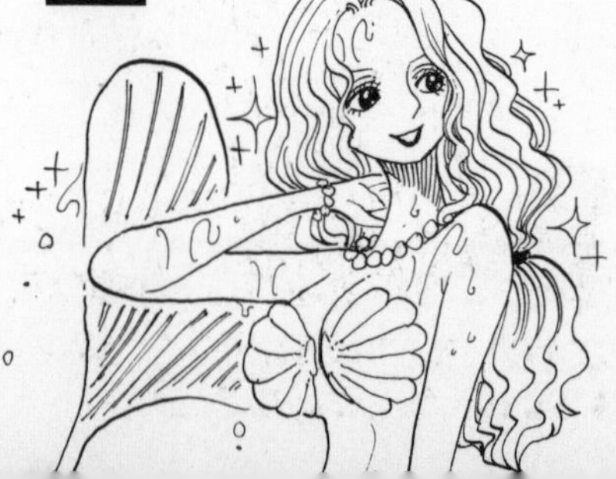

After

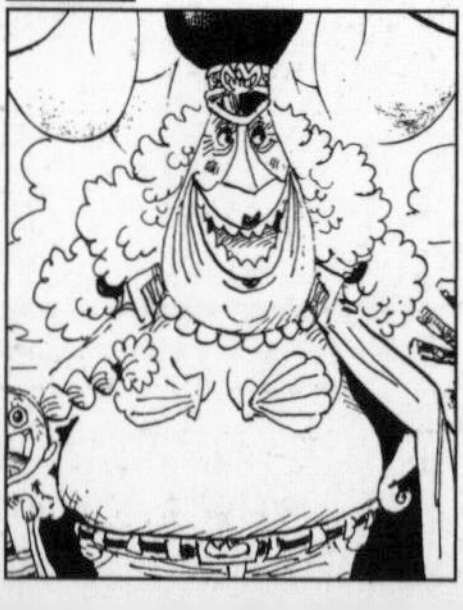

Chaper 656:

ADVENTURE ON THE BURNING ISLAND

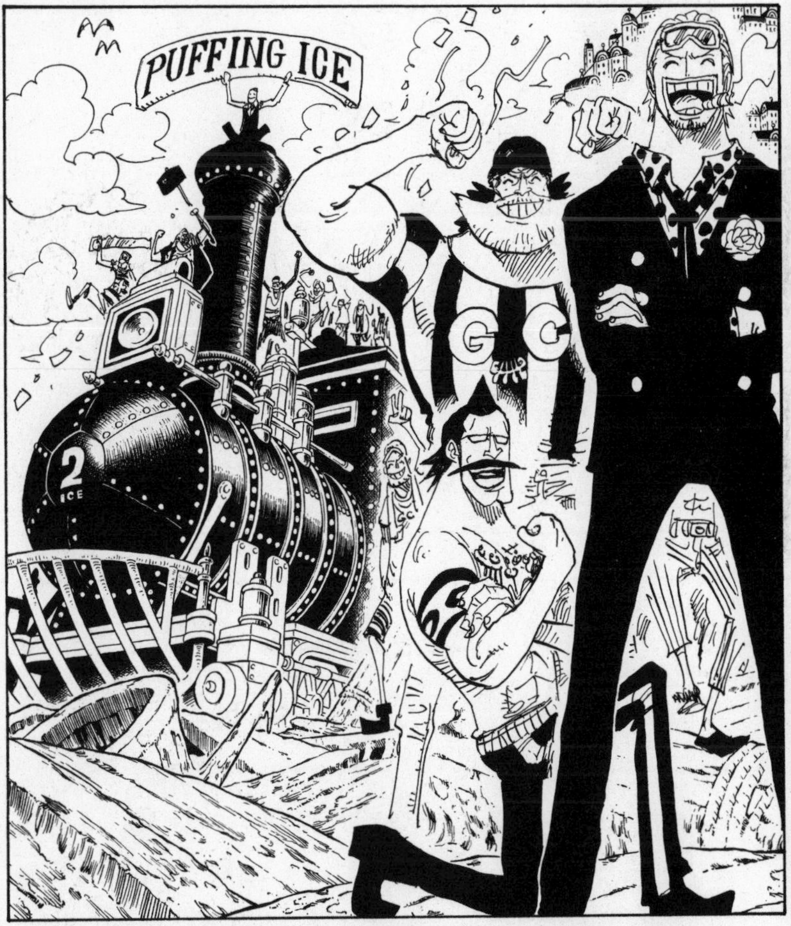
PUFFING ICE
2
ICE

DECKS OF THE WORLD, VOL. 38: "WATER SEVEN—THE SECOND SEA TRAIN IS COMPLETE"

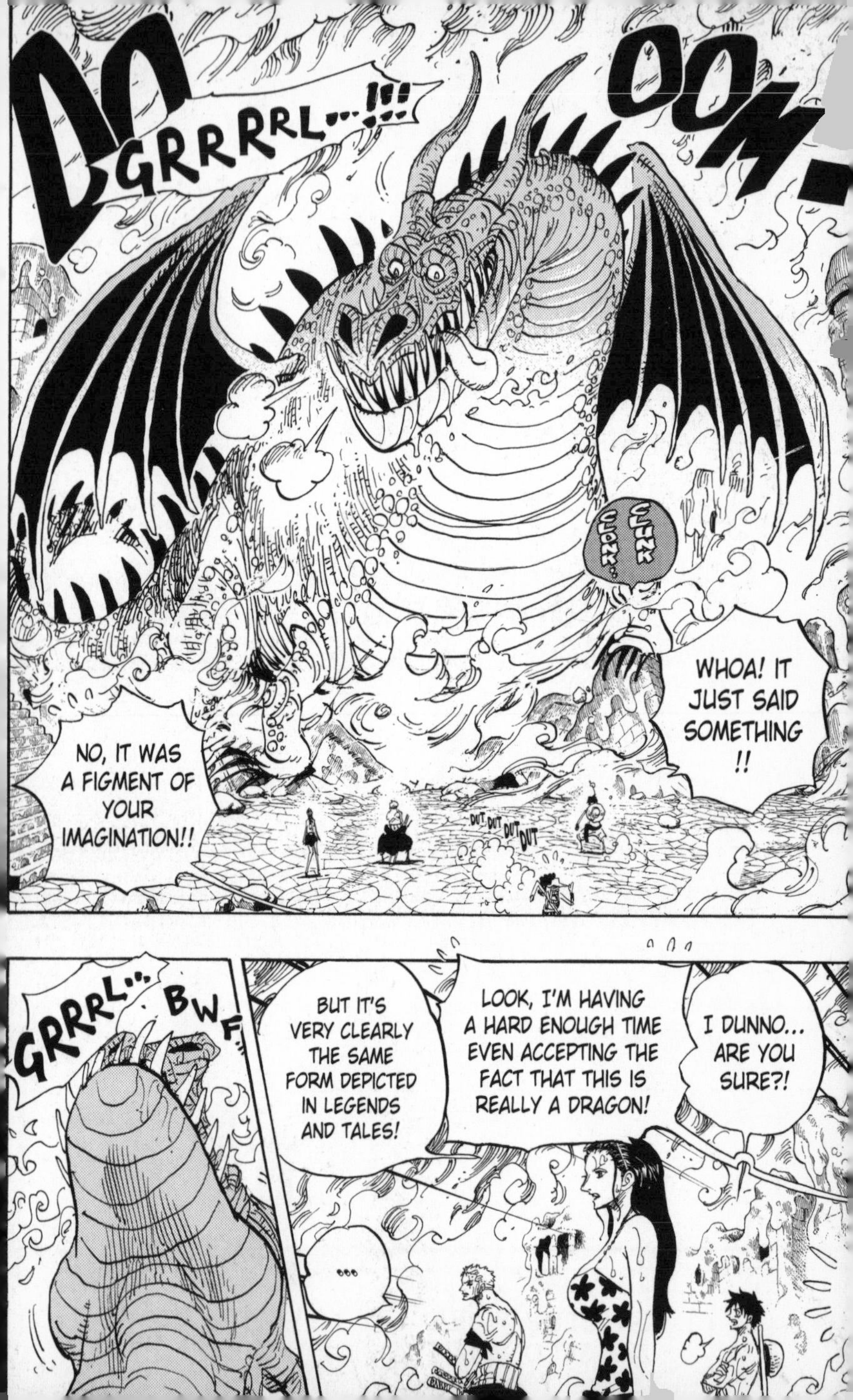
DOOOM
GRRRRL...!!
CLUNK CLUNK...
WHOA! IT JUST SAID SOMETHING!!
NO, IT WAS A FIGMENT OF YOUR IMAGINATION!!
DUT DUT DUT DUT
I DUNNO... ARE YOU SURE?!
LOOK, I'M HAVING A HARD ENOUGH TIME EVEN ACCEPTING THE FACT THAT THIS IS REALLY A DRAGON!
BUT IT'S VERY CLEARLY THE SAME FORM DEPICTED IN LEGENDS AND TALES!
...
GRRRL..
BWF

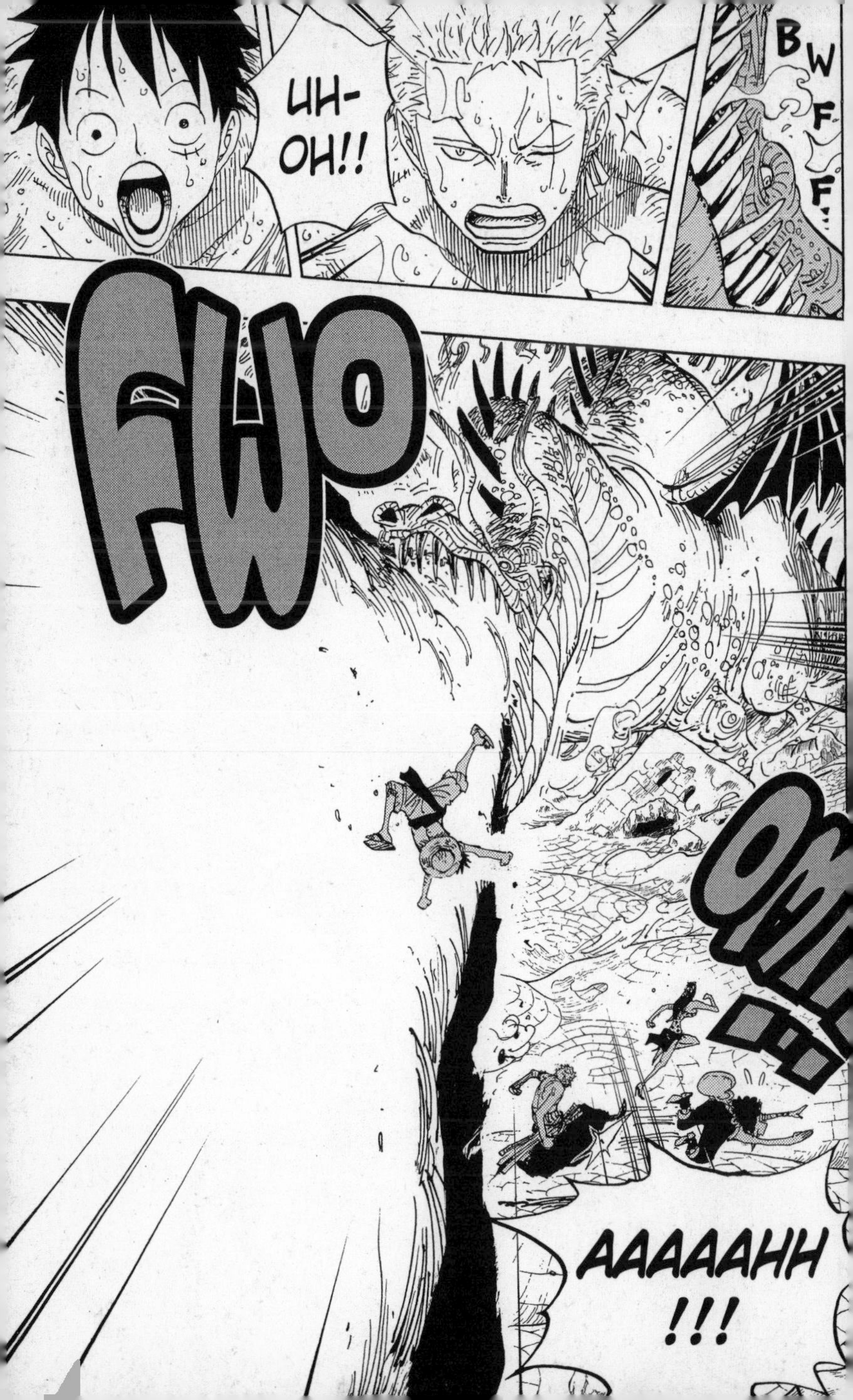
BWFF
UH-OH!!
FWO
AAAAAH !!!

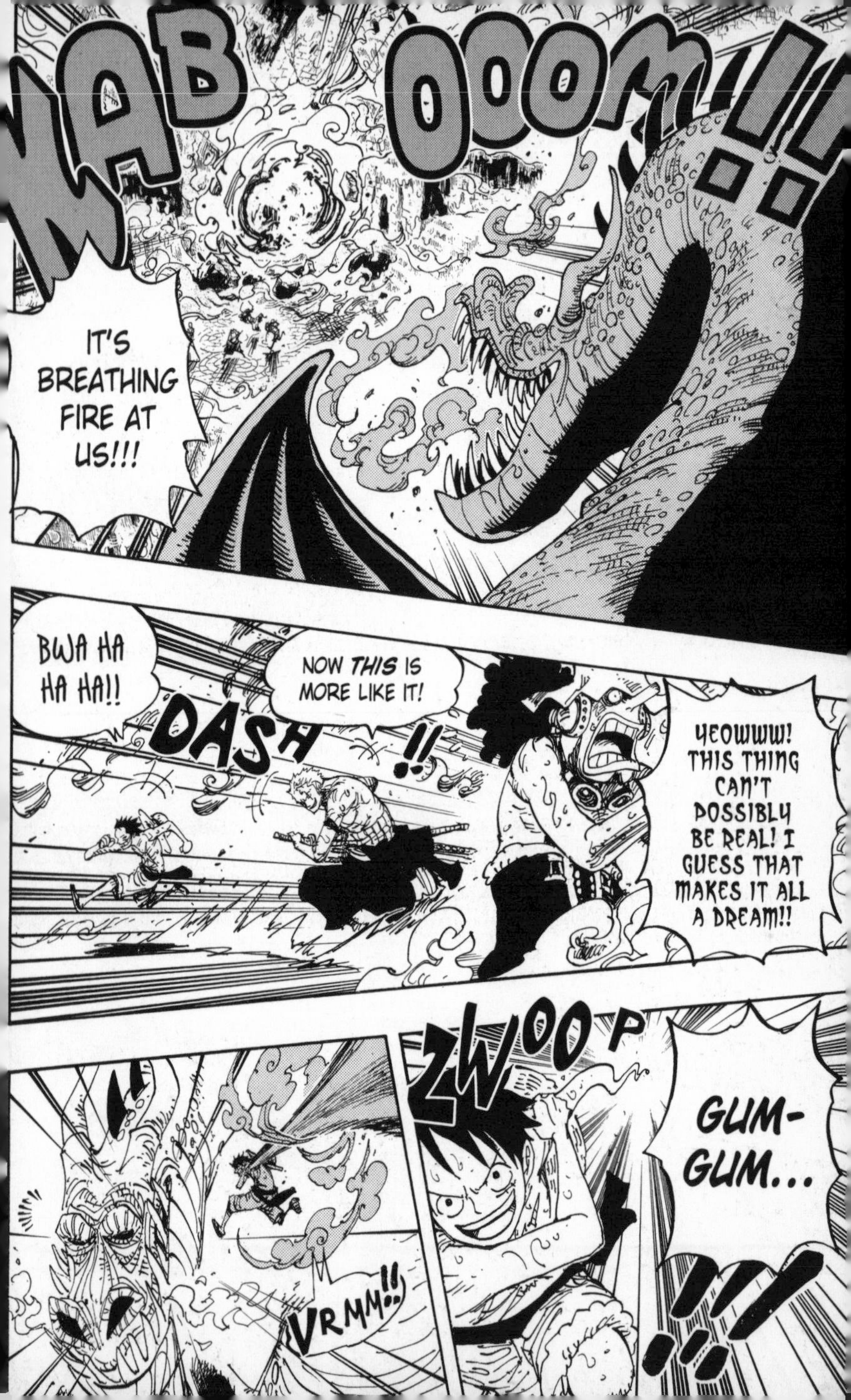
AB OOOM!!
IT'S BREATHING FIRE AT US!!!
YEOWWW! THIS THING CAN'T POSSIBLY BE REAL! I GUESS THAT MAKES IT ALL A DREAM!!
NOW *THIS* IS MORE LIKE IT!
BWA HA HA HA!!
DASH!!
ZWOOP
GUM-GUM...
!!!
!!
VRMM!!

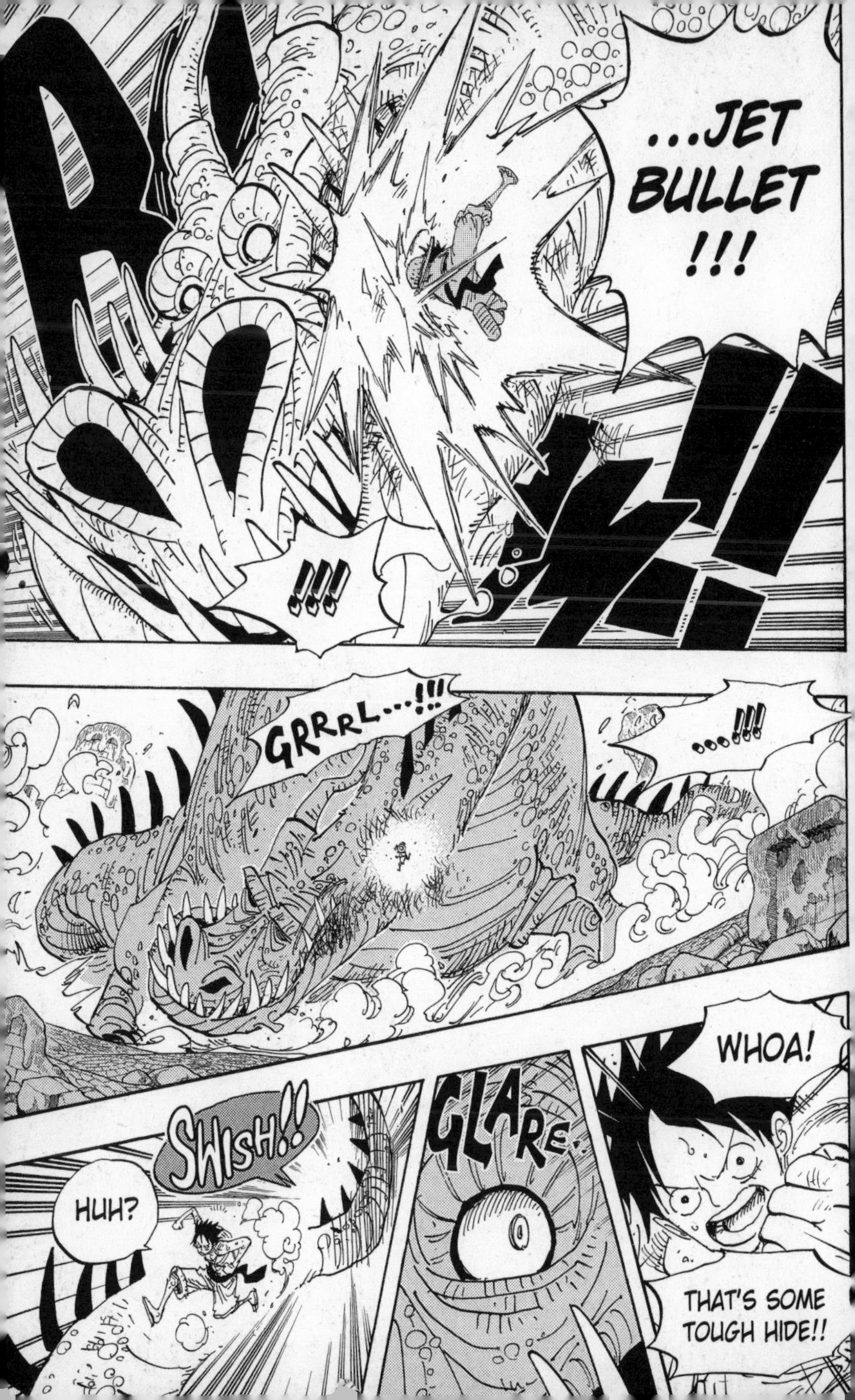
...JET BULLET !!!
!!!
GRRRL...!!!
...!!!
WHOA!
THAT'S SOME TOUGH HIDE!!
GLARE
SWISH!!
HUH?

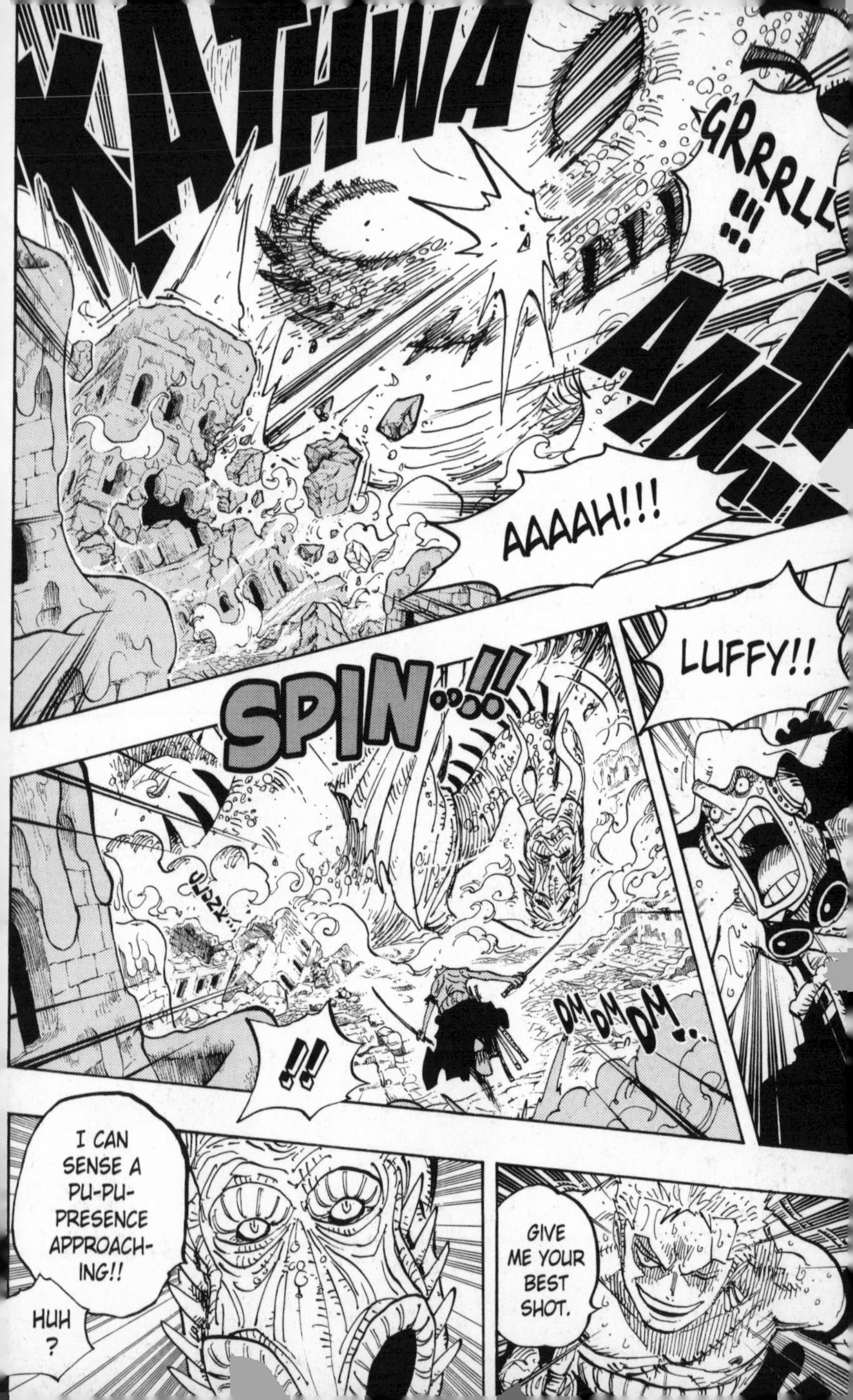
GRRRLL!!!
KATHWA
AAAAH!!!
LUFFY!!
SPIN..!!
WZZZ...
!!
DM DM DM...
GIVE ME YOUR BEST SHOT.
I CAN SENSE A PU-PU-PRESENCE APPROACHING!!
HUH?

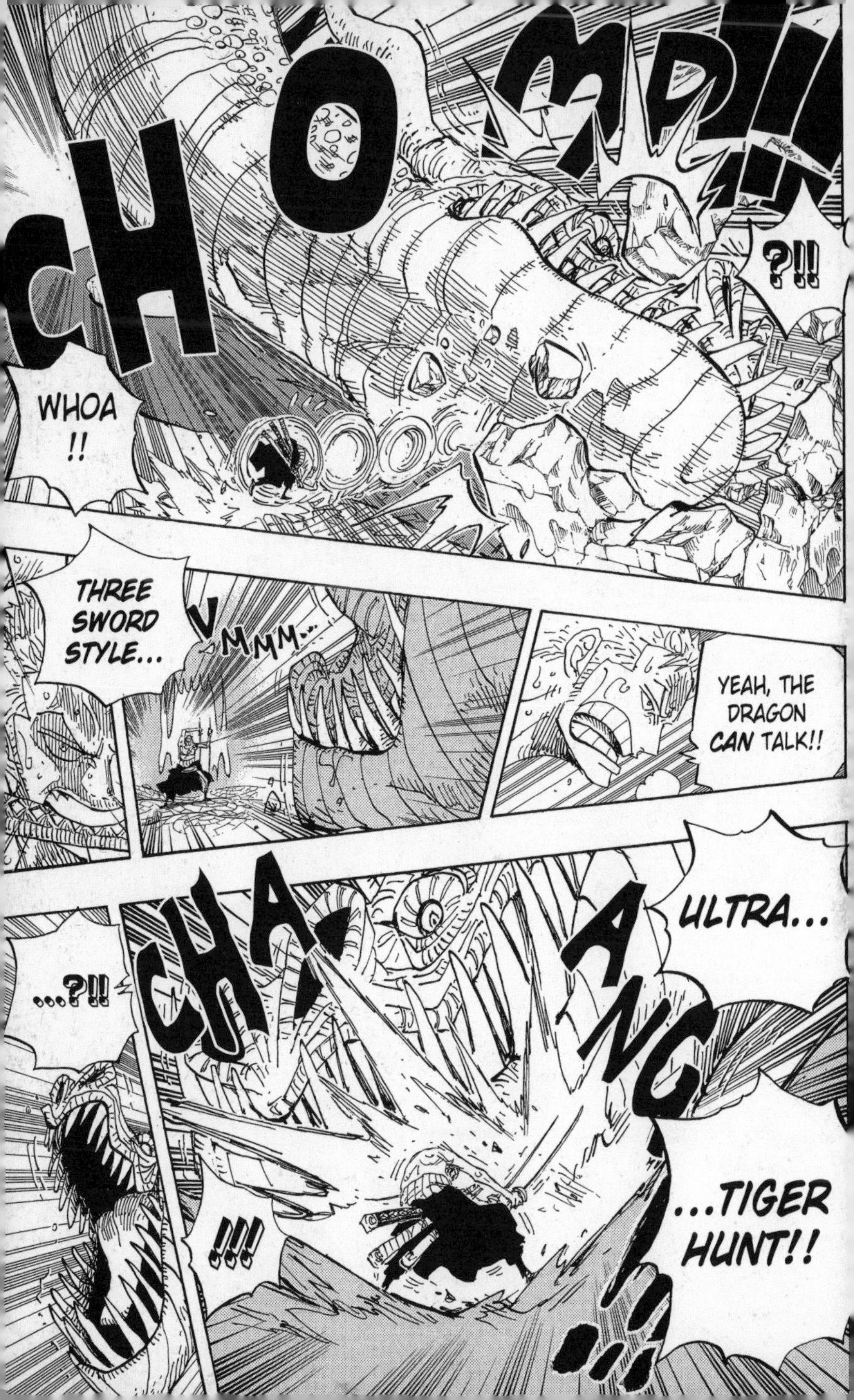
CHOMP!!
?!!
WHOA !!
YEAH, THE DRAGON CAN TALK!!
VMMM...
THREE SWORD STYLE...
ULTRA...
CHAANG
...TIGER HUNT!!
...?!!
!!!

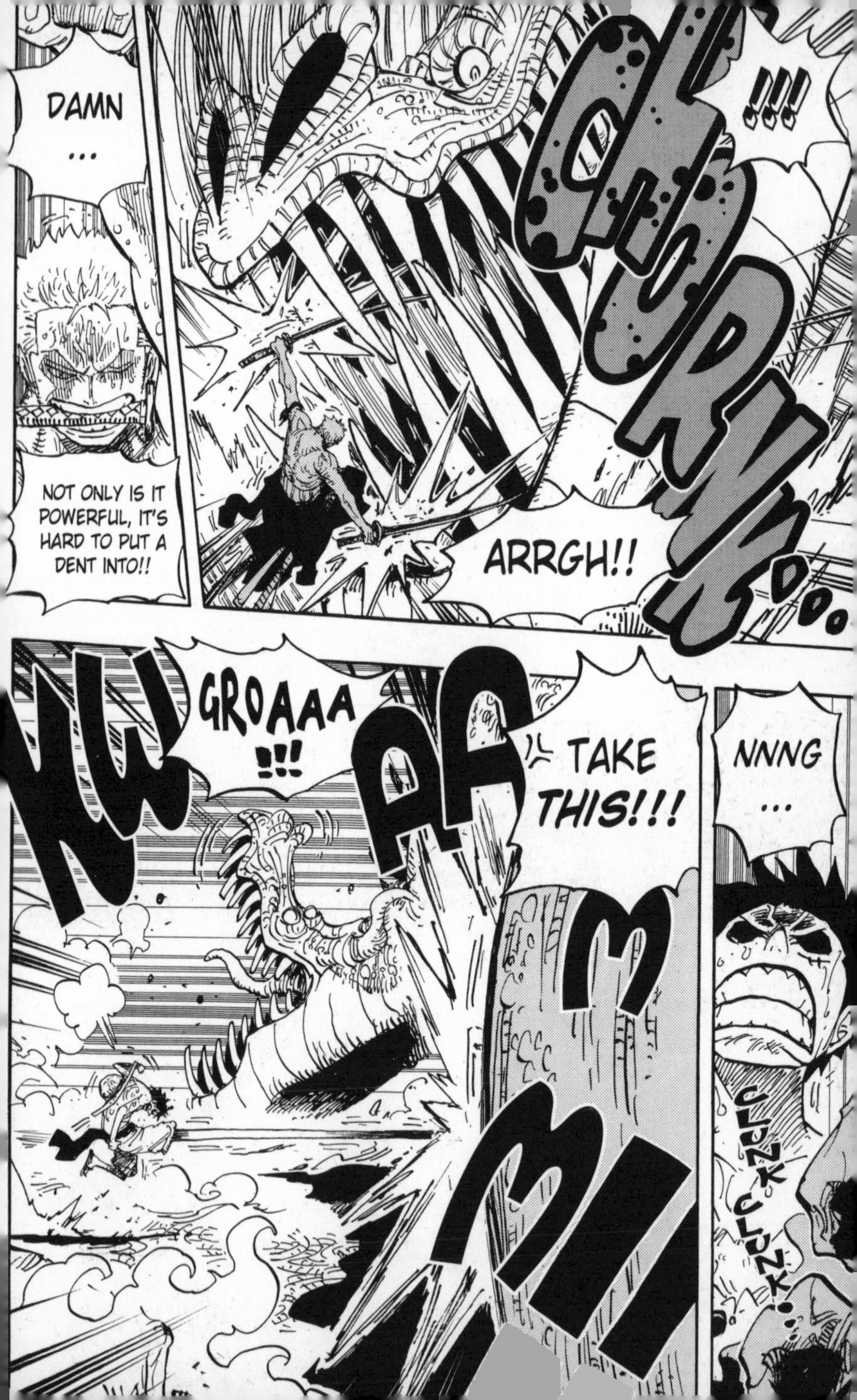
ARRGH!!
DAMN ...
NOT ONLY IS IT POWERFUL, IT'S HARD TO PUT A DENT INTO!!
NNNG ...
CLUNK CLUNK CLUNK...
TAKE THIS!!!
GROAAA !!!

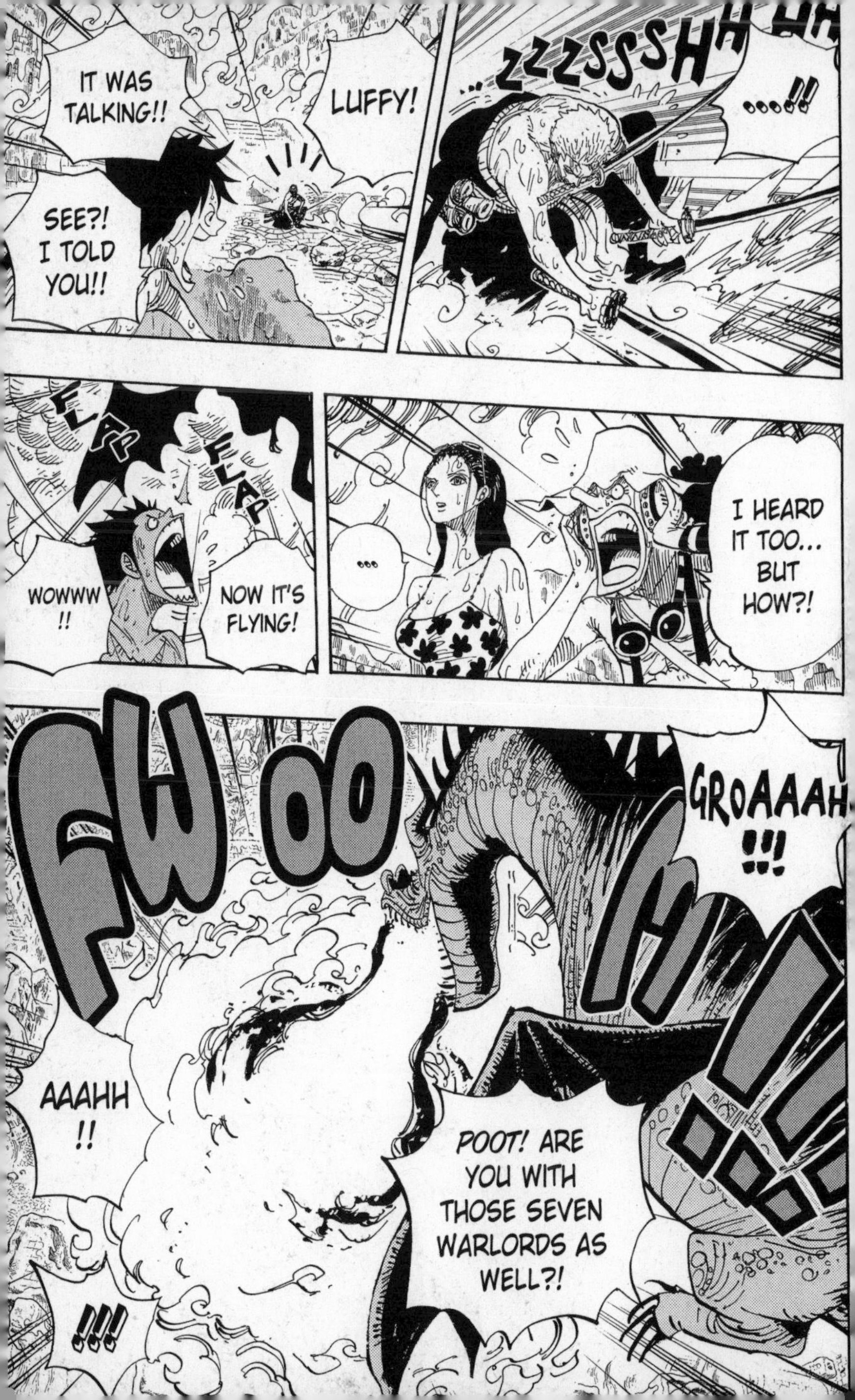
...ZZZSSSSHH
....!!
LUFFY!
IT WAS TALKING!!
SEE?! I TOLD YOU!!
I HEARD IT TOO... BUT HOW?!
...
FLAP
FLAP
NOW IT'S FLYING!
WOWWW !!
GROAAAH !!!
FWOO
POOT! ARE YOU WITH THOSE SEVEN WARLORDS AS WELL?!
AAAHH !!
!!!

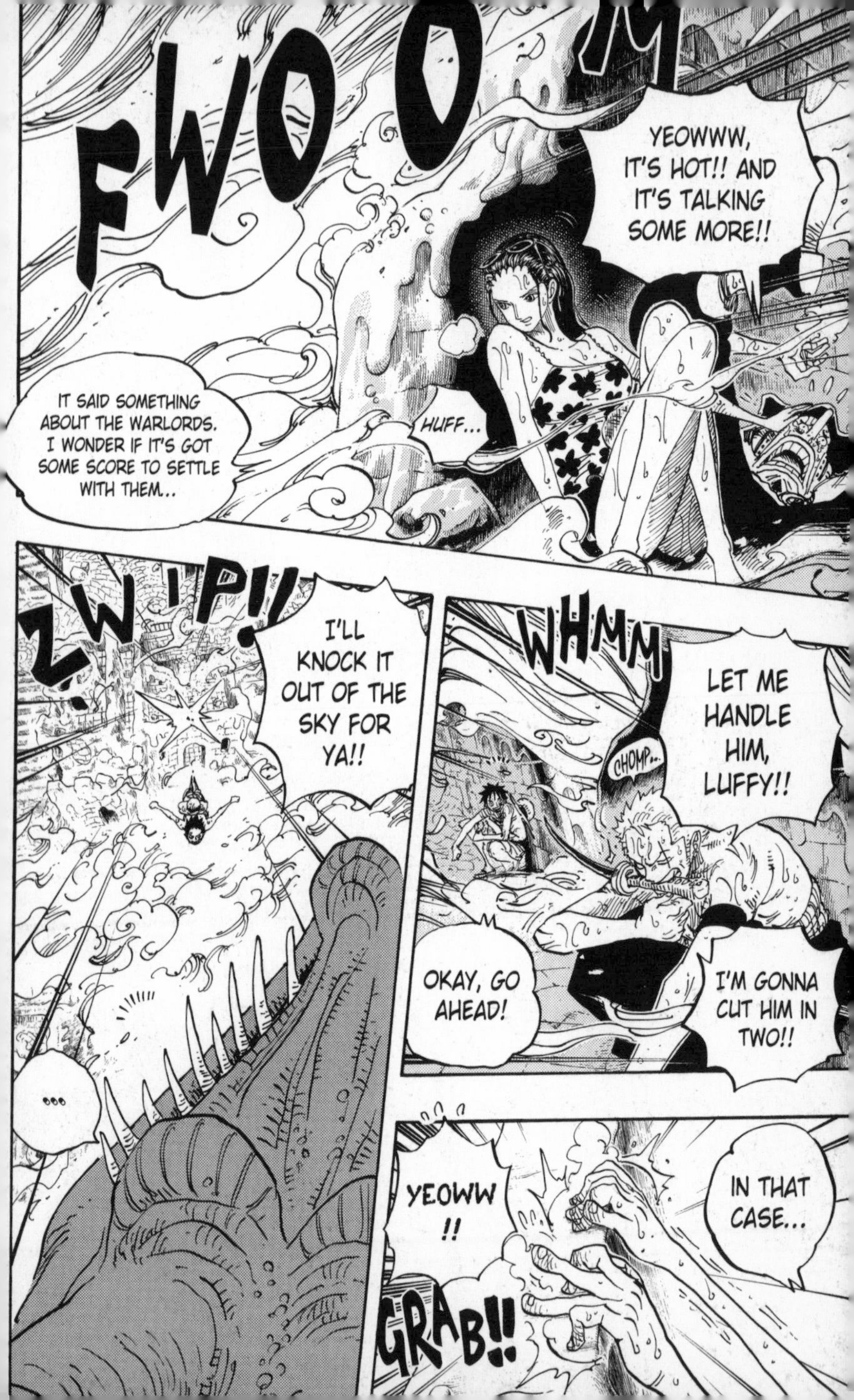
FWOOM
YEOWWW, IT'S HOT!! AND IT'S TALKING SOME MORE!!
HUFF...
IT SAID SOMETHING ABOUT THE WARLORDS. I WONDER IF IT'S GOT SOME SCORE TO SETTLE WITH THEM...
WHMM
LET ME HANDLE HIM, LUFFY!!
CHOMP...
I'M GONNA CUT HIM IN TWO!!
OKAY, GO AHEAD!
IN THAT CASE...
YEOWW!!
GRAB!!
ZWIP!!
I'LL KNOCK IT OUT OF THE SKY FOR YA!!
...

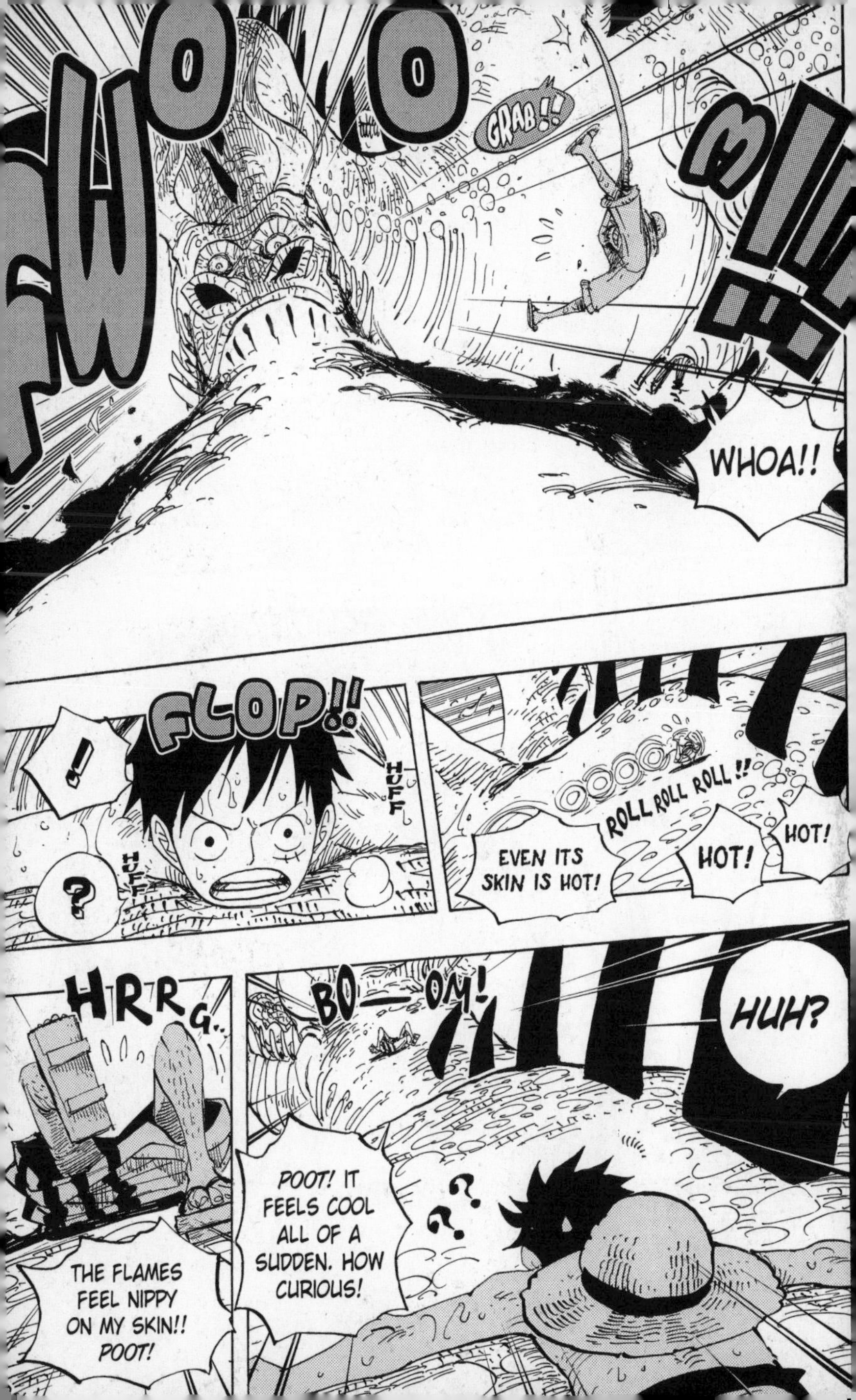
GRAB!!
WOOM!!
WHOA!!
ROLL ROLL ROLL!!
HOT!
HOT!
EVEN ITS SKIN IS HOT!
FLOP!!
!
HUFF
HUFF
?
HUH?
BO—OM!
??
POOT! IT FEELS COOL ALL OF A SUDDEN. HOW CURIOUS!
HRRG..
THE FLAMES FEEL NIPPY ON MY SKIN!! POOT!

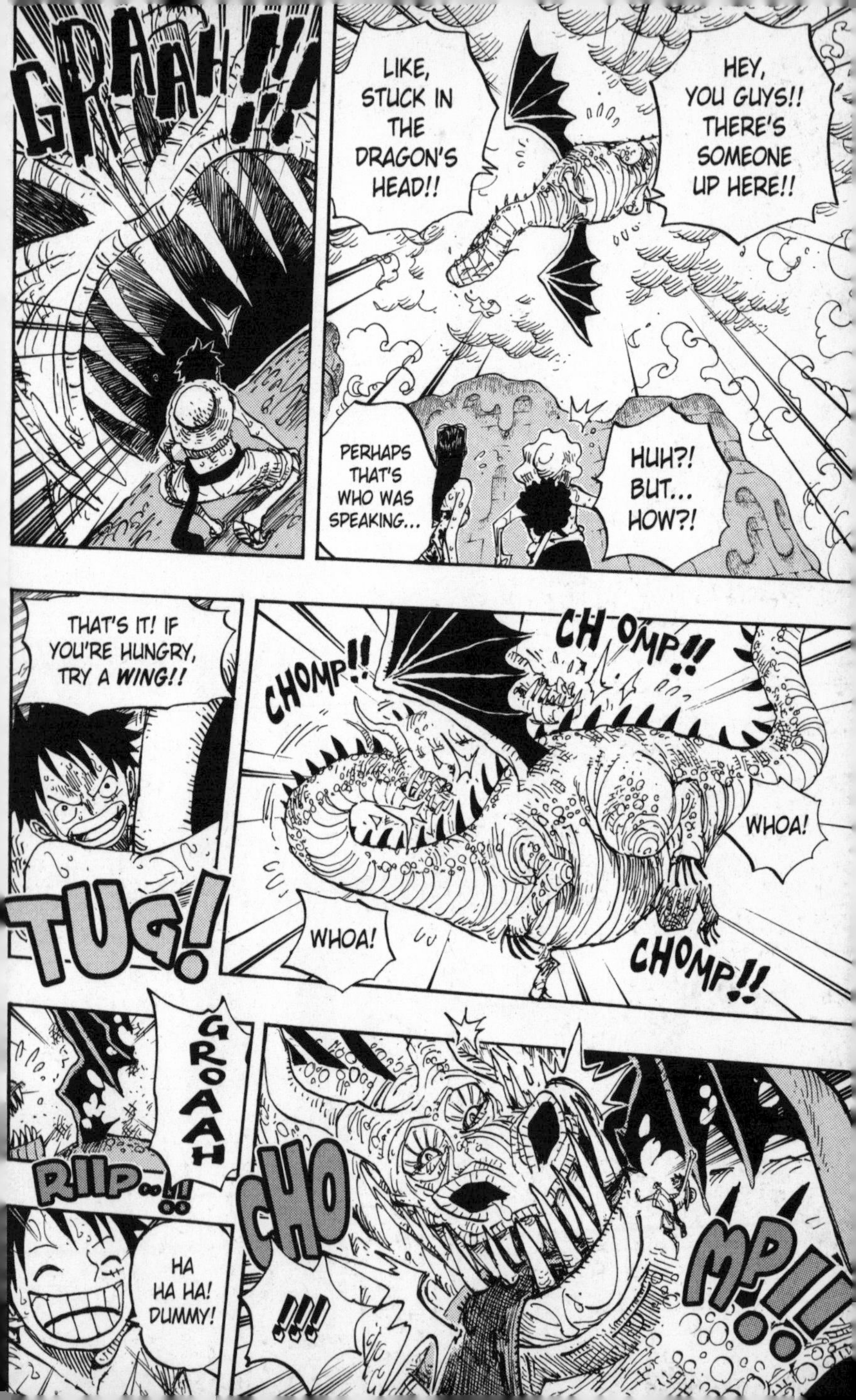
HEY, YOU GUYS!! THERE'S SOMEONE UP HERE!!
LIKE, STUCK IN THE DRAGON'S HEAD!!
HUH?! BUT... HOW?!
PERHAPS THAT'S WHO WAS SPEAKING...
GRAAH!!!
CH OMP!!
CHOMP!!
WHOA!
WHOA!
CHOMP!!
THAT'S IT! IF YOU'RE HUNGRY, TRY A WING!!
TUG!
CHO MP!!
!!!
GROAAH
RIIP..!!
HA HA HA! DUMMY!

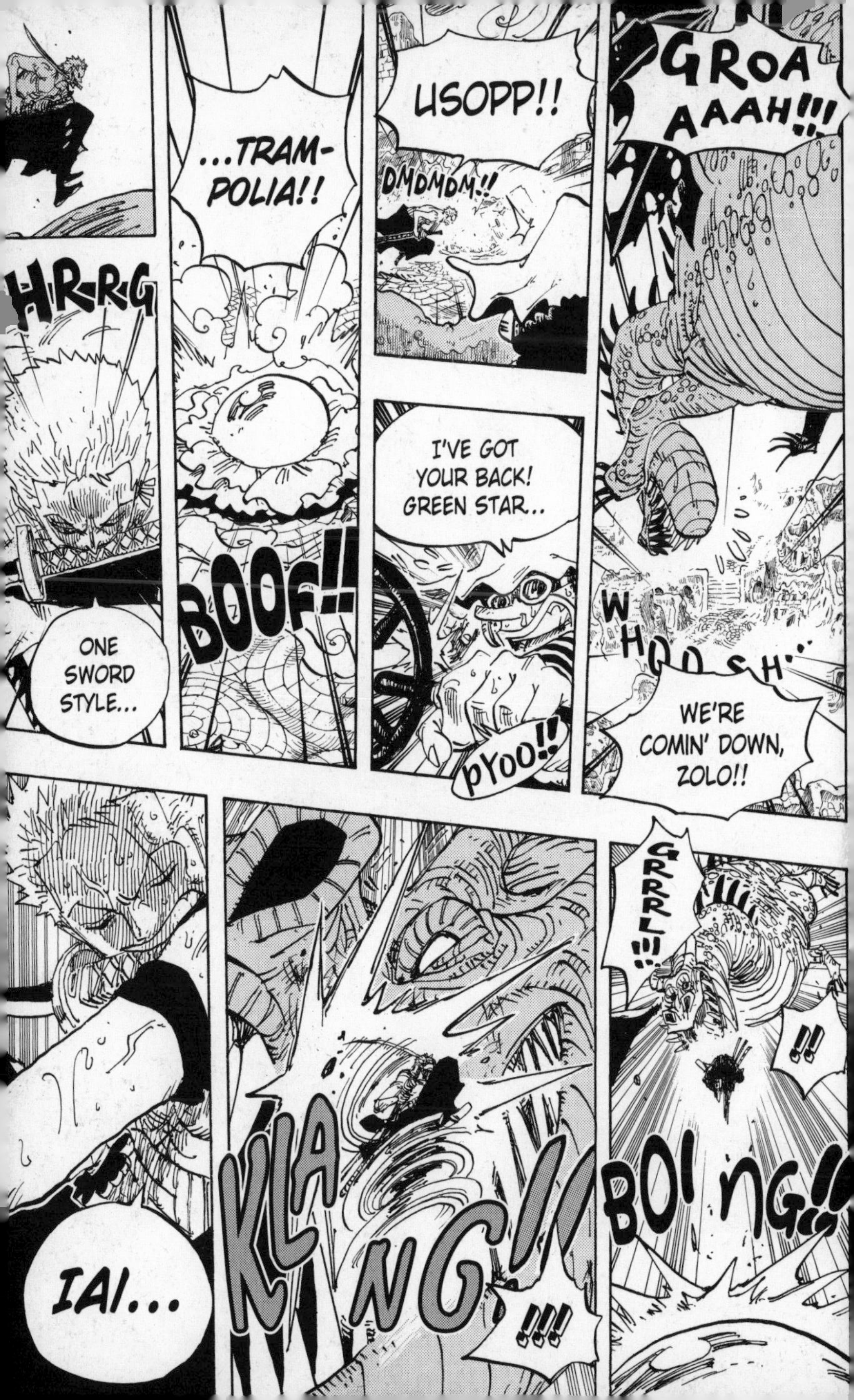
GROA AAAH!!!
WHOOSH
WE'RE COMIN' DOWN, ZOLO!!
USOPP!!
DMDMDM!!
I'VE GOT YOUR BACK! GREEN STAR...
PYOO!!
...TRAM-POLIA!!
BOOF!!
HRRG
ONE SWORD STYLE...
GRRRL!!!
!!
BOING!!
KLANG!!!
IAI...

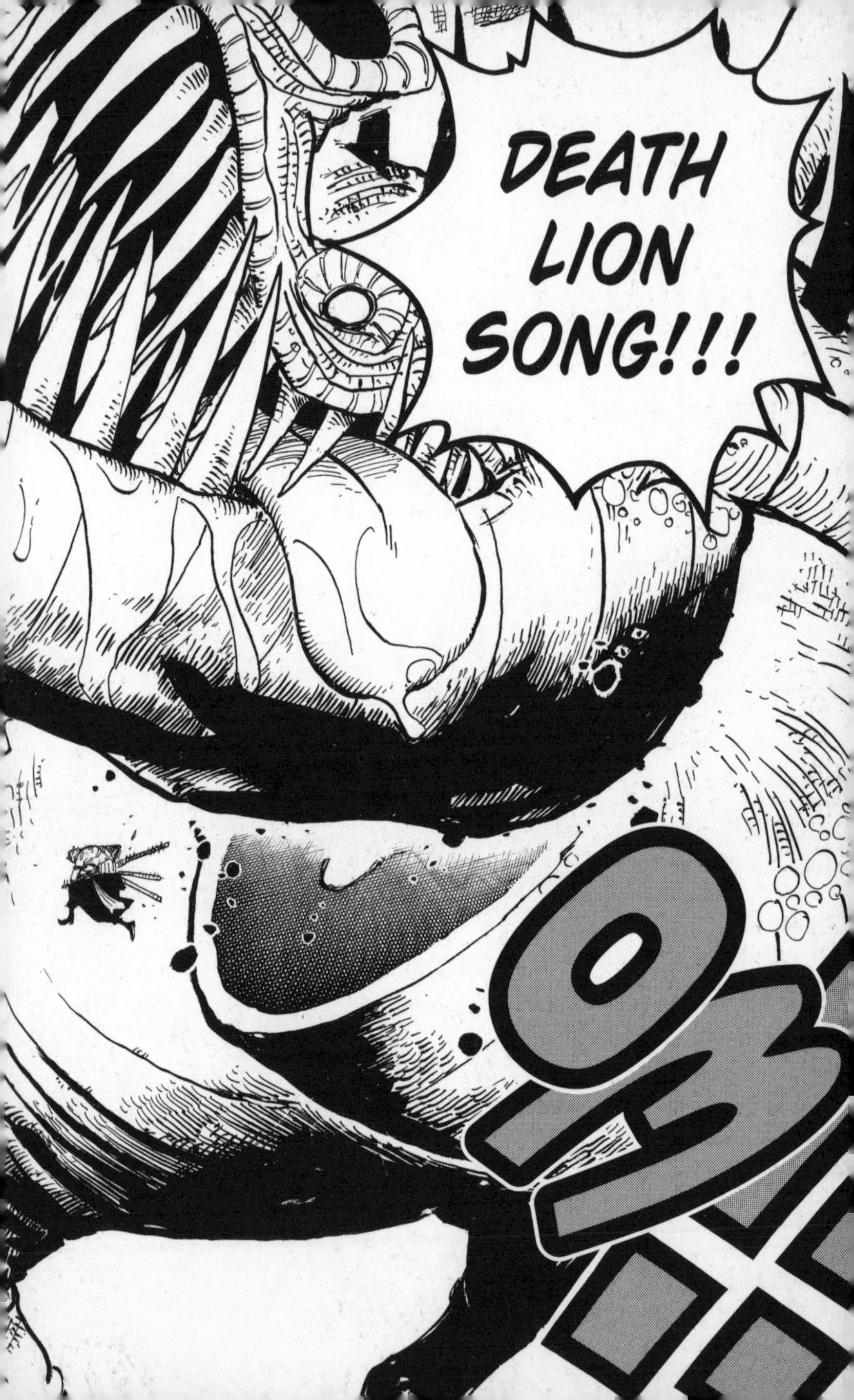
DEATH LION SONG!!!

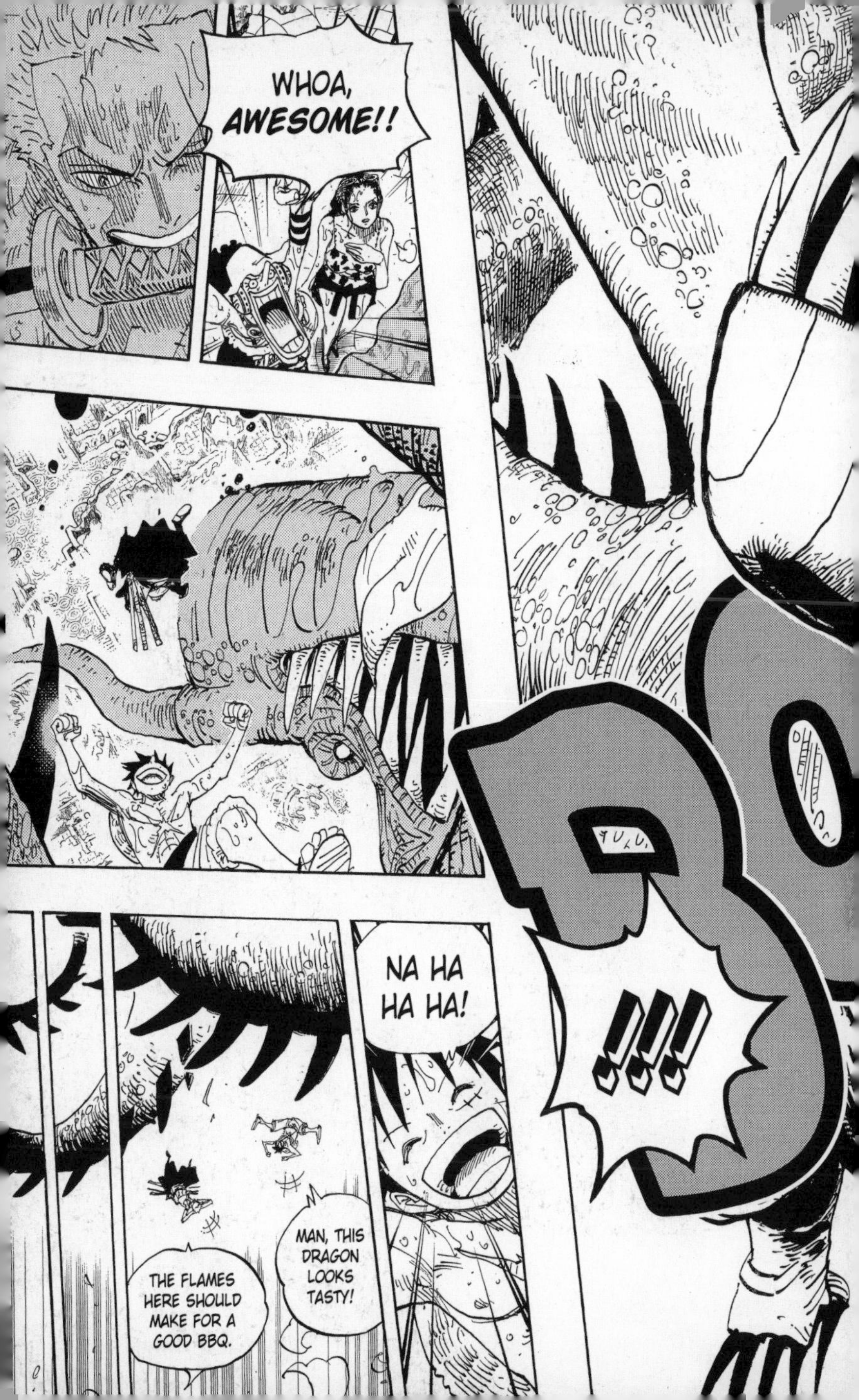
BO!!!
WHOA, AWESOME!!
NA HA HA HA!
MAN, THIS DRAGON LOOKS TASTY!
THE FLAMES HERE SHOULD MAKE FOR A GOOD BBQ.

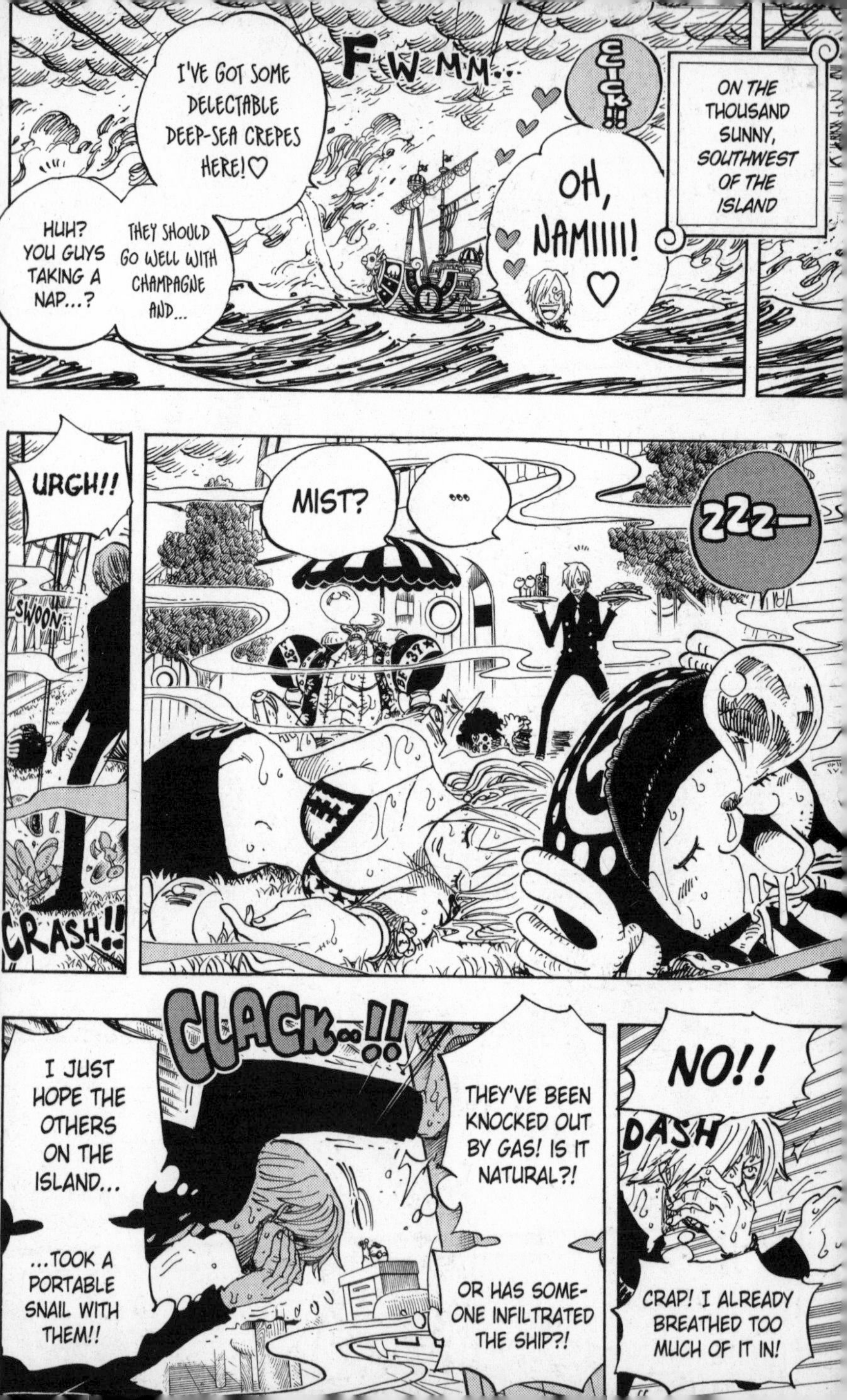
ON THE THOUSAND SUNNY, SOUTHWEST OF THE ISLAND
CLICK!!
OH, NAMIIIII! ♡
FWMM...
I'VE GOT SOME DELECTABLE DEEP-SEA CREPES HERE! ♡
THEY SHOULD GO WELL WITH CHAMPAGNE AND...
HUH? YOU GUYS TAKING A NAP...?
ZZZ—
...
MIST?
URGH!!
SWOON
CRASH!!
NO!!
DASH
CRAP! I ALREADY BREATHED TOO MUCH OF IT IN!
CLACK..!!
THEY'VE BEEN KNOCKED OUT BY GAS! IS IT NATURAL?!
OR HAS SOME-ONE INFILTRATED THE SHIP?!
I JUST HOPE THE OTHERS ON THE ISLAND...
...TOOK A PORTABLE SNAIL WITH THEM!!

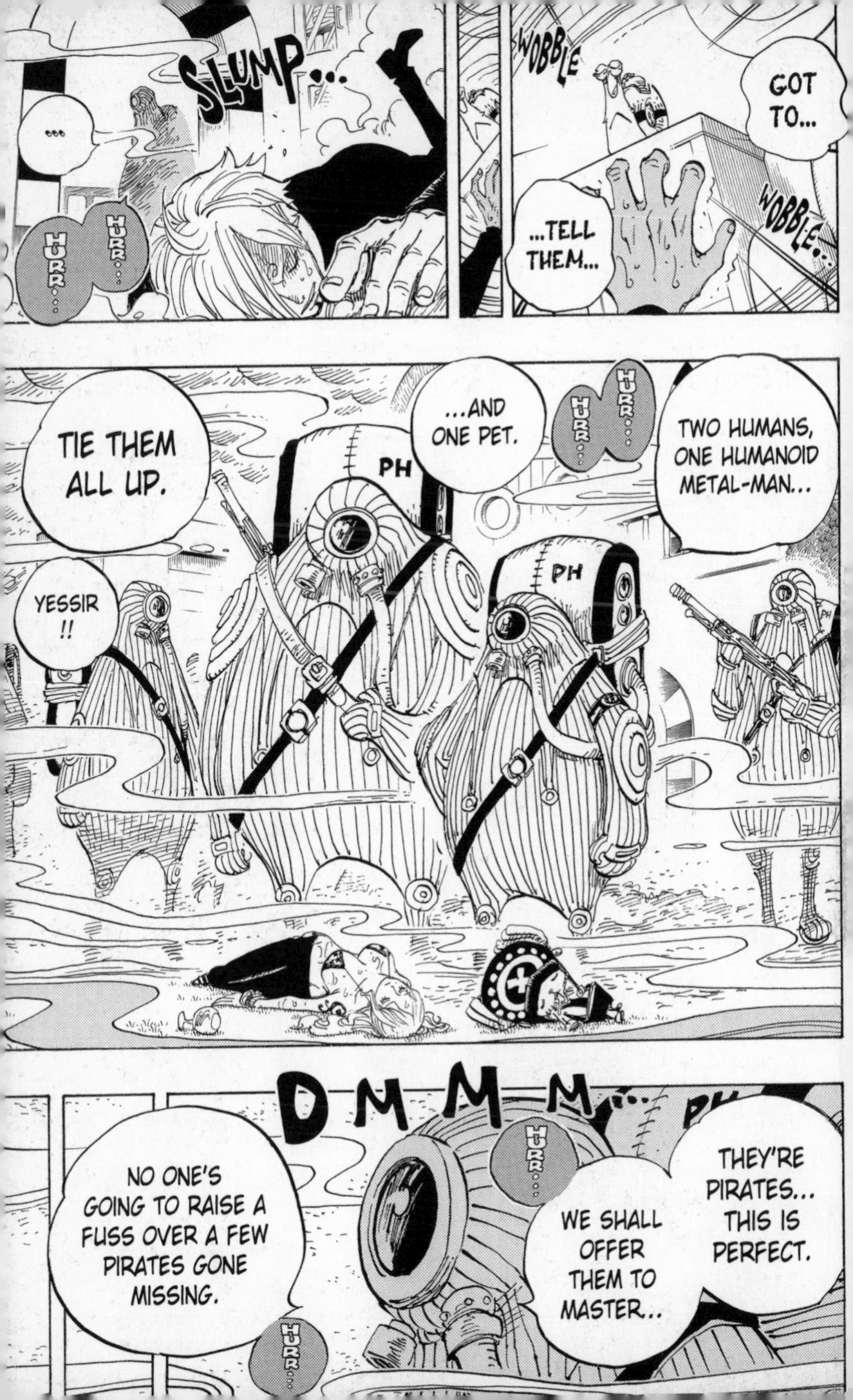
WOBBLE
GOT TO...
WOBBLE...
...TELL THEM...
SLUMP...
HURR...
...
HURR...
TWO HUMANS, ONE HUMANOID METAL-MAN...
HURR...
HURR...
...AND ONE PET.
PH
TIE THEM ALL UP.
PH
YESSIR !!
DMMM...
THEY'RE PIRATES... THIS IS PERFECT.
HURR...
WE SHALL OFFER THEM TO MASTER..
NO ONE'S GOING TO RAISE A FUSS OVER A FEW PIRATES GONE MISSING.
HURR...

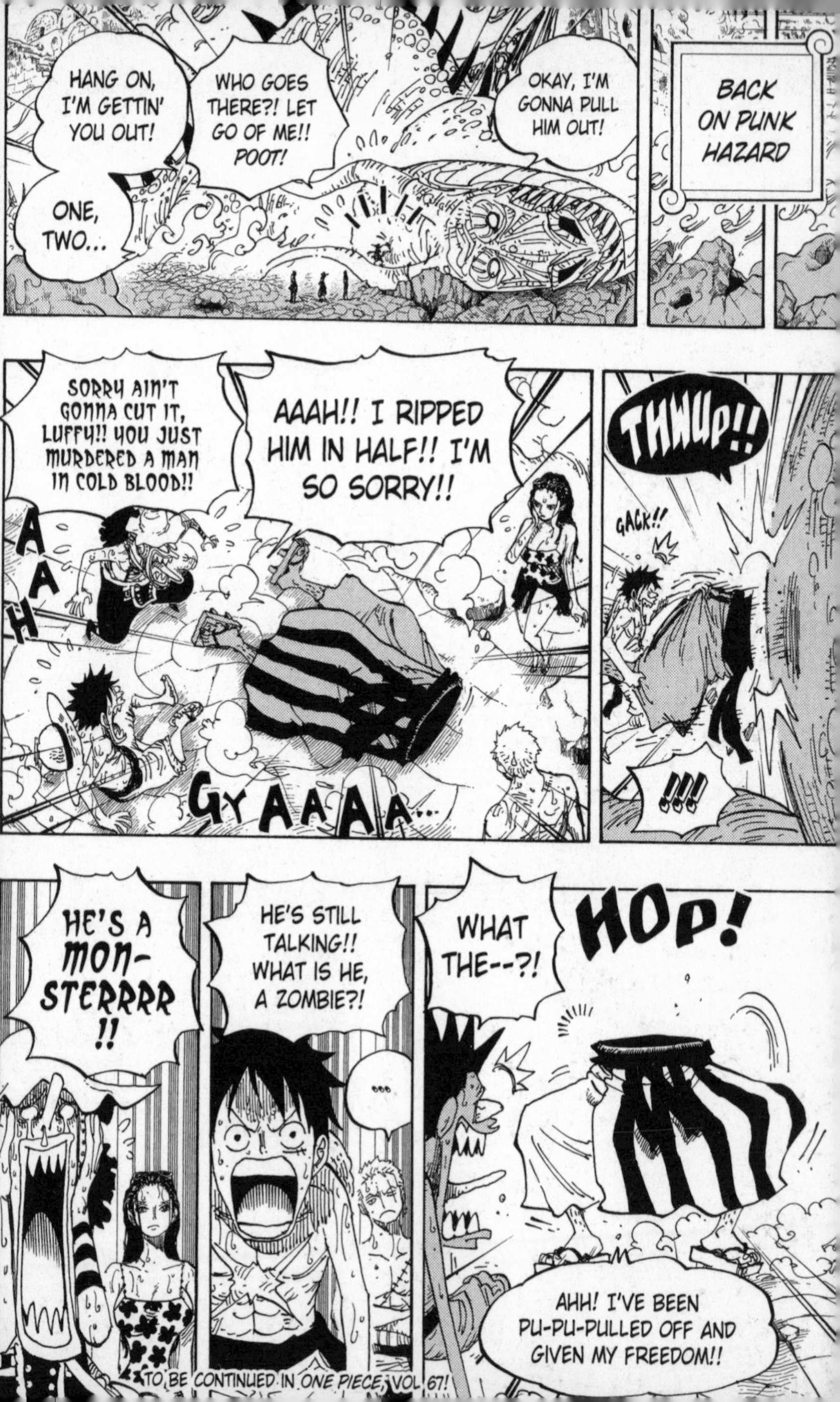
BACK ON PUNK HAZARD
OKAY, I'M GONNA PULL HIM OUT!
WHO GOES THERE?! LET GO OF ME!! POOT!
HANG ON, I'M GETTIN' YOU OUT!
ONE, TWO...
THWUP!!
GACK!!
!!!
AAAH!! I RIPPED HIM IN HALF!! I'M SO SORRY!!
SORRY AIN'T GONNA CUT IT, LUFFY!! YOU JUST MURDERED A MAN IN COLD BLOOD!!
AAH
GYAAAA...
WHAT THE--?!
HOP!
AHH! I'VE BEEN PU-PU-PULLED OFF AND GIVEN MY FREEDOM!!
HE'S STILL TALKING!! WHAT IS HE, A ZOMBIE?!
...
HE'S A MON-STERRRR!!
TO BE CONTINUED IN ONE PIECE, VOL. 67!

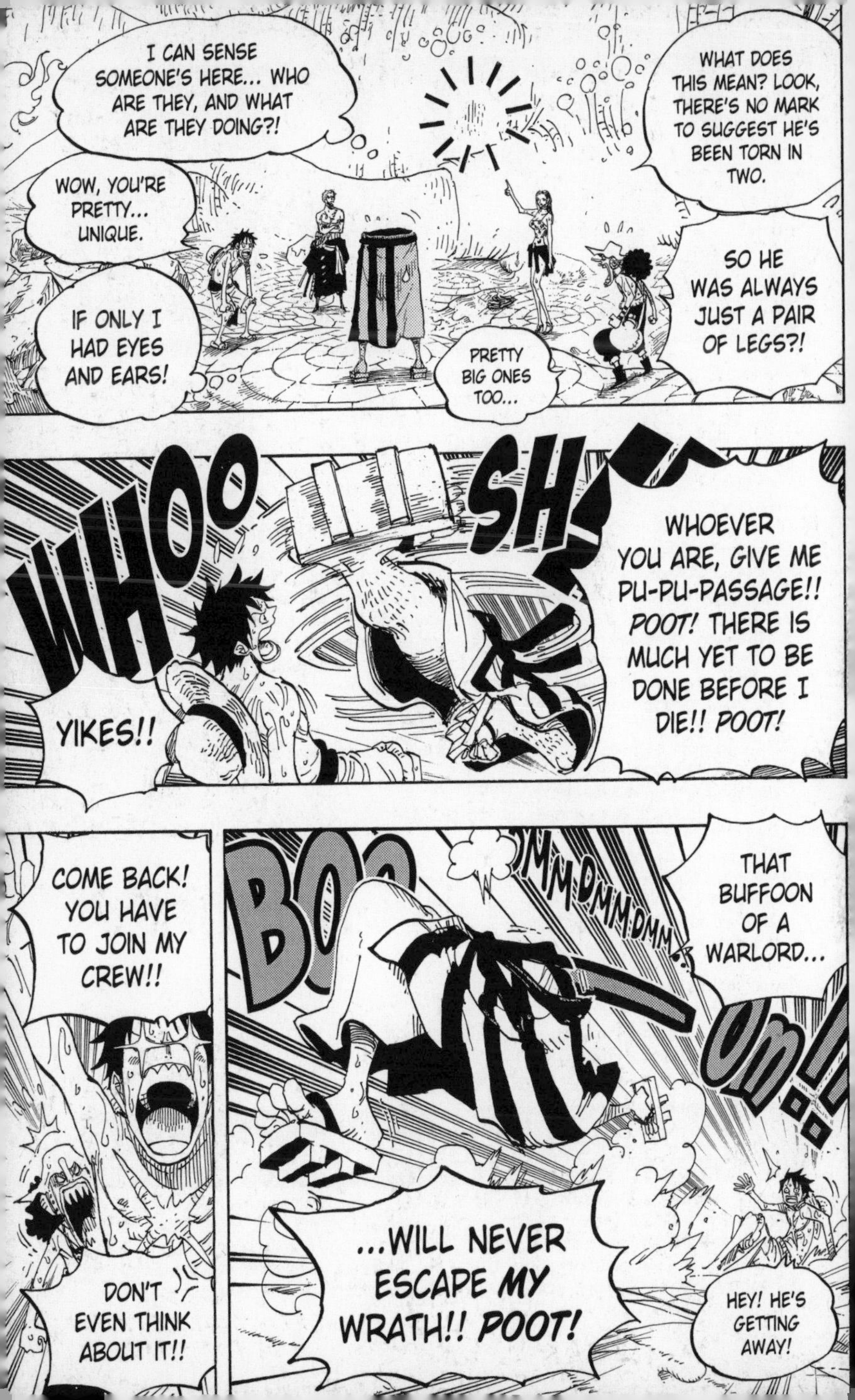
WHAT DOES THIS MEAN? LOOK, THERE'S NO MARK TO SUGGEST HE'S BEEN TORN IN TWO.
SO HE WAS ALWAYS JUST A PAIR OF LEGS?!
PRETTY BIG ONES TOO...
I CAN SENSE SOMEONE'S HERE... WHO ARE THEY, AND WHAT ARE THEY DOING?!
WOW, YOU'RE PRETTY... UNIQUE.
IF ONLY I HAD EYES AND EARS!
WHOOSH
WHOEVER YOU ARE, GIVE ME PU-PU-PASSAGE!! *POOT!* THERE IS MUCH YET TO BE DONE BEFORE I DIE!! *POOT!*
YIKES!!
THAT BUFFOON OF A WARLORD...
BOOOM!!
DMM DMM DMM
...WILL NEVER ESCAPE *MY* WRATH!! *POOT!*
HEY! HE'S GETTING AWAY!
COME BACK! YOU HAVE TO JOIN MY CREW!!
DON'T EVEN THINK ABOUT IT!!

★ Hello, hello! I've received many postcards asking about another One Piece movie. After Strong World in 2009, we did a fun little thirty-minute 3D CG movie, but it's been a full three years since there was a feature-length animated One Piece film. Well, it's coming on December 2012, which is still several months away at the time I'm writing this...But at least it's all been announced now! Woohoo! Clap clap clap!!

★ Two and a half years ago, I did a bunch of magazine and newspaper interviews where I flatly stated, "I will never work on a movie again." I mean, I honestly thought it was going to kill me. There was so much work to do, yet my bosses and readers would be angry if I skipped a week in Shonen Jump, while the movie staff got impatient if I spent too much time on the manga. What am I supposed to be, some kind of middleman?!♪ Talk about stuck between a rock and a hard place!!

★ So anyways, my dialogue with movie staff over the last two and half years has gone like this. They'd ask, "What's next?" And I would respond, "I'm not doing it."
"Oh, can you at least take a look at what we have so far...?"
"Oh, interesting."
"So here's the rough plot."
"Hmm, this part isn't really up to snuff."
"What about this?"
"Ahh, that's much better."
"We'd like to use this character in the movie."
"Wait...then I have to think of what would happen after the two-year skip...But the fans aren't going to like this, are they?!"
"Okay, then could you just do that?"
"Fine, but that's it."
"Also, this."
"Okay, just this."
"Also, can you just check this real quick?"
"Okay, but that's it."
All right, already!!♪ I'll do it!!! ♪

Executive Producer: Eiichiro Oda

Geez, talk about heavy!! But I said I'll do it, and I'll stand by my word!!! I'm not taking half-measures with this movie!! Of course, there's lots of stuff I can't reveal at this point. All I can say is that there are some incredible people working on this film. There'll be more information in future volumes. I hope you're all excited! The movie staff sure is!

COMING NEXT VOLUME:

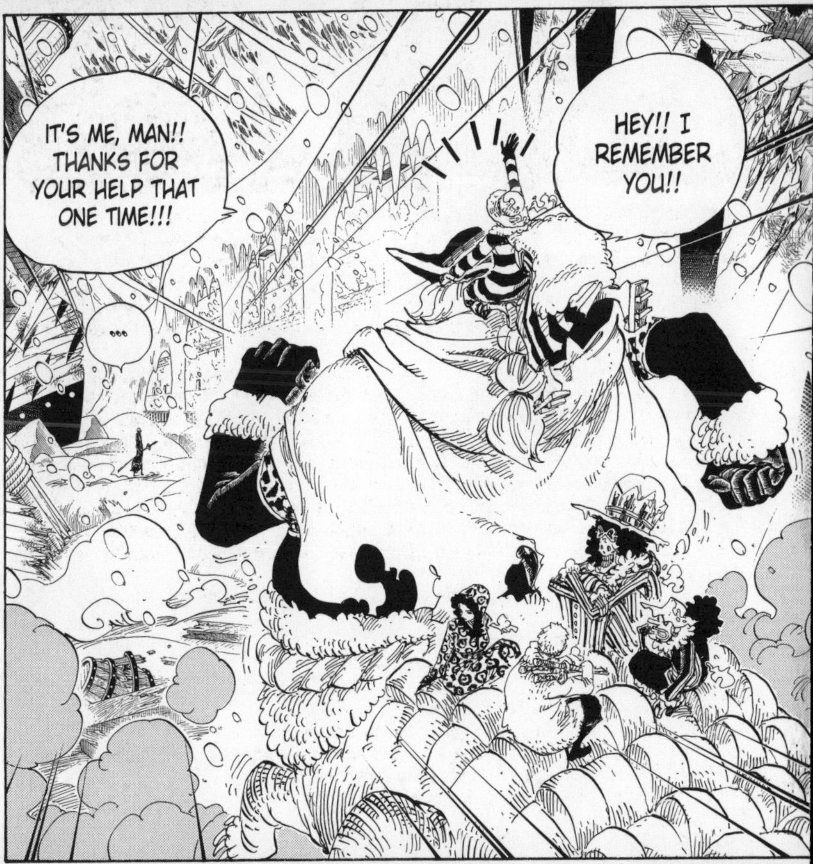
HEY!! I REMEMBER YOU!!
IT'S ME, MAN!! THANKS FOR YOUR HELP THAT ONE TIME!!!
...

Dragons, samurai, and knockout gas! The Straw Hats find themselves on the mysterious Punk Hazard Island, and things quickly go from bad to worse! The crew may have defeated the powerful New Fish-Man Pirates, but new troubles await as they make their debut in the New World!

ON SALE JUNE 2013!

You're Reading in the Wrong Direction!!

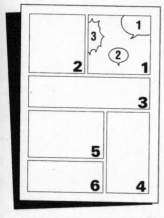

Whoops! Guess what? You're starting at the wrong end of the comic!

...It's true! In keeping with the original Japanese format, **One Piece** is meant to be read from right to left, starting in the upper-right corner.

Unlike English, which is read from left to right, Japanese is read from right to left, meaning that action, sound effects and word-balloon order are completely reversed...something which can make readers unfamiliar with Japanese feel pretty backwards themselves. For this reason, manga or Japanese comics published in the U.S. in English have sometimes been published "flopped"— that is, printed in exact reverse order, as though seen from the other side of a mirror.

By flopping pages, U.S. publishers can avoid confusing readers, but the compromise is not without its downside. For one thing, a character in a flopped manga series who once wore in the original Japanese version a T-shirt emblazoned with "M A Y" (as in "the merry month of") now wears one which reads "Y A M"! Additionally, many manga creators in Japan are themselves unhappy with the process, as some feel the mirror-imaging of their art skews their original intentions.

We are proud to bring you Eiichiro Oda's **One Piece** in the original unflopped format. For now, though, turn to the other side of the book and let the journey begin...!

—Editor